Selected Works
of
John Calvin

Iohan Calvin.

Selected Works

of

John Calvin

Tracts and Letters

Edited by Henry Beveridge
and Jules Bonnet

Volume 7

Letters, Part 4

1559-1564

Edited by Jules Bonnet
Translated by Marcus Robert Gilchrist

Baker Book House

Grand Rapids, Michigan 49506

Reprinted 1983
by Baker Book House Company

Seven-volume Set
ISBN: 0-8010-2493-5

Volume 7 is a reproduction of
Letters of John Calvin, vol. 4
(Philadelphia: Presbyterian Board of Publication, 1858)

Printed in the United States of America

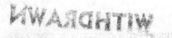

CONTENTS.

(3)

LAST DISCOURSES OF CALVIN.

APPENDIX.

1534.

CALVIN'S LETTERS.

DXXII.—To William Cecil.[1]

Hopes connected with the accession of Elizabeth. Wishes for the establishment of the pure gospel in England.

Geneva, *29th January,* 1559.

I SHALL make no tedious apology, most distinguished sir, for now writing to you familiarly, though personally I am unknown to you; for relying on the information of some pious individuals, who have extolled your courtesy, I trust that you will be naturally disposed to give a favourable reception to my letter, and especially, when, after having perused it, you shall be aware of the motives which dictated it. Since the time when, dispersing the fearful cloud of darkness that had well nigh reduced to despair all pious minds, a new light has miraculously shone forth—the fame is rife that you are strenuously engaged in directing the no common influence which you possess over the queen, to scatter the superstitions of popery which have overshadowed your land for the last four years, and to cause the

---

[1] William Cecil, Baron Burleigh, secretary of state under Edward VI., and one of the ablest ministers of Queen Elizabeth. He took a leading part in the convocation of the Parliament, the promulgation of the thirty-nine articles, and the adoption of the different measures which re-established the Reformation in England. He died in 1598. Informed by Peter Martyr of the death of Mary, and the accession of a princess known for her attachment to the Protestant faith, Calvin hastened to offer to Cecil his wishes and counsels.

(15)

uncorrupted doctrine of the gospel and the pure worship of God again to flourish among you. One thing, however, I may suggest, that what you are now doing you should go on to do with increased activity and a constancy which is not to be overcome; and that no vexatious difficulties, struggles, or terrors, should ever, I do not say, defeat, but even for one moment retard your holy endeavours. I doubt not indeed but obstacles are every now and then occurring, or that even dangers openly menace you, which would damp the resolution of the most courageous, did not God sustain them by the marvellous efficacy of his Spirit. But this is a cause above all others for the defence of which we are not permitted to shrink from any kind of labour. As long as the children of God were exposed to open and avowed slaughter, you yourself held your place along with the others. Now at last when by the recent and unlooked for blessing of God greater liberty has been restored to them, it behoves you to take heart, so that if hitherto you have been timid, you may now make up for your deficiency by the ardour of your zeal. Not that I am ignorant how much mischief is sometimes produced by undue precipitation, and how many persons retard, by an inconsiderate and headlong zeal, what they strive to drag all at once to an issue. But on the other hand you are bound gravely to ponder—that we are doing God's work when we assert the uncorrupted truth of his gospel and all-holiness, and that so it should not be set about with slackness. From your position you can better ascertain how much of progress it will be expedient to make, and where it may be fitting to adopt a prudent moderation; still, however, remember that all delay, coloured by whatever specious pretexts, ought to be regarded by you with suspicion.

One thing, which, as I conjecture, you have to fear, is a popular tumult, since among the nobles of the kingdom are not wanting many sowers of sedition, and should the English be torn by domestic broils, their neighbours are there, ever on the watch to improve and aggravate every opportunity. Nevertheless as her most excellent majesty, the queen, has been raised to the throne in a wonderful manner by the hand of God, she cannot otherwise testify her gratitude than by a prompt alacrity in shaking off all obstacles and overcoming by her magnanimity all impediments. But since it is scarcely possible that in so disturbed and confused a state of affairs, she should not, in the beginning of her reign, be distracted, held in suspense by perplexities, and often forced to hold a vacillating course, I have taken the liberty of advising her that having once entered upon the right path, she should unflinchingly persevere therein. Whether I have acted prudently in so doing, let others judge. If by your co-operation my admonitions shall bring forth fruit, I shall not repent of my advice.

And do you also, most illustrious sir, continually keep in mind that you have been exalted by providence to the rank of dignity and favour which you now occupy, in order that you should give yourself entirely up to this task, and strain every nerve for the promotion of this great work. And lest you should feel any supineness stealing upon you, let the momentousness of these two things be ever and anon presenting themselves to your mind: first, that religion which has fallen into such wretched abasement, the doctrine of salvation which has been corrupted by such execrable errors, the worship of God which has been so foully polluted, should recover their primitive lustre, and the church should be cleansed from her defilements; next, that the children of God should be at liberty to invoke his name in purity, and those who have been scattered again assembled together.

Farewell, most illustrious and most respected sir. May the Lord govern you by his Spirit, protect you, and enrich you with every blessing.

[*Calvin's Lat. corresp.*, Opera, ix. p. 113.]

DXXIII.—To the Prisoners of Paris.[1]

He apologizes for the silence which he has kept with respect to them, and exhorts them to persevere in the profession of the truth.

18th February, 1559.

The love of God our Father, and the grace of our Lord Jesus Christ be always upon you, by the communication of the Holy Spirit.

Dearest Brethren:—If I have delayed till now to write to you, it has not been for want of good will to employ myself in whatever I might think calculated to give you some consolation, or confirm you more and more in that holy constancy which God has bestowed on you; but because I was quite confident that our brethren of your city acquitted themselves of their duty, I did not think my letters very necessary nor greatly desired by you.

Now since I see that they may be profitable, I should consider myself void of humanity if I did not defer to your request. True it is, I am obliged to claim your indulgence if I do not satisfy it entirely, nor even in such a manner as I could wish. For a quartan ague, which I have had for four months, and which has not yet left me, prevents me from discharging the third part of the affairs to which I ought to give my attention if I were in better health. When I compare the slight suffering under which I pine, which is almost nothing, with the afflictions which oppress you; when I reflect also what succour I receive, and on the contrary how cruelly you are harassed and maltreated, I have occasion not only to take patience and feel myself relieved, but to be moved to the deepest compassion and

---

[1] *In a note:* "He wrote this letter to the three prisoners who were in the *Conciergerie* of Paris. One of them was named Meric Favre, and had been apprehended in the assembly of the Rue St. Jacques."

These prisoners were not put to death, but were condemned to perpetual banishment. But one of the companions of their captivity, John Barbeville of Rouen, perished at the stake on the 6th of March, 1559. The flame having consumed his bonds, he raised his hands thus let loose to heaven; "and peaceably without any great signs of pain, rendered up his soul to God." *Hist. des Martyrs.* L. vii. p. 457.

to groan for the temptations with which you may be assailed—
as also to pray our bountiful Father that he would mitigate
your sorrow and strengthen you against assaults, which if you
find hard and difficult to support, be not surprised, knowing
that the virtue of our faith is not to be insensible, but to strive
against our passions; nay that God wills us to feel the aid of
his Spirit by our infirmities—according to the answer given to
Paul.   Especially as your long imprisonment cannot but
annoy, at the same time that it humbles, you doubt not but God
bears with your weakness when you strive against it.   In the
meantime invoke him, as need calls for it, that he may endow
you with perseverance to lead you to a full victory, and that he
may fortify you with those arms which you have hitherto proved
to be sufficient to defeat Satan and his agents.   You know in
what strife you are engaged, it is that God may be glorified,
the truth of the gospel approved, and the reign of our Lord Jesus
exalted in its dignity.

That should stir you up to much greater efforts than those
of men who every day expose themselves to death for the service
of their earthly princes, whose silly ambition or hopes are
animated by the prospect of acquiring favour and credit.   Now
when we see these poor blinded mortals thus rushing into perils,
we have wherewithal to contemplate ourselves in the mirror of
their example, and not to lose courage, when we are called upon
to march where the heavenly King summons us.   Nay, since
he never sets us to work but for our own salvation, and our
state is not made worse by our death, but on the contrary, if he
is pleased to conduct us even to that extremity, he converts it
into a blessing and a gain for us.   And in fact he has no need
of us for his witnesses or advocates to support his cause.   But
it is so much honour he confers upon us when he employs us in
a matter so precious and honourable.   For the rest, take it for
granted that though you are in the hands of your enemies you
are not the less for that under the protection of Him who has
the issues of death in his hand, as is said in the psalms, and who
has thereby infinite means of delivering you, if it be his pleasure.
But whatever happen—prepare yourselves to make to him the
sacrifice of your lives if he be pleased to demand it.   And let

not your zeal be cooled by the mockeries and threats of the ungodly, for though they vent their malice on our simplicity, it
ought to suffice us that it is well pleasing to God.   Accordingly
laying before your eyes the example of Jesus Christ, who was
assailed by the like scoffings of the despisers of God, put in
practice what is taught in the 119th psalm: Let thy mercies
come also unto me, even thy salvation according to thy word, so
shall I have wherewith to answer him that reproacheth me.
Again, the proud have had me greatly in derision, yet have I
not declined from thy law.   Again, the wicked have laid a
snare for me, yet I erred not from thy precepts.   Again, princes
have persecuted me without a cause; but my heart standeth in
awe of thy word.   Again, princes have sat down and taken
counsel against me, and thy servant has meditated on thy
statutes.

And learn with Isaiah to take God for protector, in order not
to be terrified by the haughtiness and presumption of those who
thus vent their rage against the heavens.   Nevertheless fail not
to practise modesty and gentleness, to see if you may not gain
them over, not only to abate their animosity against you, and
draw them to yield obedience to God.   Only do not decline
from the good path on which you have entered, and in which
you have continued up to the present time; but having raised
your eyes to heaven, aspire to the palm which is prepared for
you—to which end we pray God to grant you his grace, showing himself your protector, making you feel it and giving such
an issue to your afflictions, that we may have all subject to bless
his holy name.   My brethren unite in this last wish, though I
trust that Monsieur de Racam[1] will write to you separately.

Your loving brother,

CHARLES D'ESPEVILLE.

[*Fr. copy.—Library of Geneva.*   Vol. 107.]

---

[1] Or Macar, a minister of the Church of Paris, then at Geneva.

DXXIV.—To the French Church of Frankfort.[1]

Warning on the subject of the new doctrines disseminated in this church.

Geneva, 23d *February*, 1559.

The love of God our Father, and the grace of our Lord Jesus Christ be always upon you, by the communication of the Holy Spirit.

Dearly beloved seigneurs and brethren, though the long malady with which God afflicts me is not without its discomfort,[2] and though the desolation of the poor church of Lausanne torments me much more than my own personal sufferings,[3] yet the troubles which I have heard that Satan has anew stirred up among you have not failed to cause me a fresh distress and anguish. The experience of the past ought assuredly to restrain those who have again begun to break the unity and concord which God of his goodness had established among you. But if you perceive any so wedded to their own opinions that their ambition and curiosity tend to the ruin of the church, it is for you to apply a remedy. And if they are so obstinate as not to yield to remonstrance, you cannot but apply the usual remedy, that of excluding them from your society. I am aware that in giving you advice, I cannot avoid subjecting myself to the accusation of undertaking too much, instead of confining myself to the duties of my charge, without wishing to extend my direction so far. But it is enough for me to have God for my

[1] Long a prey to intestine strife and divisions, this church was threatened with new perils, by the invasion of mystical and Anabaptist doctrines, the contagion of which had spread rapidly over some of the Reformed churches of Germany.

[2] " The year 1559, (Calvin) was attacked by a long and severe tertian ague, during which he was forced to his great regret to abstain from reading and preaching. . . This disease left him in such a state of debility, that he never afterwards recovered his full strength." Beza, *Vita Calvini.*

[3] The deposition of the minister Viret by the Seigneurs of Berne (20th January, 1559) was succeeded by the abdication of forty of his colleagues, who like him had in vain called for the establishment of an ecclesiastical discipline. Ruchat. *Hist. de la Ref.*, T. vi. p. 256, and the following. Among the ministers who threw up their charges, were Theodore Beza, Raymond Merlin, Berault, who became the ornaments of the new Academy of Geneva.

witness that the love which I bear towards you and the zeal which I have for your salvation excite and constrain me, and to my own great regret too, to interfere in your affairs. I am also persuaded that most (I might venture to say all) of you are convinced of it, though some who are vexed when good is done, murmur at what they themselves feel to be proper and useful.

Nevertheless I had rather hope, when all shall see that my efforts tend to unite what has been dispersed without offending any, that there will not be a single individual who will not feel obliged to me for having busied myself on this occasion. I entreat you then, my brethren, let me have wherewithal to rejoice, and console me for my other afflictions, on learning that my letters shall have been profitable to you and contributed to bring you to a good intelligence. The greatest misfortune is that even your two pastors are at variance,[1] for if parties and contentions among private persons are a plague in the church, what must it be when the messengers of peace are at war? And it is for that reason we should lose no time in applying a remedy, for fear, the evil having gained head, we come too late to correct it. If Paul deigned to take upon himself the task of reconciling women, and has on that subject written to the whole church of the Philippians, inasmuch as they had laboured along with him for the gospel, how much more, if there be a difference among pastors, whose office it is to settle all quarrels, should every one strive to bring succour, as if we had to extinguish a fire which might consume everything?

However, I pretend not to judge the point at issue, except with regard to some pamphlets which certain persons have wished to introduce or to approve of, I mean the *German Theology*—and *concerning the New Man*.[2] Respecting that

---

[1] Francis Perucel and William Olbrac. The latter was then on the point of quitting Frankfort to go to Strasbourg. These two ministers were at variance respecting the Lord's supper.

[2] Is it the work entitled, " *Theologia Germanica*, libellus aureus, quomodo sit exuendus vetus homo, induendusque novus, ex Germanico anonymi equitis Teutonici, translatus studio Johannis Theophili," Basileæ. 1557, translated from Latin into French with this title : " *German Theology*, a treatise in which is handled how to put off the old man, and put on the new man." Antwerp, 1558, 8vo ?—A remarkable monument of the ancient German mysticism, published by Luther, translated by Castalio ; this book might offend the rigid orthodoxy of Calvin, but not incur the censure of the Lutheran

subject, if I have ever attained any knowledge or proper appreciation of the word of God—I could have desired that the authors had abstained from handling it. For the work contains no notable errors, yet there are in it conceits contrived by the craft of Satan to perplex all the simplicity of the gospel. And if you look into it more narrowly, you will find there a hidden and mortal venom fit to poison the church. Wherefore my brethren, above all things I pray and exhort you in the name of God to shun like a pestilence all those who shall endeavour to infect you with such trash. I entreat those also who up to this moment have given heed to it, to be better advised and no longer to feed the evil which they shall be unable to remedy when they will. Meanwhile strive towards this end that your pastors be united in good brotherhood to do their duty. Beware of all contention which should break the bonds of peace and increase the dispersion of which the evil beginnings are already but too visible. Whereupon I pray our heavenly Father to give you counsel and prudence, to mortify all disorderly passions; and in general to have you in his keeping, to fortify you with his invincible power, and to prevent what he has built up in you from falling into ruin. My brethren greet you, and I especially desire to be commended to your fervent prayers.

[*Fr. copy.—Library of Geneva.* Vol. 107.]

DXXV.—To Augustin Legrant.[1]

Severe admonitions.

GENEVA, 23d *February*, 1559.

SEIGNEUR AUGUSTIN:—I am truly grieved because of the affection I entertain for you to hear such painful news of you, and

magistrates of Frankfort. Is it not more likely that the writing in question, the publication of which occasioned new troubles in the French Church of Frankfort, was the mystical and Anabaptist work of the physician Vadius, entitled according to some : "Summary of Christian Doctrine and Life;" according to others : Treatise touching the manner and way of human life, or respecting the beatitudes of man. See Bayle, *art. Velsius*, and Lutheran Documents of the Church of Frankfort.

[1] Augustin Legrant, one of the elders of the French Church of Frankfort. He began to sign in this capacity the registers of this church, on the last of February

still more to be obliged to write to you in harsher terms than I could wish. Though I have perceived in you too great an impetuosity of mind, and outbreaks that I could well have desired to have been moderated and kept down, nevertheless I should never have expected so much thoughtlessness on your part as you have shown, in going to seek for the deceptions of the devil in that accursed school which is calculated to annihilate all religion, inducing men by crooked ways to give themselves in the end a license to turn God and all religion into derision. Experience shows how much you have profited in it by your spreading about vain conceits full of mortal venom, which is of itself too great an evil, but which, moreover, has been the occasion of sowing dissensions in that poor church that has been so violently torn, that it will be possible to restore it only by little and little. You were already reminded of that, and have only shown yourself so much the more thoughtless—precisely like Saul when he had recourse to the sorceress.

Reflect on this saying: Woe to him by whom scandal cometh. I spare you not in order that God may spare you. And in truth I desire to make you feel the enormity of your fault, in order that you may be the more disposed to submit with a willing mind to the remedy—which is, that forsaking these inconsiderate levities to which you have given too much way, you return peaceably to the fold, and testify that it is not your fault if there is not good concord. When you shall do this, be persuaded that all those who loved you heretofore will have the sweet satisfaction of loving you more than ever. For myself in particular, if I receive these welcome news, preserving no recollection of what our heavenly Father shall have buried in oblivion, I shall cherish you more than before, and shall have the weight of my sorrow diminished. Wherefore I will pray God to direct you by his Holy Spirit, and bless you along with your family.

[*Fr. copy.—Library of Geneva.* Vol. 107.]

1558. The adversary of Valeran Poulain, he had disputes with this minister which terminated but with the death of the latter, in 1557; a partisan of the new theology, he drew upon himself the censure of Calvin, who no doubt had known him at Frankfort.

DXXVI.—To Martin Micronius.[1]

Progress of the Reformation in Sweden—The dispatch of a writing—News of Geneva and Lausanne.

GENEVA, 23d *February*, 1559.

If I but seldom write to you, my dear brother, I am persuaded that you do not take it amiss, for should I send you a letter, most of the charm arising from it would be dissipated in consequence of the distance which separates us, or rather the letter itself would be lost on the road. Just as it happened to the one containing a refutation of the ravings of Memnon,[2] which you declare never reached you; and yet the brethren of Frankfort had promised to deliver it to a trust-worthy messenger. At present I do not send you one of mere compliments; for I have a commission to charge you with,[3] one, however, which I trust you will find neither troublesome nor disagreeable—for it will not put you to much inconvenience to present or to cause to be sent to a pastor who is a neighbour of yours a letter which I am now writing to him.

My second request is rather more difficult to comply with. It is that you would contrive to communicate to Philipperius, the contents of the letter I now address to yourself. For though I am afraid you have but few opportunities of sending into Sweden, yet I fancy Philipperius at his departure must have taken steps for establishing some communication backwards and forwards between you. I have not hesitated to have recourse to your co-operation and kindness to obtain what I so greatly desire.

I have been requested by a certain Frenchman resident in Sweden (whose name has escaped my memory, for I have

---

[1] Expelled from London along with the congregation of foreign Protestants, on the accession of Mary, rejected from Wismar by the intolerance of the Lutheran clergy, Micronius, after having long wandered in the north of Germany, had become pastor of the Church of Norden, in the present Hanover.

[2] The Memnonite heresy, spread over the north of the Netherlands, renewed the ancient errors of Eutyches respecting the humanity of Christ.

[3] See the following letter.

mislaid his letter, I do not know how) if I had anything in hand that I should dedicate it to the king of the Swedes, and especially for the sake of his son, whom he asserts to be animated by a wonderful spirit of piety, that by this incitement he may be still more stirred up.

I have been induced by these reasons to comply with his request. But as I have no means of sending copies of the books, I inform Philipperius of all the circumstances of the case and give him this commission—that having procured one copy he may offer it to the king. It is of great importance indeed that a goodly quantity of copies should be dispatched there, because in a nation so remote, the name of the king would prepare a favourable reception for the orthodox doctrine. And this was my principal motive. In the meantime, it would not be polite to neglect to let the king know how much his conduct is approved of by all the children of God even at a distance, in laying the foundation of pure religion in his dominions; and above all it were well that his son, who is everywhere spoken of as a most prudent prince, should be more and more animated by the prayers of the pious to persevere in his activity.

Of the state of our affairs I scarcely dare to speak. Our city tranquil in the interior is cruelly harassed by its neighbours. I do not speak of the two monarchs between whom peace can scarcely be confirmed except by our ruin, and thus as far as they are concerned we are daily marked out for destruction.[1] But our allies who hesitate to protect and defend us are deterred by no considerations of alliance or ties of a common religion from proceeding to all extremities against us. Nor is it surprising that they should act with such hostility towards us when at home they have plunged everything into confusion.

Because Viret was rather more urgent than they wished in exacting discipline, they have deposed him and two of his colleagues from the ministry, and not content with this they have pronounced against him a sentence of banishment. He is re-

---

[1] The month of June this year, the monarchs of France and of Spain being reconciled conspired the destruction of the seat of heresy at Geneva. An expedition against this city resolved upon by common consent, and commanded by the Duke of Alba, was prevented only by the sudden death of Henry II.

tained only till he promise upon oath that he will submit to their decision. Thirty-two have been summoned that they may undergo to-day at Berne the same judgment. Beza has acted more wisely, who has spontaneously anticipated their decision. A great many terrified by this barbarous conduct will follow his example. The dispersion of that church is a sad and horrible thing. But so it behoved matters to turn out, that at length the cloud of darkness being dissipated, God might bring us some light.

Farewell, most excellent brother, salute all our friends in my name. May the Lord preserve you all in safety, govern you by his Spirit, strengthen you with fortitude, and bestow on you his blessing.—Yours,

JOHN CALVIN.

[*Lat. Copy.—Library of Zurich, Simler.*   Vol. 94.]

DXXVII.—To the Prince Royal of Sweden.[1]

Dedication of a writing to Gustavus Wasa.

GENEVA, *26th February, 1559.*

If any one should tax me with temerity, most excellent and noble king, for having taken the liberty of dedicating a public work to your father, the same person will most probably conceive that I have doubled my fault in not hesitating privately to address your majesty in the present letter, just as if an humble individual were permitted to hold familiar intercourse with you. I expect, however, a much more indulgent judgment from

---

[1] Eric (XIV. of that name), appointed King of Sweden during the lifetime of his father, Gústavus Wasa, did not merit the eulogiums which Calvin had publicly bestowed on his taste for letters and his piety. See on this subject the preface to the Commentary on Hosea dedicated by Calvin to Gustavus Wasa. In praising Eric, the Reformer pays the most splendid and merited homage to his father :

" You need not be surprised, most noble king, that a homage is paid to your majesty from so distant a country and by a person almost unknown to you, who on account of the distinguished and heroic gifts both of mind and body in which he has understood that you abound, professes himself entirely devoted to you."

Gustavus Wasa having died the 29th of September, 1560, Eric succeeded him, was driven from the throne in 1568, and perished by a violent death in 1577.

your well-known urbanity which is so loudly commended. And to confess frankly the truth, relying most confidently on your patronage, I have set my heart on this dedication, which should serve as a token of the profound respect I entertain for all your royal house, but above all that I might associate with the heroic virtues of your father, and inscribe on my work, your name as in due time to be the heir to them. For I have learned from two countrymen of mine who have been protected by you and are in your service, what distinguished favour you have shown them as professors of polite letters, which favour you also extend to all those who have faithfully bestowed their labours in purging the doctrine of pure and uncorrupted piety from shameful superstitions and barbarous ignorance; and that I was also deemed by your majesty a labourer in this work. What talents I have brought to this task in order that my labour should not prove unsuccessful, it is not for me to judge. But as I have an entire conviction that in my studies I proposed to myself no other end than to cause the uncorrupted worship of God to flourish, and that the doctrine which is from heaven being restored to its original purity should obtain in the world that reverence to which it is entitled, I willingly accept your judgment on that point. It is for that reason I have not feared to beg of your majesty in this letter not only favourably to accept the homage I now respectfully tender you, but also to interest your father in behalf of my book, that its utility sanctioned by such authority may be more widely disseminated. For ambition has not engaged me to grace my book with your illustrious names, but my desire was that my labour should give an additional impulse to those already disposed of their own accord to run the good race, and that it might be profitable at the same time to the men of your nation. Farewell, most excellent and noble prince. May the Lord long preserve your majesty in safety and prosperity, govern you by the spirit of wisdom, fortitude, and equity, and enrich you more and more with every excellent gift. Amen.

Your most devoted,

JOHN CALVIN.

[*Lat. Copy.—Library of Geneva.* Vol. 107 *a.*]

DXXVIII.—To Farel.[1]

Dispersion of the Churches of the Pays de Vaud.

GENEVA, 26th February, 1559.

Since you passed through this country, my dear N——, the sad dispersion of the Church of Lausanne has taken place. When Viret was not to be shaken from his purpose, he was deposed from his office along with two of his colleagues. As the whole class associated themselves with his cause, they were confined in the citadel. Afterwards having pledged their faith to appear before the tribunal they were set at liberty. They are now expecting the sentence which is to send them into exile, to such a degree has been carried the rage of those whom God has struck with a spirit of giddiness. Though all the godly are now in sorrow and mourning, the wicked wantonly insult Christ and his faithful followers. Nevertheless God, who is wont to make light to arise out of darkness, will bring round a more favourable issue. With regard to myself, I have been now for upwards of four months suffering from a quartan ague which has kept me hitherto confined to my bed-room, because my body is emaciated and my physical strength exhausted. At present a slight relaxation in my complaint gives me some hopes of a return of health. Again, farewell.

[*Lat. Copy.—Library of Geneva.* Vol. 107 *a.*]

DXXIX.—To Madame de Coligny.[2]

False tidings of the deliverance of the Admiral. Consolations on that subject.

GENEVA, 27th February, 1559.

MADAME:—The common rumour respecting the deliverance of Monseigneur gave us a momentary joy which has only enhanced our regret at learning so shortly after that we have been

---

[1] Without an address. This letter seems written to Farel who had just undertaken a new journey for spreading the gospel at Metz.

[2] Transferred from the Castle of l'Ecluse to the Castle of Gaud, the Admiral still continued the captive of the Spaniards. He did not recover his liberty before the month of April, 1559, after the conclusion of the peace of Cateau-Cambresis.

disappointed in our desire and opinion. But though matters have not fallen out according to our wishes, nevertheless it is your duty to put in practice what the Scriptures teach us of the long expectations of faith, and that the patience enjoined us is not that of a year or two's duration, but that we are called upon to keep our affections in suspense till the favourable opportunity come round; and continually I have recourse to Him to whom it belongs to determine it, praying him to hear our requests, support our infirmities, and for the time that it will please him to let us languish, to fortify our constancy. The main point is that we should make it the business of our lives to acquiesce in all submissiveness and humility to his good pleasure, for that supposes that he should have the peaceable enjoyment of us, that we should be captive to his obedience, and should even make to him a voluntary sacrifice, to die and live according as he shall be pleased to dispose of us. Moreover this affliction is not so severe as to preclude you from many sources of consolation, with which to remain contented till his return. At the same time, Madame, I entreat you to be prepared to hold out against the alarms that may then be got up against you. For however excellent may be his inclination to dedicate himself to God, I fear whether he will be able to remain unshaken by the murmurs and threats of his uncle,[1] or the solicitation of his brother.[2] Reflect also that it is your duty by your example to aid him in taking courage. On our part we will pray God to endow him with greater magnanimity than that of him who had begun so well, but who did not continue in the same manner.[3] Nevertheless whatever difficulties we may

---

[1] The Constable, Anne de Montmorency, a zealous Catholic and the avowed enemy of the Huguenots. A member of the trumvirate in 1561, he signalized himself by the havoc he committed in the preaching assemblies of Paris, and so acquired the nickname of Captain *Brule-banc* (Bench-burner.) He was made prisoner at the battle of Dreux in 1563, and was slain in 1567 at the battle of St. Denis.

[2] Odet de Coligny, Cardinal of Chatillon. He had not yet pronounced in favour of the Reformation.

[3] Allusion to d'Andelot. See the letter, vol. iii., p. 450. Reprimanded by the ministers of Paris, d'Andelot acknowledged his fault and promised to amend it:—"Nevertheless admonished by our brother Gaspar he did not long defend his cause, but sorrowing ingenuously confessed it, and said that he would henceforth strive openly to worship God."—François de Morel à Calvin, 27th December, 1558. (MSS. of Gotha.)

have to encounter, the promise given us that God will provide for every thing and find out a remedy ought to suffice
to prevent us from yielding to temptation, and teach us to think
more wisely, fixing our hearts upon that life which is in heaven,
so that the world shall seem nothing to us, at least that we shall
pass through it as pilgrims and strangers, having this maxim
continually engraven on our memories—that we must be conformed to our Lord Jesus in his afflictions, if we would be partakers of his glory.

Whereupon, Madame, having humbly commended me to your
kind favour, I will supplicate our heavenly Father to have you
in his keeping, to increase in you the gifts of his Spirit, to support you by his power, and grant you the grace to persevere in
serving and honouring him to the end.

[*Fr.Copy.—Library of Geneva.*   Vol. 107.]

DXXX.—To Peter Martyr.

Calvin's illness—Death of Lactanzio Ragnone—Troubles of the Italian Church.

GENEVA, *2nd March,* 1559.

Respecting myself, most accomplished sir and respected
brother, I have nothing to write, except that the violence of my
fever has abated.   But my bodily strength as well as my vigour
of mind has been so much shattered that I do not seem greatly
relieved by this mitigation.   Nay, I even feel a greater degree
of lassitude than when I had to struggle against more violent
attacks.   The debility of my stomach is especially a cause of
suffering to me, and it is increased by a catarrh which brings
along with it its accompaniment a cough.   For as vapours
arising from indigestion trouble my brain, the evil reacts in its
turn upon my lungs.   To all this has been added for the last
eight days a pain occasioned by hemorrhoids from which it is
not possible to force the blood, as they are of that kind which
are commonly termed blind.   If any dependence is to be placed
on the order of the seasons, the only remaining hope I have lies

in the near approach of spring, but the Lord in whose hand are life and death will direct the issue.

Of the death of our most excellent brother Lactanzio,[1] others have no doubt written to you, and it is with reluctance that I awaken a sorrowful recollection. In him the Italian church has certainly sustained no common loss, but what is worse, I fear that God will avenge the ingratitude and arrogance of certain persons by the difficulty of finding a good and fitting pastor. You would hardly believe with what unworthy contempt he was treated, and how little account was made of those remarkable virtues which made him an object of well merited respect among all right minded persons; and though I have sternly and openly denounced them with the punishment which they have deserved, yet I wish to have the benefit of your assistance and counsels lest the goodly structure which God has built up should fall to ruin. Another wound has been inflicted by one Sylvester, whose name probably is not unknown to you; for he lived in England, and is I believe a countryman of your own. Since he had given many indications that he had participated in the impiety of George, and as he had been rather roughly handled by Simon the catechist of the church who had exposed his perfidy, he turned round on Simon and accused him of a disgraceful and abominable crime. At last we discovered that boys had been suborned by him to bear false witness. He himself absconded. One of the witnesses in the case who had obstinately persisted in his false testimony was banished. Simon was acquitted in presence of the Italian congregation by our sentence and that of the elders, but only of what related to the infamous charge brought against him; for he was censured for not having maintained the dignity becoming a minister, and also because he had positively denied all the things laid to his charge, some of which were nevertheless true, though not involving a grave accusation. How atrociously the Bernese have vented their rage and fulminated against the poor brethren, as it pains me to hear it, I shall not write to you concerning it. It is

---

[1] Lactanzio Ragnone of Sienna, third minister of the Italian Church of Geneva. He succeeded, the 24th October, 1557, the Count Celso Martinengo, and died on the 16th February, 1559.

better that the whole matter with all its circumstances should be
explained to you, which it will be I trust ere long. Other details you will learn from our excellent brother, who in returning
to his own country has resolved to take your town in his way
for the purpose of visiting you.

Farewell, most accomplished sir. May the Lord extend his
protection to you and all your colleagues, govern you with his
Spirit and enrich you with his blessings. Amen.—Yours,

JOHN CALVIN.

[*Lat. Copy.—Library of Paris, Dupuy,* 102.]

DXXXI.—To JEROME ZANCHI.[1]

Call to the ministry in the Church of Geneva.

GENEVA, 14th *March,* 1559.

I suppose the tidings of the death of our most excellent
brother have already reached you, and I am convinced they
have produced the same feelings of regret as among us. Assuredly the Italian church has sustained no ordinary loss,
towards which he strove to perform all the duties which can be
desired of a faithful and active pastor. And now that you
have been elected his successor by the suffrages of the people,
see that you do not disappoint the wishes of your countrymen,
and abandon an unhappy flock in its utmost need. I know and
remember the numerous objections which you formerly represented to me when at the request of all I tendered you a call.
At that time I was unwilling to press you too earnestly, lest in
forcing your inclinations I should consult neither your own

---

[1] Jerome Zanchi of Bergamo, one of the most distinguished disciples of Peter
Martyr, quitted Italy in 1543, in order to retire to Switzerland, and merited by his
learned writings to be classed in the first rank among the theologians of the Italian
emigration. Appointed in 1553 professor in the school of Theology at Strasbourg,
from which the ultra Lutheran intolerance represented by the minister Marbach was
to drive him ten years later, he beame successively professor at Chiavenna and at
Heidelberg. He died in the latter city in 1570. Melchior Adam, *Vitæ Theologorum
Exterorum,* p. 77, and Gerdes, *Specimen Italiæ Reformatæ,* p. 351.

private interests nor the public advantages of the church. At present, in my judgment, the case is altogether different.

A flock bereaved of its pastor and unable to find elsewhere a person fitted for the discharge of the pastoral functions, makes an appeal to your fidelity. Unless they be speedily succoured, it is to be feared that a dispersion will take place, which would be to us matter of the deepest distress. Satan is watching his opportunity, and unless there be some extraordinary authority to restrain certain individuals, their perverseness will speedily break out. How fruitful your present labours are I have no means of knowing, except that with great sorrow I have heard that your auditory is thin and almost deserted. If this is the case, it is not the consideration of public utility which will make you hesitate, and we are thoroughly convinced that you are swayed by no regard to private interest or your own ease and indulgence. So much more urgent are the motives and binding the obligation, which should decide you on taking such steps as may correspond to the high confidence reposed in you by your countrymen.

I am aware that you are not at liberty to abandon your present position till you be relieved from the tie which binds you to it, but the whole deliberation turns on this point, if your labours, where you now are, are sterile, and if here an abundant harvest awaits them, which is the most forcible tie, the one by which God draws you hither, or the one that detains you there? When once you shall have yielded to this consideration, you will have no difficulty in obtaining your discharge, nor is the necessity of soliciting it imposed on you, for our senate will petition yours to grant you permission to establish yourself here. If then your intention be to bring succour to an afflicted church, remember the old proverb: He gives twice who gives speedily.

Farewell, most distinguished sir and respected brother. May the Lord govern you in this deliberation by his Spirit, stand always by you, keep you in safety and bless you.—Yours,

JOHN CALVIN.

[*Lat. Copy.—Library of Geneva.* Vol. 107 *a.*]

DXXXII.—To Francis Boisnormand.[1]

Regret for not having been able to have him called as Professor to the Academy of
Geneva.

Geneva, 27th March, 1559.

I do not wonder, most excellent brother, that the burden
which you sustain appears to you heavy and irksome, and that
labours full of innumerable vexations and dangers, should so
diversely distract your mind as to make you sigh for their termination and a deliverance from them. I rather wonder how
you have been able hitherto to cope with such severe trials,
under which you must have sunk a hundred times unless, miraculously supported from on high, you had not risen superior to
what mere human strength can perform. But amid these commencements which promise something beyond vulgar expectation, we dare not tear you away from your post. When seven
or eight months ago our senate had decided to appoint professors of three languages, the brethren were desirous to call you
hither, provided a suitable successor could be readily found for
you. While these things were under discussion among us, a
report brought us respecting Emmanuel Tremelli broke off our
purpose.[2] For he himself indeed had written twice or thrice
that nothing would be more consonant to his wishes than if he
obtained permission to come and settle here. The Prince of
Deux Ponts gave us a courteous reply, that he could not possibly part with Tremelli except to the great detriment of his
academy. Meanwhile, as we were still in suspense, took place
the calamity of the church of Lausanne, the tidings of which
it is probable have penetrated as far as you. Thus, then, on
the present occasion was elected Anthony Chevallier, Tremelli's
son-in-law; at least, Chevallier's wife is a step-daughter of Tremelli. This I wished briefly to inform you of, that you might
not suppose that you had been slighted by us, who, as you see,

---

[1] One of the chaplains of the King of Navarre, and versed in the knowledge of the
Hebrew Language and Literature.

[2] See the Letter to Emmanuel Tremelli, vol. iii., p. 464.

adopted a decision from a sudden and unexpected circumstance, for both religion and a sense of decorum urged us to provide for a pious brother who had been so cruelly ejected. And in that appointment both the authority of our academy and the expressed wishes of Chevallier were satisfied. But for this circumstance the situation had been destined for you. Now that you have been deprived of this opportunity, weigh well whether it would be expedient that you should abandon the post in which God so advantageously employs your labours, unless the brethren who consider you as in some sort bound up with them should counsel you so to do. Neither is it just moreover, nor do we desire that matters should be exposed to peril to comply with our wishes. Thus it will be better for you on that matter to deliberate with the brethren, and if you listen to me you will do well if above all you comply with the advice of our friend Henry,[1] since he has always faithfully and actively assisted you, shared with you all his vows and connected himself so closely with you, that it were wrong to have any separate counsels from him. Excuse the brevity of this letter, since the quartan ague still has its hold on me, debilitating me excessively, and other symptoms give me no little uneasiness. May the Lord always stand by you, govern and sustain you, and shield you and your wife with his safe protection. Many salutations I pray you to the brethren.

[*Lat. Copy.—Library of Geneva.* Vol. 107 *a.*]

DXXXIII.—To M. De La Gaucherie.[2]

Dissentions at the Court of the King of Navarre—Spanish refugees—Salutations to the young Prince of Bearn, afterwards Henry IV.

Geneva, 16*th May,* 1559.

When it was my intention to confide a letter for you to our

---

[1] Henry de Barran, second minister of the King of Navarre.

[2] Francis de la Gaucherie, preceptor of the young Prince of Bearn, later Henry IV. Jane d'Albret, in a letter to Theodore Beza (6 December, 1567,) thus appreciates the excellent cares bestowed on her son by La Gaucherie :—" My son, says she,

friend Francis[1] who was returning among you, I was prevented
from putting my purpose in execution by a sharp and violent
pain in my leg, which though it is now a little mitigated nevertheless continues to give me great uneasiness. To this was
added another cause of delay, inasmuch as this excellent man
entreated us to give him a letter of recommendation. But
while he kept waiting to no purpose for Coulonges, and thus
spun out the time, I gave the letter which had been prepared
for the king to be conveyed by a nobleman who is not unknown
to you. His name is Givré. You will perceive from the perusal of this letter, which the secretary, I trust, will readily communicate to you, how faithfully, with what bland entreaties,
with what serious exhortations, I have studied to appease the
mind of the king, that he might not preclude an honest and
sincere servant of Christ from an opportunity of spreading
more widely the gospel. And though it is possible that the
authority of Francis may have been a little too rigid, and his
zeal in dispute excessive, when I consider however for what
just reasons he opposed that licentious and perfidious monk,
I think the vehemence which has brought such odium on himself redounds to his honour, nor do I insist so much for the purpose of mitigating the resentment of the king, as of correcting
his timidity. That the counsels of the courtiers had disposed
the mind of our friend Henry[2] also to too great weakness, I
congratulate him as on a feeling that was only momentary in
both. In turn we have exhorted Francis not to give any one
offence by an excess of moroseness, and especially not to separate himself from faithful and prudent fellow-workers such as he
has found in you. I return to the bearer of this letter. He is
a Spaniard in whom we have found a genuine zeal for piety.
When I was informed by your letter that the king of his own

owes to him, and his colleagues, that root of living piety which by the grace of God
has been so well implanted in his heart by good admonitions that at present (for which
I praise our heavenly Father) it produces branches and fruits. I supplicate Him
that he will grant him grace to continue to go on from well to better." These favourable dispositions did not hold out against the corrupting influence of the court of the
Valois. La Gaucherie died in 1566, and had for successor Morelli, (MSS. of Geneva,
vol. 197 b.)

[1] Francis Boisnormand.   [2] Henry de Barran.

accord was disposed to grant an asylum to refugees from that nation, I did not hesitate to add my own recommendation.[1] Of you I ask nothing, but that according to your wonted courtesy you show him all those friendly offices which it will be possible for you to do without putting yourself to any inconvenience. Though this recommendation, in truth, seems also superfluous, because you will desire without being solicited to aid a person whom you recognize to be worthy of your affection and that of all pious men. Only let him perceive that he has been thought worthy of my testimony in his favour.

Farewell, most accomplished sir, and my highly esteemed brother. May the Lord always stand by you, support, protect, and continue to govern you by his Spirit. If you do not conceive that it will be unbecoming, will you do me the favour of offering my most auspicious wishes to the prince, your pupil, and presenting him with my best respects.—Yours,

JOHN CALVIN.

[*Lat. Copy.—Library of Zurich, Simler*, 95.]

DXXXIV.—To M. DE COLONGES.

Preliminaries of the Synod of Paris—Sending of several ministers.

GENEVA, 17th May, 1559.

I wish we had been earlier informed of your next assembly.[2] Perhaps, that we might not be altogether without our confession of faith, some measure not to be slighted might have presented

---

[1] Vol. iii., p. 487.

[2] The deputies of the principal Reformed churches of France were on the point of assembling to draw up a confession of faith, an ecclesiastical discipline, and lay the foundations of a common organization which was destined to unite the congregations that had hitherto been separated, and without any other connection than that of their common faith. It was on the 29th of May, 1559, and during the violence of the most fiery persecution that the deputies of eleven churches met at Paris, thus forming the first representative Assembly of French Protestantism. Beza, *Hist. Eccl.*, vol. i., p. 172. It appears that some differences had manifested themselves between the ministers of Paris and those of Geneva respecting the expediency of this meeting and of the new confession of faith that was to spring from it.

itself to our minds. But as the day approaches, it is scarcely
to be hoped that a letter dispatched with whatever speed would
arrive at its destination in time; we shall therefore pray God
that governing your minds he may demonstrate that his Holy
Spirit has presided over the whole transaction. If so obstinate
a zeal for promulgating a confession of faith stimulates certain
persons, we call men and angels to witness that this ardour has
not very much displeased us. The rashness of the brethren of
Tours, who had blown their trumpet so unsuccessfully, will serve
as a proof that they should not advance too eagerly. That
there should be so much anxious bustle and trepidation among
us is to me matter of deep regret. So much the more it behoves you to set about the task to which the prophet exhorts
you; namely, to confirm the weak hands and strengthen the
feeble knees. If they are so lukewarm, and if they forsake
the assembling of themselves together, I fear that we shall
send you fresh assistance to no purpose. Respecting Vesener
we have come to another decision. Arnold is substituted in his
place, a man well versed in polite letters ;—though Peter Gilbert
has not the advantages of a liberal education, yet he possesses
no common degree of knowledge in solid theology to which add
acuteness and a sound judgment. Both of them are right-
minded men and inflamed with zeal for duly establishing the
church. When they shall have heard from you your plans, and
learned as it were their apprenticeship, let me know in a friendly
way your intentions respecting your return or your longer stay.
You will see better what may be expedient in the present circumstances. Only fail not to apprise me that due respect has
been shown you as a private individual, and that your public
authority has had the pre-eminence assigned it which it deserves. You will hear the same injunction from Des Gallars,
whose arrival, if it give you pleasure, is disagreeable to our
society, and his absence inconvenient for his brethren at the
present moment. For I cannot discharge the slightest part of
my ministerial functions, and have but very slender hopes of
being able to do so in the future. So then you will press him
to return here as soon as possible. I thank you for having
written back to me so distinct, so detailed, and yet at the same

time so succinct an account. The pain in my limb prevents
me from imitating your example, and perhaps the narrative of
our transactions will afford you more pleasure when delivered
to you orally. Farewell, most excellent brother, worthy and
faithful servant of Christ. Many salutations to your fellow pastors. May the Lord direct, protect, sustain, and bless you all.

[*Lat. Orig. Min.—Library of Geneva.* Vol. 107 *a.*]

DXXXV.—To Hotman.[1]

Quarrels of Hotman with Francis Baudouin.

GENEVA, *27th May,* 1559.

I would have had you laugh at the excessive warmth of your
anger, that you might not yourself stir up laughter in some, and
sorrow in others. But from your letter I conclude that you are
not one whit more appeased to-day than you were in the first
transports of your passion. I wish indeed that you would learn
either to laugh at or despise those vexations which give you
such immoderate torment, lest the violence of your temper, to
whose sallies you unconsciously give way, should hurt your reputation among many grave and excellent men. I do not speak
of that sluggish fellow, whose lukewarmness and torpor you,
however, supported with moderation, till in a private affair of
yours, in which you wished to be all fire, he conducted himself
rather coldly.

But others, believe me, unless you speedily check your irasci-
bility, will pass a silent judgment on your character, which will
deservedly occasion you more sorrow than the numberless trifles

---

[1] The Academies on the banks of the Rhine were troubled by the violent quarrels
of Baudouin and Hotman. For a short time united at Strasbourg these two eminent
jurisconsults, of whom the former was celebrated for the versatility of his religious
opinions, the second for the fervour and asperity of his zeal, had commenced a controversy, and the departure of Baudouin for Heidelberg had not reconciled the two
rivals. Though he had to complain of the latter with whom he afterwards engaged
in a bitter controversy, Calvin deplored these polemical excesses from which he was
not always himself exempt. See Hotomanni *Epistolæ,* and the Book of M. Dareste,
Essai sur François Hotman, pp. 3, 4.

about which you are too anxiously striving. For if from polite-
ness and kindly feelings they may forgive you, they do not for
that approve of the faults of which I now more freely remind you.
I grant that Baudouin by his evil proceedings is bringing ruin
on himself, provided you do not attack so keenly what is rather
to be deplored.

For what means that very anxious investigation respecting
the salaries? Why does the mention of a successor so exasperate you? For what matters it if he desire that place to be
occupied by another than you, before he be forced to ask for
his discharge, in order that he may have it in his power to depart with less infamy and odium? Certainly till the effer-
vescence of your bile subside, it will often exhaust its ebullitions
about nothing. Remember these counsels are given you by a
man, who, though he is conscious of possessing a more vehement
temper than he could wish, nevertheless is daily supporting,
without any outbreaks of passion, attacks, in comparison of
which your strife with Baudouin is mere child's play.

Polier some eight or ten days after he arrived here, being reminded by your messenger, paid me a visit. Having strictly
questioned him about those mysteries of which you sent me an
account, I could scarcely get a word out of him.[1] As I had repeatedly requested you to write back to me some positive information respecting the grandson of Pomerai, I am surprised
that you have hitherto maintained silence, for I do not know
what you mean by saying that you think your solicitude and
that of M. Sturm was testified by a certain letter. I have
recovered from my tertian ague, but I can scarcely yet support
myself on my legs. To-day, however, I preached sitting. By
degrees I shall gain strength.

Farewell, distinguished sir and honoured brother.[2] Salute
affectionately your wife, your little boy, and our friends. May
the Lord protect, govern, and bless you all.—Yours,

JOHN CALVIN.

[*Lat. Orig. Minute.—Library of Geneva.* Vol. 107 *a.*]

[1] Allusion to some secret negociations which had for object to give for chief of the
French Reformation the King of Navarre. See the letter of Calvin to Sturm, p. 61.

[2] To the date of the letter, Calvin here added, that it was written the day before
the departure of the messenger, who was to be the bearer of it.

DXXXVI.—To the Marquise de Rothelin.[1]

Sends one of his writings to the young Duke de Longueville. Exhortations to the
Duke's mother.

GENEVA, 26th May, 1559.

MADAME:—Being informed that my first letters had been
well received by Monseigneur your son, and that if I continued
to write to him I might further his progress in the good path,
I should not have so long delayed the fulfilment of this task,
had I not been prevented during the greater part of the time
by severe personal sufferings. Nor would even this circumstance
have prevented me, had I not reflected that he enjoys instructions
by word of mouth, from those who are around him much more
ample than any I could send him by letters. These then I entreat him to listen to with docility.

In respect of the book which I had forwarded to him, I find
that the person to whom I entrusted it made a mistake when he
informed me that the young prince was well versed in Latin.
Now I had selected a lesson which was very suitable for him,
because the prophet Amos lays open and rebukes the vices of
the court without sparing any. For he sets about his task with
all the rustic plainness of a cowherd or shepherd, which was
indeed his profession when he was called to the office of public
teaching. I should have been well pleased then that the said
seigneur could have contemplated there, as in a mirror, how he
ought to guard against all the corruptions in vogue, and have
been reminded how they fail not to be condemned of God, however much the world wallows in them and applauds them. On
your own part, Madame, if they still continue to have spies set
round you and threaten you from afar, in order to fill you with
fears, never, I entreat you, be weary of God's service, but

---

[1] Encouraged by the Marquise de Rothelin and the ministers of the Church of
Paris, Calvin kept up a correspondence with the young Duke de Longueville to whom
he had just addressed his commentary on the lesser prophets : *Joannis Calvini præ-
lectiones in duodecim prophetas quos vocant minores, Geneva*, 1559. This commentary
was dedicated to the King of Sweden.

rather inure yourself by the struggles which you have already maintained to such perseverance that God may be glorified by you in the end. And I doubt not but you faithfully labour to that end, that even the rejoicings of these days have been to you so much the more vexatious that they always bring with them some consequences to displease and afflict the children of God.[1] And in truth Paul takes it for granted that the faithful will take no interest in the pleasures, delights, and dissolute revellings of the world, so as to find a charm therein, when he redoubles his exhortations to them to rejoice in the Lord.

Though in truth unbelievers have no idea what true joy is, since they do not possess a peaceable conscience towards God, nor can truly enjoy the goods which he has showered down upon them, however abundantly. For this very reason we have better motives for supporting with patience the vexations which may annoy us, inasmuch as they cannot prevent us from continually savouring the goodness of our God and Father and the love he bears towards us, till we be fully satisfied with them in the place of our everlasting rest.

Madame, having commended myself most humbly to your indulgent favour, I will supplicate the Father of mercies to have you always in his keeping and guidance, to support and fortify you by the power of his Spirit, and to increase in you every good and prosperity.

[*Fr. Copy.—Library of Geneva.* Vol. 107.]

---

[1] While the Parliaments were redoubling their rigour against the Reformers, magnificent fêtes were being prepared for the celebration of two marriages, that of Elisabeth, the king's daughter, with Philip II., and that of Margaret of France with Emmanuel Philibert.

DXXXVII.—To the Duke de Longueville.[1]

He exhorts him to abstain from all participation in the idolatries and disorders of the age.

Geneva, *26th May,* 1559.

Monseigneur :—I thank our merciful Father, that you have received my letters with a spirit of humility, and that you take pleasure in the admonitions which they contain. For I consider it as highly important that my labours in your behalf have been crowned with success, because of the profit which I hope you will reap from them, for the salvation of your soul, and also because of the advantages which will accrue from them to the church of God; and especially for the advancement of the reign of our Lord Jesus Christ. It is that which gives me boldness to write to you repeatedly, as I believe that you are convinced of the need you stand in of being continually stirred up, considering the seductions that surround you, by which you might easily be turned aside from the straight path, were you not fortified from on high to resist them. Now not only you have many thorns to prevent the knowledge of the gospel of our Lord Jesus Christ from fructifying in you, but also many agents of Satan who will heartily strive to tear it from your heart. Wherefore, monseigneur, you ought the more carefully to seek for remedies to preserve you in the fear of God and the purity of his service. On my part I shall spare no pains, as far as I shall have it in my power, to aid you in that task. For one cannot strive too much to stay such a deluge of corruption as that which we now witness in the world. You have also to con-

[1] Leonor d'Orleans, Duke de Longueville, and Count de Neuchatel. Educated by his mother in the Reformed faith, this young seigneur took pleasure in the writings and exhortations of Calvin. In 1562 he made a journey to Geneva of which we read an account in the registers of the Council :—" The Duke de Longueville arrived at Geneva accompanied by a number of noblemen. He was complimented on the part of the Council by the Syndic Francis Roset, Baudichon, Chevalier, and Bernard, accompanied by M. Calvin, who made a speech. The said Duke de Longueville was present to-day at the sermon, to which he listened with great attention—Our Lord causes him to advance in the Reformation of his holy gospel." 29th January, 1562.

sider your own age, the position in which you are placed, and the countless temptations which might well shake the resolution of the most determined.

I will not allege to you the ordinary train of the court. I shall only adduce one particular instance of the dazzling pomp accompanying the marriages a few days ago, or which it is possible is not yet all over.[1] I am not so austere as to condemn the fêtes of princes, nor the rejoicings with which they celebrate their nuptials. But I am convinced, monseigneur, that when you enter into reflection with yourself, having recalled your thoughts from the pomp, vanities, and excesses by which they may have been led astray for a moment, you will pronounce these things a gulf of ruin and disorder. I only point out to you in a small and trifling matter how necessary it is for you, amid so many idolatries, that you should be fortified in perseverance by God, and that on your own part you should strive to keep yourself as it were shut up under his direction, applying your studies to advance more and more in the knowledge of his holy word, and praying him to increase in you the gifts of his Spirit, in order that your faith may remain victorious even to the end.

I durst not venture, monseigneur, to exhort you with so much frankness, were you of the number of those who are ashamed of submitting to God, on account of their earthly rank and dignity, and who wish to be exempted from all correction and admonition. As I am confident that all the illusions of the world will never dazzle your eyes to such a degree, as that you shall not be prepared to offer up to the Son of God, our sovereign King, the homage of your soul and of your body, it is for this reason that I do not hesitate to confirm you more and more in this good resolution. But as I fear to fatigue you by too long letters, I will content myself with entreating you to read daily the holy instructions which will edify you in all good and virtue, in order that the example of your life may touch and persuade many of those poor ignorant creatures that are not incorrigible, and stop the mouth of the obstinate enemies of the truth of God.

[1] See the preceding letter, p. 43, note 1.

Monseigneur, having humbly commended me to your indulgent favour, I entreat our heavenly Father to have you in
his protection, to govern you by his Spirit in all prudence and
integrity, and cause you to prosper in all good.

[*Fr. Copy.—Library of Geneva.* Vol. 107.]

DXXXVIII.—To WILLIAM CECIL.[1]

He exculpates himself to this minister of the imputations brought against him on
account of a writing of Knox's.

GENEVA, *May*, 1559.

The messenger to whom I had given my commentaries on
Isaiah to be offered to the queen, brought me back word, that
my homage was rather distasteful to her majesty, because she
had been offended with me on account of certain writings that
had been published in this city. He also repeated to me, most
illustrious sir, the substance of a conversation he had with you,
in which you appeared more harsh towards me than your usual
urbanity led me to suppose, especially when from my letter you
were informed how much I promised myself from your affection
towards me. Now though just causes prevent me from excul-
pating myself by a laboured refutation, lest, however, I should
seem by my silence to confess that to a certain extent my con-

---

[1] Letter without a date—written no doubt in May, 1559, as seems to be indicated
by Cecil's answer to Calvin of the 22nd June following. Public opinion had been
warmly excited by Knox's pamphlet against the government of women. See vol. iii.
pp. 37, 38. Directed against Queen Mary, this book was appealed to by ardent
sectaries against the authority of Elizabeth herself, and Calvin's name was associated
with that of Knox, in the controversies to which the writing gave rise. The Reformer
judged it necessary then to offer to Cecil explanations indirectly addressed to the
queen herself. Cecil showed himself satisfied with them, if we may judge by his answer to Calvin : "In what concerns you, I know most certainly that, for many reasons,
all writings of this kind are displeasing to you. And if some of our countrymen afflicted with this mania have affirmed that you had answered, 'though in the ordinary
course of things, as we say, and in virtue of the Divine word the right of governing
is forbidden to a woman, nevertheless there are extraordinary occasions in which it
may be permitted,' this distinction, I venture to affirm, you by no means approve of."
Queen Elizabeth's secretary signed his letter to Calvin, "Yours most affectionately,
and with the warmest zeal for the evangelical profession. W. C."

science blames me, I have thought proper to put you in possession of the main facts of the case.

Two years ago, John Knox in a private conversation, asked my opinion respecting female government. I frankly answered that because it was a deviation from the primitive and established order of nature, it ought to be held as a judgment on man for his dereliction of his rights just like slavery—that nevertheless certain women had sometimes been so gifted that the singular blessing of God was conspicuous in them, and made it manifest that they had been raised up by the providence of God, either because he willed by such examples to condemn the supineness of men, or thus show more distinctly his own glory. I here instanced Huldah and Deborah. I added to the same effect that God promised by the mouth of Isaiah that queens should be the nursing mothers of the church, which clearly distinguished such persons from private women. Finally I added in conclusion, that since by custom, common consent, and long established usage, it had been admitted that kingdoms and principalities might be by hereditary right transmitted to women, it did not seem proper to me that this question should be mooted, not only because the thing was odious in itself, but because in my judgment it is not permitted to unsettle governments that have been set up by the peculiar providence of God. Of the book I had not the slightest suspicion, and it had been published a whole year before I was aware of its existence.

Informed of the fact by some persons, I testified in the most unequivocal manner that the public was not to be familiarized with paradoxes of that kind. But because the remedy did not depend on me, I conceived that an evil which could not be redressed had better be hushed up than publicly canvassed. Ask of your father-in-law, when he reminded me of it through Beza, what answer I made. Mary being then still alive, I could not be suspected of an intention to flatter. Of the contents of the work I am ignorant; but that the tenor of the discourse I had with Knox is such as I have described it, he himself will confess. But though I was affected by the complaints of pious individuals, yet as I had not been informed in time, lest greater disturbances should arise out of it, I did not venture to make any loud outcry.

If my slackness offends any one, I think I had reason to fear, if the affair had been brought to a trial, that for the inconsiderate vanity of one man, an unfortunate crowd of exiles would be driven not only from this city, but from almost every part of the world, especially as the evil now admitted of no other remedy than the exercise of indulgence. Besides that I have been loaded with undeserved blame, for that very reason I still less merited to have my book rejected, as if a pretext had been sought to throw the follies of others upon me. Your queen, if the work did not please her, might with one word have refused to accept my proferred courtesy. That would have been more straight-forward, and assuredly it would have been more agreeable to me than, besides the disgrace of a repulse, to be charged at the same time with false accusations. I shall nevertheless always cherish the most profound respect for your most excellent queen; and you too, renowned sir, I shall not cease to love and honour on account of your extraordinary talents and other virtues, though I have found you less friendly than I had expected, and though you may not in future reciprocate my feelings of affection. I am unwilling, however, to augur this last result.

Farewell, most beloved and honoured sir. May the Lord always stand by you, govern and protect you, and enrich you with his gifts.

P. S. Because I am in doubt whether you received my former letter, I have thought proper to send you a copy of it.

JOHN CALVIN.

[*Lat. orig. autogr.—Library of Geneva.* Vol. 107 *a*.]

DXXXIX.—To the Brethren of France.[1]

Perseverance in the faith—Patience in persecution—Trust in God, who will sooner
or later take in hand the cause of his innocent followers.

GENEVA, *June*, 1559.

Dearly beloved and honoured brethren, inasmuch as you are
all in general afflicted, and as the storm has burst out with such
violence, that there is no place that has not felt its ravages; as
moreover we are not informed of your individual necessities, we
have thought that we could not do better than address to you a
common letter to exhort you, in the name of God, whatever
alarms Satan may create, not to faint, or by withdrawing from
the combat to deprive yourselves of the fruit of the victory
which has been promised and confirmed to you. It is most
certain that if God did not give freer reins to Satan and his
agents, they could not thus molest you. And for that reason
you should come to this conclusion, that if your enemies plot
your ruin it is because God on his part has granted them such
a permission in order to prove your faith, having means without
number at his disposal to check all their fury when he shall

---

[1] The long struggle between Spain and France had procured a momentary truce to
the Reformed Churches. The peace of Cateau-Cambresis increased their perils by
reconciling the two monarchs in a common design, the extermination of heresy.
Irritated by the resistance of several of the counsellors of the Parliament of Paris,
and the courageous words of Anne Dubourg, Henry II. gave the signal for new executions. "Whereupon, says Beza, the king having left Paris, (June, 1559,) came to
Escouen, the seat of the constable, from which place he sent letters patent to the
judges of the provinces, enjoining that all the Lutherans should be destroyed; declaring that heretofore he had been prevented by his wars, and that he perceived that
the number of the said Lutherans had greatly increased during those troubles, but
now that peace having been concluded between him and Philip, King of Spain, he
was quite determined to employ his whole time in exterminating them, provided that
on their side they were not slack. * * * For if they acted otherwise, and spared
them as he had heard that some of them had formerly done, to them the blame should
be imputed, and they should be made an example to others. These letters were well
calculated to stir up great troubles if God had not provided for it. Nevertheless,
the churches sought consolation in the promises of God, continuing in prayer and
persuading themselves that God would finally hold out a helping hand to his church;
in which confidence the foreign churches greatly confirmed them, encouraging them
to remain unshaken in their vocation."—*Hist. Eccl.*, vol. i., pp. 194, 195, and *Hist. des
Martyrs*, p. 462.

have glorified his name by your constancy. Now when you are called to this trial all that remains for you to do is to prepare yourselves for the confession of the faith which God requires, as a sacrifice which is well-pleasing to him, however much the world despise and scoff at our simplicity. And if it is necessary that you should be sacrificed in order to seal and ratify your testimony, he thus wills you to take courage to surmount all the temptations which might turn you aside from making it. For it is but reasonable that we should suffer ourselves to be governed by the hand of so good a Father, though it may seem to us heavy and unfeeling. If we were exposed to be forsaken of him, then might we feel consternation. But since He who has taken us under his protection has himself willed to try us by all the combats into which we shall be brought, it is for us to subdue our affections, nor to think strange the condition to which we are called. We are perfectly aware what terrors you shall have to endure, when we reflect that you are not armed with insensibility, but feeling on the contrary much repugnance and many conflicts in your flesh. But notwithstanding all that, assuredly God must prevail. It was well said of the death of Peter, that he should be led by a way which he did not choose. So he subdued the natural man, so as to be conducted at God's good pleasure, that is, with a hearty good will. Therefore, following his example, wage a valiant warfare against your infirmities in order to remain victorious over Satan and all your enemies.

Great are their rage and cruelty against the poor church, their threats terrible, and the preparations are such that we might well deem that all must be ruined. So far, however, is that from being the case, that our persecutions are by no means so intense as those which our fathers endured. Not that the devil and his children are less hardened and bent upon doing evil than ever, but because God bearing with our weakness keeps them enchained like so many wild beasts. For it is certain that if hitherto he had not interposed his hand, we should have been destroyed a thousand times, and if he did not still continue secretly to watch over us, we should be speedily swallowed up. Knowing then by experience the pity and compassion that God feels for us, so much the more should we, with a feeling of security, repose on his protection, trusting that he will prove how dear our lives are to him. Meanwhile we must despise and count them as nothing when we are called to employ them in his service, and among other things maintain his holy word, in which he desires his glory to shine forth. It is thus, according to the saying of our divine Master, that we shall possess our souls in patience, because he will be the faithful guardian of them. And, moreover, if with our free-will we lose this frail and perishable condition, we shall recover it far better in the heavenly glory. And this is the principal lesson which the holy Scripture requires you now to meditate upon when it calls us pilgrims in this world; namely, that nothing should turn us aside from that enduring inheritance to which we cannot aspire with well-grounded confidence, as we are bound to do, unless we are prepared to quit this earthly habitation whensoever it shall please God to summon us away.

We shall not accumulate here all the testimonies that might contribute to fortify your patience, for we should never have done, since the whole Scripture is filled with them. We shall not deduce either how we must be partakers of the death of the son of God our chief, if we are to rise up again with him; that we must be conformed to his image, and supply what is wanting in his sufferings, in order to share in the repose which he has promised to us. This should be a doctrine common to all of us, that as he entered into his glory by many afflictions, so we are bound to follow the same course. For the present, it is sufficient to fix in our memories that all the oppressions which fall out against the church are for the trial of the faith of the elect according as God shall be pleased to ordain in the fitting time. Now since Jesus Christ did not spare his own blood in order to confirm the truth of the gospel wherein lies our salvation, it is but just that we should not refuse to make him our example, especially as we are assured that whatever our enemies devise against us shall all be converted to our salvation. And that you may take more heart, doubt not, when the evil ones shall have exhausted all their cruelty, that there will be one drop of blood that will not fructify so as to increase the

number of the believers. If it does not seem to you at first
sight that the constancy of those who have endured trials brings
forth fruit, do not for all that cease to acquit yourselves of your
duty, and leave to God the advantages that will accrue from
your life or death for the edification of his church; for from
them he knows well how to bring forth fruits in his own time
and way. And the more the wicked strive to exterminate the
memory of his name from the earth, the more efficacy will be
bestow on our blood to cause that memory to flourish more and
more. And in very deed we cannot fail to see that God intends to exalt his name at the present moment and advance the
reign of Jesus Christ. Only let us suffer the darkness of the
present eclipse to pass over, waiting until God produce his light
to rejoice us, though indeed we are never deprived of it in the
midst of our afflictions, if we seek for it in his word in which it
is offered to us and where it never ceases to shine.

There, then, it behoves you to turn your eyes during these
great troubles, and to rejoice that he has esteemed you worthy
of suffering affliction for his word rather than of chastisement
for your sins, which we should all deserve did he not support us
by his grace. And if he promises to console poor sinners who
received patiently correction from his hand, be confident that
the aid and comfort of his Holy Spirit will not fail you, when
reposing your trust on him you shall accept the condition to
which he has subjected his children. And wait not till the
great ones of this world point out to you the way, who most
frequently corrupt their brethren and cause them to backslide
rather than further their progress. What is more, let not each
man look on his fellow to say like Peter: *And this man, what
of him?* but let each man follow as he shall be called, seeing
that each must give an account for himself. Look rather at the
invincible courage of so many martyrs who have been set before us as an example, and take heart to join yourselves to so
goodly a company; which for this reason the Apostle compares
to an immense and thick cloud, as if he said their numbers are
so vast as in a manner to blind our eyes. What is more, without going further, the examples which God every day offers us
being duly considered, as they deserve, should be sufficient to

fortify us against the stumbling blocks thrown in our way by the baseness of many.

Moreover, according as each is placed in a higher station, let him reflect that he is so much the more bound to take the lead, and on no occasion to yield to dissimulation. Let not the noble and rich and people of rank think that they are privileged, but on the contrary let them acknowledge that God has chosen them, to be more highly glorified in them. When you shall march with such simplicity, invoking God to look upon you with compassion, it is certain that you will thus feel more relief than if each thought of escaping by subterfuges. We do not mean to say that you should with your eyes open, or without discretion, expose yourselves to the jaws of the wolf; only beware of withdrawing from the flock of our Lord Jesus Christ in order to avoid the cross, and fear more than all the deaths in the world the dispersion of the church. Otherwise what excuse will you be able to plead when our Lord Jesus Christ, his Father, and all the angels of paradise shall bring against you this reproach, that having made a profession of confessing God in life and in death, you have betrayed the faith which you had pledged? What a shame it will be, if after having separated yourselves from the defilement and pollutions of Papal idolatry, we should return to wallow a second time therein, and become doubly abominable in the sight of God! In one word, if all our felicity consists in being a disciple of our Lord Jesus, knowing that he will disavow and denounce all those who do not confess him before the ungodly, steel your hearts to endure reproaches as well as persecutions, and if you desire to have God for your stronghold, sanctify him, in despising the fears of the unbelieving, as we are exhorted to do by St. Peter.

Be persuaded also that the pride of these lions and dragons, and the rage with which they foam, will inflame so much the more the wrath of God, and hasten the execution of his vengeance. Finally, do not take it to heart to be despitefully treated by such mad men, since your names are written in the Book of Life, and God approves of you, not only as his servants, but also as his children and heirs of his glory, members of his only Son Jesus Christ, and companions of angels. Nevertheless let it suffice you to oppose to their fury, prayers and tears, which God will not permit to fall to the ground, but which he will preserve in his phials, as is said in the Psalm.

We have here briefly touched on what should be your conduct during this fiery trial. The main point is that each of you should diligently exercise himself in the reading of the word, and that you mark and retain the exhortations that are addressed to you by the mouth of God, to serve him with all perseverance, never wearying, whatever befall you.

If we could make manifest to you the care and compassion which actuate us for you, the desire and the good-will are not wanting to us for that purpose, just as we are convinced that the dangers which are impending over ourselves affect and stir you up to recommend us to the keeping of God, whom we entreat that of his infinite goodness he would make you feel that he is a protector both of the body and the soul; that he would govern you by his Holy Spirit, that he would support you by his power, that he would triumph in your persons, by scattering all the counsels, enterprises, and strength of his enemies, and your own.

[*Fr. Histoire des Martyrs, Lib.* vii., p. 462.]

DXL.—To the Church of Paris.[1]

Inutility of the steps taken in favour of the French Protestants—The helplessness of men—Fidelity of God.

GENEVA, 29*th June*, 1559.

Dearly beloved seigneurs and brethren, if we have delayed to answer you longer than you could have wished, it has also been

[1] At the top :—To the Brethren of the Church of Paumiers. An inexact title arising from the blunder of a copyist. It is—To the Brethren of the Church of Paris. The Church of Pamiers did not yet exist at the date of this letter, (29 June, 1559.) It could hardly be said to exist two years afterwards, (August, 1561,) according to the positive testimony of Beza.—*Hist. Eccl.*, vol. i., p. 866. Subjects of the King of Navarre, the Protestants of Pamiers had not moreover to suffer from the increased rigour which signalized the last days of the reign of Henry II. Now it is a persecuted church which Calvin addresses, and his anticipations as well as his coun-

to our own great regret.   But having once let slip the opportunity of writing to you by a messenger who was repairing to your city, up to this moment we had not been able to find another. Now I have no need to protest to you that if you are in perplexity and anguish for the dangers that are impending over you, we also feel our share of them; for we are convinced that your opinion of us is such that you cannot suppose us so destitute of humanity as to forget those with whom we are connected by fraternal ties through the faith, those too who are doing battle for the cause of our salvation; but the evil afflicts us so much the more keenly that we are destitute of all means of relieving you, and have nothing left us to do but groan with compassion.   Be persuaded that we have employed all the human means in our power to try to appease the rage of the enemy either wholly or in part, and even at the present moment we would spare nothing were there any hope that we could be of service to you.   But he whom they entreated[1] has so arrogantly rejected the request of the princes several times reiterated, that it seems that God would thereby teach us to make himself our whole stay, both in praying him to protect us, and in devoting ourselves entirely to his obedience whether for life or for death.   On our part, we do not know how soon the blow may light on ourselves.   One thing is certain, we are menaced more than all others.[2]   But you who are already exposed as a prey to the spoiler, knowing that God is the protector of his followers, commit your ways to him, and if, in the meantime, it be his pleasure that you should suffer for his name, prepare yourselves for that sacrifice, for we shall never be disposed to follow the gospel till we lay our account with being patient in persecutions.   If you are weak, God will know well how to support you; but if he bring you to the trial, you must

sels sufficiently designate the Church of Paris, the first exposed to the attacks of persecution. The trial of the most illustrious of its members was already begun, the prisons were replenished with captives doomed to death, while the court inaugurated by magnificent fêtes the destruction of heresy.

[1] King Henry II., struck, the day after the Reformer wrote this letter, by the lance of Montgomery.

[2] Henry II. had uttered terrible threats against Geneva, and Pope Paul IV. preached a crusade against the seat of heresy.—*Hist. de la confederation Suisse,* vol. xii., p. 24.

put in practice the doctrine of possessing your lives in patience. For this purpose you must raise your eyes to heaven, for otherwise it would be too difficult to quit the world, and there is nothing that can fortify us in all combats but the firm persuasion that we cannot be frustrated of this inheritance. Place before your eyes then our Chief, the Son of God, who has risen from the dead that we should feel no evil in dying with him in order to be partakers of his heavenly glory. Wherefore, dearly beloved brethren, knowing on what condition we are called, continue to advance, confirming yourselves more and more in the faith of our Lord Jesus Christ, which will be victorious over the whole world, and in withdrawing yourselves from idolatry, remain unmoved and peaceable, endeavouring by your good and holy life to cover with confusion all the agents of Satan.

Whereupon, having commended ourselves to your fervent prayers, we will also beseech our heavenly Father to condu you by his Holy Spirit, in order that his holy name ma glorified in you even to the end.

[*Fr. Copy.—Library of Geneva.* Vol. 107.]

DXLI.—To the Count D'Erbach.[1]

He offers him Christian congratulations, and consults him about a project of dedicating to the Elector Palatine the Book of the Institution.

Geneva, 1st *July,* 1559.

When the preceding year Theodore de Beza and John Budé, on their return from a visit to you, most noble and illustrious

---

[1] Eberard, Count of Erbach and the brother-in-law of the Elector Palatine, early displayed, as well as his brothers, the warmest attachment to the Reformed faith. See the eulogy of this seigneur in a letter of the learned Olympia Morata from her retreat at Heidelberg, *Opera*, pp. 216, 217. Gifted with an elevation of mind very rare at this period, Count d'Erbach deplored the sacramentarian disorders and ardently desired the conciliation of the churches on the grounds of faith and charity. "What is no less to be deplored is that under the splendid and fruitful light of the gospel there should still be found so much darkness, so great a discrepancy of opinions, that those who ought to be members of one head and one body, persecute one another with reproaches and revilings not less than the members of Antichrist are wont to do." Without disapproving of the project of dedicating to the Elector, Calvin's Christian

seigneur, among your other rare virtues highly extolled your courtesy; they could not hold their tongues, at the same time, respecting your affection towards me, and as they were fully persuaded that should I write to you, my letter would be very acceptable, they warmly pressed me to acquit myself of this duty. As, however, I was already of my own accord sufficiently disposed to undertake this task, not so much out of deference for them as for the sake of testifying my profound respect for you, I know not what cause has hitherto occasioned my delay or my sluggishness, so that laying aside all ideas of excusing myself I am forced to entreat your pardon for my dilatoriness. But now a new opportunity having most providentially presented itself, I have mustered up courage, most excellent seigneur, not only to congratulate you on your accession of honour and dignity, but also to express to you the unfeigned pleasure which I have lately conceived therefrom. For I had heard long ago from trustworthy witnesses how disinterested your integrity and constancy were, in the defence of the sound and pure doctrine, and I again hear what all pious men in your country expect from you. Though then I wish and pray for all prosperity and happiness to you, as an individual, yet I rejoice more for the public cause of the church than for your own sake, that you have been raised to this high post of honour, and assuredly you are a great ornament to that dignity which would itself have adorned any other sprung from a less illustrious family. I doubt not but the Elector Palatine counts it not the least part of his good fortune that he has found a count among the highest ranks of the nobility, fitted above all others to have this charge confided to him, and who will not hesitate, from his well-known feelings of modesty, to undertake it. But as the prudence of the prince is to be lauded in this choice, so I doubt not but that you have been commended to this post of eminence by the hand of God, first that by your

---

Institution, Count Eberard expressed some doubts respecting the seasonableness of this act. "For it is to be feared, if any troublesome and suspicious men should learn that your attempts and labours give pleasure to the prince, that they will come with less alacrity to the conciliation of which I have spoken." Letter of the 8th August, 1559, vol. of Geneva.

ability, equity, diligence, and activity the state of the principality may flourish in inviolate and well-established order, that
the laws and public ordinances should be vigorously administered, temperance and moderation prevail; next that religion, the
spots which still adhere to it being wiped out, should regain its
unalterable purity and be thoroughly purified from the corruptions of Popery. That despising the spite and murmurings of
the ill-affected, you should ply courageously and strenuously
this holy and pious task, as I deem it unnecessary to exhort
you, most noble seigneur, I shall confine myself to vows and
prayers that the Spirit of God would animate you to invincible
constancy, that by virtue of the same, all obstacles being happily overcome, you may triumphantly fulfil the course of your
calling.

How rooted a hatred of all sincere piety exists in the heart
of the French king, and how implacable is his cruelty towards
the servants of Christ, was lately made very manifest by one
example. When he had heard that the Parliament of Paris was
deliberating about relaxing their former severity, he immediately
flew thither, and having heard three judgments pronounced, he
ordered the two judges to be arrested, who had given it as their
opinion that milder measures should in future be adopted with
regard to those who had hitherto been too cruelly oppressed.
And to these two persons he also afterwards added some others
suspected by him of similar lenity. If you should chance to
feel any wish for making yourself more fully acquainted with
the chief points of this affair, I have thought proper to send
to you the letter which was written from Paris. As he is of
opinion that the doctrine which has been disseminated over all
parts of his kingdom, emanated from here; with what ardour he
is inflamed for razing and destroying this city is evident, though
he himself indeed dissembles it.

Assuredly we are not standing safe and sound up to this
moment, unless by the marvellous protection of God. In the
mean time as my Institution re-written and so altered as to have
almost the appearance of a new work, is now in the press, and
will be brought out at the time of the fair, some of my friends
have suggested to me that the apology prefixed to it addressed to

King Francis, should remain as a testimony both to the father and the son.   They think, however, that I should dedicate to your illustrious Elector the book itself, which holds the principal and far most conspicuous place among all my lucubrations.   I, however, did not dare to adopt a measure of this importance, unless you should give me some token of your approval of such a resolution, and now, if I have been inconsiderate in mentioning the matter to you, I beg you will excuse my presumption.   If, however, you shall have no objections to communicate anything to me on that subject, Hotman the jurisconsult who lives at Strasbourg will take care to have it transmitted to me.

Farewell, most excellent and illustrious seigneur.   May the Lord continue to govern both you and your noble brothers along with your families, to protect you and enrich you with every blessing, and to foster between you a holy and blessed unity.— Yours,

JOHN CALVIN.

[*Lat. orig. autogr.—Library of Geneva.*   Vol. 107 *a.*]

DXLII.—TO FRANCIS DANIEL.[1]

He pleads with Daniel in favour of one of his sons who had taken refuge at Geneva
for the sake of religion.

GENEVA, 25*th July,* 1559.

Sir and well beloved brother, I have delayed till now to write to you about your son, both to be better able to decide with

---

[1] Francis Daniel, an advocate at Orleans, the fellow student and friend of Calvin at the university of this city.   Won over in early youth to the Reformed doctrines which he no doubt derived from Calvin himself, he nevertheless remained outwardly attached to the Catholic church in spite of the censures of the Reformer.   The eldest of his sons, Peter Daniel, an advocate of the Parliament of Paris, cultivated letters with some success, and kept up a correspondence with Joseph Scaliger (MSS. de Berne, vol. 141).   The second Francis Daniel, inclined by his tastes to the study of theology, but crossed by his father who destined him for the bar, fled from Orleans and repaired in 1559 to Geneva.   Welcomed affectionately by the Reformer, and docile to his counsels, he consented a year afterwards to return to the parental roof, and follow the career of the law.   See the Latin correspondence of Calvin, 1559, 1560.   There

time what I ought to communicate to you, and also because I had no opportunity of a sure and fitting messenger. I make no doubt but that you are angry at his departure, being disappointed in the hopes and intentions which you had founded on the career which you wished him to pursue. But I beseech you not to give such loose to your passions as not to judge equitably, in order that you may think favourably of what he has done, if it is of God. If you had such courage as most certainly you ought to have had in acquitting yourself of your duty, you would long ago have shown him the example. But if you are cold and tardy in emerging from the gulf in which you are plunged, at least bear no grudge against your children if God delivers them from it, but take occasion from their example to bestir yourself to make every effort to escape from it.

As far as I have observed, it seems to me that your son has by no means been impelled or induced by thoughtlessness, but that the fear of God has constrained him to withdraw from superstitions with which God is offended. You ought not to feel hurt that God's authority has been preferred to your satisfaction. What makes me conclude that the young man has been swayed by no other consideration than a desire to serve God in purity, is that here he conducts himself with modesty, and without any marks of a behaviour different from that of a sincere Christian. As yet he has had no succour from me, though it only depended on himself to accept what I offered with a good heart, and I shall always be ready, for the love I bear to you, to aid him as far as my slender means will permit. But above all I desire that you should be appeased towards him. It is not as if he had quitted you in the manner of debauched lads—but since he has been zealous to follow God, you have much reason to be satisfied with him, and to that end I most affectionately implore you. I hope, after having had some answer from you, to write to you more fully; in the meantime, having cordially commended me to you, to your mother, and your wife, I will supplicate our heavenly Father to have you

---

exists (*Library of Geneva*, vol. 196) a letter of young Francis Daniel to Calvin soliciting the favour of studying at the same time theology and law. This letter is dated from Orleans, 5th April, 1561.

continually in his holy keeping, to govern you by his Spirit and increase you in all prosperity.

Your humble brother and entire friend,

CHARLES D'ESPEVILLE.

[*Fr. Copy.—Library of Berne, Coll. Bongars.* Vol. 141.]

DXLIII.—TO JOHN STURM.[1]

Complaints about the weakness and inactivity of the King of Navarre.

GENEVA, 18*th August,* 1559.

It was neither from laziness, nor indifference, nor parsimony, that after Hotman's departure I did not write a word about the affair that had been agitated between us. But a lack of matter kept me silent, for I felt ashamed to write to you an unmeaning letter void of information. Since that time we have had daily new and contradictory rumours respecting Varranus. Indeed it was announced to me more than ten times, that the following day or two days after he was expected at the court, when all the time he was distant from it more than seven days' journey. For as soon as it was known that an expedition had been undertaken by him, it was believed that he would make all possible haste not to lose the opportunity. But advancing at a snail's pace, he scarcely accomplished four French leagues a day. In this state of doubt you have no reason to be surprised that I remained inactive. And yet I have sharply reprimanded the man whom I had charged to have an interview with him for not having advanced to meet him. What answer he will give me as yet I know not.

[1] Active negotiations were then entered upon between Strasbourg and Geneva. While the young king Francis II., ruled by the Cardinal de Lorraine, signed every day orders for fresh executions, Sturm and Hotman urged Calvin to unite his efforts with theirs to come to the aid of the cause of the gospel, gravely compromised in France. Some Protestants believed they might rely on the King of Navarre, but neither Calvin nor Sturm had any confidence in this prince, though in the actual state of things it seemed to them impossible not to invoke his aid. It is this prince who is designated by the name of *Varranus* in Calvin's letter to Sturm. See Ch. Schmidt, *La vie de Jean Sturm,* p. 103.

From these circumstances our counsels are kept in a great measure in suspense. As long as Henry was alive, it was better for this man not to show himself. But the change which has occurred by the death of the former, forces us to have recourse to this necessity. Nay, as I am ignorant whether your prince still persists in the same opinion, I should not dare to attempt anything unless I were informed of his intentions for fear my activity should turn out rash or foolish. But as in the beginning it was my opinion that Varranus, whose inconsistency I suspected, should be left out, so at the present moment, it is necessary, whether I will or no, to learn what are his intentions. If he had arrived at court in time as was the general belief, already informed by his answer of what was necessary to be done, I should not have delayed one moment. But because it was neither safe to send a letter except by a man on whom we could depend, nor was it even ascertained where he was to be found, it was my duty to abstain from acting.

If any news shall be brought which may concern your affairs, I shall spare no expense. Among the followers of Guise there is much audacity, but of that kind which is to be found among men of desperate fortunes. The Queen Regent[1] after having made liberal promises to our party has performed none of them. We shall be able to form a more correct judgment then after the arrival of Varranus. Before that it is neither useful nor even possible to take any steps. But of him you may say that he trusts neither in God nor men. His like you will not find in our party.

Farewell, most accomplished sir. May the Lord govern, protect, and bless you.

[*Lat. Copy.—Arch. Eccles. of Berne.* Vol. vi. p. 847.]

---

[1] Catherine of Medicis.

DXLIV.—To the Duke de Longueville.[1]

He warns him of the dangers and temptations of the court.

Geneva, *22nd August,* 1559.

Monseigneur:—I hope you will not find it strange that
I continue to exhort you several times, not only to persevere,
but also to profit and grow in the faith of the holy gospel, and
show by your efforts that this very precious seed which God has
sown in you has fallen upon good ground, and has taken deep
root to produce fruits during your whole life.   And even should
the opportunity present itself of stirring you up oftener, I trust
that my diligence will not be disagreeable to you, and that you
will feel sufficiently convinced of the need you will have of it in
the midst of the many temptations which Satan contrives against
you, which it is difficult to resist, and would be altogether impossible, if you were not armed by more than human wisdom.

It is for that reason that I do not doubt but that you desire
to be fortified by good and holy admonitions to do your duty,
since you are aware that we gain nothing by flattering ourselves
in our weakness, if we do not render to God the service and
honour which is his due.   For whatever we may allege, since
his glory ought to be more precious in our eyes than a hundred
thousand lives, we have no excuse for not confessing the truth
of his gospel when he has made us acquainted with it, as it is a
sacrifice which he strictly requires of us.   And it is on this
subject that Jesus Christ says that no one is worthy of being
his disciple unless he forsake father and mother and wife, and
everything that is in the world.

Now, Monseigneur, you have a great advantage, inasmuch as
your mother desires nothing more than that you should walk
straightforwardly in the fear of the Lord, and she could receive
no greater pleasure from you than that of seeing you virtuously
profess the faith of the gospel.   If on the other hand there is
any obstacle, you must summon up courage to surmount it, and

---

[1] See the letter, p. 44.

not give way in any manner that might cause you to defraud God of the right which belongs to him in order to gratify men. There is no earthly kinsmanship that should not be trampled under foot, in order to yield and give place to the honour of our sovereign and only Father, to do homage to our Lord Jesus Christ on whom all the ties of relationship depend.

You know from experience, Monseigneur, that I do not say this without cause, inasmuch as you are constrained to bear many contradictions to which it is not lawful for you to give ear, without being disloyal to Him who has purchased you at so great a price, to the end that you should be dedicated to him. Wherefore it is necessary that you should put on such magnanimity, that neither favour nor hatred should turn you aside from glorifying him who deserves the preference over all mortal and perishable creatures. And in fact, the only means of aspiring to this spiritual kingdom, is to despise what keeps us entangled here below. But that you may be inclined to support all these combats, I entreat you, Monseigneur, carefully to exercise yourself in reading and hearing the word of God, and the pious instructions that may guide you to the understanding thereof, that you may have in your heart a lively sense of what St. Paul says, viz: that the gospel is the doctrine of truth, and that by this means you may maintain with invincible courage the struggle which most certainly awaits you.

For, here is the cause of the coldness and cowardice which we see in many,—it is that they do not make it their study to form their resolution upon good grounds, so that they might say according to the admonition of St. Paul, that they know in whom they have believed, and that He who is the infallible truth, will show himself faithful in keeping what they have entrusted to him. For which reason, Monseigneur, take courage, I pray you, to do battle in order to arrive at the crown of righteousness, which is bestowed on us, it is true of free grace, but on this condition that we confess the name of Jesus Christ whom it cost so dear to purchase it for us. And in order that God may work in you, and support you by the power of his Spirit, I pray you also, Monseigneur, to beware of the allurements and delights of the world, with which it is impossible that you should not be surrounded, that you may be the more on your guard against them, reflect that they are so many sorceries of Satan, so many mortal poisons to draw you to perdition. Now God of his infinite goodness has willed to call us to a much better condition. Though, then, many of those who call themselves believers, give themselves a license to abandon themselves to their pleasures full of corruption, be not disposed to follow their example for fear the light which God has given you should be extinguished; but learn to bear the yoke of our Lord Jesus Christ, which you will find easy and light, if you will suffer yourself to be governed by him.

Whereupon, Monseigneur, having humbly commended me to your kind favour, I entreat our heavenly Father to enrich you more and more with his spiritual gifts, to confirm you in his obedience, to have you in his protection and to maintain you in all prosperity.

[*Fr. Copy.—Library of Geneva.* Vol. 107.]

DXLV.—To the Marquise de Rothelin.[1]

He urges her to show herself always more firm in the profession of the truth.

GENEVA, 22d *August,* 1559.

MADAME:—I make no doubt but that in these changes and revolutions, you have to endure many alarms, and that you are agitated from all sides. If obstacles are thrown in your way, you know to whom you must have recourse to obtain succour. We have the promise of Him who has all strength in his hands, that our faith shall be victorious over all the enemies of our salvation. Let us then place our stay on him; let us call upon him in all our necessities, and we shall never be disappointed in our hope that he will stretch out to us a helping hand. I pray you, Madame, though others advance tardily, or even go back, not to swerve from the straight path, but to pursue triumphantly

[1] Letter enclosed in the preceding one to the Duke de Longueville, with these words:— *To the Marquise, his mother.*

the holy vocation to which we have been called, till you have
attained the mark.   For we are elected and adopted by too
good a Father ever to tire of pleasing him and conforming our
whole life to his will.   And the inheritance to which we are
called is too excellent not to be pursued to the end.   We have,
indeed, reason to praise God, Madame, for what we have heard
of you.   But when the question is to honour God, you can
never set about it with such courage as not to leave room for
desiring something still better, as I trust that you will always
aim and strive after a still higher degree of advancement.

You will see the letter which I have written to your son.
Because I know how much the house with which he is connected[1]
is for the most part hostile to the gospel, I have not scrupled to
point out to him that he should be so much the more on his
guard, not to be seduced, corrupted, or turned aside by any
considerations whatever, from the pure simplicity to which we
ought to cleave in our Lord Jesus Christ.   I believe, also, that
you will not conceive such an admonition unsuitable, considering
the necessity there is for it.

Whereupon, Madame, having humbly commended myself to
your kind favour, I will entreat our heavenly Father to have
you in his holy keeping, to guide you always by his Spirit, and
cause his name to be more and more glorified in you, even to
the end.

[*Fr. Copy.—Library of Geneva.*   Vol. 107.]

DXLVI.—To Peter Martyr.

Sufferings of the French Protestants—Gloomy apprehensions respecting the future.

GENEVA, *4th October,* 1559.

It fell out opportunely, venerable brother, that two days after
your letter came to hand this messenger was starting, to whom
I could with safety confide mine, though indeed nothing occurs

---

[1] He was nephew of Mary of Lorraine, Queen dowager of Scotland, married in
first nuptials to Louis II. of Orleans, Duke de Longueville.

to me at the moment to write to you about but what is sorrowful. I am unwilling also to make you a sharer in my vexations, but that I know that the present subject of anxiety is one which is common to both of us. The unhappy state of our brethren in France, who have at heart the interests of sincere piety, afflicts me with great sorrow, and torments me with no less inquietude and apprehension. A prompt remedy for these evils was in the power of the King of Navarre, and he had promised wonders. But now he has added treachery to his cowardice, which was already sufficiently disgraceful. The mother-in-law of the Prince of Condé[1] had obtained of the queen-mother that one of the ministers of the church of Paris[2] should be admitted to an interview. After being sent for, he is dismissed with mockery.[3] Meanwhile all things are tending towards a horrible butchery, because those who had professed themselves the disciples of Christ, and had frequented the secret assemblies, were denounced by apostates. The thing is passing sad. Yet must we wait patiently and calmly till our Avenger appear from on high, who will come at the appointed time, that I know. But we must also entreat him to support infirm minds. I will not exhort you and your colleagues to recommend the deliverance of these poor brethren to God, because I know that you are spontaneously inclined to this duty.

Farewell, most distinguished sir and sincerely honoured brother. Salute friends. May the Lord protect you and your wife from all evil, govern and strengthen you, and enrich you with his gifts.   Yours,

JOHN CALVIN.

[*Calvin's Lat. Corresp.—Opera*, ix. p. 136.]

---

[1] The Countess de Roye.   [2] The Minister la Roche Chaudieu.

[3] Peter Martyr entertained no false illusions respecting the sentiments of Catharine of Medicis. Here is the manner in which he judged this princess whose countryman he was:—" Others are perhaps astonished at the queen. I am not. For hitherto I have never perceived any sincere marks of her pious sentiments in respect of religion." Educated in the school of Machiavelli, this princess deceived all parties with the same duplicity, and remained faithful to but one maxim—To sow divisions in order to reign.

DXLVII.—To Bullinger.

Reply of a German prince—Beza at Strasbourg—Deplorable situation of the French
Reformed—Preludes of Civil Wars.

GENEVA, *5th October*, 1559.

The native of Saxony whom you recommended to me, my venerable brother, has found an honest and courteous host in Macar,
one of our colleagues, at whose house he will lodge very com-
fortably. In congratulating me on my better health, you act
according to your wonted kindness and fraternal affection for me.
You have also acted the part of a friend in informing me of
things which, though they were not in all respects agreeable,
were yet useful to be known. Herman had written the same
thing to me about the answer of the Count of Erbach. I had
received a short time before a letter from his brother Eberard,[1]
in which he lets me know that he had always hitherto professed
a great desire that the princess should decide upon a conference
for the purpose of putting an end to dissensions. As he is a
man of remarkable prudence, and altogether devoted to our
party, I do not think he expresses himself thus without some
solid reason. If he entertains favourable hopes of the result,
the opportunity ought not to be neglected. For he threw out
various hints on that subject, about which I have never written
even a syllable. But for that very reason, I have wished to
put you in mind that if you think proper you may consult with
M. Peter Martyr and the other brethren what answer we should
return.

Our brother Beza has gone to Strasbourg. What he will do
I know not, or rather I suspect he will do nothing; but as an
expedition of great importance which concerns us is undertaken
by certain persons, and Sturm earnestly demanded to have an
interview with me or Beza, we thought it right to concede a
little to his wishes lest he should fancy himself slighted.[2] At

---

[1] See p. 56.

[2] They were then discussing at Strasbourg projects of resistance to the oppression
of the Guises, projects which were destined to terminate in the conspiracy of Amboise.
Calvin did not hesitate to disapprove beforehand in the most absolute manner of the

Paris the cruelty of the enemies of the gospel rages more furiously than it appears hitherto to have done. Commissaries have orders to go over the whole city, and inquire from house to house in what manner each person conducts himself, and whether he goes to mass on all the feast days. They not only make their way into bed-chambers, but rummage beds, chests, and coffers, that they may forthwith drag to prison those in whose possession they find a suspected book. They turn all the household furniture upside down, and menace with punishment the masters of families, if they shall be discovered to have sheltered a Lutheran in their houses. They strictly enjoin all neighbours to keep a careful watch on each other, under severe penalties for their negligence, if they are slack in the performance of this duty.[1] Under this pretext not a few houses have been pillaged. There lately took place an occurrence which will inflame the rage of these men. Some fifteen persons of noble rank were dining in a tavern. In a moment the commissary is at his post. His beadles break through the windows. As the affair had a tumultuous and hostile aspect, these foreign guests having drawn their swords began to repel force by force. One of the beadles was killed, a good many wounded. Thus, unless God provide a remedy in time, there will be no end to the effusion of blood. A much greater number of men has been cast into fetters than during the two preceding years. The most loathsome dungeons are crowded with wretched individuals. Every now and then along the thoroughfares numerous persons are summoned by sound of trumpet to appear. The property of the absent is plundered.

In Provence the brethren, attacked by private individuals with the sword and outrage, have begun to defend themselves.

---

general intention of having recourse to force, and this opinion, which he shared with Sturm, was opposed by Hotman, whose influence finally prevailed in this unfortunate enterprise.

[1] In order to discover more readily the Reformed, images of the Virgin were placed at the corners of the streets and over the doors of the houses, and wo to him who did not salute them. He fell under the blows of the populace rendered fanatical by the monks. Did one wish to deliver himself from a troublesome creditor, he had but to cry out, The Lutheran, the Lutheran ! and the debt was expunged, and the debtor profited moreover by the spoils of his creditor.—D'Aubigné, *Hist. Univ.*, vol. i., p. 91.

Hitherto they have had the upper hand, and have slain but few, though they might have exterminated all to a man.[1] We have till now kept back the Normans, but it is greatly to be feared that if they be excessively provoked they too will rush to arms. God then is to be entreated that of his admirable goodness and wisdom he would calm these troubled billows. In the meantime, I pray him that he would protect, govern, and bless you, your family and colleagues. Viret and the others cordially salute you. You will salute affectionately in my name our friends and brethren.

Farewell, most accomplished sir and most respected brother.

Yours,   JOHN CALVIN.

[*Lat. Orig. Autog., Library of Leyden.*]

DXLVIII.—TO MADAME DE GRAMMONT.[2]

Consolations on the subject of a domestic affliction.

GENEVA, 28*th October,* 1559.

MADAME:—I could have wished much, had it pleased God, to have a more agreeable subject to write to you upon for the first time, but it is highly proper that we resign ourselves to be governed according to the will of him to whom we belong, and who has all superiority and empire over us; though it is our duty not only to consider his power and the obedience which we owe him, but also to reflect when he afflicts us, or visits us with the rod, that it is for our instruction and profit, and that he will know how to bring our distress to a favourable issue, if we shall patiently wait for it.

I shall not lay before you in detail the uses of adversity,

---

[1] The occasion of these troubles was the cowardly assassination of Antony de Mouvans, known to be a Protestant. The Parliament of Aix, instead of pursuing the authors of the crime, caused the corpse of the person assassinated to be thrown into the fire.

[2] Doubtless Helen de Clermont, only daughter of Francis de Clermont, Seigneur de Toulangeon and Treves, married in 1549 to Anthony de Grammont, Viscomte of Aster. Impelled by ambition to join the Huguenot party, which he was one day to betray, this seigneur exercised important functions at the court of the King of Navarre, and died in 1576.

because this subject would occupy me too long, and also because
I know that you have been instructed by the Scriptures to what
purpose we ought to apply it, whether it be to teach us to quit this
world more willingly, and in the meantime, while we are in it,
to subdue all our carnal desires, or to humble ourselves, to show
our obedience, and exercise our faith by prayer, to groan over
our faults, in order to obtain pardon ; and, in one word, to be
dead to the world, in order to dedicate ourselves to God as a
living sacrifice.

Passing by these things, then, which I suppose you to be
thoroughly acquainted with, I now entreat you, Madame, with
regard to the domestic misfortune which distresses you, to impress on your mind that such trials are sent to hold us captive
in our affections, and so subdue them as to submit to what God
knows to be just and equitable. I easily conceive what sorrows
you endure, when you see your yoke-fellow continuing unfaith-
ful to you, and that even after having given you some hope of
his amendment, he again returns to his debaucheries of former
times. But the consolations which the Scriptures hold out to
us should needs have so much the more power over your heart
to alleviate your sadness. I will only suggest to you, that had
all your wishes on this subject been satisfied, how much you
might have been carried away by vain pleasures, by the delights
and allurements of the world, so as in part to forget God. But
even though you should not know the cause of God's thus dealing with you, it nevertheless becomes you so far to honour him
as to deem this point unquestionable ; namely, that, since he is
all goodness and all justice, we are bound humbly to receive
what he sends us, and that there is neither objection nor reply
to be made to his dispensations. Exhort yourself then to patience by the word of God, and strive to overcome all temptations, by which I have no doubt you are greatly agitated. In
the mean time, pray God continually to convert the heart of your
husband, and on your own part make every effort to win him over
and fix him in the right path. I know what a hard task that
will be for you, because you have been already several times
deceived, and it is not difficult to perceive by different signs
that he has sat but too long in the seat of the scorner. But

nevertheless you must still labour to that end, as therein lies the true remedy.

As to your intention of quitting him, though I confess it is but what he deserves, yet I beg and exhort you, Madame, in the name of God to renounce this purpose, unless you follow it up in the lawful way. For if he shall be convicted of adultery before the tribunals, you will be held to be excusable in separating from him. And you are aware that if every one assumed the liberty of divorce of his own authority, without a public sentence, there would be no end to disorder. Above all, you should weigh well the scandal that may accrue from your person, and what a handle it would give to the enemies of God to vomit forth their blasphemies and defame the gospel. When you shall have duly reflected on these things, you will find that it is not lawful for you to separate from him, till at least you have observed the due formalities, and a public sentence have been pronounced. And even should you be unsuccessful in obtaining your rights, it will be evident that it did not depend on you that the cause was not judged. Your proceedings will so far vindicate your innocence as to stop the mouths of those who would seek a pretext for slander, as you are not ignorant how we are watched on every side, especially those of us who are most known and esteemed, because the devil and the ungodly have thereby more ample matter for their triumphs. But as in such extremities it is not easy always to hold the proper course, the most important point is to pray God to guide you with all prudence and the uprightness of his Spirit, so that you undertake nothing which may not be approved of and agreeable to him. On my part, also, Madame, I will supplicate him to strengthen you by his power that you faint not under the burden ; to moderate all your distresses, so as they shall not prevent you from blessing his holy name ; to increase you in all spiritual blessings, to have you in his holy keeping, and show you that you are the object of his care. Whereupon I will conclude, having humbly commended me to your kind favour.

[*Fr. Copy.—Library of Geneva.* Vol. 107.]

DXLIX.—To John Knox.[1]

Answers to different ecclesiastical questions.

GENEVA, 7th November, 1559.

If I answer your letter, most excellent brother, later than you expected, your fellow countryman who brought it to me will be the best witness that laziness was not the cause of my delay. You yourself know also how seldom a suitable opportunity of writing to you occurs, because in the disturbed state of affairs all access to your country is difficult. It was a source of pleasure, not to me only but to all the pious persons to whom I communicated the agreeable tidings, to hear of the very great success which has crowned your labours.

But as we are astonished at such incredible progress in so brief a space of time, so we likewise give thanks to God whose singular blessing is signally displayed herein. This affords you ample matter for confidence for the future, and ought to animate you to overcome all opposition. As I am not ignorant how strenuous you are in stirring up others, and what abilities and energies God has endowed you with for going through with this task, I have deemed it superfluous to stimulate the brethren. Meanwhile we are not less anxious about your perils, than if we were engaged along with you in a common warfare; and what is alone in our power, we join our vows to yours, that our heavenly Father would strike all your furious adversaries with the spirit of folly and blindness, scatter all their counsels, and defeat all their attempts and preparations. Certainly they labour under great difficulties in arming their fleet; especially for want of money. So much the more obstinately will the old

---

[1] By a letter of the 27th August of the same year, Knox had addressed to Calvin two questions relating to the administration of baptism and to ecclesiastical property. The message of the Scotch Reformer terminated with these words : " I am prevented from writing to you more amply by a fever which afflicts me, by the weight of labours which oppress me, and the cannon of the French which they have now brought over to crush us. He whose cause we defend, will come to the aid of his own. Be mindful of us in your prayers. Grace be with you."

dragon essay to throw everything into confusion, rather than
not attempt something.

Respecting the questions of which you ask for a solution,
after I had laid them before my colleagues, here is the answer
which we unanimously resolved to send. It is not without
reason that you inquire whether it be lawful to admit to the
sacrament of baptism the children of idolaters and excommunicated persons before their parents have testified their repentance.
For we ought always to be carefully on our guard that the
sanctity of this mystery be not profaned, which it certainly
should be if it were promiscuously administered to aliens, or if
any one received it without having such sponsors as may be
counted among the legitimate members of the church. But as
in the proper use of baptism the authority of God is to be considered, and his institution ought to derive its authority from
certain conditions, one of the first things to be considered is
who are the persons that God by his own voice invites to be
baptized.

Now God's promise comprehends not only the offspring of
every believer in the first line of descent, but extends to
thousands of generations. Whence it has happened that the
interruption of piety which has prevailed in Popery has not
taken away from baptism its force and efficacy. For we must
look to its origin, and the very reason and nature of baptism is
to be esteemed as arising from the promise of God. To us then
it is by no means doubtful that an offspring descended from holy
and pious ancestors, belong to the body of the church, though
their fathers and grandfathers may have been apostates. For
just as in Popery it was a pernicious and insane superstition,
to steal or forcibly abduct their children from Jews or Turks,
and forthwith to have them baptized; so likewise, wherever the
profession of Christianity has not been altogether interrupted
or destroyed, children are defrauded of their privileges if they
are excluded from the common symbol; because it is unjust,
when God, three hundred years ago or more, has thought them
worthy of his adoption, that the subsequent impiety of some
of their progenitors should interrupt the course of heavenly
grace. In fine, as each person is not admitted to baptism from

respect or regard to one of his parents alone, but on account of
the perpetual covenant of God; so in like manner, no just reason
suffers children to be debarred from their initiation into the
church in consequence of the bad conduct of only one parent.
In the mean time we confess that it is indispensable for them to
have sponsors. For nothing is more preposterous than that
persons should be incorporated with Christ, of whom we have no
hopes of their ever becoming his disciples. Wherefore if none
of its relations present himself to pledge his faith to the church
that he will undertake the task of instructing the infant, the rite
is a mockery and baptism is prostituted.

But we see no reason for rejecting any child for whom a due
pledge has been given. Add to these considerations that the
manner of proceeding adopted by a church now arising from its
ruins, and that of one duly formed and established are two very
different things. For whilst a church is being composed out of
that horrible state of dispersion, since the form of baptism has
prevailed through a long series of ages down to our times, it is
to be retained, but with the progress of time the abuses which
have crept in are to be corrected, and the parents forced to present their children themselves and become the first sponsors.
For if in the first commencements an absolute perfection is
severely exacted, it is greatly to be feared that many laying
eagerly hold of this pretext will continue to wallow in their
corruptions.

We confess indeed that we should not attach so much importance to anything as to swerve even a hair's breadth from the
line prescribed to us by God; but we imagine we have demonstrated in a few words that if we exclude from baptism those
whom we have had proofs of having been domesticated, as it
were, in the church, the exclusion would be too rigorous. In
the mean time, therefore, waiting till greater progress have been
made, and discipline have gained strength, let children be admitted to baptism on the condition we have mentioned, viz: that
their sponsors engage that they will make it their business to
have them brought up in the principles of a pious and uncorrupted religion. Though in the mean time we do not deny, that
idolaters, as often as children are born unto them, should be

sharply admonished and stirred up to devote themselves truly to God, as also excommunicated persons to be reconciled to the church.

To monks and priests it is certain that maintenance is not due from the public that they may live uselessly in idleness. If any of them then are fitted for edifying the church, let them be called to take a part in that labour. But as most of them are ignorant and void of capacity, it seems proper that we should act towards them with humanity. For though they have no claim to receive public support, inasmuch as they contribute nothing to the service of the church, yet it would be cruel that those who have been inveigled by ignorance and error, and have spent a part of their life in idleness, should be reduced to destitution. They are to be admonished indeed rather to seek their livelihood from labour, than devour the substance destined for the ministers of the church and the poor. A middle course is also to be pursued, as for example from rich benefices a part might be set aside for pious uses. In the mean time, however, provided the church recover by their death the ecclesiastical property, it does not seem fitting to raise a strife about the annual revenue, except that its present possessors are to be reminded that they retain by indulgence and forbearance, not from approbation, what they had never had any right to possess. They are also to be exhorted not to pamper themselves, but contented with a frugal manner of living, to restore to the church what belongs to it, rather than suffer it to be deprived of faithful pastors, or the pastors themselves to be starved.

Farewell, most excellent sir and our very dear brother. The whole assembly of the pious in our name wish you prosperity; and we pray God that he may govern you all by his Spirit even to the end, sustain you by his power, and shield you with his protection.

[*Calvin's Lat. corresp.*, Opera, ix. p. 201.]

DL.—To Francis Daniel.[1]

News of young Daniel studying at the Academy of Geneva.

GENEVA, 26th November, 1559.

Your allowing me to implore you in behalf of your son, and granting him forgiveness at my earnest entreaties, is a favour very grateful to me, and which brings back the pleasing recollections of our early friendship which I perceive you have not forgotten. The young man himself I have seriously admonished not to abandon the study of the civil law. At first he replied that he had no great taste for that science, from which he expected to derive no advantage; and when he represented to me the numerous corrupt practices that now almost universally prevail in civil actions, I confess he had very plausible reasons for not engaging willingly in such pursuits. But after I had reminded him of his duty, and that he could not escape from the charge of ingratitude unless he complied with your wishes, he promised that he would submit to whatever by your orders I should prescribe. But though overcome by my authority he yielded, not to conceal from you any thing, I must say that I perceived that against his inclinations this consent was wrung from him. As far, however, as my occupations will permit, I shall make it my business to watch over him and prevent him from overstepping the limits of authority at the caprice of his own will. For there is no reason to fear that he will give himself up to the excesses which too often characterize the impetuosity of his age, though perhaps in time I may perceive that he will not have made the progress in civil law that one could wish. We shall have to take counsel from circumstances, for you know how difficult a thing it is to force generous natures. I shall also take care that he apply himself to the politer branches of learning, to which he may at the same time add the study of theology. Assuredly it is especially necessary, whatever be the career for which you destine him, that he should be carefully imbued with sentiments of piety. Hitherto I do not see why his departure

[1] See the letter to the same, p. 60.

should cause you any regret, since from it very desirable effects have already resulted. Would to God that in your turn you too could extricate yourself from the snares in which you are held entangled. He shall receive monthly the allowance about which you have given me directions in your letter. Moreover, as the coat with which he left home was stolen from him at Lyons, it was not possible to refuse to let him have another which cost very little, in order to protect him from the winter's cold. So much for the present. If anything new shall occur in the course of time, I shall not fail to inform you of it most punctually. Since I cannot otherwise consult for the eternal welfare of our friend Flamberge, I will pray that he may be endowed with a sounder mind than to waste his life in his present filthy dregs. Of the father of *Bonrepos*[1] what can I say, who acquiesces with but too much security in all the pollutions of Popery? May God govern you all with his spirit, protect and sustain you by his power, enrich you with heavenly gifts, and pour out his blessing more and more upon your family.

Again and again, farewell, most excellent sir, and honoured friend.—Yours,

JOHN CALVIN.

[*Lat. Copy.—Library of Berne, Coll. Bongars.* Vol. 141. p. 47.]

DLI.—To MONSIEUR DE CLERVANT.[2]

Marks of sympathy on the occasion of the exile to which this seigneur was condemned.

GENEVA, *November,* 1559.

SIR, and honoured brother, when I exhorted you some time ago not to yield, I meant not only that you should hold out

---

[1] In the original text : Quid de *patre Bonae quietis* dicam?

[2] Anthony Claude de Vienne, Baron de Clervant, banished from Metz in 1558, on account of his attachment to the Reformation. He returned there the following year, by the protection of the German princes, and caused the gospel to be preached at his château de Montoy, by the minister Peter de Cologne, whom he had brought with him from Geneva. This minister wrote to Calvin : "I am still with M. de Clervant in his château, which is about a mile distant from the town. I there preach two sermons on the Sundays, and one on the Wednesdays. A few peasants from the neighbouring

courageously in your chateau, but also that whatever should happen, you should not flinch from your constancy in the faith; as our most impregnable stronghold is to call on God, and in the confident hope of his assistance to resist all the opposition which Satan and his agents contrive against us. And in truth it is now more than ever that it behoves you to put in practice this doctrine; for you are exposed to no small temptation in being compelled to quit your house and earthly goods, and bid farewell to your country, in order to remain constant and unshaken in the profession which you have made of following the uncorrupted truth of the gospel of our Lord Jesus Christ. Thus as your enemies have had permission to carry their evil intentions so far as even to wish to have the place razed, which you had dedicated to the word of God for the instruction of yourself and many believers, you have now to combat in another fashion. It is true that during your absence your house cannot be a sanctuary of God in which he is served and adored, but this blessing remains, that wherever you go, you will carry his temple along with you. On the other hand, I hope that this storm will ere long blow over, so that the evil intentioned will find their designs defeated; and when they fancy that they have gained their ends, and ruined what God by your means had erected, all will be anew established. For when they seem like thunderbolts to destroy everything, God causes them to be scattered like clouds, without doing the tenth part of the evil which was apprehended.

I conceive a part of the anguish with which you must now be

---

villages, and also some persons from the town come together to hear them." 11th March, 1559, MSS. of Paris, Dupuy, 102. The death of Henry II., it was thought, should have operated some change in the sad condition of the Protestants of Metz; but letters of Francis II., written at the instigation of the Marquis of Senneterre, governor of the town, enjoined the persons professing the Reformed religion to quit the country: "and Clervant was expressly ordered to abstain from holding any assemblies or conventicles, on pain of having his house pulled down and razed, and his person proceeded against according to the enormity of his fault." *Hist. Eccl.* Vol. III. p. 443. The Protestants of Metz obtained a year's delay, to put their affairs in order, and M. de Clervant, yielding to the storm, withdrew to Strasbourg. He returned to his country after the edict of January, and played a distinguished part in the religious wars. See *Hist. Eccl.* Vol. III. pp. 478 and 479, and Ancillon, *Vie de Farel*, Amsterdam, 1694, pp. 267 to 270.

afflicted; but since you have long repeated your lesson in the school of the Son of God, I trust that you will neither be overcome nor discouraged, though you should still have much more to endure. You must even prepare yourself for greater and ruder assaults, as I have no doubt but God will soon grant you an opportunity of returning to the place which you have quitted, in order to oppose the enemies more vigorously than ever, and hold them more closely in check. Though we know not the revolutions which it is the will of God to bring round, yet most certainly we perceive very striking signs of them. Nevertheless, though everything should be involved in tenfold greater confusion, all we have to do is to hold on our course. You know what cause it is which you defend, and that even should things take the worst turn, the fruits of our victory are reserved for us in heaven, and cannot fail us. I am very sorry that I am not nearer you, to be able to acquit myself a little better of my duty in consoling and fortifying you. But our merciful Father will not fail you. I trust also that you will derive much comfort from our brother who has followed you, as well as from M. Emmanuel Tremelli.

To conclude, sir, having affectionately commended me to your kind favour, I will entreat the Father of mercies to keep you always under his protection, to sustain you by his invincible power, and provide for you and your family, as he shall find it expedient.

[*Fr. Copy.—Library of Geneva.* Vol. 107 a.]

DLII.—To the Brethren of France.[1]

He exhorts them to redouble their faith to meet their redoubled persecutions, and to live and die for the confession of Jesus Christ.

Geneva, *November*, 1559.

DEARLY BELOVED BRETHREN:—I have no doubt but certain persons will think me importunate for writing to you at the pre-

---

[1] The death of Henry II. (10th July, 1559) and the accession of the young king Francis II., who was ruled by the Guises, rendered the situation of the Protestants

sent moment, while the cruelty of the ungodly rages with such
fury against the Christians, and while it requires so little to
exasperate it more and more. But those who think so are mistaken; for it is in times like these that you have most need of
exhortations to give you courage. Persecutions are the true
combats of Christians to try the constancy and firmness of their
faith. Wherefore being assailed, what ought they to do but to
fly to arms?

Now our arms to combat valiantly in this cause, and resist the
enemy, are to fortify ourselves by what God shows us in his
word. And just as each of us feels himself more timid, so ought
he to seek for the remedy. And herein we see how much most
men are apt to flatter themselves in their infirmities, for those
who are from weakness most disposed to be thrown into consternation are those who most refuse to seek strength from God
by the means which he has appointed. Learn then, my brethren,
that this is the true season to write to you, when the fire of persecutions is lighted, and when the alarms of the poor church of
God are carried to an extremity. We see that the worthy martyrs
followed this practice—to be so much the more vigilant in stirring up one another by holy admonitions, as they saw their
tyrants employing greater efforts to ruin Christianity. There
then is an example for us to follow. And in fact we hear that
our Lord Jesus Christ, after having warned the disciples of the

more cruel. Informers multiplied the number of suspected persons whom the *chambres
ardentes*, instituted by the edict of Blois for that purpose, handed over to the executioner. " From the month of August to the month of March of the following year,"
says the historian of the martyrs, " there was nothing but arrestations and imprison-
ments, pillage of houses, outlawries, and massacres of the servants of God. God,
however, amid these storms and tempests preserved the residue of his church, and
the preaching of the gospel was not abandoned." The language of Beza is not less
expressive:—" We may say of this reign which lasted only seventeen months, what
Jesus Christ says in St. Matthew, viz : ' Except those days should be shortened there
should no flesh be saved; but for the elect's sake those days shall be shortened.'
Notwithstanding this He who suffers not his own to be loaded beyond what they can
bear, gave such assistance to his lambs, that were for the most part only newly born,
and in like manner to the pastors who had just begun to arrange them in little flocks,
that amid all those storms, they not only subsisted, but, what is more, assumed a
regular order, and increased their numbers in many parts of the kingdom."—*Hist.
Eccl.* Vol. I. p. 212, and *Hist. des Martyrs*, Liv. vii. p. 464. Disseminated from
church to church, and multiplied by pious hands, the letters of the Reformer spread
everywhere courage and self-denial.

great troubles which were to come, and of which we see a part, adds: *Rejoice, and lift up your heads, for your redemption is at hand.* If we do not rejoice, at least we ought to strive to correct the vice which prevents us from so doing.

I know the dangers to which you are exposed, and I would not from inconsiderate zeal put a new sword into the hands of these enraged enemies; but yet it is necessary to set bounds to our own fears, so that those who have need of being strengthened by the word of God be not deprived of such a blessing; I leave you to judge if you do not see much unbelief among you, inasmuch as many are downcast as if God were no longer a living God. Thence you may judge that it is the more necessary for me, as much as in me lies, to endeavour to correct this defect, in order that the grace of God be not altogether quenched in you. It is no new thing for you to be like sheep in the jaws of the wolf; but the rage of your foes is at present more than ever inflamed to destroy the poor flock of Jesus Christ. And it is not only in one place; reflect that your brethren who are members of the same body, have to suffer like you for the same cause in distant countries. It is therefore the time to show more than ever that we have not been taught in vain. We are bound to live and die for Him who died for us, for our faith is not styled a victory over the world merely to make us triumph in the shade and without a struggle; but much rather that we should be armed by it to overcome Satan with all that he can devise against us; and the doctrine of the gospel is not for us to speculate about at our ease, but to demonstrate, by its effects, that the world should be held cheap by us in comparison of the heavenly kingdom.

Wherefore those that are so terrified in the time of persecution that they know not how to act, have not profited much as yet in the school of God. If there is terror, that is nothing new; for as we are men, it is not possible that we should not be environed by human passions. And since God supports our infirmity, it is but reasonable that we should do the like. Even those who feel themselves shaken with astonishment ought not to lose heart, as if they were already vanquished. But the capital point is that instead of indulging this weakness we should seek to shake it off and be re-animated by the Spirit of God.   I say then that nothing is more opposite to Christianity, of which we make a profession, than that when the Son of God our captain calls us to the combat, we should be not only cold and faint hearted, but seized with such consternation as to desert his standard.   Let us then strive against our flesh, seeing that it is our greatest enemy, and that we may obtain pardon of God let us not pardon ourselves, but rather let us be our own judges to condemn ourselves.   Let each as he finds himself tardy, push himself on, and let all of us collectively, knowing that we do not do our duty, be pleased to be stirred up by others, and may God let us feel the spur as often as he knows that our indolence requires it.

The thing most calculated to terrify us is the enormous cruelty practised against our poor brethren.   In fact it is a frightful spectacle, and one which might well make the inconstant shudder.   But we ought on the other hand to contemplate the invincible courage with which God has endowed them.   For in some way or other they surmount all the torments which the ungodly can devise to cast down their courage.   So then Satan, on the one hand, is contriving everything to trouble the poor brethren to make them swerve from the truth and turn aside from the path of salvation.   With unbridled rage he vents against them all his spite.   While on the other, God mean while assists them, and though they suffer extreme anguish according to the weakness of the flesh, yet still do they persevere in the confession of his name.   In that you see they are victorious. Should then the cruelty of the adversaries, which in spite of all their efforts is vanquished, have more weight with you to deaden your hearts, than that power from on high, with which God aids his children, ought to have to increase in you the perseverance which you should maintain in his truth?   You see the assistance of God which remains victorious and will you not repose your confidence in it?   You see the faith which triumphs in the martyrs, who endure death, and shall it be the cause of annihilating yours?   Wherefore, my brethren, when the tyrants exhaust all their fury, learn to turn your eyes to contemplate the succour which God affords his followers; and seeing that they are not forsaken by him, take new comfort and cease not to war against the temptations of your flesh, till you have attained the full conviction that we are happy in belonging to Christ whether it be to die or to live.

I am aware what reflections may here present themselves to our minds; that in the meantime the servants of God do nevertheless suffer, and that the wicked from the impunity with which they commit their acts of cruelty, break out more and more into all sorts of excesses. But since it is our duty to suffer, we ought humbly to submit; as it is the will of God that his church be subjected to such conditions that even as the plough passes over the field, so should the ungodly have leave to pass their sword over us all from the least to the greatest. According then to what is said in the psalm, *we should prepare our back for stripes.* If that condition is hard and painful, let us be satisfied that our heavenly Father in exposing us to death, turns it to our eternal welfare. And indeed it is better for us to suffer for his name, without flinching, than to possess his word without being visited by affliction. For in prosperity we do not experience the worth of his assistance and the power of his Spirit, as when we are oppressed by men. That seems strange to us; but he who sees more clearly than we, knows far better what is advantageous for us. Now when he permits his children to be afflicted, there is no doubt but that it is for their good. Thus we are forced to conclude that whatever he orders, is the best thing we could desire.

If we are not satisfied with that, he shows us that as much as our faith is more precious than gold or silver, so it is the more reasonable that it should be tried. Also it is by this means that we are mortified, in order not to be rooted in our love for this world, and more evil affections than we can imagine are thus corrected, were it but to teach us humility and bring down that pride which is always greater in us than it ought to be. By it he also wishes to put us in mind of the esteem in which we ought to hold his word; for if it cost us nothing we should not know its worth. He permits us then to be afflicted for it, in order to show us how very precious he considers it. But above all by sufferings he wishes us to be conformed to the image of his Son, as it is fitting that there should be conformity between the head and the members.   Let us not then suppose that we are forsaken of God when we suffer persecution for his truth, but rather he so disposes matters for our greater good. If that is repugnant to our senses, it is so because we are always more inclined to seek for our rest here below than in the kingdom of heaven.   Now since our triumph is in heaven, we must be prepared for the combat while we live here upon earth.

Moreover, my brethren, from the example that is now set before you, learn that God will strengthen you in proportion to your necessities.   For he knows well how to adapt the measure of our temptations to the strength with which it is his will to endow us in order to endure them.   We are sufficiently admonished, besides, by the Scriptures, that tyrants can do nothing more against us than what our merciful Father permits them. Now in permitting them, he knows who we are, and will thus provide for the issue.   The cause then of our great consternation is that looking at our own weakness we do not turn our eyes to the succour which we ought to expect and demand of God.   So it is but just that he come not to our aid since we do not seek for him.   We must even hope, that when he shall have tried his church, he will bridle the fury of the tyrants and cause it to cease in despite of all their efforts.   In waiting for such an issue it is our duty to possess our souls in patience. Most certainly he will accomplish what he has promised in the psalm, which I have already quoted, viz: *that he will break the cords of the plough which they drag over us to cut and destroy us*, and in another passage—*that the sceptre of the ungodly will not remain for ever in their inheritance, for fear the just stretch out their hands to do evil.*   Whatever happen, do you profit by the constancy with which you see your brethren endure persecution to support the truth of God, that it may confirm you to persevere in the faith.

It has been said of old that the blood of the martyrs is the seed of the church.   If it is a seed from which we derive our origin in Jesus Christ, it should also be a shower to water us that we may grow and make progress, even so as to die well. For if this blood is precious in the sight of God, it ought not to be unprofitable for us ; thus we see that St. Paul boasts that his bonds have contributed to the advancement of the gospel and expects that in his death the name of Jesus Christ will be exalted. The reason is that when we are persecuted we are called by God to maintain his cause, being, as it were, his attorneys ; not that he has need of us or that we are proper for that, but since he does us the honour to employ us therein, it is not his will that we should lose our pains. Wherefore we ought to have in the utmost detestation that blasphemy of ancient hypocrites who murmur against those who glorify the name of God, even to the offering up of their own lives, just as if by the confession of their Christianity these martyrs created scandal. Such persons have never known what Jesus Christ is, but have forged to themselves an idol under his name, when they reckon for a scandal what ought to stand for a signature to ratify more and more to our consciences the truth of the gospel. And since they are not ashamed to despise the servants of God for their rashness, because the latter expose themselves to death to defend the cause of God's Son, they will feel one day to their sore confusion, how much more agreeable this temerity, as they style it, is to God than their wisdom, or rather the diabolical cunning which they display, in denying the truth in order to exempt themselves from all danger. It is horrible that those who call themselves Christians should be so stupid, or rather brutalized, as to renounce Jesus Christ as soon as he displays his cross. As for you, my brethren, hold in reverence the blood of the martyrs which is shed for a testimony to the truth, as being dedicated and consecrated to the glory of God ; then apply it for your edification, stirring yourselves up to follow their example. But if you do not yet feel in yourselves such an inclination, pray God that he may give it you, groaning because of your infirmity, which holds you back from doing your duty ; for, as I said in the beginning, it is far too dangerous a thing to flatter ourselves in our infirmities. For faith cannot be long lulled to sleep without being at last quenched, as the example of these worldly-wise dissemblers shows us, who, desiring with their false pretences to play fast and loose with God, come at last to lose all knowledge of the gospel, as if they had never heard of it. Meanwhile, since you see that the poor flock of God's Son is scattered by the wolves, repair to him, praying him have to compassion on you and strengthen your weakness, to stretch out his mighty arm to repel them, to shut their bloody mouths and break their claws, or finally to change them into harmless lambs. Above all, pray him to make manifest that he is seated on the right hand of God his Father to maintain both the honour of his majesty and the salvation of his children. It is in this way that you will derive relief from him, humbling yourselves with tears and prayers, and not in murmuring and gnashing your teeth against the tyrants, as some do who seek not the refuge to which persecutions ought to drive us. For my own part, I could wish that God had given me the means of being nearer at hand to assist you, but since that is not possible I will pray our merciful Father that since he has once confided you to the keeping of our Lord Jesus Christ, he would cause you to feel how safe you are under so good a protector, to the end that you may cast all your cares upon him; and that he would be pleased to have compassion on you and all those who are in affliction, delivering you from the hands of the ungodly. And as he has once made you partakers of the knowledge of the truth, that he would, from day to day, increase you therein, making it bring forth fruits to his glory. Amen.

[*Fr. Copy.—Library of Geneva.* Vol. 107 *a.*]

DLIII.—To Bullinger.

Complaint of the unjust proceedings of Berne with respect to Geneva.

GENEVA, 25th *January*, 1560.

I did not dare, when I wrote to you lately, to make any mention of the injuries we are daily suffering in order not to din your ears with vain complaints.[1] But our friend Prevot has

[1] The settlement of the difficulties pending between Berne and Geneva, (see vol. iii., pp. 309, 339, 348,) had been submitted to an assembly convoked at Moudon, the 22d of January 1559, and presided by the arbiter of Bâle. The Bernese demanded the execution of the sentence of the Bailiff of Ternier; the Genevese that it should be

done well in laying an undisguised account of them before you. We give you our most hearty thanks, moreover, for having deigned with your well-known equity and courage resolutely to undertake this cause. Our society would wish, also, to testify in a formal manner their gratitude, but as that is not permitted them, they willingly acknowledge how much they are indebted to you. You could never believe to how many unworthy insults and vexations we have been exposed, during nearly a whole year. Nor have they proceeded against us with any colour of justice, but in the mere insolence of pride. At length, rendered somewhat favourably disposed by the blandest of admonitions, and even by our obsequiousness, they have shown some signs of relaxing their obstinacy. For they wrote that they would send deputies hither to arrange matters to our satisfaction. The deputies arrived with a profusion of promises. But when we were to hold a conference, they begged to be excused, saying they had received no positive instructions. The deputies were expected two days before the arrival of our friend Prevot. It is thus evident that they had been watching for an opportunity to overreach us. For they had indicated, through their deputies, that they were prepared to come to an amicable adjustment of all the points in dispute between us. Meanwhile their conditions were intricate, doubtful, and full of ambiguity. They refuse to ratify any thing, unless the sentence of the arbiter of Bale should be previously annulled, a concession which we could by no means make. But because they exhorted our senate to send a deputation to the Swiss diet in order to recommend to

annulled. The two parties could not come to an agreement, and the arbiter of Bale did not venture to pronounce judgment. On the 5th of August following, he gave sentence in favour of the Genevese, but the Bernese refused to submit to it, and appealed to another tribunal, which confirmed the sentence of the arbiter, and settled the difference by the mutual agreement of the parties. During this long contestation between the two cities, the property of the refugees had been sold to cover the expenses of justice. The Seigneury of Berne presented on this subject a last reclamation to that of Geneva.

25 Nov., 1560.—" Letter of Messieurs of Berne, by which they beg us to restore the property of the said condemned persons.

" Resolved to answer them that it is impossible for us to restore to the said condemned persons their pretended property, and that had there been more of it, it would not meet the costs and damages sustained by us."

(Extracts from the registers of the councils.)

them the liberties and tranquillity of this city, and that moreover no alliance should be concluded with the Duke of Savoy
in which there should not be included a special proviso guaran-
teeing to us our rights and security, that point was willingly
conceded. Nay, it had been previously decreed. But as they
entertained suspicions of us, they wished by this recommendation to discover what were our intentions, or if there should be
any delay or hesitation on our part, that it might furnish them
with a decent excuse in case they should conclude any treaty
with Savoy to our detriment. Deputies will be sent to Baden
accordingly. Now the advice and protection of your illustrious senate are much desired by us in this affair. It was not
agreeable to the plan adopted by us that I should write to your
senate. Instructions have consequently been given to our friend
Prevot to be communicated to private friends which will serve
the same purpose as far as the nature of the question will permit. I will not urge you and our friend Gualter at greater
length to persist in the course of the pious office you have so
happily commenced, as I know from the account of our brother
and friend how much you have the matter at heart, and he himself, with his well-known address, will effect more than I could
obtain by a letter.

Farewell, then, most excellent sir and honoured brother, along
with M. Peter Martyr, M. Gualter, and your other colleagues.
May the Lord protect you all, govern you by his Spirit, and
enrich you with every blessing.—Yours,

JOHN CALVIN.

[*Lat. Orig. Autog., Arch. of Zurich, Gest.* VI., 166, p. 45.]

DLIV.—To FRANCIS DANIEL.[1]

Counsels for the education of young Daniel.

GENEVA, 13*th February,* 1560.

Your son has followed his cousin to the town to which you
ordered him to repair. You judge wisely that the disposition

---

[1] See p. 77. Young Francis Daniel had quitted Geneva to go, at his father's request, and study law at the University of Orleans. In writing to Calvin to thank

of the young man requires the rein to prevent it from being carried away hither and thither by its natural facility; but more especially that he may confine himself to one branch of study, and devote himself to a solid erudition, rather than ambitiously run over the circle of the sciences in acquiring a smattering of each. He has great quickness of parts, and has been tolerably well trained. Let only his excessive impetuousness, the common fault of his years, be corrected, he will produce excellent fruits. I am very confident of these future good results, for he has a great deal of modesty, and a very short period of time has already spontaneously given a certain maturity to his ideas. If you desire him to apply seriously to civil law, you will have to stimulate him, for otherwise he has not much taste for that study. The seven and twenty gold crowns which he received from me have been paid down to me. I was ashamed, indeed, to accept them when I reflected that I have been so long in your debt. Nor, in truth, had I been a little richer would I have suffered a single penny to have been paid back to me. But I would have you believe that I am wholly at your service, and the little that I possess I shall always hold at the disposal of you and yours. Only you will allow me to send what I have long purposed to do, a gold piece to each of your daughters, as a kind of New Year's gift, that they, at least, may have some slight token of my gratitude.

Farewell, most worthy sir. May the Lord protect, govern, and support you and your family.—Yours,

CHARLES PASSELIUS.

[*Lat. Orig. Autog.*—*Library of Berne, Coll. Bongars.* Vol. 141. p. 49.]

him, the latter recalled to him the friendship which they had contracted at school:— "I beg you to be thoroughly persuaded of this that there is nobody who keeps up more faithfully and religiously than I do a friendship contracted in early youth. Farewell, most excellent friend. My mother and my wife salute you most cordially."

DLV.—To John Sturm.[1]

Severe judgment respecting the conspiracy of Amboise.

GENEVA, 23d *March*, 1560.

Though during the last six weeks matters of great importance have been going forward, yet such contradictory and perplexed accounts respecting them have prevailed, that having nothing sure to communicate to you, my uncertainty has stayed my hand; and now I feel ashamed to send you a letter so barren of facts, because in such an infinite variety of subjects I am at a loss where to begin and where to end. When I was at first consulted by those who were the prime instigators in this business, I frankly replied that their whole manner of proceeding displeased me, but that the transaction itself was what incurred my greatest disapprobation, because what they had foolishly resolved they next set about childishly. At present, I regret their sluggishness, because I am well informed that what they had determined to put in execution before the 15th of March had not been attempted by them till five days after that period. Just now we are in momentary expectation of what will be the upshot of their boastful attempts.[2] You judge rightly in thinking

---

[1] The death of Henry II., and the accession of Francis II., the husband of Mary Stuart, and governed by the Guises, gave rise to grave changes in the attitude of the Reformers. After having undergone without a murmur for twenty-five years the most iniquitous persecutions, they began to ask if the passive submission which Calvin had always counselled was a duty for them in the new circumstances in which they were placed. The execution of Anne Dubourg, (23d December, 1559,) put the finishing stroke to their exasperation. They consulted, says the historian La Planche, the opinions of Jurisconsults, to know if resistance to the tyranny of the princes of Lorraine was not legitimate. They formed plans of defence, to which they associated the King of Navarre, and the Prince de Condé. These terminated in the conspiracy of Amboise, the rash undertaking of a party maddened by persecutions, and of which the failure necessarily aggravated still more the situation of the French Protestants. Consulted at Geneva respecting the suitableness of a rising in arms, Calvin blamed in the most energetic terms all recourse to force. But his words were not listened to.

[2] The object of the conspirators was to seize on the person of the King, and to substitute in stead of the guardianship of the Guises the government of the princes of Bourbon favourable to the Reform. Undertaken on the 20th of March, the attempt failed, in consequence of the vigilance of the princes of Lorraine. In writing to Sturm, Calvin was yet ignorant of the death of La Renaudie, and the sad lot of the principal conspirators.

that every thing turns upon their gaining over the King of Navarre
to their enterprise. I have a lurking suspicion, however, that of
the chiefs who give themselves airs of superior address, there are
some who are but too much inclined to ingratiate themselves into
his favour. Before two or three days something will certainly
transpire. Meanwhile, in certain towns of the provinces godly
men have been emboldened to undertake more than I could have
wished.[1] I had advised them not to make a public demonstration before the royal progress of the court; now their precipitancy will engender greater disturbances. The convulsions of
Europe which I had in mind long anticipated are at last placed,
as it were, before my eyes. Yet I am not for all that so perplexed as not to be prepared to undertake a journey should
necessity require it. You will excuse the brevity and sterility
of this letter. Should any thing worth knowing take place, I
shall spare no expense to make you acquainted with it, that we
may further what has been successfully commenced, and provide against or deplore what shall have turned out unfortunately.
I shall inform you in good time of all fitting remedies to be applied, and if need be fly to your assistance.

Farewell, most accomplished and respected sir.

Yours,   JOHN CALVIN.

[*Lat. Copy.—Arch. of Berne.* Vol. VI., p. 854.]

DLVI.—To JOHN GELLIN.[2]

He exhorts him to leave France in order to retire to Geneva.

GENEVA, *Easter day,* 1560.

It is not indolence, my most excellent brother, which will
occasion the brevity of my letter, but fatigue and lassitude.
Already half my former vigour, partly from diseases, partly
from labours, has become impaired; nor on account of the numberless occupations that almost overwhelm me, is it in my power

[1] See the letter to the Church of Valence, 15 April, 1560, p, 95.
[2] To Master John Gellin at Tolose.

to go beyond the circuit of the city for recreation or even to
enjoy a brief breathing time. If now I do not simply beg you
to excuse my silence, it is because as often as I found a safe
opportunity of sending you a letter, I had no leisure to write
it, and I am not in the habit of having letters ready written
lying by me, waiting for the chance of a messenger to convey
them. In a former letter you asked me if there might be any
room for your services among us, and if so, you hinted that you
would speedily hasten hither and with prompt zeal willingly
discharge whatever functions should be assigned you. I by no
means disapprove of your intention, but I would not have you
ignorant of our manner of proceeding in never calling in any
one from foreign parts, when we have fitting persons at hand.
But I would spare no good offices of mine to promote your
interest, if after you proceeded hither, your health permitted you
to prolong your stay among us; and in one word that you may
see that I am pledging myself heartily, I am induced to do this,
not only from considerations of your being a countryman, but
also from the ties of affinity. Moreover, I think I have discovered in you marks of piety and disinterested affection, conjoined with modesty, to say nothing of your erudition, which,
nevertheless, also deservedly conciliates good will towards you.
Again, when you consult me, now that your father is dead, about
the line of conduct which I think you ought to hold, the importunate entreaties of your relations are calling you back to your
native place; on the other hand your widowed mother is urging
your return, who both by her natural claims and her tears ap-
peals to your filial piety. It is cruel to refuse her, especially as
she is burdened with other children and distracted by a variety
of cares, as is usually the lot of widows. Of her purpose there
can be no doubt. She claims you to aid her in the management
of her household—that the sorrow she has conceived from the
death of your father, may by your presence be alleviated; in a
word that she may transfer to you the direction of all her
domestic affairs, and that you may contribute, in part at least,
by your forensic gains to the support of the family. I am not
indeed so barbarous as peremptorily to exhort you to forsake her.
But what God has suggested to your mind, take care you weigh

more diligently, lest you entangle yourself in snares of such a kind as it may not be easy to extricate yourself from afterwards. And grant that you escape, yet this will neither be very speedily, nor without running imminent risk, perhaps not without falling away altogether from religion.

No sooner shall you have entered your native city than according to the wonted rudeness of our nation, the eyes of all will be fixed on you to see whether you comply with the public usages, whether you will have masses said for your deceased father, whether you be sufficiently superstitious. If they remark in you any deviation from common custom, then you are the object of universal obloquy. Should the obligations of your duty drag you thither, better would it be to shut your eyes, than from fear of dangers to withdraw yourself from the commands of God. For what is this but rashly to expose yourself to tempt God. Beware, then, lest he, withdrawing his helping hand, should punish your temerity. If in so embarrassing a matter you are held in too great suspense, and as it is difficult to comprise in a letter addressed to you where you are now resident all the considerations which would require to be examined on both sides, I think you would do well to come here forthwith, and before your views suffer any change—just as you have already signified that you wished to do. Then by weighing all the reasons for and against any decision, we may be able by the guidance of God to resolve upon something.

Farewell, my most excellent and well beloved brother. May the Lord govern you by his Spirit and accompany you with every blessing.—Yours,

CHARLES PASSELIUS.

Salute in my name all the godly who are in your parts.

[*Lat. Copy.—Library of Paris, Dupuy*, 102.]

DLVII.—To the Church of Valence.[1]

Christian exhortations—The sending of a pastor.

GENEVA, 15*th April*, 1560.

The love of God the Father, and the grace of our Lord Jesus Christ be always with you, by the communication of the Holy Spirit.

BELOVED SEIGNEURS AND BRETHREN:—Since it has pleased God that matters have come to such a crisis among you, you must prepare yourselves to maintain great combats, as there is no doubt but ere long Satan will stir them up against you, and he is already setting his agents to work to plot the destruction of the whole edifice of God. But whatever be the result, you have to fortify yourselves, not to resist the rage of the enemy by the aid of the fleshly arm, but to maintain with constancy the truth of the gospel in which consists our salvation, and the service and honour of God, which we are bound to honour more than our own bodies and souls. We cannot do better than pray with you that our heavenly Father would keep you under his protection. For indeed when you shall be assailed it will not

---

[1] The seat of a celebrated university, and of a bishopric administered by a tolerant prelate, John de Monluc, Valence could early boast of many persons professing the Reformed faith who assembled in secret in the suburbs of the town. Founded in 1559 by an old advocate of Metz, Peter Bruslé, confirmed by the preaching of Gilles Solas, and of an Angevin nobleman named Lancelot, the Church of Valence had a turbulent and stormy origin.—"As to Dauphiny, says Beza, there were terrible convulsions which began first at Valence. For some petulant spirits who were not satisfied with a moderate and peaceable state of things, wished to make a public demonstration; others were averse to it. Thus began their divisions and the source whence sprung much mischief afterwards."—The most ardent party, composed of noblemen and students in 1560, in spite of the consistory seized upon the church of the Cordeliers, installed their ministers in it, and kept an armed watch around the meetings. These imprudent acts, imitated at Romans, at Montelimart, and severely blamed at Geneva, produced sad reprisals. Maugiron, lieutenant of the Duke of Guise, having entered the town by surprise caused two of the ministers to be beheaded, and three of the principal citizens to be hanged as fomenters of sedition. This was the origin of the long troubles which agitated the whole country, and which preceded the breaking out of the civil wars in Dauphiny. *Hist. Eccl.*, vol. i. p. 219, 342, and the following: D'Aubigné, *Hist. Univ.* L. ii., and de Thou, L. xxv.

be long before the blows will fall upon us. But he who holds our life and death in his hand will discomfit all the efforts of those who hate us, only because we are his followers. This resource should suffice to prevent you from ever being thrown into consternation. In the mean time in compliance with your request, we have selected the brother who is now on his way to you.[1] He has heretofore faithfully laboured in the work of the Lord. I trust he will continue to do so in the time to come, and that God will reap such fruits from his labours that his name shall be glorified by them, and all of us have reason to rejoice.

Whereupon we pray God to have you in his holy keeping, to animate you with invincible constancy, and increase in you the gifts of his Holy Spirit.

[*Fr. Copy.—Library of Geneva.* Vol. 107.]

DLVIII.—To the Church of Montelimart.[2]

Eulogy of the Minister Francis de St. Paul—Prudent counsels.

Geneva, *April*, 1560.

Beloved seigneurs and brethren, as we bless God for the good pleasure he has bestowed on you to assemble yourselves in his

---

[1] The minister Lancelot, originally from Anjou.

[2] Without date. April, 1560. At the period in which, according to the expression of Beza, the churches were multiplied with astonishing ardour in the towns and villages of Dauphiny, " those of Montelimart also, succoured by the seneschal of the country of Valentinois, named Bourjac, and directed by a cordelier, named Frère Tempeste, who preached the truth with sufficient boldness in his Monk's frock, established their church by the ministry of Francis de St. Paul, also sent to them by Geneva." *Hist. Eccl.*, vol. i., pp. 219 and 343. It is the minister whom Calvin mentions in his letter to the brethren of Montelimart. Renowned for his learning and eloquence, which rendered him worthy of taking a part in the conferences of Poissy, Francis de St. Paul had been pastor of the French Church at Berne, and a preacher of the Reformation in Saintonge and Poitou. The troubles which broke out in Dauphiny, in 1560, did not permit him to make a long stay at Montelimart, which he was obliged to quit the following year, in order to comply with the call of the Church of Dieppe. The gospel continued not the less to make progress in this country, as is proved by a letter of the synod of Valence to the society of Geneva of the 8th June, 1562 :— " As the zeal for the service of God which we perceive in the people of this country gives us infinite delight, so we cannot think of the want we have of pastors, nor

name, to call upon him, and be instructed and confirmed in the
doctrine of salvation, so we have not wished to be awanting
on our part to aid you in that purpose, as far as our means permit us. Now as we have been informed that it was necessary
to send you a man of competent learning and prudence, we
have requested the bearer of the present letter to take upon him
this office, because we had no one at our disposal who, in our
judgment, is better calculated to give you satisfaction, which
however we had rather that you should know from experience,
than we should enter into longer details on that subject. And
the same motives induced us also to press this service more
urgently upon him; for, in truth, he had some reasons which
might have excused him had he declined it; but in fine he consented to devote his labours to you on the conditions which we
found and judged to be equitable, among which the principal is,
that he may be at liberty to return to another church towards
which he has contracted obligations, provided it please God of
his infinite goodness to remedy the dispersion which has taken
place in it.[1] For though according to men he might quit those
who had conducted themselves in a dastardly manner in the
hour of trial, yet according to the duty of a true and faithful
servant of Jesus Christ, he withdrew from them only for a time,
offering to return when the flock should be reassembled. Not
to give occasion then to those who are but too weak, to become
lukewarm, or altogether alienated from the truth, we have not
dared to insist farther than that he should go and minister to you
as long as it might be in his power, without doing any wrong to
those who are still counting on his services. Thus we beg you not
to take it amiss if you have only, as it were, a loan of him, and let
him not be accused of inconstancy should he be forced to perform the promise which he has made elsewhere. This neces-

---

hear the lamentations of the poor people without great sadness. *For in this province,*
where a thousand ministers would not suffice, there are scarcely forty."—MSS. of Geneva, Portfolio I. See also (vol. 196) two letters of the Church of Montelimart to
Calvin, of the 18th July 1561, and of the 29th March, 1562.

[1] Is it the church of Poitiers? We read in the registers of the society, March,
1559 :—"About that time Mr. Francis de St. Paul was chosen to go and preach the
gospel at Poitiers, instead of M. de Brueil." But Beza does not mention any dispersion in the history of this church in 1560.

sity falling out, however, we shall not fail to provide for you as
well as God shall permit us. And we hope that he will not
fail you withal in your need, but that he will guide you moreover by his Spirit to choose such a man as shall be useful to
you. There is another circumstance which I must mention; it
is that the person who is now on his way to you cannot remain
long absent from his wife, because for the service of the church
he has already left her for a long time in bad health, and should
he continue to do so, he might be esteemed not very humane.
Wherefore, should it please God that he take up his residence
with you, it will be necessary for him to send for his wife and his
household furniture that he may be at greater liberty to acquit
himself of his functions. Meanwhile we beg you affectionately
to take into consideration their support, as each of you may
easily conceive what must be the regret of a Christian man in
quitting his family and leaving it in penury and want. For we
can testify that he has never heaped up the goods of this world,
so that should they not be succoured by you, his wife and children would be reduced to suffer hunger and thirst during his
absence. But as we are convinced that you will be disposed of
your own accord to act with perfect humanity in this respect, it
is sufficient for us to have reminded you. What is of most importance is, that you welcome him as being addressed to you by
Jesus Christ to bring to you the uncorrupted truth of the gospel, which is that inestimable treasure in which lies all the perfection of felicity. For, in truth, this is also what he aims at,
and above all desires to witness the fruits of his labour, when
he shall faithfully bestow his pains on the work of your salvation. Now, if you show such reverence as you ought for the
word of God, which he will announce to you, we trust that you
will not fail in any thing else.

To conclude, inasmuch as the brother you have sent to us
gives us to understand that you are deliberating about establishing ere long the public preaching of the word among you,
we entreat you to abstain from that purpose, and not to think
of it till God give you a better opportunity. It is true, that
this advice is dictated by a desire to spare you. But at the
same time we do not see that you are called upon to hazard

so premature a step.[1] On the contrary, it seems to us that
it is quite sufficient that you should endeavour and put forth
all your efforts to increase the flock, collect the poor scattered
sheep, and in the meantime refrain from all public demonstrations, by making no innovations respecting the temples, provided only you keep yourselves separated from the pollutions
that are committed in them. When you shall hold your assemblies peaceably in private dwellings, at least the rage of your
enemies will not be so speedily inflamed, and you will render to
God what he requires of you; namely, to glorify his name in
purity and preserve yourselves undefiled from all superstitions
until it please him to open for you a wider door. Whereupon
we supplicate him, beloved seigneurs and brethren, to govern
you by his Spirit with such prudence, virtue, and simplicity as
he shall see fit, and in the meantime to have you in his holy
keeping, and fortify you with such perseverance that at the last
we may be gathered together into his eternal rest.

[*Fr. Orig. Minute.—Library of Geneva.* Vol. 107 *a.*]

DLIX.—To the Bishop of London.[2]

Recommendation of the French Church of London—Eulogium of Des Gallars—Wish
for a complete Reform of the Anglican Church.

GENEVA, *May*, 1560.

Though you do not expect me to thank you for an office of
piety performed by you to the Church of Christ, yet the case is

---

[1] The prudent counsels of the Reformer were unfortunately not listened to. The
minister Francis de St. Paul was seditiously installed in the church of the Cordeliers,
and the Reformers of Montelimart, like those of Valence and Romans, kept an armed
watch around their pastor. "If the wisdom of the better advised, says Beza, had
been able to overcome the impatience of some, there is much likelihood that by far
the greater part of the country would have come over to the sound doctrine of their
own accord, and their affairs would have taken a much more favourable turn."

[2] Without date—May 1560. We get the date of this letter from that of the letter
from the French Church in London to Calvin asking for a pastor, in which they
say : "What a glory would be added, not only to the foreign churches, but also
to the Anglican, if Viret or Th. Beza or Nicholas des Gallars should join himself
to us!" March, 28th 1560, *Dupuy*, vol. 102. The Bishop of London had accompanied
this request with the most urgent recommendations. A refugee on the continent during

different with regard to the protection which you have deigned to afford those of our countrymen who inhabit the principal city of your diocese. By your cares, they have had permission, through the indulgence of the queen, not only to invoke God in purity, but also to send over to us a demand for a faithful pastor ; if then for these acts of kindness, I did not profess myself bound to you, I should be deservedly chargeable with folly and a want of common courtesy. And since you have not hesitated of your own free impulse to ask and entreat me to see that a fitting pastor should be selected for my countrymen, I have no need to recommend to your fidelity and protection the persons for whose salvation you are so solicitous. And assuredly as, in assisting them so liberally up to this moment, you have given a rare and singular proof of your pious zeal, so now you will of your constancy in continuing your good offices to the end. In what concerns ourselves, both because the situation seemed to require a man furnished with eminent gifts, and because the foreigners among you particularly desired that one of our society should be accorded to them, we have preferred to despoil ourselves rather than not comply with so holy a desire. For that reason we have granted to their request our brother Nicholas des Gallars one of the three whom they themselves named in the beginning.[1] Now though it was painful for him to be torn away from us whom he knew to entertain no ordinary degree of affection for him, and though he quitted with reluc-

---

the reign of the intolerant Mary, Edmond Grindal had learned how to appreciate the Reformers of Swisserland and professed for Calvin the most affectionate admiration. He wrote to him in 1563 : " Our church and nation are greatly indebted to you, illustrious brother, . . . it is then with the deepest sorrow we have learned the deplorable state of your health. Most assuredly it is the excess of your labours that has occasioned this illness. Renounce then these prolonged vigils, otherwise the evil will increase, and you will no longer be of such utility to the church. Recall to your recollection Gregory of Nazianzen, who, as he advanced in age being unwilling to relax from the austerity of his youth, was forced almost always to keep his bed, and thereby became less useful. Since you and Bullinger remain almost alone among the pillars of the house of God, we desire to enjoy you, if the Lord shall think fit, as long as possible." (*Library of Geneva*, vol. 113.)

[1] Nicholas des Gallars was elected (the 26th April, 1560) minister of the French Church of London. On the 3d of May he took leave of the Seigneurs of Geneva. " The Lord," say the Registers of Geneva, " has seen fit to make use of him for his own glory and our joy and consolation."

tance a station in which he had long rendered services not less
productive than faithfully performed, yet vanquished by our
entreaties he has undertaken this office, because he hoped that
he should thus contribute in no small degree to the spread of
the kingdom of Christ.

Certainly nothing but necessity could have wrung from us our
consent to be separated from him, but we feared that it was not
possible otherwise than by his arrival among you to provide for
the wants of a rising, and as yet but imperfectly organized
church.   For this place will incur no slight loss by his departure,
where he was held in high esteem, and where he bore himself in
a manner worthy of a servant of Christ.   As far as my personal
feelings are concerned, the greatest intimacy and affection
having subsisted between us, I did not without the most poignant
sorrow give my consent to this disruption of our familiar intercourse.   But everything was to be endured rather than refuse
the aid so anxiously implored by our destitute and distressed
brethren.

Wherefore I feel the greater solicitude, that he should at least
find among you a welcome station to alleviate and solace his
sorrow at quitting his country.   When a closer connection,
which your natural courtesy makes me confidently expect, shall
have revealed to you his real character, you will be sufficiently
convinced, Reverend Sir, without any foreign recommendation,
how worthy he is of your affection.   In the mean time if I hold
any place in your esteem, I entreat you again and again to
honour with your favour and kindness a man whom you see to
be so cherished by me.

It is a matter of deep regret that the churches of your whole
kingdom have not yet been organized as all good men could
wish, and as in the beginning they had hoped.[1]   But to overcome all difficulties there is need of unflagging efforts.   Then
indeed it is expedient and even absolutely necessary that the
queen should discriminate, and you in your turn should lay
aside, nay, cast from you entirely whatever savours of earthly

---

[1] This regret was shared in by Grindal himself.   In his letter to Calvin of the 18th
March, 1560, we read : "I commend to your prayers, and those of the other brethren,
the state of our churches, not yet settled sufficiently according to our mind."

domination, in order that for the exercise of a spiritual office you may have a legitimate authority and such as shall be bestowed on you by God. This indeed will be her supremacy and pre-eminence; then she will hold the highest rank of dignity under Christ our head, if she stretch forth a helping hand to legitimate pastors, for the execution of those functions that have been enjoined us. But as neither your wisdom stands in need of counsel, nor your magnanimity of incitements, I shall only have recourse to prayers, and supplicate God, my most excellent and honoured sir, to govern you by his Spirit, sustain you by his power, shield you with his protection and bless all your holy labours.

All my colleagues most respectfully salute your reverence.

[*Lat. Orig. Minute.—Library of Geneva.* Vol. 107 *a.*]

DLX.—To CHARLES UTENHOVEN.[1]

Tokens of lively interest for the French Church of London—Perils of Geneva.

GENEVA, *May,* 1560.

I trust that the French Church in your parts, for which you had so anxiously solicited us, has been well provided for. To us, indeed, it was a severe trial to be deprived of Nicholas des Gallars, who has hitherto proved himself a faithful colleague and fellow-worker with us, but since you are of opinion that among you he will reap a more abundant harvest of his labours, we dared not let pass this opportunity. It is to me a source of great joy that liberty has been restored to you. The protection of the Bishop, moreover, will be of no small service to you in all your affairs, for the man who held that dignity in the time of King Edward, being too much addicted to empty pomps, was not sufficiently propitious to you. I have also endeavoured by a letter to confirm his favourable dispositions towards you, and such is his natural kindliness that I have the satisfaction of

---

[1] Charles Utenhoven, sprung from a noble family of the Low Countries, and one of the elders of the Church of the French Protestants in London. While John Utenhoven, his brother, had followed Laski to Poland, he had not quitted England.

knowing that I have not lost my pains. As the Earl of Bedford had testified by words that he had the greatest inclination to serve you, I have exhorted him[1] to continue to watch over both churches, and to show to the foreigners any offices of kindness that might be in his power. It afforded me pleasure that you found an opportunity of making Lord Burleigh[2] acquainted with my apology respecting the pamphlet. Though to confess frankly the truth, I am not under any great uneasiness about conciliating court favour. Some ill-disposed person by a malicious whisper exposed me to obloquy. The slander was but too eagerly received. If the truth is admitted, I esteem my character sufficiently vindicated; if not, there are other things which as they touch me more closely so they give me greater uneasiness. For that we still exist safe and sound is a thing incredible to all, since we were condemned long ago by the judgment of the whole of France, Germany, and Italy; and those who had fairly given us up as ruined are astonished that we have not perished a hundred times. Add to this, that if this church is still flourishing, or at least undisturbed, all the odium falls upon my head. Thus it is necessary for me to harden my heart towards both parties. It is my wish, indeed, to be serviceable to others, but only indeed according to the measure of my ability. Meanwhile I shall always cherish with an undisturbed mind those in whom I perceive the seeds of piety, and even should they not reciprocate my feelings, I shall never suffer myself to be alienated from them. It would be absurd to prolong my letter any further, since a common friend and brother is to be the bearer of it, who, though he should be charged with no commissions by me, will nevertheless carry along with him the mind of the writer.

[*Lat. Copy.—Library of Geneva.* Vol. 107 *a.*]

---

[1] See a second letter addressed to this nobleman, (June, 1560.)

[2] See the letter to Cecil, p. 46.

DLXI.—To Bullinger.

Renewed disapprobation of the conspiracy of Amboise—Account of the intrigues of Renaudie at Geneva—Vain opposition of Calvin.

GENEVA, 11th *May*, 1560.

Lest any contention should spring up between us, venerable and dearest brother, I will not touch on the subject which I perceive is so distasteful to you,[1] provided always that a harmony of views subsist between us respecting the principal points of doctrine. In other matters, let each of us leave the judgment of the other unfettered. What I deemed right and useful I have endeavoured to persuade you to, but since my freedom has given offence it is better to forbear. One thing only I should wish you to bear in mind; it is that I have long ago despaired of those creatures who ape Luther, nor is much reliance to be placed on James André and such like persons. But what wrings my heart is that brethren united to us in the faith should be oppressed by a barbarous tyranny, nor yet find any succour to alleviate their distress. For how many, think you, are there who with silent prayers desire a helping hand to be held out to them, and groan to find themselves deserted by us! But I pass to other subjects.

You have not hesitated to repel the odious charges brought against us of fomenting the insurrectionary movement in France.[2] You might do so with a safe conscience. When eight months ago these designs began to be agitated, I interposed my authority to prevent them from proceeding further, secretly and quietly it is true, because I feared if any report about the affair should reach the ears of the enemy, lest I should be dragging all the godly to a horrid butchery. I fancied, however, that all violent movements had been quashed and even quieted down, till an individual of no personal merit came to me from France and

---

[1] Allusion to the reiterated efforts of Calvin to bring about a better intelligence between the Church of Zurich and those of Germany, and thus provoke a concerted action between the Swiss Cantons and the Lutheran princes in favour of the French Protestants. See vol. iii., p. 410.   [2] To suppress the conspiracy of Amboise.

boasted that he had been appointed the leader of the enterprise.[1]
I immediately, however, put a stop to his bragging, and professed my utter abhorrence of his conspiracy. The next day,
this needy wretch, who was hunting in all directions for booty,
that he might catch in his nets a rich friend, and under pretext
of a public collection, scrape together a good round sum of
money, told a barefaced lie, declaring that I did not disapprove
of the conspiracy, but that to avoid odium I declined to take any
public part in it. Suddenly roused upon hearing this, and calling together my colleagues, I sharply exposed his groundless
assertions. More than that, I demonstrated that he himself before
he left Paris had been most distinctly informed, how perfectly
averse I was to that project. But though it was everywhere
known that he was an object of suspicion to me, yet as he lived
at Lausanne on account of its vicinity, and as he had a caressing manner, and was versed in the art of cajoling, he won the
affection of many among us, so that in the space of three days,
his principles corrupted this city as if it were by contagion.
Many men among the nobility, as well as among the lower classes
and the working people, began to hold secret meetings, not so
peaceably, however, but the din of them reached my ears. How
greatly this conspiracy displeased me, I took care to demonstrate
both in public and in private, and without any dissimulation.
When I gained nothing by these proceedings, I complained that
our body possessed so little authority that in a matter so deeply
important our advice was despised. A hundred times I declared
that this was a new kind of fascination; of the sorrowful issue I
made such predictions that many almost repented of their folly.
I entreat you then that, with your wonted kindness and for the
sake of our mutual friendship, you will go on without any mis-
givings in vindicating our character. The other details you
may ask from M. Peter Martyr, for a headache prevents me
from spinning out my discourse any further. For the same
reason I shall be obliged to claim the indulgence of our excellent brother, M. Wolf, for not having written an answer to
his letter. In my name you will thank him for the labour he

---

[1] Godfroy du Barry, Sieur de la Renaudie.

has undertaken in my favour, and you will salute both him and your other fellow-pastors.

Farewell, distinguished sir and honoured brother. May the Lord govern, protect, and support you—and bless you and your whole family. Amen.—Yours,

JOHN CALVIN.

[*Orig. autogr.—Arch. of Zurich, Gallicana Scripta*, p. 46.]

DLXII.—TO PETER MARTYR.

Reverts to the conspiracy of Amboise—Troubles in France—Dangers of Geneva.

GENEVA, 11*th May*, 1560.

You will pardon, most accomplished sir, my prolonged silence. For six whole months overcome by a concentrated sorrow, I have abstained from writing letters, unless perhaps some which necessity wrung from me. The cause of this sorrow was the inconsiderate zeal of the men of our party, who imagined they could obtain by disorder the liberty which was to be sought for by other measures. Already eight months ago they had asked my opinion. I fancied they had been brought to a sounder mind by my one answer. Some time afterwards (too late, however, for there was now no room for a remedy) I asked them what, having repudiated my advice, they counted upon doing. About sixty persons have left this place notwithstanding my remonstrances.[1] I told them plainly that they were under the influence of a kind of fascination.

They attempted to show that they had not taken up arms rashly, by saying that a promise had been made them by one of the princes,[2] who by the ancient usage of the kingdom and its written laws claims as his right, during the absence of his brother, the highest rank in the supreme council. For it had been agreed upon that he should present to the king the con-

---

[1] Among the noblemen who left Geneva, people remarked the Seigneurs of Castelnaud and of Villemongis, who were destined to perish miserably on the scaffold at Amboise.

[2] The Prince of Condé.

fession that had been drawn up among us, and that if the partisans of Guise should offer any violence, or make his action the
subject of a criminal accusation, as many persons as possible
should be prepared to undertake his defence. But not even
this plausible pretext satisfied me at first, unless they should be
perfectly on their guard not to shed blood, for I declared it to
be an inevitable consequence that from a single drop would immediately flow streams that would inundate France. But the
affair undertaken with imprudence was still worse managed; and
certainly one worthless fellow, who had audaciously thrust himself into the business, occasioned the ruin of all by his foolishness. But though nothing has fallen out which I did not anticipate, it affords no consolation of a future disaster to have
foreseen it, or to speak more correctly, that men predestined to
a manifest and distinctly announced destruction should have
been at last precipitated into ruin by a too tardy movement.
Had not the measure been opposed, our people would have taken
forcible possession of the churches, as was done in Dauphiny.
But in their manner of acting there was the same thoughtless
giddiness. Those who listened to my advice still hold out and
are prepared to meet death courageously. There was not the
same moderate conduct everywhere, for in a celebrated faubourg
of Paris, in the presence of an immense concourse of people, the
Cardinal was hanged in effigy, and when by an order of the
parliament, archers of the guard were sent to put an end to this
ignominious exhibition, means were found secretly to set fire to
the gibbet which was consumed along with the effigy. Procla-
mations against the house of Guise are hawked up and down,
and daily published in the principal cities. These are the beginnings of sorrows, as far as the French are concerned, but
they also for the most part bode no good to us. Nevertheless
we await with calm what the Lord shall determine. Perils are
staring us in the face, when powerful bodies of troops are everywhere being armed, but because we know that we are under the
Lord's protection we keep watch and abstain from tumult.

The young men whom you recommended to me will feel how
highly both I and my fellow-pastors value your recommendation. They have found, I hope, a very suitable lodging.

Farewell, my ever honoured brother. May the Lord always
stand by you, govern, protect, and bless you along with your
wife, whom as well as our brethren, M. Gualter and the others,
I most cordially salute.—Yours,

JOHN CALVIN.

[*Lat. Copy.*—*Library of Paris, Recueil, Hist.* t. xix. p. 29.]

DLXIII.—To STURM AND HOTMAN.[1]

Treacherous policy of the Guises—New appeal addressed to the German Princes—
Petition to the king.

GENEVA, 4th June, 1560.

Although for a season we have been almost paralyzed by
sorrow, nevertheless the unhappy condition of our brethren compels our grief to break out into action, both because the most
urgent necessity stimulates us, and an opportunity not to be
despised seems to present itself. The party of the Guises have
been struck with a certain degree of consternation, which may
wring from them at least some relaxation of their rigour and
cruelty; and it is probable that the defeat which the Spaniard
has lately suffered in a naval engagement, has produced such
an effect on their minds that they will bridle in for some time
their wonted ferocity. Meanwhile, whatever concessions have

---

[1] The edict of Romorantin, which soon followed the conspiracy of Amboise, had
displeased all parties in France (May 1560). The Guises were preparing to strike a
new blow at the Reformed, and endeavoured to enrol against them the German *Reitres*
of whom they had convoked the chiefs at Meiningen. To dissipate this peril, Calvin
warmly urged Sturm to exhort the German princes to send an embassy to the king. It
was to advise him to re-establish peace, not by violence and punishments, but in correcting the abuses of the church, and thus preparing by a moderate reform the conciliation
of hostile minds. But could the Guises, absolute masters of the king and chiefs of the
Catholic party, possibly consent to any concessions of which the first result would
have been to draw on their own ruin? Was the queen mother Catharine de Medicis
sincere in the promise she had made to convoke a council to put a term to the troubles
of France? Was the intervention of the German Princes, in fine, likely to be more
favourably received than had been the petitions of the churches and the counsels of
moderate men, at the head of whom the Chancellor L'Hopital was soon about to place
himself?

been made to the godly, we cannot but see have been yielded
with a fraudulent and insidious intention, that their enemies,
having first secured a state of greater tranquillity, may ere long
crush them when off their guard with much greater facility.
Certainly nothing can be more fluctuating than their conduct
in its inconstancy. Witness their virulence, which, however
carefully they disguise it, always betrays itself by numerous
symptoms.

It is for that reason that we have need of an external remedy,
and we hope to be able to obtain it by your co-operation, provided only you make a slight effort. But it would not only be
superfluous but absurd to urge you too vehemently to do us this
service, for we are by no means unacquainted with your pious
solicitude for the welfare of our brethren, and with the ardour
of your zeal. Now this is the point in question—that the
German princes by a solemn embassy should partly supplicate,
partly exhort the king, that as the best means of appeasing disturbances he should resolve not to strike terror with fire and
sword, but to purge the church of its corruptions and settle it
on a better foundation. For it is quite impossible that without
some sufficient reformation so many thousands of men will ever
hold their peace. But that you may have a clearer conception
of what we desire, we have thought proper to write out on a
separate sheet the very formula of our petition. Moreover
while you shall be engaged in this undertaking, we will make it our
business by all the means in our power to rouse the King of
Navarre to claim the regency of the kingdom that had been
wrested out of his hands,[1] nor will he want a pretext for his
demand, for it is notorious that the kingdom is in jeopardy from
these commotions, and is every day on the brink of ruin from
the perfidy or supineness of the Guises, nor can their arrogance
and avarice be any longer endured without involving everything
in destruction.

[1] All the efforts that had been tried till then to stir up the King of Navarre and inspire him with energetic resolutions had been useless. Hotman wrote to Bullinger
the 2nd Sept., 1559. "The King of Navarre has most miserably disappointed the
hopes of all. If you knew how earnestly he has been admonished, what conditions
have been offered him, what subsidies placed at his disposal, and with what sluggishness he has slighted them all, you would be truly astonished."

Certainly unless I am deceived, the king's council, when they shall feel themselves reduced to such straits, will be roused from their lethargy to consult for the public safety. Above all, the queen mother must be goaded on by the sharpest stimulants to act along with us, for unless by force it will never be possible to detach her from the party of the Guises. Nevertheless, she will adhere to whatever she is persuaded will be for the advantage of herself and her children. Other details you will learn from the messengers, who, when you shall have made their acquaintance, will stand in need of no recommendation; and for the cause itself we know that as a matter of course it brings its own recommendation along with it in your eyes no less than in ours.

Farewell, then, most acccomplished and highly esteemed sirs. May the Lord sustain you by his power, govern you by his Spirit, and bestow on you every blessing.—Yours,

JOHN CALVIN.

What follows is in the handwriting of Theodore Beza:

This seems a fitting moment for the most illustrious princes to send an embassy to the king, for though the faction of the Guises are still possessed by the same obstinacy, and there are but small hopes of their being brought to equity, yet as the fear with which they have been struck has troubled their reason, so it will compel them to put on at least some appearances of moderation. But as matters now stand in France, if they should make ever so small a concession, and abate somewhat of their rigour towards their adversaries, the pure religion would in a very brief space of time acquire such a strength as it would not be in the power of all its enemies afterwards to diminish. If the most illustrious princes then have ever taken an interest in the welfare of the French, who profess a zeal for true piety, now an opportunity is offered them by Divine providence, of making use of their authority for the succour of these afflicted men. To procrastinate on the contrary and attempt no remedy, would be highly dangerous, because as often as the Guises see a certain calm re-established, they again commence to give vent to their rage with the same license as before. Besides, unless our friends be spurred to action anew, whatever the council of the king has promised will end in nothing. There is a necessity for us then to ply our task sedulously, lest the evil should gain such ground as no longer to admit of a remedy. Now the following summary of our petition, if it meet with the approbation of the most illustrious princes, will be highly useful.

First of all, then, it would be desirable that they should declare their extreme satisfaction and offer their congratulations to the king, because he has decided upon convoking a council for the purpose of removing the abuses and corruptions with which it is notorious that all the sincere worshippers of God are so much scandalized, that they would rather a thousand times suffer death than pine away for ever amid such pollutions ; for that this is the only means by which all troubles can be quieted, the issue of which will be disastrous unless his majesty provide a remedy before it be too late.

In the next place, the deputation might proceed to expose that the most illustrious princes exhort the king and his council not to desist from so just and advantageous a purpose, though in thus exhorting them they refrain from offering their services, inasmuch as they are an object of suspicion to the Popish priesthood ; that nevertheless they most ardently desire to confederate to the extent of their ability in the furtherance of this cause, and that in any matter in which the king may deem their good offices of any utility to him, he may confidently count on them.

In the third place, the deputies may state that they have undertaken this journey chiefly for two reasons—to consult first for the security and tranquillity of the king and for the public welfare ; that the illustrious princes are of opinion that this object cannot be secured otherwise than by the abolition of superstitions, which exasperate the minds of all good men to such a degree that they hold their own lives cheap in comparison with the legitimate worship of God, and should deem themselves traitors did they even manifest a semblance of assent to what their conscience repudiates ; that the second object of their mission is to represent that persons should not be treated with rigour who worship God in purity, and keep themselves apart from the defilements of Popery; on the contrary, if they are obedient to the king, as their duty requires, and stir up no troubles, but confine themselves in their private capacity to the observance of the faith which they have embraced, that they should be tolerated till a reformation of the universal church by fitting remedies be provided for.

If the king as well as his council shall deign to take into consideration this representation, that then the most illustrious princes are already disposed and will most cordially hold them, selves prepared to lend him their aid; but if, on the contrary, he deal harshly with his subjects, and refuse all just reforms, that they cannot but fear the most unhappy results; and for that reason, as well as for the good-will and profound respect which they entertain for the king and kingdom of France, they not only advise but beg and implore, that he will not neglect so excellent an opportunity of establishing peace on a firm basis, in continuing to struggle against necessity.

[*Lat. Minute.—Library of Geneva.* Vol. 107 *a.*]

DLXIV.—To John Lusen.[1]

Anxieties about the Churches of Poland—Refutation of the errors of Stancari.

GENEVA, *9th June*, 1560.

You write to us, honoured brother in the Lord, that Vergerio keeps gadding up and down, and poisoning with his admixtures the pure doctrines of religion. Respecting his conduct, complaints had long ago been made to us both by John Laski and others, who do not approve of such subtile devices. But since it does not belong to us to impose silence on a man naturally inclined to crooked ways, we have only to entreat God to check his career. The Seigneur Palatine of Wilna should also be put in mind to guard against his insidious arts, a task which we were just on the point of undertaking, had time permitted; though as he is a silly, meddlesome creature, he can scarcely

[1] *On the back:* To John Lusen, Minister of a Church in Poland.

deceive a second time any one possessed of even ordinary common sense. We are surprised, notwithstanding, that he has carried his impudence so far as also to have been tampering in England, but the more he brings himself forward the less dangerous, we fancy, he will prove, since people shall thus have an opportunity of ascertaining not only his deceit but his foolishness. We have not thought proper to attack the supporters of Stancari,[1] partly because they are unknown to us, and partly because we believed that they might be more easily brought back to a sound mind, should they not be stigmatized by any peculiar mark of disgrace. For, if they show any deference to our judgment, they will learn from our letter to you that they ought to retrace their steps. And to put an end to all this shuffling, know that Stancari has falsely put forward our names among you to screen himself. Perhaps before the time of the Frankfort Fair, our letter will be published in which we proclaim that we hold in perfect abhorrence his extravagant dogma.[2] Moreover, you will be made aware by our answer to him that we disapprove of what is written by you about the eternal priesthood of Christ, as if Christ were not necessarily eternal since he was appointed to be a priest not less than a mediator. If you listen to our advice, you will make some change in that passage, lest your adversaries should make a handle of it for calumniating you. We have not had leisure to write to the illustrious Bishop of C——,[3] because we have had all our time absorbed by continual writings, and it is incredible what a pressure of business overwhelms us from the state of affairs in France. The unfortunate churches of that country are oppressed by the most cruel tyranny. Would to God that half the liberty, at least, were allowed to them which you state to be enjoyed by those of Poland, though the Saxons,

[1] Francisco Stancari, a native of Mantua, and a distinguished Orientalist, was one of the principal apostles of the Antitrinitarian doctrines in Poland. He maintained that Jesus Christ is a mediator between God and man, only in virtue of his humanity, and while pretending to steer at an equal distance from the errors of Tritheism and Arianism, overthrew the dogma of the Trinity by subtle interpretations.

[2] Answer to the Polish Brethren respecting the manner in which Christ is mediator, in order to refute the error of Stancari. 1560, in 8vo. *Opera,* vol. viii.

[3] A word illegible in the text.

without employing the sword or other weapons, yet by practising
one species of tyranny, are almost a match for Antichrist and
his satellites in cruelty. Unless God from heaven provide a
remedy for so many evils, a frightful dispersion is impending
over all the churches. But whatever happen, let us hold on
with constancy in the course of our vocation.
Farewell, distinguished sir and renowned brother. May the
Lord always stand by, protect, and strengthen you to the end.

[*Lat. Orig. Minute.—Library of Geneva.* Vol. 107 *a.*]

DLXV.—TO NICHOLAS DES GALLARS.[1]

Counsels for the direction of the Church—Domestic news.

GENEVA, 16*th June*, 1560.

We have learned that certain persons of your congregation
have made themselves busy in order to have the charge of su-
perintendent, which was entrusted by the Queen and her council to the reverend father, the Bishop of London, transferred
to another. If that is true, you must do your endeavour to
check their importunate officiousness, for which there will be
found no other motive than private cupidity. For the pretext
which they bring forward, that it is uncertain what the character
of his successor may turn out to be, is of no sort of importance
to you, since the inspection over your churches has not been
accorded to any Bishop of London whatsoever, but to this upright, faithful, and sincere protector of your liberty. Should
any other equally fit be at your disposal, still, in my judgment,
it would be better for you to make no change, because it is not

---

[1] By a letter of the 3d June, Des Gallars informed Calvin of the gracious reception
which he had met with from the Bishop of London. " I presented to him your letter, says he, which he read with an appearance of great satisfaction. He testified to
me his gratitude for it, and seemed pleased that you had written to him in so friendly
a manner and in reminding him of his duties. He then offered me his friendly services with a ready access to his person as often as I should desire it." Ecclesiastical
discords, which seemed to be the sad lot of the French congregations abroad, and the
state of his health, abridged Des Gallars' stay in England. He became pastor of the
Church of Orleans in 1561.

advantageous for you to alienate from you the good-will of the man who has embraced you with the warmest affection, who has undertaken to defend the repose of your church, whose activity and courage in procuring you tranquillity you have already experienced, and whose authority, in a word, is more than ever necessary to you. Now, since it is probable that this matter has been canvassed among a good many of you, should any report of it come to his ears, and should you suppose that he has been offended, you will, I trust, undertake the office of interpreter, that he may pardon the folly of those who have erred from an ill-judged excess of zeal. Assuredly he must be appeased, that he may not cease to extend to your church the same favour which he began to entertain towards it. And should you discover any persons of untractable dispositions, lose no time in letting them know that for another end you had been sent over to them than that of being mixed up with their turbulent counsels, and that carried away by them you should neglect the common welfare of the flock.

Your son Amos was lately tormented during four days by so severe an attack of colic that we hardly entertained any hopes of his life. He is not yet quite recovered, but the pains being abated he is out of danger. Your wife is gradually recovering strength. She now goes abroad, and we are in hopes that she will continue to enjoy tolerable health.

Farewell, most excellent brother and faithful servant of Christ. May God always prosper you, direct you by the spirit of wisdom and fortitude, and keep you in safety. Salute all friends.

[*Lat. Copy.—Library of Geneva.* Vol. 107 *a.*]

DLXVI.—To the Earl of Bedford.[1]

Agitations of Europe—Wishes for the re-establishment of peace, and for the marriage of the Queen of England.

GENEVA, *June,* 1560.

During the short interval that has elapsed since I wrote to

---

[1] Without date: To the generous and most noble seigneur, the Earl of Bedford. . . . Member of the Privy Council, this nobleman took an important part in the measures which prepared the definitive triumph of the Reformation under Elizabeth.

you, most illustrious and generous seigneur, by our colleague, Nicholas des Gallars, nothing has occurred to furnish me matter for a letter, except that France being occupied with her preparations for the Scottish war,[1] the terrible threats with which this city was assailed from all sides are momentarily suspended. In the space of four years we were a hundred times marked out for destruction, nor are we yet exempt from danger if our enemies were only delivered from their apprehensions in other quarters; but the loss of the Spanish fleet has fallen out very opportunely for us, and your Queen keeps the French on the alert, who, by their caresses, confess their fears of her power. Would that disturbances being settled, and the din of arms appeased, you could enjoy a little tranquillity for firmly establishing piety, and purging the worship of God from all the pollutions of Popery, and that those who without a cause seek our ruin would leave us a little repose, since we desire nothing but to live unnoticed in peace with all the world, and beyond the reach of harm in our little corner, like the tortoise in its shell. But as many conspire for our destruction, God will shelter us under the covert of his wings. It is very painful to all pious men, that in organizing a church conformably to the model held out to us in the Scriptures, your progress should be so very slow; and, to unbosom myself freely to you, it is no less a matter of regret to them that your Queen does not consult the good of posterity, and give her mind to raise up a race of children to succeed her.[2] For what will take place, think you,

---

[1] The first religious disturbances broke out in Scotland in 1559. The lords of the congregation took possession of Edinburgh, whilst the queen regent, Mary of Lorraine, withdrew to Leith with the French troops that had come to her assistance. An English fleet was going to blockade the port of Leith and support the Reformed. See *Hume's History of England*, chap. xxxviii., § 9 and 10.

[2] The hand of the Queen was then sought by the Archduke Charles, second son of the Emperor, as well as by Casimir, son of the Elector Palatine, and as this latter prince professed the Reformed religion, he thought himself, on that account, better entitled to succeed in his addresses. Eric, King of Sweden, and Adolph, Duke of Holstein, were encouraged by the same views to become suitors, and the Earl of Arran, heir to the crown of Scotland, was by the states of that kingdom recommended to her as a suitable marriage. Even some of her own subjects entertained hopes of success—The Earl of Arundel, Sir William Pickering, and Lord Robert Dudley. The policy of the Queen was not to disgust any of the pretenders to her hand by too absolute a refusal. See *Hume*, chap. xxxviii., § 14.

should she die without leaving any offspring? But transported by my anxiety, and my love of country, I overstep the bounds which I had prescribed to myself. I could not, however, refrain from making a tacit allusion to the solicitude of those who wish a continual duration of good fortune to your nation. In the meantime, most illustrious seigneur, I rejoice that you are unwearied in your holy zeal for piety, and advancing the progress of the church, and I pray God from the heart, to preserve you more and more, enrich you with his gifts, and shield you with his protection.

Farewell, most noble and highly esteemed seigneur.

[*Lat. Copy.—Library of Paris, Dupuy*, 102.]

DLXVII.—To the Waldenses.[1]

He exhorts them to keep up friendly relations with the Reformed churches of Poland.

GENEVA, 1*st July*, 1560.

After the brother from whom I received your letter had, in a private interview, exposed to me your instructions, as I perceived that he had been sent not to me individually, but also to my colleagues, I exhorted him to repeat the same before our society. My answer will, therefore, express the common opinion of all. And, in the first place, we return you no common thanks, because you have not hesitated to send to us brethren who should be witnesses, and, as it were, vouchers of your affection towards us, and of your brotherly connection, and therefore we have the more willingly welcomed this act of courtesy

---

[1] To the Waldenses (or Vaudois) of Bohemia. Though commonly designated by the name of Waldenses, the members of these primitive churches of Bohemia seemed rather to be an offshoot of the religious revolution of which John Huss was the leader and the martyr. In a letter to Calvin, dated from Carmel in Bohemia, they had manifested a desire to connect themselves more closely with the Reformed churches. "We see the enemies of our Lord and of the whole church lending one another mutual aid, and evidently conspiring to oppress the truth. As it is our duty vigorously to resist them, so we should take care to be all as one body in the Lord." Calvin replied to this pious desire in exhorting them to make some concessions on the question of the sacraments, and to contribute for their own part to appease the religious discords which agitated the churches of Poland.

on your part, because it flowed from a sincere zeal for piety. We desire, in our turn, that you should be equally persuaded how much our inclinations prompt us to cherish a holy unity. And assuredly, when we are separated from each other by such extensive tracts of country, and surrounded on every side by enemies that occupy nearly the whole world, to enjoy this consolation of our dispersion is dear and delightful. Let us then bear witness, with common consent, that we have one Father in heaven, and that we form one body under Christ our Head. This we are confidently assured you will do, and we will make it our business to make you feel that this is in reality what we have most at heart. Now, we are convinced that there is no better bond for cementing and strengthening concord than not to lend too credulous an ear to evil reports that people circulate about one another. And, in truth, in this point we do not think that we have at all failed in our duty towards you; for, with respect to the letter written to the Poles, about which the brother in your name seemed indirectly to complain, we are not conscious of having committed any fault, and you yourselves, having in your equity duly considered our reasons, will find that being consulted on that cause we could not have given an answer with greater courtesy, nor with more moderation. Certainly we did not mention you invidiously, and as far as the case permitted we strove to mitigate the offences which had arisen to obviate worse dissensions, and so to reconcile the parties on both sides, that at the very outset you might be fellow-workers with the Poles in erecting the kingdom of Christ. We were on the point of writing to you, also, had an opportunity presented itself; but it cannot escape your observation how difficult the means of communication are between countries lying so remote from each other; now that a more favourable opportunity has been offered, we shall frankly make known our sentiments. Do you yourselves in your wisdom maturely reflect, even if we said nothing on the vast importance of your holding out a hand to the Poles, in order that the pure doctrine of the gospel may make progress among them. For no one can doubt that your dissension, if it be remarked by the enemy, will throw obstacles in the way of undertakings already so well and happily begun.

The brother has assigned to us some reasons more specious than real, why you should dread to contract a more intimate union with them ; namely, that you perceive them to be rent by perverse factions. Now this motive should act the other way, and stimulate you to form a closer connection, in order to counteract the evils which are springing up and spreading so fast. For the authority of so many churches lending one another mutual aid would curb those wild spirits, that, in a state of dispersion, claim to themselves a license to breed tumults and disturb all order. At present, the pious brethren, deprived of your co-operation, have a much harder task to perform. If Satan directs the attacks of Stancari, George Blandrata, and others against Poland, is it not your duty to come to the rescue? If you neglect it, reflect whether the aid of your brethren may not one day fail yourselves. For it will not be always in your own power to escape contentions from which God has hitherto kept you exempt. The controversy respecting the imparting to us of Christ's flesh and blood is what prevents people from coalescing with one another. We have given it as our opinion that on this point a fitting and unambiguous explanation, given and received by the two parties, is the way to remove this stumblingblock. If this advice displease you, experience will one day prove it to have been sound and salutary. Two things, perhaps, have given you some offence ; first, because we have written that there is an obscure and ambiguous brevity in your confession, and that it stands in need of greater precision in its definitions ; and next, that in your apology there is too much vehemence and animosity against all those who, not content with the bare form of the expression, would like to have the light of a sound interpretation thrown on these words, in which you assert that the bread is the body of Christ. We know the plausible plea of those who, under the shade of the Augsburg confession, consulting only their ease and a quiet life, fly from every thing which might give them trouble ; in one word, from the odium of the cross itself. What opinion M. Philip Melancthon, himself the author of the confession,[1] entertained on this

---

[1] Melancthon died in the month of April preceding, his heart broken by the ecclesiastical disorders of which he had been the sorrowing but powerless witness, deplor-

matter is not unknown to you, and I shall be forced perhaps to
let the whole world know it, in consequence of the double dealing of those men who endeavour to spread darkness over a
transparent light. And yet, though we reverently cherish the
memory of Philip, we do not make use of his authority to crush
our adversaries; we only show how unfairly they shelter themselves under the confession of Augsburg, when nothing can be
conceived more alien than they are from the sentiments of its
author. We, however, persist in our opinion (let this be said
without giving you offence) that the formula of your confession
cannot be adopted simply as it stands without danger, and that
to subscribe to it before it had received a suitable interpretation,
would be the origin and subject of many evils to the Poles.
We have no difficulty in overlooking your vehemence, for it gives
us no pleasure to rake up old griefs, when it is our desire that
they should be buried in oblivion. Only this we may be allowed
to say, that it cannot decently be denied that the author of your
apology exceeded the bounds of moderation. With regard to
the charge with which your messenger has reproached me, (for
the sake of retaliation, no doubt,) that I too in some of my
writings break out into sallies of passion, though I do not entirely deny it, yet it is irrelevantly brought forward. If I, indeed, inveigh rather too sharply against some unprincipled mis-
creants, the manner of your apology is altogether dissimilar,
for it confounds without discrimination or distinction many pious
and learned men with the enemies of the truth. Certainly if
it was your intention to assail the error of certain persons, you
were bound to draw a line of demarkation so as not to involve
in one common charge the innocent and the guilty. But to put
a stop to all contention, we only beg and entreat you, if we have
candidly pointed out the way which we judged most efficacious

---

ing, however, his own weakness. Calvin, in one of his writings, paid him the most
eloquent homage :—" O Philip, who art now in the bosom of Christ, and in peace
expectest us, how often fatigued by the combat, and reposing thy head on my breast,
hast thou said to me, God grant me to die upon this heart! and I too have a thousand times wished that we had lived together. Thou wouldst have shown more
courage for the battle, and they who triumphed over thy great goodness, which they
styled weakness, would have been restrained within bounds which they would not
have dared to pass."—*Calvinus contra Heshusium, Opera*, vol. viii.

for healing strife and banishing angry passions, that you should
not consider that as any slight put upon you; nor have we so
overweening an opinion of ourselves as not to bear patiently
being blamed or admonished, if it should chance that we have
at any time acted with too little circumspection.

Farewell, most excellent and respected brethren. We pray
our heavenly Father to govern you continually by his Spirit, to
shield you with his protection, to enrich you with his gifts, and
to bless all your holy labours.

JOHN CALVIN,

In the name of all.

[*Calvin's Lat. Corresp.—Opera*, ix., p. 14.]

DLXVIII.—TO THE DUCHESS OF FERRARA.[1]

He apologizes for not having been able to send her a minister—exhorts her to free
herself from the obligation of an oath they have imposed on her, and to show herself more firm in the profession of the gospel.

GENEVA, 5th July, 1560.

MADAME:—Though I have been often required and solicited
on your part, I have never been able to decide upon sending
you a man such as you demanded, fearing lest those who
brought me word, might from excess of zeal have gone
further than your intention. For I had no letters from you to
certify if what they told me was exact or not; and even at present, Madame, I should have very much wished to have been

---

[1] This princess was on the point of quitting Italy. Widow of Hercules d'Este (3d
October 1559), she began her journey to return to France in the month of September
1560, followed by the homage and regrets of the population of Ferrara : "The loss of
this royal princess gave great sorrow to the population of Ferrara, because attaching
everybody to her by the liveliness of her disposition and her pleasing manners, she
was in the highest degree beloved by every body. And so much the more that she
had not her match for her liberalities, nor was she ever tired of relieving the poor
with her alms." Muratori, *Antich. Estensi*, vol. ii. p. 389. Aunt of the young king
Francis II. and of the regent Catherine of Medicis, the Duchess of Ferrara hoped to exercise at the court of France an influence useful to the Reformed party. Her departure
from Ferrara excited the regrets of Calvin, who had never ceased to found on this
princess great hopes for the propagation of the gospel in Italy.

better assured, in order to write to you more freely. Not that I distrust the bearer, who has given me pretty good proofs to convince me that he was sent by you, but you know, Madame, how many persons may be suborned to draw from me things that might occasion you much trouble and regret.

As to the oath[1] which you have been constrained to take, because you have failed in your duty and offended God in taking it, so you are not bound to keep it, any more than a superstitious vow. You know, Madame, that Herod is not only not approved of for having too well observed the oath which he had taken in an unguarded moment, but it is imputed to him for a two-fold condemnation. This I say to you, not to importune you to write to me, but that you may have no scruples about what God leaves you free to do, and of which he absolves you. I have discharged my duty in letting you know.

With respect to the journey which you have resolved upon, though the captivity in which you are, and have been too long kept, is hard and worthy of compassion, nevertheless, I must declare to you, Madame, that you will not have gained much by having escaped from one gulf to be plunged into another. For I do not see in what this change can better your condition. The government with which they intend to mix you up is at present in such disorder that everybody utters a cry of alarm. Should you take some share in its proceedings, and should your opinions be listened to, I am tolerably satisfied things will not go on quite so badly. But that is not what they are aiming at. They want to screen themselves under your name, to foster the evil which people can no longer endure. Now to go and thrust yourself into the middle of these disorders is manifestly a tempting of God. I desire your prosperity, Madame, as much as possible; but if the elevation and grandeur of the world should prevent you from approaching to God, I should be a traitor to your interests in making you believe that black is white. If you were thoroughly resolved to conduct yourself with straightforwardness and greater magnanimity than you have done hitherto, I should entreat you forthwith to take a greater share

---

[1] Hercules d'Este, on his death-bed, had exacted of his wife an oath that she would no longer keep up a correspondence with Calvin. (Library of Ferrara.)

in the management of affairs, than what they offer you; but if it is only to say amen to everything which is condemned both by God and men, I have nothing to say, but that you beware of falling from bad into worse. I do not mean, however, Madame, to advise you to continue in your present state of bondage, nor to go to sleep in it, for there has been something too much of that in times past. Only I beseech you to make such a change as may lead you to serve God unfeignedly, and tend towards the right mark, and not to entangle yourself in snares it might be difficult for you to break, and which might fetter you as much as, and even more than the former ones.

However that may be, Madame, at any rate, you are continuing too long in a languid state, and if you do not take compassion on yourself, it is to be feared that you may seek, when it is too late, a remedy for your malady. Besides what God has so long taught you by his word, age admonishes you to reflect that our heritage and eternal rest is not here below, and Jesus Christ certainly deserves that you should forget for him both France and Ferrara. God has also by your widowhood rendered you more disencumbered and free, in order that he might draw you entirely to himself. I wish I had an opportunity of demonstrating more fully these things to you by word of mouth, and that not once, but from day to day; but I leave you to meditate on them in your prudence, more fully than anything I have written could suggest.

Madame, having commended me humbly to your gracious favour, I entreat our heavenly Father to have you in his protection, to govern you by his Spirit, and to increase you in all good.

[*Fr. Copy.—Library of Geneva.* Vol. 107.]

DLXIX.—To Bullinger.

Mission of Theodore Beza in France—Counsels to the churches of that country—
Sending off of four pupils to Zurich—Death of a minister of Geneva.

GENEVA, 6th September, 1560.[1]

Had I been informed in time of the departure of this messenger, I should have written to you at greater length; but as
I write to you after supper and fatigued by my day's labour,
you will excuse my brevity, especially as I am obliged to prepare
myself for to-morrow's sermon. Respecting the troubles in
France, I doubt not but many and various rumours are flying
about among you as nearly everywhere. Of most that is going
on I am ignorant. What many people expect it is unnecessary
to write, not to mix myself up with their foolish conjectures.
Beza at my request has undertaken a mission both troublesome
and dangerous, and which will expose him to all sorts of inconvenience. I do not, however, repent of my advice.[2] Unless I
had interposed, many districts would have been involved in a
dreadful conflagration.

If God bless our counsels, there will be ample matter for congra-
tulation. Whatever fall out, all good men, after being thoroughly
acquainted with the circumstances, will judge that we have not
attempted any thing rashly. The object of our efforts is to
prevent our coreligionists from stirring up tumults. Hitherto
we have met with much success. The events of futurity are in
the hand of God. In the meantime an excess of confidence has
turned the heads of our people. For in opposition to what we
have always forbidden, they seize upon the churches or preach

---

[1] To the date is subjoined : "on the eve of the messenger's departure."

[2] The object of this mission was to make another attempt to decide the King of
Navarre to repair to the court and avail himself of the approaching meeting of the
States General, in order to destroy the power of the Princes of Lorraine. But Hotman and Beza could obtain nothing of the weak and vainglorious Bourbon. Here
are the terms in which the registers of the society of Geneva announce the mission
of Beza : " The twentieth of July of the same year (1560) our brother M. de Beza was
sent into Gascony to the King of Navarre in order to instruct him in the word of
God."

in public places. The brethren sent by us make this excuse for themselves that they are dragged forward contrary to their inclination or compelled by necessity, as there is no private dwelling capable of containing four thousand people. But I am straitened for time—ere long I shall let you know more.

The senate has commissioned me to make a request to you and your brethren about a matter in itself most reasonable and which will not be disagreeable to you. It has resolved to bring up at the public charge in your city four young lads, to be instructed in the branches of a liberal education, and to learn your language. The youths of whom in the judgment of their schoolmasters the fairest hopes are entertained, have been pitched upon. Now in the name of the senate I make an appeal to your friendship to see them provided with lodgings, where they may be kept under a pious and virtuous discipline. I should not like to be troublesome to you, but because I am fully convinced that all of you will be inclined to render us this service, I have not hesitated to demand of you what will not put you to much inconvenience, and which of your own accord you would have granted. I should like to discourse with you and your brethren at greater length, but as my duty calls me off, I defer that pleasure to another opportunity.

Farewell, most excellent sir and brother, whom I venerate with my whole heart along with your fellow-pastors. May the Lord protect, govern, preserve, and support you all even to the end. I add no salutations from any one, because no one was aware that I was about to write to you.—Yours,

JOHN CALVIN.

I am overwhelmed with grief for the recent death of our most excellent brother Macar.[1] In him the church has lost a most faithful pastor, we, a most affectionate colleague, and I personally am bereaved of a most upright brother and of almost

---

[1] The minister Macar had scarcely returned from his perilous apostleship at Paris, where he devoted himself to the care of the poor, and to visiting those who were ill of the plague. He was speedily attacked by the disease, and died about the end of August, 1560, much regretted by the republic and the church of Geneva. (Gaberel, vol. ii. p. 164.)

one half of my soul. The whole city mourns, but a weight of sorrow preys upon the more serious part of it.

[*Orig. autogr.—Library of Geneva.* Vol. 107 *a.*]

DLXX.—To Theodore Beza.[1]

Troubles in France—Faults committed by the chiefs of the Reformed party—Sluggishness of the King of Navarre.

GENEVA, 10*th September*, 1560.

As I suppose that my letter has miscarried in which I signified to you what I am about to write, I am obliged now to repeat it. Our Hotspur[2] had been informed in time of the change in their purpose, and I had previously informed him that, for important reasons, nothing ought to be attempted by him, till something had been accomplished by you. Thus by his rash haste he has been guilty of a grave fault. Another untoward accident kept your letter of the 25th August nearly four days on the road, through the negligence of I know not what muleteer, who had engaged to deliver it four hours after it was put into his hands.

---

[1] This letter designedly obscure was written during the gravest conjunctures. Before Theodore Beza had arrived at Nerac bearing the instructions of Calvin, the King of Navarre and the Prince of Condé had conceived, the former with hesitation, the latter boldly, projects which were destined to terminate in the momentary insurrection of the provinces in order to overthrow the authority of the Guises. Young Ferrières, Seigneur of Maligny, entering secretly into Lyons with 1200 men, was to have seized on the fortress by surprise, Paul de Mouvans was to stir up Languedoc and Provence, and Monbrun, Dauphiny, while the King of Navarre setting out from Nerac should call around him the nobility of the South to the rallying cry at once monarchical and religious : Christ and Capet. This project failed like the preceding ones, in consequence of the irresoluteness of its principal chief, and the want of concert among the conspirators. Invariably opposed to every armed insurrection of the churches, Calvin had in vain essayed to moderate their ardour, and transform a plot into an imposing but pacific manifestation of opinion. He could not, however, abandon a cause which was dear to him, in the moment of danger, and exhorted the King of Navarre to avail himself of his rights as the first prince of the blood, not to withdraw himself from the authority of the king, but to overthrow the usurped domination of the Guises.

[2] In the text, *Fervidus noster*—a covert allusion to the name of Ferrières de Maligny, who, for having put in execution too soon his attempt upon Lyons, had received a severe check, and saw himself reduced to the necessity of evacuating the place. See de Thou, lib. xxv. and Claude de Rubys, *Histoire de Lyon*, p. 386 and the following.

Exhausted by a sorrow of eight days' duration I had thrown myself into bed, after my return from a very melancholy expedition, for I had accompanied the funeral procession of our most excellent brother.[1] I got up immediately and wrote to beseech *Hotspur*, to take care to have transmitted to the place indicated in my letter, an account of whatever preparations had been made, or to be the bearer of it himself. In the mean time, to make some apology for his excessive precipitancy, he has sent this person with a letter whence it is permitted to conclude that he would not suffer himself to be guided by any sober counsels, and for that reason the messenger himself who then coincided with him in opinion will give a much better account of the whole affair. I have selected him from among all, chiefly because no one was better fitted for surmounting obstacles. How disgracefully that foolhardy man came off who would listen to no advice, I forbear for the moment to tell you. You shall hear it all when we meet. But now for fear this adverse stroke should take by surprise our chief and our standard-bearer, I determined immediately to dispatch some one to acquaint them with what had happened. There was another motive for sending to them, viz: that they might know how faithfully we had looked after those things, which we had promised to manage. I will begin with this last consideration. Our neighbours had either broken faith, or given way to cowardice, unless I had most energetically recalled them to their duty. Their spirits seemed revived by the presence of the person who to my reproaches added both prayers and threats. Three days after, we heard that they had again lost all heart. Another person succeeded to the first. The sum had already been completed, but only because we became sureties for it. Whether any adverse blast shall drive us from this course also, I cannot tell. Certainly the transaction was managed with good faith. You may assure the chief and the standard-bearer of this, that we were abundantly sedulous to accelerate matters, but that some delay was occasioned by the sluggishness of others. Then when your arrival was the most efficacious remedy for all those evils, to have no word from you was productive of much mischief. For hence it

[1] See p. 197, note 1.

happened that the individual usurped a greater degree of licence, whose vain impetuosity was so suddenly checked, and the others who believed themselves undone wavered in their duty.[1] Hence the disaster which nevertheless ought rather to whet than blunt people's courage.

From other quarters I conceive better hopes, because active collectors with instructions from me having gone to Macon, the neighbouring towns, and the whole of the maritime coast, for the sake of transacting business, will not spare their pains. What then remains to be done but that our chief should by his promptitude recruit his forces, which he will never do by sitting still and inactive. If he complains that he is unprovided with funds, he will find many persons, each of whom will stretch their own resources to furnish them. Something should have been attempted already. He would have experienced how much depends on confidence and activity. And it is to no purpose that he deliberates while his adversary executes, and is bringing forward with all zeal, machines to crush him. A rumour indeed has gone abroad that attempts have been made to cajole him by deceitful blandishments, in order that he may be gained over.

This does seem very probable to me, since the cause which he has embraced is so far advanced that there is no room for reconciliation. But if our chief should prove credulous beyond what is conceivable, how much I fear that he will soon discover, and yet too late, that these caresses are poison bedaubed over with honey. And should we admit that he could in safety abandon our cause, which it is folly to expect, yet what more ignoble than this cowardice to yield to these savage monsters, nay, to present his face for them to spit on and thus remain branded with an indelible mark of disgrace! And even should an enemy, of unbounded insolence, however, refrain from insults, yet such a deserter would be covered with everlasting contempt, and had better suffer a thousand deaths. But it is clear that should they be victorious, they will not confine themselves to insults, but will trample on their victim even unto death. Now if he

---

[2] Disconcerted by the check which Maligny had received at Lyons, Mouvans and Monbrun had laid down their arms and made an act of submission to the lieutenant of the king.

does not shrink from holding out his neck to the executioner, yet should respect for the cause weigh with him—a cause which he knows to be approved of God and recommended by the suffrages of all good men. As we are unacquainted with your situation, I dare not advance any further remarks, unless that it is necessary for you to press on him this point, and to keep dinning it into his ears—that it is, not only, neither expedient, nor honourable, nor safe, nor in one word lawful to abate any portion of diligence; but that on the contrary the most manifest and inevitable danger, both of death and infamy, is impending over his head, should he loiter even for a moment. Before matters came to a crisis, I did not spare our neighbours; at the same time I made it my business that their warlike demonstrations should be put down. I saw what might result from them. I carefully examined the subjects of their complaints. I said to our friends among whom was at that time he of whom death has bereaved us, "that it would be on my part an act of the highest cruelty,[1] to expose men so wantonly to destruction, because the auxiliary troops being removed from thence, I should be leading them forth as it were to the butcher." I turned a deaf ear to all remonstrances that I might faithfully discharge my duty.

Now when I see them exposed to so many injuries, a feeling of compassion rises up in my breast, nor can I help feeling all the bitterness of sorrow if I see them abandoned. Wherefore it is your duty importunately to assail those ears that shall be too slow to hear, or stopped by unworthy obstacles. I wish I could join you to play a secondary part, but even the task of stimulating the sluggish, by writing to them, is taken out of my hands. Do you then not only give publicity to the contents of this letter, but borrow from our school sharp arguments to prick them on, because you know with what ardour our masters here are animated when necessity demands it. It has seemed to us better, moreover, to make you the interpreter of our wishes than to charge the present messenger with letters which might perchance create discontent. Salute then most respectfully—you

---

[1] There are here several words effaced in the original manuscript, though the want scarcely affects the sense of the passage.

know whom, and farewell, most upright brother. May the
Lord stand by you all, govern, sustain, and protect you.
[*Lat. Copy.—Library of Geneva.* Vol. 107 *b.*]

DLXXI.—To Sulcer.

Movements in Italy—Causes of the troubles in France—States of Fontainebleau.

GENEVA, *1st October*, 1560.

For a long time I have written nothing to you, my worthy
sir and respected brother, because I am distracted by all sorts
of affairs, and prolonged diseases take up a great part of my
time.[1] Besides, in all parts of France, the brethren implore
our assistance, and I am not sorry now to abstain from all
writing which is not wrung from me by necessity, because I see
that my letters are immediately made public. For a short time
ago, when I had written to a friend who lives in your city, respecting the disturbances in France, I was surprised to learn
that part of my letter had been quoted in the privy council of
the king. For I was forced to recognize my words in which
nothing was changed, and yet this single reason would not for
all that prevent me from writing, (since I have learned quietly
to despise both rumours and hatred,) were it not that I do not
find in what terms I could explain matters so uncertain and
perplexed. How the Venetians and the Duke of Mantua, along
with the Emperor, are disquieting the Pope,[2] I say nothing;

[1] Amid the sufferings occasioned by the several complaints which were soon to bereave the church of Calvin, he continued to keep up a vast correspondence, which he
considered as one of his principal duties. Sulcer, in his answer to the Reformer,
thanked him in the following terms :—" Your letter was to me exceedingly agreeable,
and more than compensated for your silence. For I am not ignorant of your most
holy labours, which I should by no means wish to break in upon by desiring you to
write to me. Your letter gives me proof that the state of your health is not despaired
of, and that you still preserve a recollection of me, your most intimate brother in the
Lord."—(14 Nov., 1560,) vol. 112, Library of Geneva.

[2] To Pope Paul IV., the furious enemy of the Spanish domination in Italy, had succeeded in 1559 Pius IV., of the family of the Medicis, who was destined to inaugu-
rate a new policy less hostile to the two branches of the House of Austria.

nor, above all, what the Florentine[1] is complotting, whom I take
to be the *choragus* in this drama, for though the duchy of Milan
is offered as a reward, yet that good man most assuredly in his
secret heart destines a good deal more for himself than what
is openly held out to Maximilian.[2]

In France there are two causes of tumultuary movements ; the
government of the Guises is not supportable, and many cannot
any longer bear to see religion oppressed with so much and
such violent barbarity. The Guises, seeing their power so detested by all, have lately with foolish and childish pomp feigned
to be ready to give an account of their measures. The Assembly was very magnificent.[3] The king in his public edicts boasts
that the princes of the blood were present in it. It is certain
that only his brothers assisted at it, the elder of whom is not
yet ten years of age ; unless, perhaps, you count the Cardinal
of Bourbon, the brother of the King of Navarre, whose mind
is more lumpish than a log, unless when it is a little quickened
by wine. In what concerns a regent for the kingdom they
came to this decision, that the king should appoint a general
assembly of the orders for the month of December. This is
called in our language a meeting of the estates. Hitherto the
Guises have shrunk from a meeting of the estates. But mark
how facetiously they elude it. It has been decided by a decree
to hold previous meetings in each of the provinces in which deputies should be elected as the Guises shall direct, and such
only as give clear proofs of their being the creatures of that ill-
fated house.[4] The 20th January is fixed upon for the bishops,
not that they should decide upon any thing, but merely that
they should deliberate what may be expedient to be laid before
the general assembly, and next that they should correct abuses

---

[1] The Duke Cosmo I. See in the following letter new details about these diplo-
matic intrigues.

[2] The son of the Emperor Ferdinand and King of the Romans.

[3] Allusion to the Assembly of Fontainebleau, held on the 21st of August, 1560.
See for further details the following letter.

[4] " The Guises," says a contemporary historian, Regnier de la Planche, " had expressly
enjoined the governors of provinces to allow none to be chosen deputies but those
whose Catholic principles were clearly ascertained. Above all, they desired none but
those of their own faction, and that especial care should be taken that none of these
seditious and rebellious Huguenots should be listened to."

introduced by impious persons into the church; in other words, that they should so consolidate the old tyranny that all grounds of controversy being surreptitiously removed, there should no longer be need of any greater remedy. Meanwhile, in certain provinces there is a short truce to their cruelties, not that the Guises are appeased, but because they required a powerful army to maintain their war. Add to that, the Admiral has had the courage to present a petition in the name of fifty thousand persons, who, in Normandy, demand entire liberty to call upon God. The Guises inveighed bitterly against him. He obtained, however, for the petitioners some relaxation of rigour. The Bishop of Vienne[1] spoke with exceeding good sense on the manner of healing the evils of the church. A short time afterwards an order was signified to him to betake himself home. The King of Navarre has not declared himself, but the churches of Gascony enjoy a certain degree of repose. Our brother Beza is on a mission to him. What he may afterwards determine to do I cannot say. A quantity of arms was lately seized at Lyons. The rumour is rife about a conspiracy; nothing, however, is certain. Here you have a confused mass of information; I wish I could have made it ampler and more distinct.

Farewell, most accomplished sir and respected brother. Viret and my other fellow pastors beg me to send you their kindest wishes. God has taken from among us one of them, distinguished for his excellent qualities. We have all mourned over his ashes, and I more than others, because in private life we were intimately united. May the Lord preserve in surety you and your colleagues, govern you by his Spirit, and enrich you more and more with his gifts. Yours,

JOHN CALVIN.

[*Lat. Orig. Minute.—Library of Geneva.* Vol. 107 *a.*]

---

[1] Marillac, a prelate of an elevated and tolerating character, who was accused, as well as Monluc, the Bishop of Valence, of professing in secret the Reformed doctrines.

DLXXII.—To Bullinger.[1]

Intrigues of the Guises in Germany, and of the Emperor in Italy—New details respecting the Assembly of Fontainebleau—Speeches of the Chancellor, and of the
Bishop of Valence—Progress of the gospel in France.

GENEVA, 1st October, 1560.

I informed you some time ago, respected brother, that the
letter which you wrote to our friend Beza was delivered to me.
I also received the one you wrote to myself from a Belgian, a
neighbour of ours, five days after his arrival here. When I
learned that he had received the letter from you two days before
his departure, and that it contained details respecting the young
man whom you recommended to me, (I mean the young man
who is a native of the valley of Aosta, and has run away from
his father and the Duke,) I assure you I received this tardy
messenger rather dryly. He had no excuse for his delay, as I
am so easily to be found, since I preach every day in the morning, and give a lecture in the public school every afternoon.
But I have got inured to the rudeness of that people, and as
they border on my own birth-place I dare not speak of them
too harshly. For I am myself a Belgian, too, though it follows from our want of sympathy that we are far from resem-
bling one other. This, of course, is a joke, though, in truth,
we are any thing but polite. I now come to the subject of my
letter. What the French envoy was going to do in Germany,
men of some sagacity shrewdly guessed while he was on his
way. For they saw that the pretexts for his mission were frivolous. The only object the Guises have in view is to throw
every thing into confusion, that they may compromise as many
people as possible by their schemes.[2] I do not then doubt the

---

[1] The correspondence of Bullinger at this period shows him to be singularly attentive to the political and religious transactions of France. "I entreat you," wrote he
to Calvin, "that you would let me know, by means of your correspondents, what is
going on, and what hopes of success there are in France. I expect a better order
of things, and I pray God to have pity on us."—Library of Geneva, vol. 111.

[2] Their intrigues aimed at nothing less than placing a Prince of the House of Lorraine on the throne of Denmark, and bringing about the restoration of Catholicism
in that country.

truth of all that you have written to me concerning their intrigues. But God has impediments of his own to check their
progress.[1] For the Emperor wishes to obtain the Duchy of
Milan for his son, the King of Bohemia, that the latter may not
be without a patrimony. He has married his two daughters, as
you know, in Italy, the one to the son of the Duke of Florence,
the other to the Duke of Mantua; the latter a petty dependant
prince, the former governing the Pope by his counsels and influence, and who has made himself so much master of Tuscany
that all his neighbours, terrified by his power, are reduced to
silence. He is aiming at higher things. The Venetians, the
Duke of Ferrara,[2] and others have united in a league. Each
one consults his own private interests. This drama opened
with an act of spoliation. Contrary to all justice, the legitimate prince was stripped of his Duchy of Camerino. The Pope
restored it. But because the Apostolic See suffered by this
restitution, Placentia and Parma are demanded in exchange
for it.[3] You do not perceive that these preludes will terminate
in serious contests; that they are but the precursors of a general council, I am quite disposed to believe, nor will you, I fancy,
say the contrary. With reference, then, to what you wrote,
that we must wait till our heavenly Father dissipate their bloody
counsels, I would have you remark that sparks of his heavenly
light are already beginning to shine. Though it behoves us to
look a little deeper into the aspect of things, and, above all, to
this point that if hitherto we have been in a state of torpor,
God is now wakening us up from our lethargy. Before I relate
to you matters enveloped in greater mystery, you will learn in
what a wretched and deplorable state France is now, from a
complaint of which I send you a copy which was brought here.
You will laugh at my offering you a pamphlet written in French,

[1] Allusion to the Austrian and Spanish influence again become preponderant in
Italy. The Duke, Francis de Guise, general of the league formed by Pope Paul IV.,
in 1556, had in vain essayed to take Naples from the Spaniards.

[2] The new Duke of Ferrara, Alphonso II., needed by his docility to make the Emperor forget the part which his father, Hercules d'Este, had taken in the crusade
against the Spaniards.

[3] These two cities formed an independent duchy under Octavius Farnese, the husband of Margaret, the daughter of the Emperor Charles V.

but you will find about you translators who will explain to you
the principal points in it. It will give you a notion of the
marvellous intrigues of the house of Guise. Respecting other
subjects you will excuse my brevity, for I should never have
done were I to enter into details in so immense a field of
matters.

All the great men of the nation were lately convoked at
Fontainebleau, a place about two days' journey distant from
Paris. None of the princes of the blood royal were present,
except the Cardinal of Bourbon, brother to the King of Navarre, one you might easily mistake for a cask or a flagon, so
little has he the shape of a human being. The Guises imagined
that it would add greatly to the pomp of the assembly, if as
many as possible of those purple robed knights, who are so
proud of belonging to the order of St. Michael, were summoned
to attend it. Thirty of them made their appearance, though
formerly their number was twelve. There the Chancellor took
occasion to speak in pompous terms of the illustrious senate in
which was vested the whole authority of the kingdom. His
exordium was in a strain of the most fulsome adulation. He
then enlarged on the state of the kingdom, remarking that as
it stood in need of remedies to heal its complaints, it was their
business to investigate the cause of the evils. Here he brought
his report to a close, as if at his wit's end he had been invoking
a consultation of state doctors. The king, by a preconcerted
scheme, asked the Bishop of Valence, who was among the last
of the counsellors to deliver his sentiments, evidently because
the Guises wished to elicit the secret inclinations of all, and
suddenly, as they should find an opportunity, assail them one
by one. Contrary to the expectations of every body, the Admiral arose and presented to the king a petition in which the
inhabitants of Normandy, who wish to worship God in purity,
requested to have leave to assemble themselves in open day, in
order not to be exposed to diverse calumnies on account of
clandestine or nocturnal meetings. Being questioned how he
became possessed of such a document, he replied that he took
an interest in the public good, and was curious to know what
the Lutherans wished for ; that he would produce, moreover, the

signatures of fifty thousand men that were affixed to it, if the king desired it. In the whole assembly but two persons spoke with any degree of discretion—the Admiral and the Archbishop of Vienne. When all the speakers had delivered their opinions, of whom the greater part consisted of underlings, the Duke of Guise gave vent to his spite with an insolence that would not have been tolerated elsewhere. In a few words I will give you a sample of his stolidity. When the Admiral had expressed his disapprobation of the barbarous custom, not only of assigning to the king body-guards, but surrounding him with an army, declaring that such an education was not worthy of a nation like France, and that a youthful sovereign should not be brought up to distrust his subjects, whose affections, on the contrary, he ought to conciliate and foster by acts of kindness; that madman replied that the king had no need of tutors or governors, since he had been educated in the practice of every virtue, (I quote his words to the letter,) and if, moreover, he required any instruction, his mother was fully competent for that task. He had the audacity to say that in spite of what a thousand councils should decree, he was immovably resolved to adhere to the institutions of his ancestors. His brother, the Cardinal, with greater gravity and shrewdness observed that it was idle to demand of councils any innovation in doctrine, for it was impious to make those things which had proceeded from the Holy Spirit the subject of controversy. If any vices in conduct existed, permission should be granted to the bishops of their own authority to correct them. The Bishop of Vienne had provoked him to make this remark, having declared that it was a base and disgraceful sign of dissoluteness when bishops abandoned their churches to frequent the courts of princes. He also, in vehement terms, besought the king not to bereave churches of their pastors under the frivolous pretext of the public good, for that hence it followed as a consequence that no one was restrained by law or necessity, but every one did whatever his inclination prompted. You ask, What resulted from all this? The Bishop of Vienne betook himself home. Four or five days were spent in vain recriminations. A meeting of the estates is fixed for the month of December. The bishops are convoked for the

20th of January, not that they should decide upon any thing, but merely that they should deliberate upon what may be expedient to be laid before the general assembly. Hitherto the Guises have struggled obstinately to prevent the assembling of the estates. Now, having plucked up courage, they are devising means wittily to overreach those who expect any relief from this measure. For they have tacked a clause to the decree by which it is provided, first, that each of the provinces should examine, in the presence of their governors, what affairs it may be expedient to have discussed in the general assembly; (in this examination there will not be a shadow of liberty:) next, that they should choose their deputies according to the suggestions of the same governors; so that none will come up to the meeting but such purchased parasites as the Guises shall be pleased to name. How frivolous, moreover, and nugatory this parade of a council is, you will comprehend from the form of the decree which any of your friends will translate for you. Meanwhile, the truth of the gospel is breaking forth. In Normandy our brethren are preaching in public, because no private house is capable of containing an audience of three and four thousand persons. There is greater liberty in Poitou, Saintonge, and the whole of Gascony. Languedoc, Provence, and Dauphiny possess many intrepid disciples of Christ. Why the Cardinal is so supine he has himself hinted pretty clearly; evidently it is that ere long he may detect the imprudence of these inconsiderate people; but the Lord, I trust, will not only bring to light his accursed devices, but will defeat his impious attempts.

The King of Navarre is still quiet. He is, nevertheless, an object of suspicion, as if he were about to attempt something important. Thus, when garrisons were lately placed in ten places of the kingdom, the most effective for the purposes of the French war was stationed by the Guises in the territory of Gascony. I have not had news of Beza for some time, because the roads are blocked up. At Lyons a quantity of arms was seized. There was then a great trepidation in that quarter, and though no one marched against them, yet they conceived themselves to be in great danger, and thus their fears whetted their cruelty. Some have been already hanged, and all who come

from there are immediately dragged to prison, and put to the
rack indiscriminately. Be sure that our brother Beza did not
go there of his own accord, but because he was summoned by
a letter of the king's, in which he asked me politely and with
the greatest earnestness to grant him this highly important
favour. I thought it right not to refuse him, partly that Beza
might stimulate his sluggishness, and partly that he might counteract the turbulent counsels of many. For I never approved
of deciding our cause by violence and arms. But as I can
never crowd into one letter the immense quantity of news that
yet remain untold, I shall here come to a close. Because you
made no difficulty in undertaking the task of procuring proper
masters for the young men that are sent from here to be educated in your city, and also in seeing that they were lodged in
virtuous families, our senate begs me to offer you their warmest
thanks for the hearty good-will you have shown, and they most
willingly pledge themselves to return the favour, should an occasion ever present itself. Besides, these four who are maintained
at the public expense, some others are sent by private persons
whom I desire not less to recommend to you. I have been entreated to do so in the name of three, but as I hear that two
of them are already provided with lodgings, I am very desirous
that you should make arrangements for the third, both because
his mother is a woman of singular piety, and his father was a
dear and intimate friend of mine. His name is Michael Plan-
chan. Pardon me, if yielding to entreaties, I occasion you
more trouble than I could wish.

Farewell, most distinguished sir and my very honoured brother. You will present my best respects to your brethren, colleagues, and other friends. May the Lord always keep you in
safety, direct you by his Spirit, and bless your labours.

Yours,   JOHN CALVIN.

I know not whether I ought to thank M. Wolf for Tilmann's
book,[1] translated into Latin, which he sent me. For though

---

[1] Tilmann Heshusius, author of a pamphlet against Melancthon, translated by Marbach at Strasbourg.

that wrangling fellow deserved the critic's lash, yet I was of
opinion that he should have been passed over with contempt.
[*Lat. Orig. Autog.—Library of Geneva.* Vol. 107 *a.*]

DLXXIII.—To NICHOLAS DES GALLARS.[1]

Domestic details—News of the Church and Academy of Geneva.

GENEVA, 3*d October*, 1560.

You seem to have felt a little hurt, because you received no
answer when you had asked me for my advice on some important
matters. I fancy you had already understood how punctual I
am in attending to letters when once they have been delivered
to me. I immediately wrote back to you on the receipt of yours,
how long after its date it had been put into my hands. I also
endeavoured, as the circumstances required, to settle the business which gave you so much uneasiness. Though my letter
was rather desultory, and I had been forced by illness to dictate
a part of it, I was nevertheless unwilling to omit anything
which might contribute to relieve your anxiety. I faithfully
executed your commissions. I wrote to Roche and exhorted
him to cross over to you. There did not exist a copy of what
the Strasburgers had written about Peter,[2] and perhaps it is
better that that matter should be handled rather leniently.

---

[1] On his arrival in London, Nicholas des Gallars saw himself engaged in difficulties
which paralyzed the exercise of his ministry in the congregation of the foreign Protestants. Separated from his wife and children whom he had left at Geneva, he
suffered at the same time from the inefficacy of his services and his solitariness.
"What I should decide upon I do not clearly see. It is not my intention to abandon
this infant church, which is yet far from being well organized, to the wolves that are
still gaping to devour it, nor can I return to you unless there should be another pastor
left to replace me, and I should be called for some valid reason. I have not been
able to send over for my wife in the present doubtful state of affairs, and because I
have no means of furnishing her with what she would require to defray the expenses
of her journey. I cannot easily contemplate this prolonged absence both from you
and my family without the deepest sorrow. I say nothing of many things which I
must endure in silence, and for which I am without an assistant and an adviser."

[2] Peter Alexandre of Arles, formerly minister of the French Church of Strasbourg,
and second pastor of the Church of London.

They might complain that those things which they had communicated to us confidentially should have publicity given to
them; and he himself might raise an outcry that we acted with
inhumanity in odiously exhibiting as a criminal charge against
him those things which had been written to exculpate him. That
other manner of pacification then is preferable, if for no other
reason at least for this, that it does not compromise the public
tranquillity.

But what surprises us is, that you say not a word either about
your stay or your return. This is the more extraordinary because the letter addressed to us by the members of the congregation conjointly had set our minds at rest, for they return us
public thanks, and assert in no equivocal terms that you are
their pastor. They also beg of us, pledging themselves to be
responsible for the payment, to furnish your wife with whatever
she may stand in need of. That she might be emboldened to
ask, I have let her know that she shall want for nothing.
About the house which she occupies, she has thoughtlessly teased
you with her complaints, and you have lent but too ready an
ear to them. Hitherto I had heard nothing on that subject,
but now she has confessed to me that she had talked with Beza
concerning it a good while ago. His answer was frank and
open; if you remained in England... according to the implied
consent of the brethren, that house was intended for her, that
she might be nearer the school, but not a word has ever been
dropped on that subject, nor have they yet deliberated respecting
it, while matters still remain in their present doubtful state.
I do not suppose she invented what she wrote to you, but when
we are over inquisitive, it sometimes happens that we hear
more than we could wish. She has even formerly related things
which I never heard from any one. But if people keep babbling
this or that, does their silly gossip forsooth deserve to pass the
channel? This I affirm; nothing was ever decided respecting
the house, nor will be, till the election of your successor, and this
we have put off till now. It is fixed, however, for to-morrow.
But whatever shall take place, we will take care that she be not
obliged to remove before the winter. She might even have
made something by hiring the house, had she not wished to

show herself so liberal to foreigners, strangers, and even wealthy people. The house is still the subject of some lawsuits, but she hoped, as Beza told me, that they would soon be terminated. Hilaire is dead; Nicholas and his wife have been ill. He is not yet recovered, and his complaint it appears will be of long duration. Diseases have been raging among our townsmen since your departure, two of them are dead, Tagaut[1] and Gaspar; in fine that most excellent man Macar to the great sorrow of all has been taken from us. You can well imagine from my disposition how bitterly I have felt so many bereavements. Baduel[2] drags on as well as he can. Bernard and Chevalier have got rid of their fever. Henoch[3] and Morel are gradually recovering strength. Colic and inflammation of the blood and lungs have severely tried me. Though we have a great deficiency of pastors, yet our brethren have always put off the election of a successor to you, till lately they learned from the collective letter of your church, that you have been retained where you are. Beza's absence, besides the extraordinary burden of lecturing which it imposes on me, is for many other reasons annoying to me. I am distressed that our worthy brother should be incessantly beset with dangers, and I see but little prospect of his return. But what torments me more cruelly is the reflection that, urged by necessity, we have not hesitated to peril the life of so singular a friend and so excellent a man. Other secret griefs I kept shut up in my own bosom.

Farewell, most worthy brother. You will pardon my colleagues for not writing. As I had undertaken this task, they fancy they have acquitted themselves of their duty by my assistance. In the mean time, carefully salute all. May the Lord always protect, govern, and sustain you, for I see how laborious a function you have to discharge in directing that church; but God, who for the hardest struggles always imparts sufficient strength, will stand by you to the last. I imagine the

[1] John Tagaut, professor of philosophy in the Academy of Geneva. Bernard taught Greek in it, and Chevalier, Hebrew.

[2] Claude Baduel, formerly rector of the University of Nimes, professor of mathematics at Geneva. He died there in 1560.

[3] Francis Henoch, originally from the valleys of Piedmont, minister of the Church of Geneva. He was for some time almoner of the Duchess of Ferrara.

minister Belzan from whom new disturbances were apprehended is half crushed, now that he has been stripped of his false colours.

[*Lat. Orig. Minute.—Library of Geneva.* Vol. 107.]

DLXXIV.—To BULLINGER.

Conspiracy of Lyons—Journey of the King of Navarre—Expectation of grave events in France.

GENEVA, 14th October, 1560.

I am prevented from writing back to you at greater length, respected brother, by a violent headache, which has not ceased to torment me for the last two days. Stegner the Avoyer of Berne had already told us here what you write to me about our neighbours.[1] I think it is probable that they will purposely seize on this opportunity of making war, and will be driven to take this step, not so much by their own impetuosity as by foreign impulse. May the Lord restrain or mitigate their ferocity, and at the same time resist their perverse designs. I had heard that the King of France demanded supplies of money and troops from you, but relying on your perspicacity I did not think it necessary to remind you of the purpose of such a demand. I wrote to you lately respecting the troubles at Lyons. Certainly something was agitated, but by a few. They wished, but very preposterously, to stimulate in this manner the King of Navarre. I who was aware that that was not consonant with his plans, and who knew his mind, attempted to divert them from their project. But because they had proceeded too far, the conspiracy was partly detected. The only thing criminal, however, which was discovered in their conduct, was that they wished to open up a free course for the gospel. Nothing had been attempted against the king or his government. But what the Guises are aiming at by this new petition is sufficiently apparent, from the edict in which in the person of the king they complain that money and men are everywhere col-

---

[1] Emmanuel Philibert, Duke of Savoy, and Philip II., master of Franche Comté.

lected under the pretext of religion, and that for that reason
they forbid on pain of death any one from furnishing loans to
the princes and other great nobles of the realm; and to this
punishment is further annexed confiscation of property. The
King of Navarre summoned to court is now on his way thither.[1]
He brings his brother along with him, of whose flight you will
by and by hear something; but take care that it come to the
ears of no one before the time.[2] Troops of cavalry are disposed
in such a manner up and down in France, as to be able to in-
tercept the King of Navarre in all directions. The issue is in
the hands of God, who will perchance bring to nought what seems
so craftily contrived by them.

One chief cut off, they promise themselves an easy victory
over all. But those whom they style rebels, Guise himself
aptly designated, in the assembly of the nobles, as those
who desire to have a different religion. For when in the petition
which the admiral presented, the subscribers profess that they
are quiet and peaceable men, and will always be obedient to the
king; "There," said he, "are good and obedient subjects for
you—men who are not satisfied with the established religion,
who dictate laws to their sovereign, and many things of that
kind." Believe me, I affirm it for certain there is no danger
of a riot, because none will stir, unless they chance to make a
hostile attack on the King of Navarre, in the defence of whom I
trust many will put themselves forward. He has determined to
recover his rights in the council, but without having recourse to
arms.[3] As I know him to be feeble and vacillating, I have sent

---

[1] He had set out from Nerac in the end of the month of September.

[2] The most alarming reports were circulated respecting the intentions of the court.
The queen mother had warned Coligny and the princess of Condé that the two
brothers had been sent for only that they might be put to death. Tavanne's Memoirs,
vol. i., p. 289. Nothing but the energetic attitude of the King of Navarre could turn
aside the danger.

[3] The nobility dissatisfied everywhere offered their services to the King of Navarre.
If, without taking up arms, he had advanced resolutely to the Loire, drawing after
him his numerous partisans, and presented himself to the court as the first prince of
the blood, to claim there the authority to which he was entitled, and overturn the
government of the Guises, there is no doubt but he would have succeeded. It is the
opinion of a contemporary and an excellent judge, the Marechal de Vieilleville.
Memoires, p. 439.

a man to confirm his resolution. For Beza has disappeared, nor
is it generally known to what part of the country he is gone.
Nevertheless one of our brethren knows when he may be expected. An embassy has been sent from Spain to prevent the
meeting of the National Assembly—a mere sham this, since
the bishops will be permitted only to examine what may be expedient to have laid before the general assembly. You know
doubtless what we should not have thought possible that the inhabitants of Lucerne and the five Catholic Cantons, and along
with them the people of Soleure, have been negotiating about a
treaty of alliance with the deputies of the Duke of Savoy, which
bodes no good to us, unless you should at last be touched with
some compassion for us and anxiety for our safety.

[*Lat. Orig. Autogr.—Arch. of Zurich. Gal. Scripta.* Gest. vi. p. 52.]

DLXXV.—To BULLINGER.

Alliance of the Catholic Cantons with the Duke of Savoy—Uncertainty of the news
from France—Dearth at Geneva. ·

GENEVA, 1*st November*, 1560.

That the five Catholic Cantons with blinded fury lend their aid
to the destruction of the Helvetian name,[1] is to us a subject of
painful anxiety. Since they are so disgracefully venal, the
Lord will cause to fall on their own heads, I hope, what they
are threatening the innocent with. There is still, however,
some hope of a pacification, if it be true that a congress has
been appointed for the 28th of this month, though it behoves
your townsmen to be vigilantly on their guard. The enemy,
I have no doubt, thinks suddenly to crush you as being unprepared. For I have learned from the letter of a certain individual that such designs are just now agitated among them.
With what vigour our neighbours[2] will get themselves ready for

---

[1] Allusion to the alliance which the five Catholic Cantons of Swisserland had just
concluded with the Duke of Savoy, Emmanuel Philibert. One of the secret articles
of the treaty was the restitution to Savoy of the Pays de Vaud, and the abandonment of Geneva.

[2] The Bernese threatened in the conquests which they had accomplished twenty-
four years before by the sword of Franz Negueli.—*Hist. de la Suisse*, vol. xii., p. 18.

the contest in these conjunctures is not known. Either they are concealing with great address their preparations, or they are shunning danger by remaining inactive. And it is more desirable they should hang back than desert their allies, as they formerly did, in the middle of the struggle. We are still waiting for information respecting what was transacted in the last congress. In the meantime, at Dijon, a place of rendevous has been fixed for those troopers that are equipped with fire-arms, which the French now call pistols, whence they may, at a moment's notice, fly to whatever part their orders indicate their march. They are about five hundred in number. The same station has been named for horsemen armed *cap-a-pie*, taken out of the ordinary cavalry. Some people fancy that these preparations have been got up in favour of the Roman Pontiff, as a bugbear to frighten you into subjection to him; others, with greater probability, conjecture that they are intended to bring destruction upon us. We have been warned, but precautions will not avail us much unless God miraculously protect us. With confidence and in tranquillity we nevertheless trust that the storm will blow over and leave us uninjured. In France disorders everywhere prevail, and things seem coming to a crisis. Where Beza is, or what he is about, I know not. Of the King of Navarre[1] various rumours are afloat. My own opinion is that perceiving he would have to engage in a conflict with so many troops, he has retrograded. A civil war in France is then inevitable. The nobility of Brittany, (the ancient Armoricans are now Britons,) will declare for him. The natives of Poitou, and a good number of the inhabitants of Anjou, will also join him. From Gascony many will flock to his standard. The kingdom will be torn by a wretched and deplorable anarchy. The king is at present at Orleans, where the greater part of the municipal magistrates are said to be sentenced to be executed, which I can scarcely be brought to believe.[2] There

---

[1] The King of Navarre had arrived at the court on the 31st of October, after a journey full of delays and hesitations, in which he neither knew how to answer to the expectations of his partisans, nor how to disconcert his enemies. Once arrived at Orleans, he was at the mercy of the Guises.

[2] The inhabitants of the town had been disarmed, as being suspected of an inclination to the religious Reform, and of hatred towards the domination of the Guises.

is, indeed, no appearance of an insurrection, but the ungodly keep up a turmoil, either because they are really in trepidation, *when no man pursueth*, or rather because they feign to be alarmed, that they may throw every thing into confusion.

I would have written to you at greater length respecting the troubles in France, if I had been informed in time of the departure of our brother. But we happened to be in the consistory when he came to my house; so he found no one to speak to. Returning after supper I, at last, learned that he was to set off on the following morning. My letter would have been finished, but as I expected from day to day that something new would fall out, and furnish me with fresh matter, I purposely delayed to terminate it. About Tilmann,[1] I have as yet decided nothing. I will write to you on the first opportunity what is most advisable to be done. The affair, moreover, does not require us to be in any hurry.

Farewell, most accomplished sir and respected brother. I beg you to present my best respects to your colleague, and to all your family. I write these words, though I have not yet seen the brother who is to be the bearer of them. I could have wished that greater results had followed from your recommendation and that of M. Peter Martyr. You yourself, indeed, partly experienced how excessive the dearth of provisions is here, and the Duke of Savoy is determined to starve us to death by cutting us off from all supplies. My colleagues most cordially salute you.   Yours,

JOHN CALVIN.

[*Lat. Autog.—Arch. of Zurich.—Gallicana Scripta.* Sect. vi., p. 48.]

DLXXVI.—TO STURM.

Mission of Hotman and Beza to the King of Navarre—Apathy of that prince.

GENEVA, 5th November, 1560.

It happens very unseasonably that for the last twenty days no one has left this city to go to Strasbourg, of whose depar-

---

[1] See note, p. 138.

ture I could get any information, though I made the most diligent inquiries. For Holbrac, the pastor of our French Church,
in one of his letters had caused us some uneasiness about Hotman, for he wrote that the rector of the school and all of you
were offended at his absence, especially because he had neither
communicated to you the motive for his departure,[1] nor sent
you any excuse for absenting himself so long. I know not
whether you were acquainted with his expedition. From myself and Beza he wished to have it kept such a secret that when
he imparted it to an individual who has the reputation of being
a blab, it was only after he had bound the person in question
by an oath not to say a word on the subject among any of us.
A little later I learned that he had been seen at the court of
the King of Navarre. From there, at last, he wrote to me, but
it was after an interval of a month that I received his letter.
Now, as I myself have no difficulty in tolerating these fooleries,
so I wish that they could be indulgently overlooked by others.
It will be but what we expect, if your prudence and moderation
interpose your good offices to prevent any harsher measures from
being adopted against him, while the cause of his absence is yet
unknown. But I am so convinced that you will do so, that I deem
any entreaties and exhortation to that effect quite superfluous.

His letter had lain by me seven days waiting for a bearer,
when, contrary to our hopes, Beza was restored to us, having
escaped, as it were, by a miracle from the greatest dangers.
From him I learned that, unless he meet with some accident on
the road, Hotman will be among you before the arrival of this
letter. I need not say a word, then, of the sluggishness of that
tortoise,[2] since he shut his ears against all persuasion, and repudiated the services of a numerous nobility all entirely devoted
to him. Let him work his own ruin, since all men know that
he deserves a disgraceful end.[3] Nor do I feel much compassion

---

[1] Hotman had gone, it appears, without the authorization of the magistrates of
Strasbourg to visit the King of Navarre, in order to stimulate his ardour. His
efforts, as well as those of Beza, had as yet been quite ineffectual.

[2] Allusion to the King of Navarre.

[3] He had scarcely arrived at Orleans when he was deprived of his liberty, whilst
the prince of Condé, his brother, was arrested by an order of the king, and saw a
process commenced which was destined to end, so far as he was concerned, in a sentence of death.

even for his brother whom I had hitherto judged to be quite another sort of man. But what will become of the unfortunate churches which they have ruined by their inconstancy? It is this anxious concern which fills me with anguish. I trust, however, that God, in his usual way, will provide better for his children. I forbear to mention how much the rasher spirits have injured our cause by their silly attempts. Assuredly the effects of their ill-timed activity have given the death blow to our hopes; and now the whole fury of the enemy will fall on this hapless and unoffending city. Our only consolation lies in the protection of God, which, with an entire confidence, we hope will be extended to us.

Farewell, most accomplished and ever honoured sir.

[*Lat. Copy.—Library of Geneva.* Vol. 107 a.]

DLXXVII.—To BULLINGER.

Unsuccessful issue of Beza's mission to the King of Navarre—Scruples respecting the communication of Melancthon's letter—Intolerance of the German Theologians.

GENEVA, *4th December*, 1560.

I made a brief reply to your last letter, honoured brother, because our most excellent friend, John Liner, came to me when exhausted with a multiplicity of cares I was sitting down to supper, and told me that he was urged by his companions to take leave of us the following day. Our brother Beza will touch upon the principal points of his expedition. Those whom we wished to save would listen to no counsels, though, indeed, we took all this trouble, not so much for their sake as for that of the church. The King of Navarre, as I wrote to you, had of his own accord implored my assistance, and begged in a very courteous manner that Beza should be sent to him. If he had met with a refusal, what clamours would have been raised by everybody, that it was all our fault, if things had turned out unfortunately! We should have been reproached, not only with timidity, but with perfidiousness and cruelty. Beza accomplished every thing which his duty required of him, not only with fidelity but incredible constancy. A hundred times they changed their resolutions. Finally, that fell out, which is now a secret to nobody, that the King of Navarre and his brother were resolved to rush on their ruin.[1] If our advice had been attended to, without a drop of blood being shed, they would have effected their purpose. This was what we always aimed at. Now everybody is plunged in despair, because the soldiery are everywhere let loose, as in a conquered country. And yet our neighbours,[2] who blew the flames of sedition, now cast all the blame on us. But I will pass them by for the present.

I cannot, for sundry reasons, comply with your demand to have sent to you those letters of Philip's,[3] in which he undisguisedly professes himself to be of our opinion. They are not numerous, and are written in such a spirit that you yourself will perceive that they contain things which he poured confidentially into my bosom, but which would afford matter of ridicule to certain, that is, to unfriendly persons; to others, again, who were less intimately acquainted with him, they would hardly be intelligible. Some consideration for the memory of the dead should also have weight with us, which would certainly suffer by the revelation of some things which he wrote to me. Mixed up with them are others which it would certainly do me honour to have made public, but they would be obnoxious at the same time to the malicious carpings of Flaccius, and such like fellows. And that reminds me that when your letter was delivered to me I had already dispatched one-half of my reply to Heshusius. In it I determined to confute him, not so much by dispassionate argument as by an irrepressible burst of indignation. His baseness is so intolerable that it might well call for a lapidation.[4] We are very sorry to learn that the population

---

[1] The Prince of Condé, arrested by the king's order, turned towards the Cardinal de Bourbon, and addressed him in the following words: "Sir, with your fine promises you have delivered your brother over to death." He then repented, no doubt, but too late, to have lent a deaf ear to Calvin's advice, and surrendered himself to the fury of his enemies.

[2] The conspirators of Lyons.

[3] See note, p.   ,

[4] The names of Flaccius, Heshusius, and Westphal, recall to our minds whatever was virulent in the intolerance of the Sacramentarians. In the eyes of these men, Zwingli, Bullinger, and Calvin were "Anabaptists and disciples of Servetus."

of Glaris is still kept in suspense.[1] But Moab, in his pride, will dash himself to pieces, and beyond all doubt, God is driving headlong these Cyclops, that while they plot mischief against others they may compass their own destruction. Let them fall into their own snares, but let us stand firm on our own foundation. I abstain from writing any thing about the troubles in France, lest I should give uncertain intelligence. Ere long you will learn something.

Farewell, most accomplished and honoured brother. Best wishes for the health of M. Peter Martyr, M. Gualter, and your other fellow pastors. May the Lord protect, govern, and bless you all. We are in such jeopardy every moment that many despair, many are anxious, and others laugh. We, therefore, commend ourselves to your prayers.—Yours,

JOHN CALVIN.

[*Lat. Orig. Autog.—Library of Geneva.* Vol. 107 *b.*]

DLXXVIII.—To SULCER.

The sending of a Pastor to the Church of St. Marie aux Mines—The arrival of the King of Navarre at the court—Arrestation of the Prince of Condé.

GENEVA, 11*th December,* 1560.

To us, also, the news of the death of our most excellent brother, Peter Marbusius,[2] was very afflicting. His integrity and sincere zeal had been demonstrated by undoubted proofs. His like is not everywhere to be found; for, though with too much eagerness many thrust themselves into the ministry, yet few possess that talent which warrants their confidence, and still more rare are these virtues, that piety, ardent zeal, and constancy which are nevertheless especially necessary to render men fitting ministers. But God, having compassion on that little church, has provided to our hands a successor who will alleviate their affliction for the death of their pastor, because in no re-

---

[1] The Catholic cantons refused to maintain Glaris in the confederation, unless mass was re-established in four parishes of this country. This quarrel was not appeased till the 3d July, 1564, by mutual concessions between the two contending parties.

[2] Pastor of the Church of Sainte Marie aux Mines in the Comté of Montebelliard.

spect will he be found, we hope, inferior to his predecessor; for besides his other gifts we have always remarked in him a singular simplicity and probity. I am, therefore, perfectly confident that he will prove to your German pastor a no less suitable and welcome than faithful fellow-workman; and as far as I can discover from what the latter has written to me, he, in his turn, will hold out a helping hand to his new brother, that with pious and holy concord they may vigorously ply their task of advancing the kingdom of Christ. Not very long ago I received from you a couple of letters. I was about to send an answer to them by your countryman, Oswald, the bearer of the former, but when in passing by here he supped very merrily with us, he had the misfortune two days afterwards to break his leg while on his journey.

Respecting affairs in France, I have nothing but this to write to you: the King of Navarre, after we had conceived the highest hopes of his magnanimity and perseverance, suddenly changing his resolution, set out for the court. Immediately after his arrival his brother was arrested. He always warmly approved of my counsels, and those of Beza, which were certainly both safe and not less consistent with his dignity than conducive to his own advantage and the welfare of the church; for it was always our wish to secure his elevation as well as to guard against the effusion of even one drop of blood. And our plans had been so well laid, that, without violence or tumult, he would have triumphed over all his adversaries. But, as he is naturally of a weak and pusillanimous disposition, he was partly deceived by fallacious promises, and partly he imposed on himself; for he never apprehended what was clear to every one, that the Guises would venture to lay violent hands on his brother, but no sooner had they carried their audacity to this pitch than their insolence increased, for it is scarcely possible to express with what violence they give loose to their outrages in the very bosom of France.[1] And now when nearly all men

---

[1] The Cardinal of Lorraine had just issued the most severe orders everywhere against the Reformed. He enjoined the governors of provinces "to chastise without pity the madmen who cause so much scandal against the honour of God, and to keep a stiff hand in punishing those fine preachers, that people might hear no more of them."—Nov., 1560. MSS., Colbert, Library of Paris.

were struck with consternation, and the greater part, as it were
paralyzed by so impetuous a torrent of fury, behold again, contrary to our expectations, and all of a sudden, the hand of God
has revealed itself. For the death of the young king,[1] of which
the report is no doubt spread about among you, also must necessarily produce a notable change in every thing.

Farewell, distinguished sir and honoured brother. May the
Lord always stand by you, govern and protect you, and enrich
you daily with his gifts. My colleagues, especially Viret and
Beza, cordially salute you. I desire you, in my name, to salute yours.   Yours,
                                        JOHN CALVIN.

[*Lat. Copy.—Library of Geneva.* Vol. 107 *b.*]

DLXXIX.—To STURM.

Death of King Francis II—Inconsiderate ardour of the Reformed—Moderating action
of Calvin.

GENEVA, 16*th December*, 1560.

Did you ever read or hear of anything more opportune than
the death of the king? The evils had reached an extremity for
which there was no remedy, when all of a sudden God shows
himself from heaven. He who pierced the eye of the father,
has now struck the ear of the son.[2] My only apprehension is

---

[1] See the following letter.

[2] The young King Francis II. died (5th December) of an abscess in the ear, as his
father had from a splinter of Montgomery's lance that entered his eye. This unexpected event, which put a term to the most cruel persecution, was considered by the
Reformed as a judgment of God, and the sentiment expressed by Calvin, is likewise
developed in some verses of Theodore Beza :

> Tuque, Henrice, malis dum consultoribus utens
>   Sitis piorum sanguinem,
> Ipse tuo vecors inopina caede peremptus
>   Terram imbuisti sanguine.

> Henrici deinceps sectans vestigia patris
>   Franciscus, infelix puer,
> Clementem Christum surda dum negligit aure
>   Aure putrefacta corruit.

lest some persons in the excess of their triumph defeat the hopes of an amelioration in our condition. For one can hardly believe how inconsiderately many people exult, nay, wanton in their joy. They wish to transform the whole world in an instant, and because I do not countenance their folly they tax me with supineness. But to me it is enough that God approves of my diligence, and even more than enough to have in my favour the testimony of impartial and moderate men: these are not in a majority it is true, but I prefer their calm judgments to the noisy outcries of the multitude. They would wish me to act along with the King of Navarre in his turbulent projects, as if indeed, supposing him to be the most sagacious and vigorous of mortals, it was in his power to grant what they so preposterously demand. I on the contrary am so opposed to this precipitancy that it gave me no small accession of joy to learn that his brother was unwilling to quit his prison. I had already previously given my advice to such an effect, so that I rejoice the more heartily, that what I deemed the most salutary proceeding has spontaneously suggested itself to their minds. And certainly it will be a suitable and compendious method of crushing the enemy, if the victor retire after the justice of his cause has been recognized; for this being accomplished they must necessarily be condemned. To these considerations add this: that

> Versuti, fatui, surdi, haec spectacula, reges
> Vel sapere vel mori jubent.
>
> (Arch. of Cassel.)

> Tool of bad men, Henry, thy thirst of blood
> Fit retribution found,
> From thy pierced eyeball gushed a purple flood
> Which crimsoned all the ground.

> Following thy father in his mad career,
> Francis, unhappy youth,
> Thou felt'st God's arrow cleave thy guilty ear
> Fast closed against God's truth.

> Ye crafty, foolish, dull-eared kings to you
> These awful warnings cry,
> Or now prepare your evil deeds to rue,
> Or in your blindness die.

all the godly will not be re-instated in their rights without creating a certain prejudice.[1] Already because the crafty knave, who is by no means a friend to piety, will have to be dragged in to take a part in the business, and because we cannot dispense with him—the progress will be slower. Therefore in so perplexed a state of affairs, it is desirable that people in the beginning should content themselves with obtaining for those who have been exiled from their homes and stripped of their property, a restoration to their primitive condition; their next object should be to secure liberty to the pious worshippers of God to abstain from all pollutions and to hold private assemblies to adore God. Should all acts of cruelty cease and fear of peril be removed, a wonderful revolution will take place in a short time. But I cannot persuade everybody of this. The greater part rush on with turbulent impetuosity. At the same time, however, just as if the King of Navarre had instructed me respecting his intentions, I will go on, as I have begun, stimulating them to be of his party. We are not yet prepared for the measure which you thought should be attempted.

Farewell, most accomplished and respected sir. May the Lord always stand by you and enrich you with all blessings. I beg you to present my respects to all friends.

[*Lat. Copy.—Library of Geneva.* Vol. 107 *a.*]

DLXXX.—To the Ministers of Paris.[2]

Counsels respecting his conduct addressed to the King of Navarre.

GENEVA, *December,* 1560.

To let the King know that three points are especially to be examined: First, that the liberation of the prisoner do not take

---

[1] Sturm on this point shared the apprehensions of Calvin : "Even if there was the most certain prospect of establishing the gospel in France, nevertheless that kingdom will never enjoy an uninterrupted tranquillity."

[2] Without an address or date—December 1560. This memorial dictated by Calvin and containing the expression of the views and hopes of the Reformed party on the death of the young king, Francis II., was destined for the King of Navarre. The eyes

place before his sentence, and the whole process be thoroughly revised,[1] that afterwards there may remain no spot or blame on his character, which is a thing which will contribute to his personal satisfaction, and prevent him from being again troubled or molested in time to come, if any opportunities of offering him such molestation should occur. For by this means a door will be shut against all future annoyance. It will also have for consequence the relief of the other prisoners and a good settlement of the whole cause. Without this we should be continually obliged to begin again. Now the said king can see that this may be done without either danger or difficulty, as soon as the cause shall be revised before competent judges, such as you must now have, and of whom we hope you have already a sufficient number to begin with.

The second point is the principal one, because on it everything depends. It is to establish a council of regency. In this affair, if the king does not show a great deal of firmness at the very outset, there is danger that his fault may be very difficult to repair. To consent that a widow, a foreigner and an Italian woman, should have the principal power, would not only turn out very much to his own discredit, but would prove so prejudicial to the crown that he would be everlastingly blamed for such remissness. To grant her as many honours as possible will not hinder him from retaining the highest for himself. But however he may act in that respect, it is above all necessary to insist on establishing a council which can only be done by the Estates, and the said king is well aware that it would not be prudent to go about the business in any other manner, and even if the council could be well established just now without their concurrence, still the precedent would be a bad one.

Now inasmuch as the Estates which had been convoked have

of all were then fixed on this prince, and the minds of all were in suspense. To convoke in haste the Estates General, to appoint a council of regency from which Catherine of Medicis should be excluded, to bring the Guises to a trial, to establish in fine a moderate religious liberty—such were the counsels addressed to the king by Calvin.

[1] The Prince of Condé, condemned to death on the 26th November, 1560, and declared innocent by a sentence of the Parliament, on the 13th June, 1561.

no commission to undertake this business,[1] it would be necessary in the form of an amendment to convoke them anew, for some term not too distant, and in the mean time by some provisional measure to establish a temporary government in which it is very possible there will be disputes and opposition, when we reflect that the adverse party to maintain themselves in power will allege things which are indeed already laid before the board. But this point must be insisted on, viz: that those possessing rights cannot be deprived of them without an examination of the cause. And having secured some moderate and tolerable measure of a provisional kind, it will be sure to be confirmed; for the Estates will make no difficulty in doing what is desirable according to reason and equity.

There is one evil which it will be difficult to remedy all at once, that is, to cashier those who have had so much vogue.[2]   It would in that case be necessary to deliberate, whether it will be better, to assail them vigorously at once and without any delay, or to put off the attack, till criminal proceedings can be instituted against them. Were it possible, it would be a good thing to make them keep watch by the body of the defunct, as they themselves made others perform the same ceremony.[3]   But whatever is done, unless they are degraded upon solid and clearly ascertained grounds, they will have leisure to strengthen themselves; the best method of proceeding then seems to be, to watch narrowly all their motions, till it be possible to handle them as they have deserved. Remark, moreover, that if they have even an appearance of influence they will avail themselves of it to intrigue and practise mischief; so that if you would prevent them from doing evil, you must keep a tight bridle over them;

---

[1] The Estates General, convoked on the 10th December at Orleans, had but a restricted commission relating to religious questions. De Thou, lib. xxv.

[2] "When the partisans of Guise," says Beza, "knew that they had nothing further to hope for, they went and barricaded themselves in their houses, a prey to terror, till they were assured by the queen mother and the King of Navarre, that no harm should be done them." *Hist. Eccl.* vol. i. p. 460.

[3] The obsequies of the king were performed without pomp, and in a manner that but ill corresponded to the royal dignity. The Sieurs of Lansac and de la Brosse accompanied his body to St. Denis, while the Guises apologized for their absence by alleging the necessity they were under of watching over their niece Mary Stuart. *Hist. Eccl.* vol. i. p. 403. De Thou, lib. xxvi.

by no means allow them a long term to fortify their power, but strive to get the start of them. If it were possible, that their trial could be got up before the Estates will be convoked for the second time, nothing could be more desirable.

The third point is concerning religion; and here all that is to be desired is that the liberty of presenting petitions on that subject, which was accorded by the first edict, should still be maintained. True it is, the edict was changed, and the mouths of the faithful shut, so that they durst not breathe a syllable about such matters. But because this change was brought about by violence, and was contrary to the honour of the king, it seems highly probable that such a liberty will be permitted without any difficulty. Now, if petitions are received, the least thing surely we can expect from them is that they will procure a bare provision, not very cordially granted perhaps, by which an end will be put to persecutions exercised against those who shall not seek to breed riots, or extort any thing by violence. For it will be quite enough that those who cannot with a safe conscience go to mass have permission to stay away from it; and to secure such persons from being denounced as void of religion, that they shall be allowed to assemble themselves to pray to God, and hear his word with express prohibitions and interdiction, under severe penalties, to go beyond the limits prescribed by the permission, which might afterwards, however, be rendered more favourable to them. In the mean time, it might be enjoined that all those who should consent to it might be enrolled in presence of the officers and agents of the king in each parliament of justice, and that some of the most influential members of the society be held responsible for all; that is to say, they might represent as guilty of a revolt the individuals who should infringe the royal ordinance.

Having exposed these matters, you may remind the said king that I have not suggested these precautions like one who is in a place of security, and does not reflect on the struggles which he will have to maintain; but I imitate those physicians who prescribe what is necessary, that the patient, if he does not comply with all the articles of the prescription, may, at least, observe it as closely as possible.

You may also remind him that till he have rid himself of all that vermin, he will neither be able to follow good counsels, (for he will be turned aside from them at every moment,) nor will God permit him to prosper. Entreat him to read the 101st Psalm, from which he will learn that God will never dwell with him till he be cleansed from such pollutions. Moreover, that inasmuch as God has endowed him with an easy, good-humoured disposition, he should the more carefully strive to have about him none but such as will give him courage to do his duty.

And, in conclusion, let him know that I beseech him to reward me by furnishing me with as ample matter for rejoicing as he has hitherto done for shedding tears.

[*Fr. Orig., corrected by Calvin.—Library of Geneva.* Vol. 145.]

DLXXXI.—To the Reformed Churches of France.[1]

Project of assembling a council—Conditions requisite for its legitimacy.

GENEVA, *December,* 1560.

ADVICE FOR THE HOLDING OF A COUNCIL.

To put an end to the divisions which exist in Christendom, it is necessary to have a free and universal council.

Its liberty consists in three points; viz., in the place, the persons, and in the manner of proceeding.

In respect to the place, if there be not a secure access for all those who are to be heard in discussing the matters which form the subject of controversy, it is perfectly clear that this will be shutting the door on them. Wherefore it would be requisite to select a town situated in the midst of the nations that are to be present at the council, and that all the neighbouring provinces around it, through whose countries it should be neces-

---

[1] Same date as the preceding memorial. An article of the treaty of Cateau-Cambresis stipulated the assembling of a general council for the reform of abuses and the re-establishment of religious unity in Europe. But what were the characters which such a meeting should present, in order to be equally accepted as a legitimate tribunal by Protestants and Catholics? Such is the question to which Calvin replied in a memorial intended, no doubt, for the Reformed churches of France.

sary to pass, promise and swear to respect the safe conduct of those who repair to it, both in going and on their return.

Respecting the persons, first of all, it would be an iniquitous thing should none but the bishops have a decisive voice in it, since it is sufficiently notorious that they are parties concerned, and cannot therefore be competent judges in their own cause.

What is more, should the authority which they insist on being allowed them, yet it is certain that not one of them is free, inasmuch as they are all bound and subjected by the oath which they have taken to the Pope to maintain his see, a thing totally incompatible with the liberty of a Christian council.

The remedy would be that out of the party which desires and demands the reformation of the church, both in doctrine and in morals, should be elected persons, who, though not possessed of a deciding vote, should yet be empowered to oppose all resolutions repugnant to the word of God, and that they should be entitled to be heard in all their protestations, while demonstrating by solid reasons the grounds of their opposition to the things which the bishops might be inclined to enact. Above all, it is not to be tolerated that the Pope should preside in the council as chief; that is to say, with the pretensions he has recently put forth of making every thing depend on himself and his good pleasure. But even admitting that the chief place should be assigned to him, it should be an indispensable condition of presidency that he, in all things, submit to the council, and take an oath to observe whatever should be decided and concluded in it, abdicating the domination which he has usurped; the bishops, likewise, should swear to conform to the general decision, and support it when it shall have corruptions and abuses to eradicate in doctrine as well as in ceremonies and morals.

As to the manner of proceeding, it would be altogether nugatory, if the custom which has been introduced since a short time should be followed, which is, that those who desire a reformation should propose their measures verbally, or in writing, and then retire, leaving their bishops, the prelates, to decide whatever they may think fit. It is requisite then that whatever is ill-advised may be redressed, and also that it be permitted to reply to all erroneous opinions by sound and conclusive reasons.

It is, likewise, necessary to have determined beforehand the order in which the matters that will come before them ought to be treated, and to know that in the first place the points and articles of doctrine, which are now the subject of controversy, should be fully discussed; that this once settled, they may proceed to regulate the ceremonies, and finally the government of the church.

The articles of doctrine, on which at present the parties dispute, respect the service of God, and the point at issue between them is, whether it ought to be regulated purely and simply by the sacred Scriptures; or if, indeed, men have been at liberty to lay down laws of their own respecting it, and if their traditions are binding upon souls on pain of being chargeable with mortal sins if they neglect them. Under that head are comprised vows, professions of celibacy, confession, and things of the same kind. The question that will next present itself is, upon what we found our hopes of salvation, and whether we are justified by the merit of our own works, or the gratuitous mercy of God. Connected with this question are those of freewill, penances, purgatory, and others of the sort. It will be proper to examine, at the same time, how we should invoke God in conformity with the full assurance of our faith, and the right solution of this question puts an end to the intercession of the saints.

In regard to the second point, that of ceremonies, there will be here an occasion for treating of all those things which have been borrowed from the shadows of the law, of the number of the sacraments with their accessory matters, etc.

The third point, concerning the government of the church, includes the definition of the office of bishops or pastors, in order to ascertain to what persons this title belongs, and what is the scope and bearing of ranks, degrees, and orders, along with privileges and things of a like character.

Now, it would not be enough to hold a council, unless it were to be universal; that is to say, if the object of it were not to appease all the troubles of Christendom. True it is, that each king and prince can very well remedy the disorders of his own states by a national council, when he shall not find his neighbours disposed and agreeing in sentiment and desires with himself. But should a partial council be held, which, notwithstanding, should be called a universal one, this would only kindle with greater violence, and spread more widely the brands of discord. Wherefore, it is indispensably necessary that those who demand a reformation, should accept the council which will be held, in order that all Christendom may be united, or that those who shall be unwilling to range themselves under the banners of unity and concord be declared and held for schismatics.

[*Fr. Orig.Minute.—Library of Geneva.* Vol. 145.]

DLXXXII.—To the King of Navarre.[1]

He exhorts him to pursue with ardour the restoration of the gospel in France.

Geneva, 16*th January*, 1561.

SIRE :—If I thought that my letters were disagreeable to you I should fear to importune or annoy you in writing them. But the confidence I entertain emboldens me, because as I feel that you are convinced of the respect I bear towards you, and of my good intentions to strive to render you service, so I am sure you will receive graciously the testimony which I endeavour to give of them. Wherefore, sire, though I am aware that you have no need of my counsels, yet I do not cease to entreat and even exhort you, in the name of God, to be pleased

---

[1] The weakness and ignorance of the King of Navarre had deceived the calculations of Calvin, and the just hopes of the Reformed party. " For though," says Beza, " both God and the laws called him to the government of the kingdom, and the consent of the states required it of him, in which he would neither have found want of counsel nor of force to re-establish every thing, in case of resistance, he was so far from supporting his rank that, on the contrary, he contented himself with the shadow of it, leaving willingly the body and the substance to the queen mother, without her experiencing any difficulty."—*Hist. Eccl.,* vol. i., p. 564. Nevertheless, as lieutenant general of the kingdom, the King of Navarre had it in his power to contribute greatly to the consolidation and progress of the Reformed churches. Calvin spared this prince neither warnings nor admonitions.

to take courage, in order to do combat courageously and more and more overcome all the difficulties with which I know you to be surrounded. And, in truth, the re-establishment of such a kingdom is an object for which we should spare nothing, and still more it is our most imperious duty to strive that the reign of the Son of God, true religion and the pure doctrine of salvation, which are things more precious than the whole world, should be completely re-established. The greatest obstacle that stands in your way seems to me easy to be overcome, whenever you shall be pleased, sire, to remonstrate frankly with the adverse party,[1] and let her feel keenly that she ought not to apply in thwarting you the power which she holds only by your favour. For the rest, sire, there is one subject of which I have thought it good and expedient to remind you, that your majesty may be pleased to provide for it according to your wisdom. It is not my natural disposition, nor my habit, to intrude and interfere. But it seemed to me to be my duty to recommend to you the bearer of this letter, that you may learn from him, by word of mouth, the matter in question, when your good pleasure shall decide upon giving him an audience.

Sire, having humbly commended myself to your indulgent favour, I will pray our heavenly Father to have you in his keeping, to sustain you by his power, and increase in you all good and prosperity.

[*Fr. Copy.—Library of Geneva.* Vol. 107.]

DLXXXIII.—To the Queen of Navarre.[2]

He congratulates her on her conversion, and lays before her, her principal duties as a Christian princess.

GENEVA, 16th January, 1561.

MADAME:—I cannot adequately express my joy at the letter you were pleased to write to my brother Monsieur de Cha-

---

[1] The regent Catherine De Medicis.

[2] Without date. Written no doubt at the same time as the preceding 16th January, 1561.

lonné,[1] seeing how powerfully God had wrought in you in a few hours. For though already long ago he had sown in you some good seed, you know at present that it was almost choked by the thorns of this world; as for want of daily exercising ourselves in the holy Scriptures, the truth which we had known little by little drops away, till at length it totally disappears, unless our compassionate Father provide a remedy. Now of his infinite goodness he has made provision to keep you from coming to that extremity. It is true that those who yield to indifference, take a pleasure in their inactivity, not perceiving that it is a mortal lethargy. But when it pleases God to rouse us up and draw us effectually to the fear of his holy name, and kindle in our hearts an ardent desire to serve his glory, that is an inquietude happier and more desirable than all the delights, pleasures, and enjoyments, in which poor worldings lose themselves. I speak familiarly, Madame, believing that you will without hesitation give me leave to do so, as moreover, I have derived this advantage from your letter that it has given me an occasion and a liberal access to write to you.

Wherefore, Madame, I pray you to prize the mercy of God as it deserves, not only because it has brought you all at once

Daughter of Henry d'Albret King of Navarre and of Margaret de Valois, the sister of Francis I., Jane d'Albret joined to the talents of her mother, superior judgment and a heroic soul. Betrothed in her childhood to the Duke of Cleves, and married in 1548 to Antony de Bourbon, Duke of Vendome, she inherited a few years afterwards the kingdom of Navarre. The Reform had already long before penetrated into this country, and the preachers of Geneva found support and favour at the court of Nerac. "But the queen," says Brantome, "who was a young, beautiful, and very virtuous princess, and who loved, moreover, quite as much a dance as a sermon, took no great pleasure in this innovation in religion." It was only at a later period, during the process of the Prince of Condé and the captivity of the King of Navarre, that this princess, taught by misfortune, showed herself more attentive to evangelical exhortations:—"Seeing," says Beza, "that the trust she had reposed in men was deceived, and that all human succour failed her, being touched to the heart by the love of God, she had recourse to him with all humility, and in sorrow and tears. . . so that in the time of her greatest tribulation she made a public profession of the pure doctrine, being fortified by Francis Le Guay, otherwise called Bois Normand, and Henry, faithful ministers of the word of God." *Hist. Eccl.*, vol. i., p. 326.

[1] A pseudonym of Theodore Beza. Sent on the 30th July, 1560, to Nerac, "to instruct the King and Queen of Navarre in the word of God," he acquitted himself successfully of this mission, and had commenced his journey back to Geneva in the month of November of the same year.

out of the darkness of death to show you the light of life in his Son, who is the true sun of righteousness, but also because he has deeply imprinted on your heart a faith in his gospel, giving to it a living root, that it may bring forth its due fruits.   For you have felt by experience how the vanities of this world deaden the knowledge of the truth.   We would fain swim between two currents, so that the word of God is made cold and of no effect, if the power of God be not conjoined therewith.   And this is the true and perfect covenant which he promises to contract with his own children, namely, to impress and engrave his doctrine on their inward parts.   Having then received so great and inestimable a benefit, you have reason to be so much the more zealous to dedicate yourself (as you do) entirely to Him, who has bound you so closely to himself.   And whereas kings and princes would often wish to be exempted from subjection to Jesus Christ, and are accustomed to make a buckler of their privileges under pretence of their greatness, being ashamed even to belong to the fold of this great Shepherd, do you, Madame, bethink you that the dignity and grandeur in which this God of goodness has brought you up, should be in your esteem a double tie to bind you to obedience to him, seeing that it is from him that you hold everything, and that according to the measure which each one has received, he shall have to render a stricter account.   But since I see how the Spirit of God governs you, I have more reason to render him thanks than to exhort you as if you had need to be goaded forward.   When, besides, I doubt not but you apply all your zeal to that end, as is indeed very requisite, when we reflect on the coldness, weakness, and frailty that is in us.

Long ago we had already essayed to discharge our duty with respect of the king your husband, and even more than once to the end that he might quit himself manfully.   But you will see once more, Madame, by the copy of the letter which we have sent to him, what effects your admonition has produced.

Madame, having very humbly commended myself to your indulgent favour, I will pray our heavenly Father to have you always in his keeping, to govern and direct you by his Spirit, to strengthen you by his power, and increase you in all good.

[*Fr. Orig. Minute.—Library of Geneva.*   Vol. 107 *a.*]

DLXXXIV.—To the Admiral Coligny.[1]

Encomiums on the constancy of the admiral—Recommendation of Geneva.

GENEVA, 16th January, 1561.

MONSEIGNEUR:—We have indeed occasion to praise God for the singular courage which he has bestowed on us to serve his glory and the advancement of the kingdom of his Son. It were to be desired that you had many companions to aid you in your task, but though others are slow in acquitting themselves of their duty, nevertheless you ought to put in practice the saying of our Lord, that each should follow cheerfully without looking upon others. St. Peter fearing to march by himself said to Jesus of John, And this man, what of him? The answer given to one man should be applied to all. Let every one go whither he shall be called, even if he should not have a single follower, though I trust that the magnanimity which God has hitherto caused to shine forth in you, will be a good lesson to draw out the lukewarm. Even if the whole world should be blind and ungrateful, and that it should seem to you that all your pains had been laid out in vain, let it satisfy you that God and the

[1] Restored to liberty after the conclusion of the peace between Spain and France, the admiral had openly declared for the Reform. Unshaken by the threats as well as by the seductions of the court, he had the courage to present to King Francis II. in the assembly of the Notables at Fontainbleau an address from the Protestants of Normandy demanding the free exercise of their worship, and added proudly in presence of the Guises, that in this single province fifty thousand persons were prepared to sign their names to this petition. Some months later (November 1561) he quitted Chatillon to repair at the peril of his life to the Estates of Orleans. "On leaving his house," says Beza, "he was unwilling to dissemble from his wife (one of the most Christian and virtuous ladies of her times) the dangers by which he was going to be surrounded, and without expecting from them any prosperous issue, saying, however, that he had perfect confidence that God would have compassion on his poor church and on the kingdom; exhorting the lady as well as her family to remain constant in the doctrine of the gospel, in which they had been rightly instructed, since God had given them to know that it was the only true and heavenly food, and that it was their duty to think it the greatest happiness to suffer for his name." *Hist. Eccl.* vol. i., pp. 392, 393. The sudden death of King Francis II., having disappointed the hopes of the Guises, and brought on a change favourable to the Reformed, the admiral did not hesitate to have the gospel preached in his own house at Paris.

angels approve of your conduct. And in reality it ought to suffice you that you cannot miss the heavenly crown, after having courageously battled for the glory of the Son of God, in which consists our eternal salvation.

For the rest, Monseigneur, I have made bold to address to you the bearer of this letter in order that he may expose to you an affair of which you will have a more ample detail from his mouth, whenever you shall be pleased to grant him an audience. I believe that after having listened to him you will not find the advice amiss nor the execution of it importunate; at least you will in your wisdom conclude, that I have nothing at heart but the repose and prosperity of the kingdom. I do not dissemble the desire I feel that some measures should be adopted in favour of this poor city, in order that it may not be exposed to pillage.[1] But as I am convinced that the safety of this place needs not to be recommended to you, you will not blame the anxiety I feel respecting it, especially as that anxiety tends to the public good of France, and is intimately connected with it.

Whereupon, in conclusion, Monseigneur, after humbly commending myself to your indulgent favour, I will supplicate our heavenly Father to keep you under his protection, and increase in you the gifts of his Spirit, that his name may be more and more glorified in you.

Your humble servant,

JOHN CALVIN.

[*Fr. Copy.—Library of Geneva.* Vol. 107.]

---

[1] After the peace of Cateau Cambresis and the restoration of the Duke of Savoy to his states, Geneva was constantly threatened with an attack by this prince, supported by the pope and Philip II. Emmanuel Philibert asked the Catholic powers to guarantee to him beforehand his conquest. But could France abandon Geneva without alienating the Swiss Cantons from which she drew precious succours? The independence of Geneva was necessary for the security of France. Such was the sense of Calvin's representations to the admiral, and of the admiral's to the court, of which the policy at this moment appeared more favourable to the Reformed party.

DLXXXV.—To the King of France.[1]

Reply to the accusations directed against the Church and Seigneury of Geneva.

GENEVA, 28th January, 1561.

SIRE :—Having heard the letters of your majesty, though we had a ready excuse to satisfy you, we are nevertheless exceedingly sorry that we should be charged with being partly the cause of the troubles which have lately taken place in your kingdom. The smallness of our state does not permit us to allege what services we have rendered to your predecessors, to show that we have been as well affected towards the crown of France as could have been desired of us. Thus far, sure, our good-will has never been wanting in that respect, and the effects of it, too, have been manifested as far as God has afforded us any opportunity. Wherefore, sire, for the time past, we pray your majesty to deign to accept the devotedness which we have always and for a long time displayed, and in which we have persisted as a proof of the desire which we have to serve you to the utmost of our power, for the tranquillity and prosperity of

[1] Focus of the propagation of the Reformed religion in the states of the south of Europe, the city of Geneva was incessantly exposed to the enmity of the Catholic powers. The 23d of January, 1561, the King of France, Charles IX., in a threatening letter to the council, complained bitterly of the troubles excited in his kingdom by the presence of the preachers that had come from Geneva, and summoned the seigneury to recall them. In so difficult a conjuncture, the council, assembled in an extraordinary sitting, invited the ministers to attend its meeting. "After having heard," say the registers, "the reading of the said letter, and consulted together, they have replied that they are sorry to be blamed in that manner unjustly; that no doubt they cannot deny that when any one addressed himself to them, and they considered him a proper person, they have exhorted him to do his duty to advance the knowledge of the gospel in France, as our Lord commands us, but as for the troubles that have arisen in France, they are by no means blamable for them, . . . begging the council to reply to the king that they are ready fully to justify themselves in his presence of all that is imputed to them."—Extraits des Registres, 28th January, 1561. Calvin, who was the organ of the seigneury, in difficult circumstances, was charged to reply in their name to the King of France. "Then he was told to make the reply promptly that it might be despatched by the same express that had brought the letter; and further, it was enjoined that all the seigneurs here assembled, and all the ministers, should keep secret, on pain of death, the contents of the letter, in order that it may appear to the public that the king has written to us to our advantage rather than to our disadvantage, which might cause us great prejudice."

your kingdom, and to co-operate, if an opportunity permit us, to procure for your majesty that obedience to which you are entitled. But lest it should seem, sire, that under this general expression of our sentiments we wish to conceal any thing, we protest in verity before God that we have never attempted to send persons into your kingdom as your majesty has been told; what is more, such proceedings have never been demanded of us, nor has any one ever addressed himself to us for such a purpose; so that it will be found that no one, with our knowledge and permission, has ever gone from here to preach except a single individual who was asked of us for the city of London.[1] Not that we disapprove of true Christianity being re-established everywhere, and for that reason we beg your majesty, with your council at the same time, not to suppose that we wish to perish knowingly, and work the perdition of our souls which have been ransomed at so costly a price by the precious blood of the Son of God. We could wish, therefore, that the doctrine by which our salvation is assured had free course everywhere. But we know well also what is within our compass, and we do not presume even to wish to reform extensive kingdoms, having quite enough to do to maintain ourselves peaceably and in all humility, in the lowly condition in which God has placed us. But because the letters bore that that might have been done by some of the principal ministers of our town, supposing (for the expression was ambiguous) that the words were meant to be applied to our ministers and pastors who instruct us in the word of God, we have summoned them, in order to know from themselves what grounds there were for such a charge, in order that we might promptly satisfy your majesty. They have replied, then, that they do not deny that some persons have made application to them, and that on their part, when they have found that those who had recourse to them were persons possessing instruction and piety, they have exhorted them to exercise their gifts wherever they should go for the advancement of the gospel. For since they find, and are persuaded that the doctrine which they preach is of God, tending to have him duly and purely served and honoured, that the grace which

---

[1] Nicholas des Gallars.

he has bestowed on us by our Lord Jesus Christ should be made
known, as it is entitled to be, and that all men should be made
acquainted with the right way of salvation, in order to attain
it, it is impossible that they should not desire this doctrine to
be disseminated everywhere, both that God may be glorified,
and because of the care they are bound to take of all men.
And in that, sire, they make this excuse, that they by no means
imagined that they were offending your majesty,[1] seeing that
it is the sovereign good of all kings and princes to do homage
to Him who has appointed them to reign, and that they are
especially commanded to kiss our Lord Jesus Christ in token of
obedience.

With regard to the charge of stirring up disturbances and
seditions, they protest against ever having entertained any such
intention, and declare that, on the contrary, they have employed all their influence to check and prevent them, that they
have never given advice to make any innovations, or attempted
any thing criminal with respect to the established order of the
state, but have exhorted those who are disposed to listen to
them to remain in peaceable subjection to their prince. And
if any disturbances have arisen, it has been to their great regret,
and certainly not by their having furnished any pretext for them.
And so far have they been from countenancing any such enterprises, that they would willingly have lent their aid to repress them.[2]
In short, they have declared that they never adhered to any
violent counsels, nor recommended the taking up of arms, but
have condemned them; and what is more, they never advised
the taking forcible possession of churches, for this express reason, that they wished to attempt nothing without the authority
and permission of the late sovereigns, your predecessors. And
of all such charges they have offered to justify themselves, and
prove their innocence, whenever it shall please your majesty
to give them a hearing. For our own part, sire, we are so far
from ever having given our consent to any enterprise that had
for its object to sow discord and divisions among your subjects,

---

[1] What follows is written by the hand of the secretary of the republic, and was
dictated by Calvin.

[2] Allusion to the conspiracy of Amboise. See the letter of the 16th of April, 1561,
to the Admiral de Coligny.

or trouble the tranquillity of your state, or expose your provinces to danger, that we have given orders and forbidden, on pain of rigorous punishments, any of our citizens from taking one step in such proceedings; and when you shall be pleased, sire, to inquire into the truth on this subject, you will find that it was impossible for us to have conducted ourselves with greater fidelity, just as we engage for the future to give to your majesty no occasion of thinking otherwise of us than as of persons well disposed to your person and your very humble servants; and we entreat you, sire, to do us this favour, that having recognized that we have not failed in any point of duty towards you, you will intimate to us the fact, and your majesty with your council will discover that we are ready and inclined to give you every satisfaction.

Sire, after having very humbly commended ourselves to your kind favour, we will pray God to keep you under his holy protection, to grant you a long and prosperous life, and increase your crown with all blessings.

Given at Geneva this Thursday, the 28th January, in the year of grace, 1561.

The humble servants of your majesty, the Syndics and Council of Geneva.

[*Fr. Orig. Minute, in the handwriting of Calvin. Arch. of Gen.*, 1561.]

DLXXXVI.—To the Church of Paris.[1]

He apologizes for not being able to send to it new ministers—Advice relating to the Council of Trent—Disapprobation of the excesses committed by the Reformed in the south of France.

GENEVA, *26th February*, 1561.

MESSIEURS, and well beloved brethren, I suppose that one of our friends has brought you letters, and has apologized to you

---

[1] Decimated by persecution, but recruited by an ardent proselytism, the Church of Paris demanded from that of Geneva new ministers. The minister, Flavigny, wrote to Calvin:—"If you grant us our request, you will be the cause of so great a progress that it is impossible for us to express it."—Letter of the 22d February, 1560, Library of Geneva, vol. 197 a. The Church of Geneva could not subscribe to these demands

orally, because we have not been able to satisfy your desire in sending you the man you demand. For, first, there is one of our colleagues at the present moment elsewhere,[1] and to deprive ourselves of two, all at once, would be rather too much, seeing that some of our society are ill, whose place we are obliged to supply as if they were absent. And though it is with much ado I drag myself along, still from the urgency of circumstances I am to be considered, as it were, the most robust of our body. It seems to me, also, that you should have some consideration for the threats that have been pronounced against us, which are so harsh and violent as to astonish many people. But besides all that, the person you demand is fallen ill a second time, and so gravely that should we burst like a thunderbolt upon him, it would be impossible for him to stir.

With regard to the point about which you ask our advice, we have not yet heard any thing of it;[2] though by common rumour it has come to our ears that a council was to be assembled. No one has even feigned that there was any necessity for informing us about it.[3] Now we did not know if it would be advisable to intermeddle, for there are many heads difficult to manage. At present we shall tell you, in a few words, our opinion. It is that you have no occasion to concern yourselves about the council, nor to send to it either confession or protestation. First, for an excellent reason, it would not be received, nor would there be any means of presenting it; and even if that would be done, you would only give occasion for stirring up violent tumults without any useful results. For your enemies would have excellent pretexts for falling foul of you outrageously, as having exposed the country to civil wars. Moreover,

---

continually renewed without depriving itself of its own pastors, and exposing the city to the redoubtable resentment of the King of France. See the preceding letter, as well as the Latin correspondence of the Reformer, February, 1561. Charged with replying to the ministers of Paris, Calvin, at the same time, gave them advice on several important points of policy and religion.

[1] Nicholas des Gallars, called to reorganize the French Church at London.

[2] Respecting the line of conduct they were to follow in case a general council should be assembled. See the memorial to the Reformed churches, page 158.

[3] Convoked at Trent for the feast of Easter, 1561, the council was not opened till the month of January, 1562. This assembly realized none of the conditions required by the Reformed, and which were necessary for assuring the religious pacification of Europe.

you ought to let the danger pass by, because there will be abundance of other opponents, and it is possible they will be asking for a great deal more than they are authorized to do. When you shall have considered every thing closely, you will find that there is neither opening nor grounds for your interference, and that in this matter you will do well to fold your hands and sit still. The reason is different with respect to the Estates.[1] For there it will be necessary for you to endeavour to make all the remonstrances in your power, that the council is neither Catholic nor legitimate, seeing that it is but a continuation of what has been done heretofore, to ratify resolutions full of errors and blasphemies, and entirely contrary to the word of God. There will be no liberty to examine the matters which are the subject of difference between us, nor to obtain any good reformation of abuses, as the pope seeks not to consult the necessities of the church, but only to maintain his own tyranny; and nevertheless there is need that the king with his council should provide for those things in a better manner, without expecting any thing from those who care not whether they bring confusion and ruin on his state, country, and subjects, provided their own profits suffer no diminution. That subject might be touched upon in a more conciliatory manner, but may God be pleased to give you counsel thereupon.

Of the other things which you shall have to demand, your deliberation will depend upon the state in which you will find matters at the time. Your object, nevertheless, should always be (and all your efforts should be directed singly to the attainment of this object), that some tolerable provision be made for securing your rights, and that poor innocent people should not be molested, nor persecuted, nor blood wantonly shed as heretofore.[2] You will advise among yourselves, also, how you may

---

[1] The Estates General, held at Orleans the 13th December, 1560, had been prorogued to the month of May, at Pontoise. They were to deliberate in this new assembly respecting the reform of religious abuses, and the means of restoring peace to the church.—De Thou, Lib. xxvii.

[2] In the Estates of Orleans, Jacques de Sillery, Comte of Rochefort, had presented to the king, in the name of the nobility, a petition demanding the free exercise of religious worship for the Protestants. This petition was to have been presented for the deliberation of the Estates prorogued to Pontoise.

make all lawful efforts to procure for yourselves such favour as
may enable you to obtain your request.

To give yourselves up to extravagant excesses of joy, and to
take possession of the churches, except by permission, are
things which you know I have never approved of. As often
as it has been done, it was in despite of me.¹ If they go on in
this manner, we shall leave the event in the hands of God. We
are afraid that this heat will be cooled by some rude storm.²

Whereupon, commending ourselves to you and to your fervent prayers, we will supplicate our heavenly Father to have
you in his keeping, to fortify you by the power of his Spirit,
to direct you in all your affairs, and to give to them a prosperous issue.

[*Lat. Copy.—Library of Geneva.* Vol. 107.]

DLXXXVII.—To John Lening.³

Hostilities of the Duke of Savoy—Diversion in the valleys of Piedmont and at Nice—
Unexpected preservation of Geneva.

GENEVA, *14th March*, 1561.

As your letter testifies how deep an interest you take in the
state of this city, and what anxiety its dangers occasion you,
honoured brother, I return you most sincere thanks for your
pious and fraternal zeal. What you indicate with sufficient and
more than sufficient probability has been already discovered; for
the tendency of that clandestine league, purchased at the expense of so much penury by the Duke of Savoy, was no mystery

---

¹ In some localities in the south of France, the Protestants had taken forcible possession, and in spite of Calvin's remonstrances, of several edifices consecrated to the
Catholic worship. See the Latin correspondence of the Reformer of the years 1561–'62.

² What had taken place at Valence is a proof of this. See letter, p. 95. The
Marechal Damville, also, exercised severe reprisals on the Protestants of Languedoc.

³ An unknown personage, probably a minister of Switzerland. This conjecture is
confirmed by the following passage of a letter from Lening to Calvin, February 22nd,
1561. "Bullinger will be able to tell you who Lening is, and where he lives and
with what zeal he has hitherto preached the word of God, for more than thirty years."
Library of Paris, Dupuy, 102.

to any one. He had indeed repeatedly attempted to form an alliance with the whole Helvetic nation, but not succeeding in his project, he has had recourse to the five Catholic cantons. At length he attracted to his schemes the inhabitants of Soleure and Fribourg, not that he hoped they would openly and declaredly take up arms against this city; but because, when the Swiss should be by his combinations distracted by intestine discords, he had resolved to attack us suddenly, as persons who should then be left exposed to his mercy. For he had placed his hopes of victory in the belief that no succour would come to us from our allies the Bernese. But the divisions among the Swiss being healed, he was deceived in his calculations. Add to this that God had called his attention to another quarter. For his subjects who inhabit the Alps, though they had recently been pillaged and cruelly maltreated for professing the gospel,[1] have not for all that apostatized from the true faith, and when he again sent against them some troops of soldiers, by whom these unfortunate people were driven to despair, they began to defend themselves and repel his tyrannical violence. For they had been despoiled of all their fortunes, their houses had been burned down, and they themselves with their wives and children had taken refuge in the lurking places of the woods.

Summoning up courage then, they fought a second and even a third time so successfully, that the forces of the Duke were all cut to pieces. Moreover he is still more hardly pressed in another quarter. For the Turkish fleet is just coming up, and cannot be driven back from the port of Nice which is situated in his dominions, and where he himself very narrowly escaped being captured last summer. For certain, his escort was partly slain—partly taken—and a good many of them carried off. He himself fled in great trepidation and with the greatest disgrace. To all this add that he is so desperately poor and so overwhelmed with debt, that he can find nowhere a creditor to lend

---

[1] By a brief of 1560, Pope Pius IV. exhorted the Duke of Savoy to take the severest measures against heresy. Notwithstanding the generous representations of Margaret of France, who secretly professed the new opinions, the magistrates were ordered to keep an eye on the Reformed, and to the toleration which the churches of Piedmont had for some years enjoyed, a most bitter persecution succeeded. Muston, *Israel des Alpes*, vol. i. *passim ;* and Giles, Perrin, Leger, etc.

him anything. Thus God scatters the counsels of the ungodly
like clouds. We are on our guard against snares however.
Though indeed there seems nothing to be feared for the moment,
and we trust that God will continue to be the guardian of an
innocent city which he has hitherto protected.
Farewell, most excellent brother. Viret cordially salutes you,
and I will pray from the heart the Father of our Lord Jesus
Christ to govern you by his Spirit, and support you by his
power even to the end.

[*Lat. Copy.—Library of Geneva.* Vol. 107 *a.*]

DLXXXVIII.—To the Admiral de Coligny.[1]

An account and solemn disavowal of the conspiracy of Amboise.

Geneva, 16*th April*, 1561.

Monseigneur :—I have been apprised by my brother,[2] who
is at present among you, that you thought it fitting and desirable
that I should publish a printed apology to clear myself of the
blame which has been laid to my charge, with respect to the enterprise of Amboise, as if I had given my consent to it. It is
true that long before this time and from several quarters, I have
been required and solicited to do this, and I might easily have
done it, if I had consulted nothing but my own person; but I
have forborne for two reasons: first, many persons would have

[1] In a note, by another hand : " He clears himself of participation in the enterprise of
Amboise."

As a bold attempt of a religious minority maddened by persecution, the conspiracy
of Amboise was the first act of the political and religious Protestantism which was
henceforth to be associated with the Protestantism of faith and martyrdom. It had
for agent La Renaudie, for instruments the Protestant nobility, for secret chief the
Prince of Condé, for motive the insupportable tyranny of the Guises under a king in
his minority. Coligny, who felt an aversion for the employment of arms in the cause
of religion, and who wished to obtain liberty of conscience by conciliation and the
progress of time, remained a stranger to this enterprise. Calvin, who was accused of
having been the instigator of it, had made every effort to prevent it, and publicly dis-
owned it by his letters. See pp. 91, and 106.

[2] Antony Calvin, then entrusted with a mission in France.

esteemed it cruel to insult the calamity of poor people whose
only crime was to have been actuated by inconsiderate zeal; and
next, because it might have been thought that I had waited for
the issue in order to square my sails according to the winds.
Wherefore I have chosen to suffer patiently to be wrongfully
accused, rather than to manifest an excessive anxiety about my
reputation.   However I have never dissembled my opinion about
that transaction, when I was questioned respecting it, as on the
present occasion I am quite disposed, if you wish, Monseigneur,
to hear a brief abstract of it, to lay before you the whole truth.
Seven or eight months before the event, a certain person entrusted with the command of some troops consulted me, whether
it was not lawful to resist the tyranny by which the children of
God were then oppressed, and what means might be employed
for that purpose.   As I perceived that opinions of this sort
were becoming very generally current, after having given him a
peremptory answer that he should abandon all thoughts of this
kind, I strove to demonstrate to him that he had no warrant for
such conduct according to God; and that even according to the
world such measures were ill-concerted, presumptuous, and could
have no successful issue.   He was at no loss for an answer, and
even for one that had a certain plausibility.

For, said he, nothing was to be attempted against the king
nor against his authority, but all they aimed at was only to exact a government according to the laws of the country during
the minority of the king.   In the mean time great were the
lamentations respecting the cruelties that were practised to
abolish the Reformed religion, that they even expected hourly a
horrible massacre to exterminate all the poor brethren.   I replied simply to such objections that if a single drop of blood
were spilled, floods of it would deluge Europe; that thus it were
better we should perish a hundred times, than expose Christianity and the gospel to such opprobrium.   I admitted, it is
true, that if the princes of the blood demanded to be maintained
in their rights for the common good, and if the Parliament joined
them in their quarrel, that it would then be lawful for all good
subjects to lend them armed assistance.   The man afterwards
asked me, if one of the princes of the blood, though not

the first in rank,[1] had decided upon taking such a step, we were not then warranted to support him. I again gave him an answer in the negative with regard to this supposition. In a word I adopted so decided a tone in condemning all his proposals that I was convinced he had completely abandoned them. And that is the reason why I did not breathe a syllable on the subject, because it would only have been breeding disturbances to no purpose.

Some time after that, I was very much astonished when Renaudie,[2] on his arrival from Paris, told me that he had been entrusted with the direction of such an enterprise, demonstrating the goodness of his cause by all the sophisms he could muster up. What is more, Monseigneur, I protest that he represented you as mixed up with the affair. Now, having always known him for a man puffed up with vanity and self-conceit, I constantly repelled all his advances, so that he could never wring from me the slightest token of consent; on the contrary, I strove to turn him aside from these follies by many reasons which it would be too tedious to enumerate. Seeing himself thus frustrated in his expectations, he plotted in secret both to seduce those whom he knew to have but little judgment, and also to empty the purses of those who would have been but little disposed to march with him. All this was done in small coteries and under the seal of an oath not to disclose any thing that was going on. Now, there was one who being rather shy in opening his purse consulted Master Peter Viret, and revealed to him that La Renaudie, soliciting him for a contribution, had adjured him not to say a word about it especially to me, because I was unwilling that it should be known that I had given my consent to the enterprise. Master Peter Viret, without a moment's

---

[1] Allusion to the Prince of Condé.

[2] Godfroi du Barry, Seigneur de la Renaudie, chief of the conspiracy. "This man," says Beza, "was endowed with a good understanding. For a process that had been before several parliaments between him and Du Tillet, the Recorder of the Parliament of Paris, he had been very badly and ignominiously treated, and cast into prison, from which, having found means very adroitly to make his escape, he had retired to the territory of Berne, in Swisserland. At a future period he had obtained letters authorizing a rehearing of his cause. . . . By these letters he was to be re-established in the possession of his lands and honours. He returned to France for the homologation of the said letters, and for his other affairs."—*Hist. Eccl.*, vol. i., p. 250.

delay, came to me, as in duty bound, and forthwith I begged
Monsieur Beza to send for the man. I also called in some
witnesses, in whose presence I sharply reproved him for having
made use of my name under false pretexts. He protested and
swore that he had done no such thing, confessing, of his own
accord, that if he had spoken as he was represented to have
done, he would have been the most shameless of liars, since he
had heard from me the very contrary of what was there reported. He who had made the report was struck dumb. However, these intrigues were still continued. Even when La Renaudie had withdrawn to the Bernese territory where he had
his habitation, he gained over some who ceased not to attract
others. Hereupon I endeavoured as well as I could to arrest
the progress of the evil. When I called before me those who
had been inveigled into this wild project, every one denied it.
Nevertheless they marched away, protesting all the time that it
was to prevent all disturbance. So that seeing every thing go
wrong, I bitterly lamented, and frequently I was heard to utter
these words: Alas! I never thought to live to see the day in
which we should have lost all credit among those who are renowned for their fidelity. Is it possible that the church of
Geneva should be thus despised by her own children? In one
word, during all that time I did nothing but groan. The council being apprised that some enterprise was going forward,
although they were as yet ignorant of its nature, caused to
be proclaimed by sound of trumpet that no man should stir,
and issued similar prohibitions throughout all private houses.
Wherefore none left this city except clandestinely, and in small
numbers, so that we did not know the mischief that they were
secretly brewing. In fact, I looked upon it altogether as a kind
of childish game they were playing, and when I wished to cheer
up my melancholy a little, I used to say that it was a crusade
of knights errant, or of those of the round table who were in
verity bewitched. There is one who is at this moment my witness before God whom you have known, Monseigneur, and whom
I have no need to name.[1] When at first they broke the affair

---

[1] The Seigneur de Villemongis-Bricquemant. He had taken up his residence some
time after his wife, at Geneva.—Bolsec, Vie de Calvin, C., 15. Condemned to lose

to him, he only turned it into ridicule, and from the respect he
entertained for me flatly and laconically refused to have any
thing to do with it. Afterwards, contrary to his natural character, which was frank and straight forward, he consulted me
whether he should not undertake a journey to settle some matters with his brother who had reduced him to great straits. I
have no doubt but he was swayed by this motive, but he was
also actuated by another consideration, namely, that of not being held for cowardly, especially as La Renaudie had boasted to
him that you, Monseigneur, were favourable to the undertaking.
I told him that if he would take my advice he ought not to go.
As he affirmed and promised that he would avoid all contact
with the conspirators, and stand aloof from their projects, I
made use of these very words :—"I know you; you will not
stand aloof from it when once you are on the spot. Remain,
then, where you are." It is true, he made one exception to
his promise, and declared that if you commanded him he should
not dare to refuse. Whereupon I replied:—"Have you profited so little in the school of God as to do evil in order to
please men? On the contrary, the greatest service you could
render the seigneur, to whom you bear so great an affection,
would be to prevent him from meddling in this business, and
tell him frankly that I send him word, in the name of God, that
he does wrong if he allows himself to be entangled in so disorderly a proceeding." However, I was not very uneasy on that
score, because I was persuaded that there was no foundation for
such surmises, and that the brazen-faced bragger who had made
use of your name was screening himself under false colours.
Be that as it may, this poor seigneur having quitted me five or
six times, almost overcome by my arguments, at last told me
that he could never be at rest till he had undertaken a journey
to see you; and, in truth, I believe that such was his intention.
Nevertheless, I had conceived such apprehensions of what took
place, that I allowed him to set out with much regret. Nay,

---

his life on the scaffold, after the conspiracy of Amboise, he dipped his hands in the
blood of his decapitated brethren, and lifting them up towards heaven exclaimed :—
"Almighty God ! there is the innocent blood of thy children, and thou wilt avenge
it."—D'Aubigné, *Hist. Univ.*, vol. i., p. 94.

when he came to bid me farewell, in holding out my hand to him, I turned my back upon him to show what displeasure I felt in my heart.

If I should be asked why I did not more formally oppose the proceedings, I answer, that first of all I thought there was no great necessity for doing so, because I despised the enterprise as a childish affair. And, in fact, I always said that if the deed displeased me, the person of La Renaudie disgusted me still more. I held him for a frivolous person; I thought his project would fall to pieces of itself. Since I suspected no danger, I was unwilling to begin skirmishing that I might not give rise to great troubles, or kindle a fire that might spread too far; for it was to be presumed that many poor, innocent persons would pay for the rash presumption of others. This reason kept me back; I wished to spare the innocent whom I could not distinguish from the guilty; besides, I knew of no one to whom I could address myself to set things to rights. Nevertheless, Monsieur Coignet, who is the king's ambassador to the *Ligues*, knows what I then said to him about the business. So far was I from wishing to swim between two currents, or dissimulate from craftiness, and still farther from wishing to gratify the ardour of those who were rushing, of their own accord, to their ruin. For I always declared, without any reserve, that if their folly succeeded, I should be the most degraded man in the world, as having betrayed the church, thrown obstacles in the way of God's work, opposed myself to liberty, etc., etc.; since it is clear that I despised all these imputations, and preferred to be held for a poltroon and a coward rather than give loose reins to what I condemned. You can judge, Monseigneur, why I was constrained to hold my peace, or, at least, not to make any great outcry. And yet it is an undoubted fact that at that time people heard me preach several sermons, in which I combated their cause with as much vehemence as I was master of. This can easily be verified, inasmuch as these sermons were copied word for word as I delivered them with the date of the month and of the day, whence, it is evident, that I did not play a double part, nor avail myself of silence to spring a mine under ground.

The result having turned out as every one knows, I was in deep distress, as was to be expected, but was by no means surprised, as if any thing unforeseen had happened, because I had constantly predicted the issue, protesting that I feared to be recognized in the end for too true a prophet. Had it been in my power to adopt better measures, I should not have spared my pains, and I have often completely defeated other intrigues which had spread very widely and without apprising a single person in the kingdom of them. However, I cannot prevent people from accusing me in that quarter where I cannot be heard, but it suffices me to have God for my voucher, and all those who have intercourse with me for my witnesses; so that wherever they shall be pleased to give me a hearing, I shall open my mouth to show that they do me great wrong who charge me with accusations so calumnious. Since that time, when the King of Navarre begged me of his own good will and spontaneous movement to send to him M. Beza, he knows that my inclinations pointed at no other object than the public tranquillity of France, and the security of the king. But, besides, what he knows, I have good witnesses who can prove that by indirect means I have endeavoured to cool those whose tempers were too much inflamed. If it please certain persons, either from malice or any other cause, to impute to me all the evil that is done at a great distance from me, what should I do except to entreat them to make inquiries and learn how the matter stands? For when the truth shall be brought to light, I shall have wherewith to confound all evil disposed people who would like to blame me. Excesses have been committed in Provence.[1] Some have taken up arms, several persons have been killed, but it remains to be proved that I had any secret understanding with the authors, if I had ever seen or known them, if we had ever communicated together by letters or messages. Now it will be found that I have no less condemned all their acts than I had

---

[1] Charles de Monbrun had drawn his sword in Dauphiné and the county Venaissin, in the defence of religion. The assassination of a Protestant nobleman of Castelane, Antony de Mouvans, set the whole of Provence in flames. Paul de Mouvans, the brother of Antony, not being able to obtain justice for this murder, which had been accomplished under atrocious circumstances, took up arms, and sacked the whole country round Aix.—Beza, *Hist. Eccl.* vol. i., pp. 374–383. De Thou, Lib. xxv.

those which had taken place previously. We have also heard something of a tumult that had fallen out at Lyons ;[1] but, however that may be, the origin of all these disturbances came from elsewhere, and had it only depended on me, this thoughtless conduct would have been quietly put an end to. However, I have never seen the man to whom the fault was attributed, and if thoughtless conduct there was, it is not for me who resisted it to bear the blame of it. Nay, because at that time the gentlemen of Geneva merely heard it whispered that certain persons were making a sudden rising, they strictly enjoined all the inhabitants of our city not to stir, and notwithstanding this, people have not ceased to say that fifteen hundred horsemen had gone from here. But it would have required a very piercing sight to count what never appeared. I also allow people to say that in this town punishments were inflicted on those who had put themselves too prominently forward, though they did so rather from simplicity than evil intentions. You have here, then, Monseigneur, a brief abstract of all that concerns me ; that is to say, the naked truth of the facts by which you will judge in your wisdom whether it would be expedient, in order to clear my own character, (a thing by no means difficult,) that I should aggravate the cause of those whom I wish to protect. For I am astonished at seeing worthy people of great piety who have been circumvented, because the warning which I gave them had been maliciously kept back from them. For the rest, I ought to be on my guard against being induced by ambition to justify myself in such a manner as to cause them injury or prejudice ; nay, I desire, even if all the evil should fall on my own head, that the scandal of it should be buried in oblivion.

Monseigneur, having humbly commended myself to your indulgent favour, I will pray our heavenly Father to have you in his holy keeping, to increase you in all virtues, and govern you by his Spirit, even to the end.

[*Fr. Orig., corrected by Calvin.—Library of Paris. Dupuy*, 102.]

---

[1] "In the year 1561, those of Lyons seeing how throughout the greater part of the kingdom, and even at the court of the king, people publicly preached, took courage to do the same."—*Hist. Eccl.*, vol. iii., p. 215. These first assemblies gave rise to some sedition

DXC.—To John Knox.[1]

Explanations on the subject of a letter—Expression of satisfaction at the progress of the Reformation in Scotland and of sympathy for a domestic affliction.

GENEVA, 23d *April*, 1561.

About four months previous to the receipt of your last letter, I had received from you another, in which you took great pains to exculpate yourself, because I felt offended at being consulted a second time by your friends and countrymen, about certain questions respecting which I had already given them an answer. Here is a correct statement of the case. If they had not promised that my letter should arrive in safety at its destination, I should at least have preserved a copy of it. It was their fault, and in consequence of their pledging themselves rather inconsiderately, that I took no better precautions. When then, some time afterwards, they informed me that the answer about which they had asserted I had nothing to fear, had completely miscarried, and demanded that I should a second time undertake a new labour, I confess I was displeased, and I answered them that I had a suspicion, that what they asked was only with the intention of insidiously sounding me. But lest you should be surprised that I answered them so harshly, know that I had previously learned from a sure source that the counsel which I had given them was not to their liking. When I knew then that I had by no means given them satisfaction, I not unnaturally conjectured that they desired to suppress what displeased them, and returned to me to elicit something more in accordance with their wishes; but that you acted with any degree of dissimulation in the matter, I never said nor even suspected. And even at the moment all offence dropped so entirely from my mind that there was not the least need of making any apology. But it

---

[1] There exists but a small number of letters exchanged between Knox and Calvin. Those of the Scotch Reformer alluded to in Calvin's answer, have been lost and the letters of the Reformer of Geneva have not had a better fate. Dr. McCrie, the learned historian of Knox, affords no explanation of the loss of this precious correspondence, which leaves in history a void so much to be regretted.

grieves me that anything which has fallen from my lips should have made such an impression on your mind, as to lead you to suppose that you were taxed with craft or bad faith, things which I judge the most alien to your character. Banish then that apprehension or that inquietude.

I come now to your letter, which was lately brought to me by a pious brother who has come here to pursue his studies. I rejoice exceedingly, as you may easily suppose, that the gospel has made such rapid and happy progress among you. That they should have stirred up violent opposition against you is nothing new. But the power of God is the more conspicuously displayed in this, that no attacks either of Satan or of the ungodly have hitherto prevented you from advancing with triumphant constancy in the right course, though you could never have been equal to the task of resistance, unless He who is superior to all the world had held out to you from heaven a helping hand. With regard to ceremonies, I trust, even should you displease many, that you will moderate your rigour. Of course it is your duty to see that the church be purged of all defilements which flow from error and superstition. For it behoves us to strive sedulously that the mysteries of God be not polluted by the admixture of ludicrous or disgusting rites. But with this exception, you are well aware that certain things should be tolerated even if you do not quite approve of them. I am deeply afflicted, as you may well believe, that the nobles of your nation are split into factions,[1] and it is not without reason that you are more distressed and tormented, because Satan is now plotting in the bosom of your church, than you were formerly by the commotions stirred up by the French. But God is to be intreated that he may heal this evil also. Here

---

[1] Among the noblemen the most devoted to the cause of the Reformation, were the Earls of Arran and Murray who maintained an intercourse with Calvin : " The Earl of Arran would have written to you but he was absent. James the brother of the queen salutes you. The old man is the only one of those who frequent the court who sets himself against its impiety. And yet even he is fascinated as well as the others, inasmuch as he fears to hurl down by violent means that idol." *Knoxus Calvino*, 24th October, 1561. In this same letter, Knox announced the re-establishment of the mass in the chapel of Mary Stuart at Holyrood, and asked if it was not the duty of the Reformed, to abolish this last relic of superstition in Scotland.

we are exposed to many dangers. Nothing but our confidence
in the divine protection exempts us from trepidation, though we
are not free from fears.

Farewell, distinguished sir and honoured brother. May the
Lord always stand by you, govern, protect, and sustain you
by his power. Your distress for the loss of your wife justly
commands my deepest sympathy.[1] Persons of her merit are not
often to be met with. But as you have well learned from what
source consolation for your sorrow is to be sought, I doubt not
but you endure with patience this calamity. You will salute
very courteously all your pious brethren. My colleagues also
beg me to present to you their best respects.

[*Calvin's Lat. corresp.*, Opera, ix. p. 201.]

DXCI.—To Christopher Goodman.[2]

Pious admonitions on the occasion of the death of Knox's wife.

Geneva, *23d April*, 1561.

Your letter was for many reasons exceedingly agreeable to
me. The excuses which you make for your long silence were
quite superfluous, for I am not wont to exact from my friends
the task of writing to me, and I am thoroughly convinced that

---

[1] Knox had just lost his first wife, Margery Bowes, who had been the companion
of his exile on the continent. This domestic grief was announced to Calvin by
Goodman in a letter of the 13th February, 1561. " Our brother Knox has just been
bereaved of his wife. He himself, feeble in body but robust in mind, never flinches
from labours. His arrival in Scotland was very seasonable, and his presence there
just now is not less necessary. I pray that the course of his life may be prolonged
for years, that his services may profit his country and the church." (Vol. de Geneve,
113.) Knox remained a widower two years, and married in 1564 Margaret Stewart
a daughter of Lord Ochiltree.

[2] See vol. iii. p. 37. Associated with the vicissitudes of Knox's life on the continent,
Goodman returned in 1559 to England. He repaired to Scotland the year following,
and united his efforts with those of the Lords of the Congregation for the establishment of the Reformation in his country. McCrie, *Life of Knox*, 1847, notes, p. 408.
In a letter to Calvin already quoted, he drew a gloomy picture of the state of Scotland under the authority of Mary Stuart : " Impiety, pride, avarice, and luxury, have
seized upon nearly all, and abound in all places. People find in fine what fruits they
reap from the female government they have set up and extolled to the skies." *Geneve*,
vol. 113.

I shall not cease to hold a place in your affections. Still I receive those excuses with much pleasure, because they are so
many proofs of the tender solicitude you experience lest I
should fancy myself neglected by you. Though I am not a
little grieved to hear that our brother Knox has been bereaved
of his affectionate wife, I rejoice nevertheless that he has so far
mastered his affliction as not to suffer it to prevent him from
strenuously discharging his duty to Christ and the church. It
is no small relief to him that he has found in you a most faithful and very fitting fellow-workman ; nor in truth do I see why,
in so great a penury of labourers, you can possibly abandon your
present sphere of usefulness. On the contrary, that penury,
which you so justly deplore, ought to stir up both you and
others to continued and courageous exertion. And if necessity
has been styled the sharpest spur to activity, it ought certainly
to be so in an especial manner in the work of the Lord, in the
accomplishment of which we know that our efforts will not be
unavailing, however much the zeal of the children of the world
may often be defeated in the attainment of its object. It is my
advice then, most excellent brother, that you should persevere
until at last, due provision being made for its ministers, God
shall more firmly establish the Scottish Church.

Farewell, most worthy sir and honoured brother. May the
Lord direct you by the spirit of wisdom and fortitude, and bless
all your labours. My fellow-pastors salute you.

[*Calvin's Lat. corresp.*, Opera, ix. p. 150.]

DXCII.—To the Church of Aix.[1]

Duty of Christians to endure persecution without murmuring and without resistance.

GENEVA, *1st May,* 1561.

DEARLY BELOVED SEIGNEURS AND BRETHREN :—Be persuaded
all of you, that having heard of the extortions and acts of

---

[1] To the brethren of Aix in Provence. The Church of Aix, one of the first of that
country of Provence, which saw spring up in a single year the churches of Cabrières

violence that have been committed against several of you, we are touched with such compassion as the fraternal tie which binds us together requires. This we protest that you may not suppose that, because we are in peace and removed from these blows, we therefore are bolder in exhorting you to patience, seeing that the evil does not affect ourselves. Now though sorrow is common to us with all mankind, yet it is our duty to restrain and bridle it, and give such counsels to one another as that He who has all authority over us may be obeyed in simplicity. We are well aware that it is a plausible and specious opinion that it is lawful for us to avenge ourselves on a mutinous populace, because this is not resisting the order of justice; nay, that the laws themselves arm both great and small against robbers. But whatever reasons and sophistical excuses may be alleged, still our whole duty consists in practising the lesson which the sovereign Master has taught us, viz: to possess our souls in patience. And in truth it is the best and safest defence we can have to conceal ourselves under his shadow when we are assailed by such storms. Now it is by this resisting evil by force of arms that we prevent him from coming to our relief. And it is for that reason St. Paul, to moderate our passions, exhorts us to give place to anger, relying on the promise which God has given to sustain and protect his people after their enemies shall have vented all their rage. If what has taken place astonishes you, wait till God show you by examples what has always been known; viz: not only that the blood of the faithful will cry out for vengeance, but will form a good and fertilizing seed for the multiplication

and Mérindol, and sixty churches organized between the Durance, the Rhone, and the sea, had at first for its pastor a nobleman of Dauphiné, Claude de la Boissière. It grew up in trials and was confirmed by martyrdom. The Sire de Flassans, consul of the city in 1561, having brought the authorities to decide that the Reform should be expelled, "that was the cause," says Theodore Beza, "that not only several noblemen and other notable persons were expelled with great violence, but also that some were murdered by the fury of the population." *Hist. Eccl.*, vol. i. p. 891. It was under these distressing circumstances that Calvin, addressing the persecuted church, recommended to it patience and submission. His voice was listened to. We read in the answer of the Church of Aix to Calvin (29th May 1561): "May God give us grace in the mean time to keep in memory and observe your holy admonitions, which with great good will we all desire to hear, learn, and submit to, as much as it shall be in our power. May the Lord reward you for your labour, and bless you with every blessing." (Library of Geneva, vol. 196.)

of the church. It is not without a cause that the Scriptures insist so much on our correcting our hastiness, when we reflect how difficult it is for us to do God the honour of leaving him to do his own work in his own manner, and not according to our wishes. For though we have been so often taught that he will build up his church in a miraculous manner, we cannot suffer him to employ either stone or morter without gnashing our teeth if he does not proceed according to our likings. Now the times are such that we should labour on the one hand and suffer on the other. We call it labouring to bear ourselves manfully and overlook all obstacles when the question is to do our duty. For it were better a hundred fold to die than to flinch. But that does not prevent us from suffering with patience, and, guided by a spirit of meekness, from defeating by our silent endurance all the furious attacks of our enemies. If you accept this counsel, we have assured confidence in God, that ere long his hand will appear as your safeguard. Whereupon, dearly beloved seigneurs and brethren, we entreat him to conduct you in a spirit of prudence and virtue, and make you prosper in all good to the end that his name be more and more glorified in you.

[*Fr. Copy.—Library of Paris, Dupuy.* Vol. 102.]

DXCIII.—To Bullinger.[1]

Intrigues of Vergerio in Germany—Portrait of the King of Navarre—Progress **of** the gospel—Ardour of the French Protestants—Popular massacres.

GENEVA, 24th *May*, 1561.

I do not deny, my dearest sir and honoured brother, that my negligence is sometimes the cause why I write to you less fre-

[1] The year 1561, signalized by the first edicts of toleration, marks the culminating point of the progress of the Reformation in France. From all quarters of the kingdom they wrote to Calvin to ask him for new ministers, and Geneva was incapable of answering so many multiplied demands. The court itself, by the impulsion of the able but fickle Catharine de Medicis, showed itself favourable to the cause of the gospel, and thought of bringing together the preachers of the two religions in a solemn conference. There was for a moment even talk of calling Calvin to Paris. But the part of conciliator between the two rival churches did not suit the austere Reformer, and was in vain attempted by Th. Beza.

quently than I ought. I may assert, however, with truth, that three days never elapse without my feeling a desire to write to you about something, if an opportunity presented itself; but during the greater part of a month no one left this for your city to whom I could safely entrust a letter. An envoy of the king, indeed, in consequence of our old friendship, liberally offered me his services. But I can hardly bring myself to trust him, unless I were pressed by a more urgent necessity; for, though he is a man of probity, the office which he discharges often compels him to forget what is due to Christ. At present, I was about to write to you at greater length by Liner, if my health had permitted; but a pain in my side was too violent to admit of my making any effort. Vergerio, from mercenary motives, has procured an embassy for his nephew, in order to throw every thing into confusion. I wish you could impartially see, as I do, the effrontery of that busybody. Either there will be no religion solidly established in France, or the chief points of our doctrine will be maintained intact. I wish we could have as much confidence in the final regulation of the business. The King of Navarre is now as sluggish and versatile, as he has been always a liberal promiser; he lacks good faith and constancy. For though now and then he seems to show some sparks of a manly temper, and even flashes out into zeal, yet a moment after this flame becomes extinct. And when this fit comes on him, from time to time, he is as much to be feared as an advocate who betrays his cause. Add to that, he is wholly taken up with amorous intrigues, and a woman versed in these arts has found among the ladies of the court wherewith completely to entrap him. This story has got wind, and is the theme of the conversation of all the young gallants. Respecting these things I have reproved him with as much freedom and sincerity as I would have any individual of my own flock. Beza has handled him with not more reserve. But in listening patiently to our reproaches, and without flying into a passion, he fancies he has sufficiently acquitted himself of his duty. The Admiral is the only one on whose fidelity we can count. A colleague of ours, also, is most active in stirring up his zeal. This colleague I sent to him without consulting any body, lest any part of the

odium of the transaction should fall upon our senate. He
preaches publicly to crowded audiences at no great distance
from the palace. All our adversaries keep bawling that such
audacity is not to be tolerated. The queen entreats him, coaxingly, to desist, but to no purpose. He has determined to brave
every thing rather than flinch. The queen, moreover, did not
hesitate to say that all remedies would be useless unless I were
sent for. It is incredible with what fervent zeal our brethren
are urging forward greater progress. Pastors are everywhere
asked for from among us with as much eagerness as the priestly
functions are made the object of ambition among the Papists.
Those who are in quest of them besiege my doors, and pay their
court to me as if I held a levee. They vie with one another in
pious rivalry, as if the condition of Christ's kingdom were in a
state of undisturbed tranquillity. On our part, we desire as
much as it lies in our power to comply with their wishes, but
our stock of preachers is almost exhausted. We have even
been obliged to sweep the workshops of the working classes to
find individuals with some tincture of letters and pious doctrine
to supply this necessity. Certain outbreaks displease us, which
it is extremely difficult to moderate. In many towns, as no private building was capable of containing the multitude, they
have usurped the temples. And though they are everywhere
preaching all over Guienne, without any public disturbance,
we should have preferred nevertheless that they had followed a
line of conduct that we deemed more expedient. Nor are they
dismayed by those atrocious edicts in which the king commands
all the edifices in which a meeting may have been held to be
razed to the ground, and those who have attended it to be
punished as rebels. But there is greater liberty in Guienne.
The Parliament of Paris, which has extorted this last edict,
fulminates against our brethren with the most frightful violence.
In twenty cities, or thereabouts, the godly have been massacred
by the infuriated mob. Respecting these butcheries no investigation has been instituted, except at Beauvais. At Paris,
when the populace attacked tumultuously the house of a courageous nobleman, and he, by the aid of his friends, repelled
that furious assault, twelve individuals were killed and forty

wounded. A decree was immediately passed that he should be summoned to compear, and unless he constituted himself prisoner before the expiration of three market days, that he should be condemned by default. Now, certainly, if ever, it is the moment to implore God that he would be mindful of his unfortunate flock, and speedily come to their aid by his marvellous power to appease these storms. Perhaps ere long we shall hear of some change for the better. In the mean time, it behoves us to be prepared for enduring even worse extremities.

[*Lat. Copy.—Library of Geneva.* Vol. 107 *a.*]

DXCIV.—To AMBROSE BLAURER.[1]

News from France—Mission of new ministers—Rage of the Parliaments—Lutheran Intolerance.

GENEVA, *May,* 1561.

The state of affairs in France is not so settled as you imagine. The King of Navarre is still as pusillanimous as ever. Something is elicited from time to time from the queen-mother, but whatever she concedes is full of deceit and treachery. In many cities the Papists have broken out into tumults, not without bloodshed. At Paris, they have been twice vigorously repressed and severely handled. The court which is called the Parliament not only dissembles, but seems to consider it as an advantage to kindle animosity against us. With that it is incredible how far and wide the kingdom of God is spreading. From all quarters demands for ministers are addressed to us, and though we have no more to send, yet such is the importunity of those who ask, that we must choose certain ministers from the lower ranks of the people. The Parliament of Toulouse is more atrocious than that of Paris. Many are still in prison there. Some were burned not long ago. Unless the Queen of Navarre, who takes a much more courageous and manly attitude than her husband, had made opposition, many churches would

---

[1] A fragment, without date, and of which the beginning is a wanting, May, 1561.

have been cruelly afflicted. We should have but very slight hopes, were it not that God in establishing the kingdom of his son is wont, from perplexed beginnings, to bring more joyful issues. When I perceive springing up in the hearts of all the godly an invincible alacrity which yields to no terrors, I endure with greater confidence.

In the mean time, the Lutherans do not cease to give way to their extravagant follies. I have resolved in future to be a silent spectator of their Midianitish battles, because these men can in no way be so effectually destroyed as by their own violence. Brentz would have consulted better for his own reputation by holding his peace. Now he has broken out with such a degree of stolidity and folly that he has brought on himself more disgrace than his enemies could have wished. Certainly it is impossible that this last act will not render his interment disgraceful.

[*Lat. Copy.—Library of Zurich, Hottinguer.*—F. 43, p. 435.]

DXCV.—To the Admiral de Coligny.[1]

Pious exhortations—Renewed recommendation of Geneva.

Geneva, *May,* 1561.

MONSEIGNEUR :—We have to praise God for having prospered the journey of the man you demanded.[2] I doubt not but you have found him such as you desired, and have discovered by experience that he seeks faithfully to discharge his duty. As I know not in what nor for how long a time you intend to employ him, I shall, on that point, wait for a declaration of your good pleasure. In the meantime, Monseigneur, I pray you not to be weary in the pursuit of so good and holy a work, to which we ought to devote a hundred lives if we had them. I partly comprehend the difficulties and obstacles which might arrest you,

---

[1] Without date. The end is wanting, May 1561.

[2] The minister, John Raymond Merlin, from Romans in Dauphiné, surnamed M. de Monroy. "Master Jehan Merlin was sent to the house of the Admiral at court, who had written to have a person in such a place."—Registres de la Compagnie, ann., 1561.

or cause you to turn bridle. You feel, by experience, far more of them, but you know, Monseigneur, that in placing your stay upon Him, who has set you to work, you shall never be frustrated in your expectations. It is true, that to fortify yourself to serve him constantly, you must look higher than the world, as the Apostle also exhorts us to cast our anchor in heaven. But whatever happens, God will always cause to prosper the service which we shall offer him with unconstrained courage. I have a shrewd notion that the devil is brewing some mischief under ground, in order to produce fresh disorders. But on the other hand, I trust, that God will do his own work in some extraordinary fashion. Not that I approve of the ardour of certain persons who are in too great a haste. But since I cannot moderate their impetuosity, I shut my eyes, not knowing what God intends to do ; unless it be to cast down all human policy, in casting down by foolishness the sly devices which people anticipate on the part of the crafty. In a word, I trust that though the king will go to seek the cardinal,[1] God will draw near to him and to his people, in such a manner that these shall never be able to remove far from him. In the mean time, it is our duty to march in the path which he points out to us.

I must, also, drop one word in your private ear, Monseigneur, touching the affair[2] about which I sent to you a written memorial. If you see that the matter is followed up, I entreat you to take care that we be not forgotten in it. I believe this town recommends itself to your attention upon higher grounds. But what is certain is, that you cannot procure the good of this town without serving at the same time the interests of the king. For though it seems to be of small importance, yet what is small is not always to be despised. . . .

[*Fr. Orig.—Library of Paris, Dupuy.* Vol. 102.]

[1] Young King Charles and the court were about to go to Rheims for the fêtes of the coronation which was performed by the Cardinal Lorraine, on the 13th June, 1561.

[2] See p. 166. The point in question was to have Geneva included in the renewal of the alliance between the King of France and the Swiss Cantons.

DXCVI.—To the King of Navarre.[1]

Keen censure of the foibles of this monarch.

GENEVA, *May*, 1561.

SIRE :—Though by the letter which you were pleased to write to me lately, you have given me permission and boldness to continue to give such exhortations as necessity might call for, nevertheless I could very much have wished not to enter on a subject which it is possible will not at first sight be very agreeable to you. But I pray you, sire, to reflect on what St. Paul says, that we are sometimes constrained to make sad those whom we desire to make glad, and even if they are grieved for a short time, it is for the purpose of causing them a hundred times more joy than if we had left them in repose, or lulled them into a mortal sleep. And in fact, sire, in your wisdom you would judge that I should be both a traitor and disloyal to you, if in speaking in the name of God, who commands not to spare kings, I did not frankly remonstrate with you about what cannot and should not be dissembled. I know what modesty and discretion we should make use of, in order not to advance rashly and at random things of which we have not a proper knowledge. But at the same time the facts of which I have to give you notice are but too much divulged, and a great deal more than I could have wished. St. Ambrose complains with great justice in some passages of his writings that the world suffers

[1] Letter without any date, written probably at the same period as that one addressed to Bullinger, (25 May, 1561,) in which we remark this severe judgment pronounced on the King of Navarre :—" The King of Navarre is now as sluggish and versatile as he has been always a liberal promiser; he lacks good faith and constancy. For though now and then he seems to show some sparks of a manly temper, and even flashes out into zeal, yet a moment after this flame becomes extinct. Add to this, that he is wholly taken up with amorous intrigues, and a woman versed in these arts has found among the ladies of the court wherewith completely to entrap him." Informed by the ministers of Paris of the foibles of this prince, Calvin laid before him his duties with a pious freedom. · " Respecting these things, I have reproved him with as much freedom and sincerity as I would have reproved any individual of my own flock. Beza has handled him with not more reserve; but in listening patiently to our reproaches, and without flying into a passion, he fancies he has sufficiently acquitted himself of his duty," etc.

little children to hear, see, and speak; and it would wish to render the servants of God deaf, blind, and dumb, though a special charge has been given to them to watch, spy, question, and cry aloud, as it were, by sound of trumpet. I hope, sire, and feel persuaded that you will not be of the number of those, but that you will believe that I have not been for slight reasons moved to declare to you the deep distress I feel on learning that you have been gained, by very bad means, to a great many things which you ought to have opposed strongly and steadfastly. I only write to you, sire, what is the common talk, and with which the ears of too many have been filled. What is whispered about is that some foolish amours prevent you from doing your duty, or cool in part your ardour in the discharge of it, and that the devil has agents that seek neither your good nor honour, who by such allurements strive to draw you over to their party, or to coax you that they may not be disturbed in their plots and intrigues. If you are angry, sire, that they should entertain such an opinion of you, I pray you to reflect on the number of young girls that give occasion for it. I entreat you again and again, sire, to remark well what St. Peter says, that it is enough for the time past to have followed foolish lusts, pleasures, dissoluteness of unbelievers; for when you shall be no longer stained with these things, sire, not only will all be overlooked by God and his angels, but also forgotten by the world. But, on the contrary, God permits when we return to iniquity that what was blotted out should be brought to remembrance, and specially he places it to our account. I entreat you, then, sire, in the name of God, to rouse yourself up in good earnest. Know that the greatest virtue you can possess is to war against your affections, to retrench worldly pleasures, subdue the lusts which induce you to offend God, and trample under your feet the vanities that very soon lead us astray without our being aware of it. For though in the elevated position and royal rank in which you are placed it is difficult to curb one's self, yet it is most certain that the license which the great ones of the earth allow themselves is by so much the less excusable, as God has laid them under greater obligations. And the saying of Jesus Christ will needs be made good, that an account

will be asked of every one according as he has received. Nay,
I beseech you, sire, now to apply it for your own instruction,
for among the other distinguished favours which have been con-
ferred on you in times past, you are anew established in a position which ought to incite you more than ever to keep yourself
carefully on your guard. For not only you have to support
the charge of the public weal, but God has ordained you as a
father to relieve all his poor followers, and send them your
assistance, so that they may be able with perfect freedom to
serve and honour him in purity; nay, what is more, has appointed
you to be the steward of his truth, of pure and true religion,
of the sovereign right which belongs to him, to be obeyed by
all, and that all should regulate their conduct according to his
will.   This is a burden so weighty that there is not a creature
who would not find much difficulty in bearing it, and the devil
lays so many traps that one must be aided by singular grace
from God, in order not to sink under it.   So much the more it
behoves you, sire, to put forth all your energy, to divest yourself of all inward hindrances, in order to give yourself up more
freely to the discharge of this noble and holy commission, so as
not only to be approved of by good men, but found irreprehen-
sible before the heavenly Judge, that you may receive the crown
of glory and immortality which is more precious than all the
empires of this earth.   In the mean time, sire, though I doubt
not but you see the snares that are laid, and the nets that are
stretched out to surprise and circumvent you, and the intrigues
that are hatching, all tending to bring back that disorderly
state of things from which we fancy we have escaped, nevertheless my duty obliges me to entreat you to be vigilant and attentive in order to defeat them.

Sire, having humbly commended myself to your indulgent
favour, I pray our Lord to have you in his keeping, to direct
you in the spirit of wisdom, uprightness, and constancy, and
increase you in all prosperity to the end that you may glorify
his name.

[*Fr. Orig.—Library of Parss, Dupuy.* Vol. 102.]

DXCVII.—To the Church of Nimes. [1]

Ecclesiastical troubles, and counsels how to remedy them.

GENEVA, *1st June,* 1561.

The love of God, the Father, and the grace of our Lord Jesus Christ, be always upon you by the communication of the Holy Spirit.

Dearly beloved seigneurs and brethren, we have seen your letters, and heard the report which has been sent us by you, as well as the contents of the documents which M. Mutonis had brought for his justification.[2] On the other hand, having received some accounts of a purport somewhat different, and having duly considered all, we see to our great regret that your church is split into factions, and that every one holds out too stiffly for his own party. Now, you know, that the foundation of a church is unity, and also that it is kept up only by brotherly love and concord. Thus one can look for nothing but dispersion and

---

[1] To our very dear seigneurs and brethren, the overseers and deacons of the Church of Nimes. Glorious metropolis of the Reformed churches of the south, the church of Nimes came into existence in persecution and was inaugurated by martyrs. The first fires that were kindled against the Protestants had their origin in this city in 1537. " At Nimes, no obscure city of Languedoc, a new act of cruelty of the wicked has burst out on the poor dispersed brethren that have taken up their residence there. Two were burned, many thrown into prison, who are in danger of their lives," &c.— (Vol. i., p. 58.) The blood of the new confessors, Maurice Sécénat and Peter de la Vau, fertilized some years later (1551-1555) the field on which was destined to rise one of the most powerful churches of the Reform. It had for first pastor Guillaume Mauget, an eloquent preacher and an intrepid missionary, who wrote to Calvin on the 12th May, 1561:—"It is very true, that they make many and grievous assaults upon us, especially in this town of Nimes. For not only the magistrates attack us, and the people threaten us, but also (which is the greatest distress we experience) our own bowels; that is, a part of our consistory rises up against us, contrary to all order and discipline."—(*Library of Geneva,* vol. 197 *a.*) Informed of the disturbances which the election of a second minister had produced in this church, Calvin addressed to the consistory the most prudent counsels. See (*Ibidem*) two letters of the Church of Nimes to Calvin, (May and August,) as well as the documents contained in the portfolio 1. and entitled: *Proceedings of the Conference held at Nimes, the 20th March, 1561, on the affair between Mutonis and Manget.*

[2] Jean Mutonis, almoner of Madame de Crussol, minister of Montagnac, near Uzes, called to Nimes by the party opposed to the minister Mauget. This election was annulled.

ruin when a door is opened for strife and contentions. And, in fact, God will always make good what has been declared by the mouth of St. Paul, that those who bite and devour one another will in the end be consumed of one another. We then entreat you, for God's sake, to beware of the crafty devices of Satan, and not to yield to bitterness of spirit, in order to support any quarrel whatsoever, unless it be that which ought to inflame and consume your hearts, when you are called to do battle with a common accord against the enemies of the truth of God. We can easily perceive that you have been too much taken up with the question of persons which has impaired the rectitude of your judgments, as our Lord well reminds us; and for that reason, you were obliged to institute lawsuits which have caused great scandal, the rather that many persons might suppose the church was troubled by some envy or emulation among its ministers. For we are inclined to suspect evil much more than good. Now, as we have not found that it would be to the advantage of our church to rake up the quarrels which ought to be set at rest by the decisions which have been adopted respecting them, we were unwilling to interfere for fear of usurping the rights of others. Even if there should be any defect in point of form in these decisions, we conceive it to be expedient to keep by the resolutions that have been adopted. Thus we pray and exhort you in the name of God not only to hush up and overlook the recollection of these differences which have but too much agitated you, but also to obliterate them entirely from your minds, that there may be nothing to prevent you from holding out the hand of fellowship to one another, and acting in concert in the discharge of your duty. The bearer has made every effort to effect his object in having the said Mutonis accorded to you for your pastor, and has not failed to insist and make replies to the best of his ability. But our remonstrances were so just that finally he was obliged to acquiesce in them, for the brethren of Uzes had anticipated you, and having obtained him with his own consent, granted with only one exception, that their choice should meet with our approbation, and because we had given them an answer by an express messenger that we should by no means think of opposing an election which they had made, and that our desire was that he should labour faithfully for their edification, we were no longer at liberty to retract our words. For if we do not come near to the virtues of St. Paul, at least, we should strive to follow them at an humble distance, and put in practice the lesson he has given us, that no one may find in our conversation at once yea and nay, to make us be judged double-minded and inconstant. We do not see, then, how the said Mutonis can disengage himself from such an obligation. At any rate, it would have been a great shame for us to vary in our opinion, since we had already sent off the letters, and this apology we make, no doubt, you will accept. Now, for the present, we see nothing better for you than to listen peaceably to the instructions of our brother, M. Mauget, and seeing his labours profit among you, to take courage to further the work of your salvation. We should· not have failed to send you our brother, M. d'Anduze,[1] were it not that some of our society are absent and another is ill; but we trust that in the course of three months we shall have a better opportunity, and then we shall not fail to prove to you the desire we have of coming to your aid. If God grants us this favour that he shall go to visit you when he is on the spot, and shall have remained there some time, he will deliberate with you about every thing that may be good and proper for preserving the state of your church, pacifying all dissensions, and establishing such order for the future as that you shall not relapse into similar troubles. In the mean time, we reiterate our entreaties to you to come to an amicable agreement with your pastor, for you know we are incapable of being disciples of Jesus Christ till we have a spirit of meekness. We hope that on his side he will conduct himself towards you with so much kindly feeling that you shall have no reason to be dissatisfied with him.

Whereupon, beloved seigneurs and brethren, having commended ourselves to you and to your fervent prayers, we sup-

---

[1] "The Seigneurs d'Anduze," says Beza, "made such a profession of the gospel that one of them, having retired to Geneva, there exercised the ministry for a long time, and died afterwards a minister at Nimes, in very great renown."—*Hist. Eccl.*, vol. i., p. 214. See a letter of M. d'Anduze (Pierre d'Airebondouze) to the society of Geneva, 7 April, 1571.—(*Geneva*, vol. 197 a.)

plicate our God and Father to have you in his keeping, to
govern you by the spirit of wisdom and integrity, to sustain
you by his power, and increase you in all good.

[*Fr. Copy.—Library of Paris, Dupuy.* Vol. 102.]

DXCVIII.—To JAMES STUART.[1]

He engages him to persevere in his pious efforts for the advancement of the reign of
Jesus Christ in Scotland.

GENEVA, 11*th July,* 1561.

MONSIEUR:—Though I do not know you personally, yet the
zeal and constancy you have displayed in advancing the reign
of our Lord Jesus Christ, and re-establishing the true service
of God and religion, encourage me not only to write to you but
also oblige me to confirm you in this holy purpose.   Not that I
imagine you have any need of being impelled to the work by
others, as if it were to be feared that your courage should become
weakened or damped; but because I well know that you cannot
labour so strenuously as you do to maintain the truth of God
without having to endure many assaults.   I doubt not, when on
my side I shall endeavour to aid you by some exhortations, but
you will take it in good part; as in fact those whom God has
most fortified feel but so much the more the residue of weak-

---

[1] *The superscription:* To the nobleman, James Stuart, elder brother of the Queen
of Scotland.

James Stuart, natural son of James V., and Prior of St. Andrews, played an important part in the history of Scotland during the reign of Mary Stuart.   A declared
partisan of the Reform, he was named a deputy to Mary Stuart to invite her to
return to her kingdom after the death of Francis II. her husband.   He protected her
from the excesses of the Reformed party, was created successively Earl of Mar, Earl
of Murray, and became regent in 1567.   From that time, opposed to the queen, he constantly courted the favour and support of Queen Elizabeth.   Victorious over the royal
army at Langside, (1568,) he publicly accused Mary of the murder of Darnley her
second husband, and perished himself by the hand of an assassin of the house of
Hamilton.   Robertson, the historian, while he accuses him of ingratitude towards Mary
Stuart and of servility towards Elizabeth, pays homage to his military talents and
the vigour of his administration.   Long after his death popular gratitude accorded
him the title of the *Good Regent.*

ness that is still in themselves, and desire to be so confirmed as never to faint. You have indeed given proofs of a rare virtue in shutting your eyes on all the objects of this world which might retard your efforts, or prevent you from giving yourself entirely up to combat for the cause of the gospel; but be persuaded that the devil will never cease to return to the charge, and he has an infinite number of agents whose rage is sufficiently inflamed to overturn the pure doctrine of salvation if it were in their power.

You must be prepared then to encounter many troubles, and should fortify yourself with strength from on high in order to resist them. When you shall have long pondered in your mind beforehand, that you ought never to be weary of this great work, nothing will make you astonished. The more furiously the crafty and reprobate fight against God, we ought to be the more animated to combat under the banner of our Lord Jesus Christ for our salvation, being certain of the victory. St. Paul had accomplished much, when nevertheless he protests he had not yet attained to the end, but was striving to reach it. Seeing himself drawing near to his death, he boasts that he has not combated in vain, since the crown of righteousness is prepared for him. I doubt not but God, who has begun so well to conduct you, will continue to the end, that along with courage he will also bestow on you wisdom to resist and defeat all the evil wiles and machinations of the enemy. And you have much need of it, for certain it is that the enemy is devising nothing but disloyalty and treachery.

You will also have to keep an eye on those who half counterfeit to be Christians, and yet mix up their errors and blasphemies with the truth, that you may repel them from creeping into the church, or even cast them out of it altogether, lest it should be infected by their poison, for they are plagues of the worst and most deadly kind. Wherefore we must carefully practise the exhortation of the Apostle, not to let the bitterness of evil weeds spring up, that the good seed be not corrupted by them; and as it is our duty always to be going forward in the work of God, it will be proper for you at least to keep a strong hand, that what has been well begun fall not into decay.

Whereupon, sir, having humbly commended myself to your indulgent favour, I will entreat our heavenly Father to have you in his holy keeping, to guide you by his Spirit, to do what shall be agreeable to him, and strengthen you with invincible courage.

[*Fr. Copy.—Library of Paris, Dupuy.* Vol. 102.]

DXCIX.—To the Admiral de Coligny.[1]

He pays homage to the zeal of the Admiral and the constancy of the French Protestants.

GENEVA, 11*th July,* 1561.

MONSEIGNEUR :—Though it were to be desired that the kingdom of God should make greater advances in your country, and that the gospel had a more peaceable course, nevertheless you must not think it strange if He, who conducts everything by his admirable counsel, wishes to try the patience of his people in prolonging the term of their struggle, provided only all those who hold for the good cause, break through all restraints in order to employ themselves perseveringly and unreservedly as they ought in building up the temple of God.   And in one word you will experience that he watches more than we comprehend, to cause his work to prosper.   Let us only beware of becoming weary, and though the fruit of our labours be hidden for the present, it will appear in due time.   The efforts also of the enemies of the truth ought to be an occasion for your striving still more, in order that their audacity and presumption may be

---

[1] While under the influence of the Chancellor L'Hôpital, the government showed itself less hostile to the Reformed party, and while the triumvirate was formed for the defence of Catholicism and the extermination of heresy, the Admiral de Coligny, redoubling his energy, demanded free preaching of the Reform in France. " The admiral is the only one on whose fidelity we can count.   A colleague of ours also is most active in stirring up his zeal. . . He preaches publicly to crowded audiences at no great distance from the palace.   All our adversaries keep bawling that such audacity is not to be tolerated.   The queen coaxingly entreats him to desist, but to no purpose. He has determined to brave everything rather than to flinch. . . It is incredible with what fervent zeal our brethren are urging forward greater progress." *Calvin to Bullinger,* 24th May, 1561.

checked and defeated by the constancy which God shall have bestowed on you. It is much to be perfectly assured that whatever trouble they give you, the issue will be fortunate for you and turn to their confusion. God also holds out before your eyes a fine mirror for your encouragement, when amid fears and threats the poor brethren of France never tire in holding on their course. The state of things there is in great confusion, but we trust that God will confound the most wily, and that they will find themselves caught in their own nets. He who ought to take the lead is so indifferent that it is impossible to be more so.[1]

The enemies are more furious than ever to ruin all, if God did not bridle their rage. Even that mad fool who sometimes made war on you has lately taken about three hundred of your men prisoners in the neighbourhood of Chinon. But he received strict orders to set them all at liberty and repair immediately to court, with sharp threats if he should show himself restive.[2] At least this is a slight relief which God has afforded his children. And so, Monseigneur, being animated by such examples, you should not connect yourself with those who acquit themselves badly of their duty, but you ought rather to strive to make them ashamed and correct their cowardice, and whatever resistance Satan oppose to you, you should surmount it all by the power of Him who has promised that our faith will be victorious over the world. Reflect also that you have not only to resist open enemies, but also those of your own house who introduce themselves under false pretexts. And forasmuch as in these beginnings many fickle and ungovernable characters will permit themselves too much licence, it will be the more necessary for you to exercise a strict police. I have known a young soldier of your nation, who has not, I believe, his match

---

[1] The King of Navarre, seduced by the artful promises of the Guises, and deaf to the energetic representations of his wife, showed himself every day less zealous for the cause of the Reformation.

[2] The seigneur thus designated appears to be Jacques d'Armagnac, Duke of Nemours, the declared enemy of the Admiral de Coligny. A recent edict of the king (April 1561) had enjoined the setting at liberty of all persons imprisoned for the sake of religion. The Parliament of Paris, inexorable in its rigour against the Protestants, refused to register the edict.

for overweening self-conceit. I have no doubt but he will be intermeddling to embroil matters as much as he can. If such people were not kept in check, there would result very soon a confusion that it would be impossible to remedy. But I hope that, in everything and everywhere, God will provide you with prudence and courage to bring to a successful conclusion what he has given you the grace to commence.

Monseigneur, having humbly commended myself to your indulgent favour, I will supplicate our heavenly Father to increase in you more and more the gifts of his Spirit, that thereby his name may be glorified, to prosper you in all your actions, and to keep you under his protection.

[*Lat. Copy.—Library of Geneva.* Vol. 107.]

DC.—To the Pastors of Zurich.

A collection in favour of the Evangelical Churches of Piedmont.

GENEVA, 14*th July*, 1561.

These brethren have come from the valley of Angrogne, and the places in its neighbourhood, to ask for some relief in their necessities. In their distress we have not reproached them for having injudiciously taken up arms, although we had certainly dissuaded them from having recourse to such a measure. They are reduced to such utter destitution that their sad condition might well move to compassion all those who have any feelings of humanity. We have not been able to make up a considerable sum for them, for the third part of the foreigners who sojourn here have at present taken their flight from the city. None but the poorer classes have been left. We have, nevertheless, contracted a debt of four thousand crowns, and, at the present moment, we have acted well, if not very wisely. He who should have discharged this obligation is deaf. Thus (what will not redound greatly to the honour of the King of Navarre) we have paid down what in all justice he ought to have placed to his own account. They will now proceed as they have been

directed to you. It would have been foolish to commend them
to Beza. A letter to you it was not in my power to refuse them.
If you should judge it proper, since it is their wish to pass
through Schaffhausen, you will direct and assist them with your
kindness and authority.

Farewell, most excellent sirs and most honoured brethren.
May the Lord always govern, protect, and bless you.

Yours,   JOHN CALVIN

In the name and by the order of the brethren.

[*Lat. Copy.—Arch. of Zurich, Gest.* VI., 106, p. 839.]

DCI.—TO THE CHURCH OF SAUVE.[1]

Energetic censure of the acts of vandalism committed by a minister of this church.

GENEVA, *July,* 1561.

DEARLY BELOVED SEIGNEURS AND BRETHREN :—If every one
practised rightly the rule which the Holy Spirit has given us by
the mouth of St. Paul, to walk circumspectly and with all modesty,
so as not to give to others any handle for offence, you would
not be in your present distress, nor should we be at a loss how
to counsel and exhort you to remedy a scandal which has already
taken place, and provide that such acts should not occur for the
future. We speak of the foolish deed which was performed at
Sauve in burning idols and pulling down a cross. We are very
much surprised at such temerity in a man whose duty it was to
moderate and restrain others. For, as we have heard, he not

---

[1] On the back of the letter in Calvin's hand : "Against the temerity of the preacher
of Sauve." A letter without date, but written in the month of July, 1561, as is indicated by the answers of the minister of the Church of Sauve, of the 31st August, 1561.
Under the administration of the precarious toleration, inaugurated by the accession
of Charles IX., excesses to be regretted were committed by the Protestants of Languedoc and Dauphiny. Several Catholic churches were sacked. The Reformed population of Sauve, a small town of the Cevennes, committed acts of sacrilegious
violence which Calvin energetically blamed. Deposed by the provincial synod of
Sommières, maintained by the consistory of Sauve, the minister Sartas, the principal author of these excesses, humbled himself before the society of Geneva, and obtained from them a pardon, as he assured them that he had done nothing but out
of a worthy zeal to prevent many scandals."—*Library of Geneva,* vol. 197 *a.*

only gave his consent to the deed (which was already too bad a thing), but he stirred up the people, being the most mutinous of them all. Now, if he had forgotten himself, being surprised by some thoughtless ardour, the least thing he could do was to acknowledge his fault and profess himself sorry for it, especially as he had been warned and exhorted. But to maintain that he acted so with a good conscience is an instance of intolerable obstinacy. If he will have us believe such a thing, let him prove from the word of God what grounds he had for this proceeding. But we know quite the contrary. God has never given commandment, except to each one in his own house, and in public to those he arms with authority, to cast down idols. Now it is not without cause that it was expressly said to the people of Israel, *when thou shalt have come into the land which thy God giveth thee*, and shalt possess it, *then*, etc. Thus let this firebrand show us by what title he is lord of the land where he has issued his order for burning. Now, inasmuch as God has not authorized him to do this, his good conscience, as he calls it, is nothing else than the good intention of the Papists. In expressing ourselves thus, we are not become the advocates of idols, and would to God they were all banished from the world, even should it cost us our lives. But since obedience is better than sacrifice, we have to consider what is lawful, and restrain ourselves within bounds. For it is to act like a horse that has broke loose from the reins to attempt more than what our vocation warrants. We verily believe that Daniel and his companions, and Ezekiel, and many others, were quite as zealous as this poor man who boasts himself in the extravagance of his self-conceit. One thing is certain, as long as they were at Babylon they contented themselves with showing their contempt of idol worship, without usurping any power which did not belong to them. It were high time that this poor man, having so greatly forgotten himself, should hold down his head. But it is astonishing that he should be so stupid as not to think of the handle which he has given to the crafty to ruin every thing. But it is the height of pride and stubbornness obstinately to persist in vindicating himself, and not to yield to good counsel. Now, since such is the case, dear brethren, we entreat you, having compassion on the poor churches, in order not to expose them to massacre with your eyes open, that you would disavow this act, and declare openly to the people that have been led astray, that you have separated yourselves from him who was the principal instigator of it, and that for his rebellious conduct you cut him off from your society. Had he submitted and deigned to listen to reason, he might have been treated with more indulgence. But since he is stiff-necked, you cannot spare him without a violation and infraction of all order. It is possible, however, that God may tame his stubbornness, as we humbly supplicate him to do, as also to have you in his keeping, to fortify and govern you by his Spirit, while we heartily commend ourselves to you and to your fervent prayers.

[*Lat. Copy.—Library of Geneva.* Vol. 107 *a.*]

DCII.—To the King of Navarre. [1]

Recommendation of Theodore Beza.

GENEVA, 14*th August*, 1561.

SIRE :—We have received the letters which your majesty has been pleased to write to us. We cannot sufficiently thank you for the kind affection which you deign to entertain towards us, and we esteem ourselves very happy to have a prince like your majesty favourably disposed towards us. As to the excellent

---

[1] Docile to the counsels of the Chancellor L'Hôpital, the court had just decided on the opening of a solemn conference between the two religions at Poissy. The Protestant princes, zealous to draw thither the most distinguished ministers, wrote to the seigneurs of Geneva to ask them for Calvin or Theodore Beza. The seigneury refused the former, and consented to grant the second. Informed of these favourable dispositions, the King of Navarre wrote to the magistrates of Geneva to thank them, and hurry the departure of Theodore Beza. " We pray you again and again as affectionately as we can, to be pleased to grant him permission, and send him off as soon as it will be possible, . . . being assured that all due honour, welcome, and good treatment will be shown him, such as his probity, erudition, and talents deserve. In this you will, moreover, do the king, my seigneur, the queen, his mother, as well as myself particularly, a very sensible pleasure.—Spon, *Hist. de Geneve*, vol. ii., p., 95 ; *note de Gautier.* Beza had already quitted Geneva (14 August, 1561,) when they there received the king's letter, which Calvin was charged to answer in the name of the seigneury.

Theodore Beza, our good pastor and minister, we are forced to confess, sire, that it has been to our great regret that he undertook this journey; not that we were not both ready and willing, sire, to employ for your service our slender means as far as they can extend, but we know what loss both the church and the school will suffer by his absence.[1] But if it please God that his labour produce such fruits, as we are bound to hope, we know very well that it becomes us to forget all private considerations. Now we owe much more than that to Jesus Christ, from whom we derive every thing, and to his church. So that, in acquitting ourselves of a part of our duty, we have been extremely glad at rendering a service to your majesty. Now we shall always esteem it a great advantage for us to have the means of doing any thing which will be agreeable to you, and we pray you, sire, to deign to take into your custody a part of our treasures in the person of him whom we have no need to recommend to you.

Sire, having very humbly commended ourselves to your indulgent favour, we will supplicate our heavenly Father to preserve your majesty in his present state, to have you under his protection, and increase you in all good.

Your very humble and affectionate servants,

THE SYNDICS AND COUNCIL OF GENEVA.

[*Lat. Orig., in Calvin's hand.—Arch. of Geneva*, 1561.]

DCIII.—TO PETER MARTYR.[2]

He exhorts him to repair to the religious conferences which are about to be held in France.

GENEVA, *17th August,* 1561.

The person who lately accompanied our friend Beza to your neighbourhood is again returning to you. He is the bearer of

---

[1] Theodore Beza was at the same time Rector and Professor of the new Academy of Geneva.

[2] At the invitation which was addressed to him by Catherine de Medicis, desirous to hear one of her most eloquent countrymen in the religious conferences, which they

a letter from the king of Navarre to your senate, in which he earnestly begs and entreats that you should be speedily sent off, and in his own name he pledges that this will be very acceptable to the king and his mother. Beza has set out without having obtained a safe-conduct, and from the village to which I had retired he was escorted by my brother to the nearest relay of the couriers, that he might pass through less noticed by means of the post-horses. With regard to yourself, I make no doubt but that you have fully resolved not to play the loiterer, on so important an occasion. But it will be your duty also to see that others do not occasion any delay.

I see how many things are to be regretted, and I wrote to you already, how dissatisfied I am that this business will be handled in no very liberal spirit. I do not by any means, for all that, think that this affords you a just reason for refusing your compliance; because if it is not yet God's pleasure to open a door, it is our duty to creep through the windows, or press through the smallest holes that give us entry, rather than allow an opportunity of bringing about a happy arrangement to escape us. I learn that the queen mother is so very desirous of hearing you, that it is not now in your power to put off any longer without occasioning very general complaints. And though I am persuaded that you have the matter too much at heart to require to be stimulated or encouraged by any remarks of mine, I would nevertheless have our brethren to be well reminded beforehand, that if they take any false step in the outset, they will be exposed to blame, as also if they should not be sufficiently energetic in stirring up the council. If you are resolved to undertake this mission, your shortest road will lie through Burgundy. You will not, however, I hope, consider the abridgment of your travelling fatigue of such importance, as not to pay us a visit as you pass through.

Farewell, most accomplished sir and venerable brother. Salute most affectionately in my name M. Bullinger and all your brother pastors, whom from the heart I honour. May the

were now preparing at Paris, Martyr repaired to France. He spoke but once, at the colloquy of Poissy. He was back at Zurich by the 21st of November, 1561.

Lord continue to govern you by his Spirit and enrich you with his gifts. My best wishes for your wife and family.—Yours,

JOHN CALVIN.

[*Lat. orig —Library of Geneva.* Vol. 107 *a.*]

DCIV.—To SULCER.[1]

Journey of Beza and Martyr to France—Preparations for the colloquy of Poissy— Intrigues at the court of Wurtemberg.

GENEVA, 23*d August*, 1561.

I received your letter, most accomplished sir, written to Beza, when a short while ago he had taken his departure for France. He travelled by post-horses, because it would not have been safe for him to undertake the journey openly. We could not obtain a safe conduct, as they call it, because the queen mother was unwilling to expose herself to so much unpopularity with the Pope. The king of Navarre, however, pledged his faith in a letter written to our council. Privately also the king himself, his brother the Prince of Condé, and the Admiral earnestly urged Beza not to protract his departure any longer, because he would have need to make all possible dispatch if he wished to arrive at the proper moment. They also entreated me rather to push him forward immediately than to retard him. A safe-conduct was sent some time ago to Doctor Peter Martyr, by which he is not sent for, but which enjoins all the governors of the provinces to afford him a secure journey as he passes along. The king of Navarre afterwards asked the council of Zurich the same thing which he had demanded of ours. The messenger is not yet returned, but I shall know before three days whether he will come or not.

You are surprised that none of your doctors from Germany

---

[1] As a zealous Lutheran, Sulcer wished to see some of the principal divines of the Confession of Augsburg called to the colloquy at Poissy; whilst Calvin saw in the presence of these same divines at the colloquy, an occasion of discord which the adversaries of the gospel in France could not fail to turn to their advantage. See the following letter to the King of Navarre.

have been invited to the conference, know then that matters
have not yet reached that point, that the godly are at liberty
to profess openly that they are aiming at a secession from
Popery. They dare not for the moment put publicly forward
anything else but a remedy, which they are seeking for, appeasing disturbances. There is no mention made about a change
of religion. But even if all the difficulties were removed, I
know not why it should have entered your thoughts to wish for
a thing which would ruin our auspicious beginnings. Assuredly
among the princes whom you think we ought to be careful not
to offend, the Prince of Wurtemberg is the only one who will send
his favourite Brentz, and perhaps also P——,[1] who as I hear
now holds with him the second post of honour. Hitherto Brentz
has raved more absurdly about his *ubiquity* than the whole herd
of the Papists. Now with that satellite of his he has begun to
combat more perversely the true and real faith. Certainly, unless it be our wish to afford pleasant sport to our enemies, it is
necessary by all means to take measures to prevent these furies
from breaking in on us, with lighted torches, to stir up greater
contentions than those which have hitherto invaded Germany.
For my part I had rather undergo a hundred deaths than not
oppose vigorously such pernicious counsels.

We are to have a conflict with the Papists. Let us sound the
trumpet to proclaim this war, not for stirring up intestine
divisions. I confide to you more freely these complaints, because I am perfectly aware what the Prince of Wurtemberg was
aiming at, when he sent on a mission, the nephew of Vergerio,
whose uncle was lured, as we cannot help believing, by a bribe.
Certainly he reaped some profit for his complaisance. When
the affairs shall be mature, a method of entering on some league
will be carefully meditated, but it will be one that will not
trouble our domestic tranquillity. For those who desire the
kingdom of Christ to be restored are not so senseless as knowingly to admit among them a brand of discords. For my own
part, as I am thoroughly persuaded of the sincerity of your
mind, so I make no doubt but you will easily recede from your

---

[1] The word is illegible in the manuscript.

former intention, when you shall have more closely considered the matter.

Farewell, most accomplished sir and honoured brother. May the Lord always protect and govern you, and bless your labours. You have discharged a duty agreeable to God and the church towards the Piedmontese brethren, when by your influence some relief was afforded to their necessities.—Yours,

JOHN CALVIN.

[*Lat. orig.—Library Freyo-Grynæana of Basle.* Vol. ix. p. 93.]

DCV.—TO THE KING OF NAVARRE.[1]

Warning on the subject of the Lutheran intrigues to introduce into France the Confession of Augsburg.

GENEVA, August, 1561.

SIRE :—The sad news which we have of the state of the kingdom has forced us to write to you, and beg you to open your eyes and see what must be sufficiently notorious. For even the most blinded may perceive, as if they felt with their hands, the plottings and intrigues which have been set on foot, to break off whatever has been well commenced, and overturn from one day to another all good conclusions, and bring back things to such a point, that Jesus Christ with his gospel will ere long be banished from the kingdom.[2] Now he will not suffer himself to be thus mocked, and he will know well how to take the crafty in their

---

[1] The end is wanting. For title, " To the King of Navarre, to deter him from receiving the Confession of Augsburg.'' An intrigue ably contrived by the Duke of Guise and the Cardinal of Lorraine had engaged the Duke of Wurtemberg to demand the adoption of the formulary of Augsburg, as the symbol of the Reformed churches of France.—*Hist. Eccl.*, vol. i.. p. 691. This step, provoked by the adversaries of French Protestantism, to bring on a conflict between the two grand communions of the Reformation, unhappily divided on the question of the sacraments, had already excited the inquietude of the Theologians of both parties. Always feeble and irresolute, the King of Navarre seemed to be inclined to favour the project of the Guises. In a severe message Calvin warned him, but in vain, to be on his guard against the perfidious intrigues of his enemies.

[2] The edict of July (1561), promulgated at the demand of the Cardinal of Lorraine, had just interdicted, under pain of banishment, the religious meetings of the Reformed, before the assembling of a general council.

own trap ; but in the mean time, sire, it is your duty not to permit and suffer the truth of God to be thus betrayed in the sight
of all. It is possible you may have thought to gain something
by concessions, but the evil is springing up abundantly and
gaining but too much strength ; and if you be not on your guard
disorders will arise from it, in a moment of time much more serious than you imagine, and then it will no longer be time to
remedy them, for God will take vengeance, in order to punish
the indifference of those who shall have neglected their duty,
according to the rank and degree in which he had established
them. If we speak rather sharply, sire, believe me now is the
time to do so, or never.

On the other hand, we have heard that the Duke of Wurtemberg, suborned by those whom it is not necessary to mention,
is soliciting you to employ your influence to have the Confession
of Augsburg received in France.[1] Suppose, sire, that this man
is playing on a stage his part just as it has been distributed to
him.[2] But in God's name reflect how the confession of faith
which the French churches have sworn to follow and maintain
has been ratified, and even though it had not been signed by
the blood of martyrs, yet since it has been extracted from the
pure word of God and presented to the king and his council,
you cannot reject it, nor so huddle up the matter but that God
will oppose your designs, and show you by effects that he will
be listened to and believed. With regard to the Confession of
Augsburg, how dare the Duke of Wurtemberg beg you to receive
it, when we reflect that he and his like condemn the author of
it, who is Melancthon? However, we shall leave him out of the
question, since they have forced him to play a part in speaking
of a thing of which he is entirely ignorant. The fact is, that
the most renowned persons of that party agree like dog and
cat. We are much deceived if the person who brought you the
letters be not the nephew of one Vergerio, a foreigner from

---

[1] The Duke of Wurtemberg, accompanied by two of his ministers, Brentz and
André, had met the princes of Lorraine at Saverne. " The Cardinal," says Beza,
"having made a present of some silver plate to these two good preachers, he knew
so well how to adapt himself to them, that this simple prince thought he had more
than half converted him." . . . *Hist. Eccl.*, vol. i., p. 691.

[2] There are here some words wanting in the manuscript.

Italy, and one of the most barefaced intriguers that ever existed.[1] There is another clownish apostate, Baudouin,[2] who has already apostatized three or four times from Jesus Christ, and it is just possible he may have so insinuated himself into your favour, as to deceive you with regard to his character, if you were not apprized of it. We then entreat your majesty to be on your guard amid so many snares, and again we pray you in the name of God not to allow yourself to be shaken hither and thither, in order that the word of God may be maintained unimpaired, which it is impossible to be otherwise than by preserving to it its simplicity. There is a common saying among the people about crooked loaves in a batch, which might teach you to reject those who endeavour to persuade you by dissembling pretexts. For though at first they may make you believe this or that, we declare to you in virtue of Him who has given us authority to speak, that the issue will be unfortunate, and we warn you of it in good time, fearing lest you experience.[3] . . .

[*Fr. Orig.—Library of Paris, Dupuy.* Vol. 102.]

[1] Paolo Vergerio, formerly Bishop of Capo-d'Istria di Friuli, and Legate of Pope Paul III., at Ratisbonne. Gained over to the Reform by Melancthon, he gave up his bishopric, and took up his abode in the Grisons. Being an ardent Lutheran, he was accused of having devoted himself to the propagation of the formulary of Augsburg, from motives of personal interest.

[2] See vol. i., p. 133, note 1. A Calvinist at Geneva, a Catholic at Paris, a Lutheran at Heidelberg, Baudouin had but too well merited by his religious inconstancy, the stigmatizing epithets of triple apostate ($\tau\rho\iota\alpha\pi\sigma\sigma\tau\alpha\tau\eta s$) and outcast ($\dot{\epsilon}\kappa\beta\sigma\lambda\iota\mu\sigma s$). A deserter from all communions, he had been favourably received by the King of Navarre, who counted on employing him usefully in effecting a reconciliation between the parties.

[3] Without date. The end is wanting. But the date is furnished us by a letter of Calvin to Bullinger of the 5th November, 1561, in which we remark the following passage:—" Long ago I had discovered that the devil was plotting, by clandestine arts, a thing which is now very apparent, and three months before I had carefully reminded the King of Navarre to be on his guard against snares." The letter to which he alludes in this passage is then of the month of August, 1561

DCVI.—To Theodore Beza.[1]

Death of Guillaume de Trie—Scarcity of ministers at Geneva.

GENEVA, 27th August, 1561.

I am obliged to dictate this letter to you from bed, and in the deepest affliction from the loss of my dear friend De Varennes,[2] who has hitherto been my principal stay and comfort in all my troubles. One thing affords me no slight consolation in my sorrow, which is that nothing could have been more calm than the manner of his death, which he seemed to invite with out-stretched arms as cheerfully as if it had been some delicious enjoyment. His disease was mortal from the beginning, but it was only the day before yesterday towards the evening that we began to give up all hopes. He suddenly set in order all his domestic affairs, and so expeditiously indeed that he had finished everything in less than half an hour, and yet he omitted nothing. After that, as if he had taken farewell of his illness, and had done with this earthly life, all his thoughts and conversation turned only on eternal happiness. His discourse was like that of a man in perfect health. His life was protracted till the commencement of yesterday night. For one hour only he was

---

[1] To my well beloved brother, Monsieur de Challoné, at court.

He had arrived the 20th of August, and received the most flattering welcome from the queen mother, and the principal Protestant Seigneurs. *Hist. Eccl.*, vol. i. pp. 496, 497.

[2] See vol. ii. p. 93. Guillaume de Trie, Seigneur de Varennes, was one of the most distinguished members of that French emigration, which gave to Geneva Jean de Budé, Charles de Jonvillers, and the brothers Colladon. He inhabited a house close by Calvin's in the Rue des Chanoines. From the year 1549, the period of his es- tablishment at Geneva, he had constantly lived on intimate terms with the Reformer, with whose sentiments he entirely concurred. He showed this in a particular manner by being the first to denounce to a Catholic gentleman of Lyons the heresy of Servetus, thus provoking the first judicial pursuits, which were terminated at Vienne, as at Geneva, by a capital condemnation. The letters of Guillaume de Trie to Claude Arneys his cousin, attributed without reason to Calvin himself, and inserted in the *Mémoires* de l'Abbé d'Artigny, vol. iii. p.   , are a proof with what equal horror the negations of Servetus, were regarded by both Catholics and the Reformed, a horror which caused the destruction of the unfortunate Spanish innovator.

deprived of the faculty of speech, but he showed signs of unimpaired intelligence, till he breathed his last, and he expired with such tranquillity that no one of us could mark the transition from life to death. He then is happy—I wretched.'

At your departure lately two things escaped my memory about which I had resolved to consult you. You are aware that we had changed our resolution respecting De Collonges, and determined that no successor should be appointed to replace him, and we did so because his stay with the duchess could not be of long duration. We on the contrary from the smallness of our number are unequal to our task. Three days after your departure, Anduse was laid up with the gout, and Colladon with a fever. It is necessary that Collonges and Merlin consult each other, which of the two with least inconvenience and loss can return to us as speedily as possible. The necessity of the case will be a sufficient apology. I wished to send you word in the second place, that Hugh Reni is still detained a prisoner, and that you ought to undertake the charge of having him set at liberty, otherwise with such unjust and unprincipled judges he might rot in his dungeon. There is another in nearly the same condition that I imagined had been liberated. He is the son-in-law of M. Passy, who wrote that he did not think it lawful for him to comply with the prescribed condition, nor that he should make any promise for the time to come. He does not object to be banished. His father-in-law with great earnestness commends him to your care, I too at his request; and that he may understand that his entreaties are not of small importance, you will not only undertake this office, but in your first letter you will render an account of your activity in the affair.

Farewell, most worthy brother. May the Lord assist, govern,

---

[1] We read in Beza's answer to Calvin: "This is our condition, that we should instruct one another, not less by our death than by our life. On my departure my mind presaged something unfortunate respecting our friend De Varennes. But since he has taken his departure from among us in so blessed a manner, I rejoice that I was a false prophet. For nothing evil has happened to him, except this perhaps that by his death he has left his friends in deep affliction, whom while he was alive he never offended. He has had the good fortune to go before us, and it is my desire that we should speedily follow him." 12th September 1561.

and protect you, Amen.   Salute my brethren and friends.—
Yours,
                                     CHARLES PASSELIUS.

[*Lat. orig. autogr.—Library of Gotha.*   Vol· 409, p. 90·]

DCVII.—To THEODORE BEZA.[1]

Fresh deaths at Geneva—Distrust of the Cardinals of Lorraine and Ferrara.

GENEVA, 3d *September*, 1561.

Lest I should have to mourn but for one death, three days
after that of my friend De Varennes, the oldest pastor has followed him to the tomb. We have given up all hopes respecting
the life of Baduel. Yesterday the wife of our treasurer, after
having seemed recovered from the sufferings of child birth,
died suddenly of convulsions of the nerves. And not to
go on enumerating our losses, Nicholas Ignée was suffocated
by a catarrh in the short space of nine hours. It is some
consolation that Beraud is gradually recovering, as well as
his wife, who was lately very nearly cut off by a premature
delivery. She is now, however, doing well, and her child is
alive. I lately asked you that one of your two colleagues
should return here. Contrive to see that done as speedily
as possible. If Des Gallars were at liberty, and the church
over which he has been set should suffer no detriment, we
should like him to be restored to us. But as the matter was
uncertain we have thought proper not to stir in it. Time will
show us what is proper and advantageous, but I warn you in
time; be not put off your guard by the friendship of the Cardinal
of Lorraine. His brother, the Cardinal of Ferrara[2] had also

---

[1] On his arrival at court, the 24th August, 1561, Beza had found the most favourable
welcome from the Protestant nobility, from the regent Catherine de Medicis, from the
Cardinal of Lorraine himself, who embracing him cordially said to him, "I am happy
to have a conference with you, to hear your reasons and give you mine. You will
find that I am not so black as I have been painted." *Hist. Eccl.*, vol. i. p. 497.

[2] The Cardinal Hippolite d'Este, brother-in-law of Renée of France, whom Calvin
had known at the court of Ferrara.

imposed upon me. For when he lavished his caresses on me here some thirteen years ago, he promised that he would also be one of the best of my friends. Beware then of showing yourself too much elated and too proud towards me, because you see it would be easy for me to retaliate, especially as a Legate overtops all Cardinals whatsoever.

Farewell, most excellent and worthy brother. May the Lord stand by you, govern and protect you, enrich you with all gifts, and prepare you for all battles, arm you with prudence against snares, and fortitude against terrors. Salute very carefully our brethren. All the brethren and your friends here salute you. Again, farewell.

[*Calvin's Lat. corresp.*, Opera, ix. p. 199.]

DCVIII.—To Theodore Beza.[1]

Doubts respecting the efficacy of the Colloquy of Poissy—Policy of the Romish Prelates—Criticism of the Augsburg Confession—Divers particulars.

GENEVA, 10*th September*, 1561.

The letter which you wrote to me on the 30th of August was put into my hands yesterday. While others are feeding our expectations so liberally with favourable reports, it would not be surprising if you felt ashamed of that stinginess of yours which has left us almost famished for want of news. If you desire to

---

[1] It was not without warm opposition that the Conferences of Poissy opened on the 9th September in presence of the king and court. The council having proposed to deliberate, if the Reformed should obtain a hearing, the queen mother cut the question short by declaring that she would have no more discussion respecting a point that had already been resolved affirmatively. On the eve of the opening of the synod, twelve doctors of the Sorbonne presented themselves before the queen, to entreat her not to permit the ministers of heresies to have a hearing in presence of the king; but to their great discontent the only answer they received was that the thing had been decided, and that it was not possible to adopt any new measures on that subject. Thus the Romish prelates were reduced to the necessity of discussing, for the first time, with the ministers the principles of a religion which they had hitherto condemned without giving them a hearing; and whatever might be the result of the conference, it was a glorious day in which the gospel was about to be freely expounded by the organ of its gravest and most eloquent doctors.

give pleasure to a great many persons, profit in that school in which your name is at present so celebrated, and learn to lie a little more audaciously; for when others recount marvels,.you alone scarcely let us have one glimpse of hope. But joking apart, remember that you are writing to me who care for nothing more than to be made acquainted with the present state of affairs by a plain narrative. Whatever others may think, it has always been my conviction that the boasted results of the conference would come to nothing. Believe me, the Bishops will never proceed to a serious discussion, not that there are not among them some who, I have no doubt, are actuated by laudable desires and expectations. But those who are at the helm would rather be driven to extreme courses, than forced to be reduced to order by such a method as this. Wherefore, I imagine that the theologians whom the Legate drags about in his train in such bands, and those who have come from Spain, will be shown off on this theatre, like those of old who were wont to carry about empty trophies in a public pageant. In a word, if you listen to me, you will give yourself no trouble about the conference. If they were at liberty to lay down the conditions, there would be some mock skirmishing, but now when they see that laws have been imposed on them, they will openly decline all contest. The arrival of the Legate will also puff up their presumption; provided only the terrors which he inspires be dissipated, as I trust they will, we need scarce look for any other result. Before this letter reach you, his thunders will have sounded. Unless I am greatly mistaken, he will not launch his thunderbolt, but he will threaten most savagely before he departs. This will test you to the quick. But should the bishops, for the sake of deceiving you, present themselves to the contest, you have Peter Martyr, who, I conclude, by computing the days that have elapsed since his departure, must have arrived among you in time. Though I earnestly entreated you not to mention my name, you do not cease, as I perceive, to broach projects in regard to me, which, in my judgment, is not expedient,[1] and in

---

[1] It was the wish of the French ministers that the most illustrious interpreter of their faith, Calvin himself, should be summoned to the Colloquy of Poissy. But he could not appear there without exposing himself to the most imminent perils, " con-

my preface upon Daniel, I, on purpose, designed to preclude myself from all access to the conference; not that I grudge my pains, or would shun any dangers, but because where I see so many fit and well instructed persons, I do not imagine that my presence could be of much service, and certainly all of them, with the exception of Merlin and yourself, are sufficiently ardent in the cause. I have not written to you what I thought of the conditions, partly because I imagined that an opinion on that subject would be too late when the business had been transacted, and partly because I was greatly pleased that what the brethren had demanded had been conceded to you. Had I been in their place, I should have feared to prescribe such hard conditions. On their success I partly congratulate them. I eagerly expect to hear the termination of the affair. I suppose you keep in mind what I had declared to you beforehand, that there is no reason to fear but that, to their great disgrace, from the conclave in which they have been secretly hatching their plots, will break out a glorious victory for you, though from the height of their grandeur they look down upon you. For that reason, you must beware lest, if you should be too obstinate in asserting equal rights, the blame should be cast on yourselves. The Confession of Augsburg, as you know, is the torch of our deadliest enemy to kindle a conflagration which will set all France on fire.[1] But it behoves you to inquire for what purpose it should be obtruded on you. The author of it repented of his work when his own faintheartedness had always been displeasing to men of energetic character. In most parts, also, it is adapted to the peculiar use of Germany. I forbear to mention that it is obscure in its conciseness, and mutilated by the omission of some articles of capital importance. Besides, it would be absurd, passing by the Confession of the French, eagerly to adopt that one. Need I mention what matter for future contention will be amassed by this manner of proceeding? But I am reasoning just now as if the Cardinal and his satellites sincerely

sidering the rage which the enemies of the gospel had conceived against him, and the troubles which his very name would excite in the provinces of France, should it be known that he was there."—Letter of La Riviere to Calvin, 31 July, 1561, (Lib. of Geneva.)

[1] See page 212.

embraced that confession, whereas they are only laying snares for you, that the present business being once disposed of they may throw every thing into confusion. To that end, a pamphlet was published at Bâle. I suspect, nay, I am almost certain, that Baudouin is the author of it.[1] I should like to give the scoundrel a drubbing according to his deserts, but I am overwhelmed with the multiplicity of my private correspondence, and the little vigour I once possessed begins to flag. I shall persist, however, as far as my strength will permit. I learn, also, that I know not what decree has been published at Paris respecting the connecting of history with jurisprudence in which you are odiously reflected on. At present, Baudouin is said to be concocting some new poison along with his abettor, Cassander. I imagine you have it at heart to procure us relief by your aid. If you loiter now, he who is to come after you will have to bestir himself.

Farewell, most excellent brother, as well as all your associates. May the Lord govern you by the spirit of prudence and fortitude, may he protect and bless your labours. My colleagues send to you all their best wishes. Our friends, also, whom it would be tedious to enumerate. Would to God, that one of whom death has deprived us were still in the number.

[*Calvin's Lat. Corresp.—Opera*, ix., p. 156.]

DCIX.—To the Admiral Coligny.[2]

He puts him on his guard against the Catholic and Lutheran intrigues—Recall of the minister Merlin to Geneva.

GENEVA, *24th September*, 1561.

MONSEIGNEUR:—I can easily imagine that every day you have to bear up against alarms that are raised against you; not

---

[1] See for further details on this subject the letter to the Queen of Navarre of the 24th December, 1561.

[2] A letter written during the Colloquy of Poissy, which began the 9th September, and finished the 24th October, 1561. Present at the conferences, the Admiral showed himself every day more resolute in pursuing by legal means the establishment of religious liberty in France. Theodore Beza preached several times in his hotel, in pre-

only by those who openly declare themselves the enemies of the
truth of God, but especially by those trimmers that swim between two currents, feigning to favour the good party and yet
having all their looks turned only towards the world and entirely dependent on it.[1] I am quite sure that seeing them veer
and stagger in this manner you are often distressed. But it
is a good lesson for you, Monseigneur, when there is neither
shore nor bottom in those that are tossed by the vanity of the
world, to fix the deeper your anchor in heaven, as we are exhorted to do by the Apostle. Be that as it will, I pray you to
hold on courageously; that is more important than all human
hope, fortifying yourself more and more to despise all the hindrances which might retard you, for we cannot say with St.
Paul that we have fought a good fight to receive the crown of
righteousness, if we have not completed our course. But I take
it for granted that He that has so well disposed you for his service, and displayed in you such power of his Spirit, will not
leave his work imperfect, but will stay your hand even to the end.

I am even pretty well convinced that the arrival of the Legate[2] will have given rise to some harder skirmishing; people
demanding that all examination of the points in debate should

sence of the most considerable personages of the court. "To-day," wrote he to Calvin, "I preached at the Admiral's, who kept me to dinner. After dinner, dropped in
the Cardinal de Chatillon and M. de Montmorency, who I see stand well affected to us,
as, in truth, matters are now set in motion with a wonderful impulse."—Letter of the
25th August. MSS. of Geneva, vol. 117. Another letter of Beza's to the seigneury,
mentioned by the registers of the council, contained some familiar details which the
gravity of history will not disdain. "The said letter also mentioned that the Admiral had a parrot which kept continually screaming: *Vie, vie, la messe est abolie.* (Life,
life, the mass is abolished.) N'oserait-on parlêr de Dieu en tout lieu? (Should we
not dare to speak of God everywhere?) Parlons de Dieu en tout lieu. (Let us speak
of God everywhere.)—Extraits des Registres. [This parrot's doggerel is worth preserving, as a characteristic trait of the times, but it is impossible to render the childish
jingle of the words.]

[1] Allusion to the King of Navarre already gained over by the Guises. Beza giving
an account to Calvin of his first interview with this prince, thus expressed himself:—
"As to the king, . . . the main point of our conversation was that I said I was greatly
afraid that very soon he would not be so delighted with my arrival, unless he thought
of acting otherwise. He began to laugh, and I replied it was in sober earnest he
ought to think of it."—Letter already quoted.

[2] The Cardinal of Ferrara, Hippolite d'Este. He was charged by Pope Pius IV. to
break up the Conferences of Poissy in demanding that all the religious questions
should be brought before the Council of Trent.

be referred to this fine council. Now, Monseigneur, it seems to
me that for the diffident who tremble even at their own shadow,
here is the true point for blunting the shock of the council. It
is that the king,[1] without making more ample declaration of wishing to change the religion, should join with the Queen of England,
the German princes, the Swiss who belong to our party, to protest and declare the nullity of this Council of Trent, both because of the place where it is held, which is not of safe access,
and because it is neither free nor[2] . . so as to be able to treat
independently of the points that are to-day in litigation, seeing
that one party alone sits in it to judge every thing according to
their good pleasure, without the other party being heard, or
having any opportunity afforded them of maintaining the doctrine which the bishops already consider as condemned without
entering into further examination or debate.

I know that the German princes will require them to specify
more distinctly the causes of opposition, nay, that they will
wish to saddle them with their Confession of Augsburg.[3] But
the king will indeed have influence to make them remain satisfied with a more simple declaration, as it will not occasion them
any prejudice. Especially I entreat you, Monseigneur, to hold
firm and not allow the Confession of Augsburg to be brought
into the question, which would only be a torch to light the fire
of discord. And, in point of fact, it is such a meagre compo-
sition, so feeble and so obscure, that it is impossible to stop
short at its conclusions. As to the rest of the Swiss, it would
be expedient that the king should exhort them all to join with
him in such a protestation, which has no other object than to
reform abuses in the church, since to accomplish this end it is
necessary the points of difference should be well ascertained
and discussed, and the two parties heard each in its own cause.

---

[1] The young king, Charles IX. The queen mother, then docile to the inspirations
of the Chancellor L'Hôpital, and favourable to the Protestant party, seemed sincerely
to desire a reform of the church.

[2] A word illegible in the manuscript. Perhaps *universal*.

[3] Several theologians of Tubingen, Jacques Buclin, Jacques André, and Balthazar
Bidenach, had just arrived at Poissy. The Comte Palatine had also sent the doctors,
Michel Diller and Jean Boquin, who, says Beza, did not agree with the three others,
but supported the Confession of the French churches.—*Hist. Eccl.*, vol. i., pp. 615, 616.

I say this, because the king instead of shrinking from it will make overtures for the renewing of the alliance; not that this will have any immediate results, but after they have fretted for some time, I assure you, that this offer will produce an excellent effect a year after.[1]

I have also to beg of you, Monseigneur, that considering our urgent necessity you will be pleased to release M. de Montroy from his engagement.[2] For since his departure we have lost three members of our society. M. Beza,[3] and he who went to join the duchess,[4] are absent. Our burden then is too heavy, unless we be speedily relieved. . . . I have prolonged the term as much as I could, but I am obliged to beg of you not to be offended if, at least, he make a tour hither to relieve us till God have provided for us otherwise. I believe, Monseigneur, that in your wisdom and equity you will not take it amiss that he should return to the flock to which he is bound, and which he has not quitted. It is possible, also, that God will send to you in his stead another so suitable that you shall have no reason to regret his absence. This is not to insinuate that those who have sent him to you are not always equally ready to busy themselves in rendering you a service, but I assure you that for

[1] Swisserland was divided into two camps—the Catholic cantons, the natural allies of France, and the Reformed cantons, which a tolerant policy might dispose to enter into the circle of the alliance and the military capitulations.

[2] The Minister Merlin. The Admiral in giving him permission to return, wrote in these terms to the seigneurs of Geneva :—" MESSIEURS :—In consequence of what M. d'Espeville has written to me, I send you back M. de Montroy, the present bearer, whom I have always kept near my person, and I will tell you that I have received from him as much satisfaction by his exhortations and excellent conduct as I ever have from any man. So that I will pray you still, Messieurs, if it be at all possible that you can do without him, that you would be kind enough to do me the favour of letting me have him. I mean that you should try to procure for yourselves some minister in your neighbourhood, where it would be impossible for me to do so, and that you would consent to send back M. de Montroy to me to take up his residence with me. For desiring to make the profession which I wish to make, I should be much distressed not to have a minister. In doing this you will bind me still more to you. Whereupon, I commend myself most affectionately to your indulgent favour, and I will supplicate the Creator, Messieurs, to grant you long and happy life.—From St. Germain en Laye, this 6th October, 1561.   Your most devoted friend,

CHASTILLON."

[3] Then deputy at the Colloquy of Poissy.
[4] Francis de Morel, almoner of the Duchess of Ferrara.

the present moment we are in such straits that the instance I give you of our difficulties deserves to be favourably received.[1]

Whereupon, Monseigneur, having humbly commended myself to your indulgent favour, I will supplicate our Father and our Lord to fortify you with invincible constancy, to increase in you the gifts of his Spirit, and to keep you under his protection.

[*Fr. Copy.—Library of Geneva.* Vol. 107.]

DCX.—To MADAME DE COLIGNY.[2]

He congratulates her on her perseverance amidst many temptations and perils.

GENEVA, 24*th September,* 1561.

I should accuse myself for having so long forborne to write to you, were it not that he who makes up by his word for the want of my letters must have given you sufficient reasons for my silence. I have been led to suppose, also, that you have accepted, instead of letters addressed to yourself, the duty which I have fulfilled in that respect towards your husband. I have not ceased in the mean time to thank God for having so continued his grace in you that, amid many temptations and great difficulties, you have constantly persevered in his service to such a degree, as to be an example to those who were too weak or too timid. Now, Madame, you ought to reflect that our merciful Father having advanced you thus far, you are so much the more bound to make every effort, till you have entirely finished your course. I pray you then to practise the rule which St. Paul gives us by his own example—to forget the things which are behind—not once to look at them, and, as if, having thus laboured, you had

---

[1] The Minister Merlin became again, some years afterwards, the almoner of Coligny. He was with the Admiral on the night of the 24th August, 1572, and almost miraculously survived the massacre of St. Bartholomew.

[2] She had quitted the Château of Châtillon-sur-Loing, her usual residence, to go to St. Germain where the court was at that time. In his letters to Calvin, Beza bears testimony to the firmness of Madame the Amirale, and of her niece, the Princess of Condé :—" With a troop a hundred times greater than I could have wished, I was conducted to the house of Madame the Princess, and Madame the Amirale, whom I found marvellously well disposed."—Letter already quoted.

yet done nothing to reach forward to that which remains, till you have attained the mark to which we should be ever stretching during our whole life. For if this holy apostle having borne himself so valiantly, and having supported combats so admirable of every kind, and during so long a space of time, confesses nevertheless that he has not attained to what he was aspiring after, and in order to take better courage accounts that he would have commenced in vain, unless he held on, what should we think of ourselves, who are still very far from having made so much progress? Thus, Madame, I pray you, whatever happens, never be weary of employing yourself in the service of so good a Father; as also I am convinced that you are not of the number of those who would wish to obtain a discharge after a certain term of service, persuading themselves that what they have already done is quite sufficient. Now God does not accept of us on such a condition; but as he desires to remain our heritage, so he also desires that we should remain his followers, to dedicate ourselves entirely to his service, whether in life or in death. For, in truth, if we die not for him and in him; that is to say, in his obedience and in the faith and hope of his fatherly kindness, we cannot attain to that heavenly life which has been purchased for us at so dear a price. Though the world should turn, change, and be tossed about by every wind, let us remain firm in this conviction, and set up our rest in it, for there is no other prosperity nor happiness except that of being the people of God, according as it is said in the Psalm; and if the world does not taste that happiness, let us recognize that God accomplishes in us, by a singular privilege, what is said elsewhere, that he makes all those that fear him to feel in secret the infinite greatness of his bounty, of which he will give you an assured experience, even in this perishable life, while you are waiting to be received into that life everlasting for which we hope, in order fully to enjoy what is now concealed from our senses.

Madame, having humbly commended myself to your indulgent favour, etc.

[*Fr. Copy.—Library of Geneva.* Vol. 107.]

DCXI.—To the Comtesse de Roye.[1]

He encourages her to persevere with her daughters in the profession of the truth.

Geneva, *24th September,* 1561.

Madame:—If I have delayed so long in answering your letters, it is partly because I did not know whither to address mine, and partly from shame, inasmuch as I was unable to satisfy your holy desire, for you asked me for three men capable of being employed in the service of God and of his church, designating the places where you intended to send them, in order that I might be the more incited to make all diligence. The same message had been already conveyed to me orally by a man of Noyon, who said he had been charged with such a commission.

Now I assure you, Madame, that we are at the present moment so unprovided with ministers, that I preferred, not having found suitable persons, to delay the execution of my commission rather than send persons that might not have given you satisfaction. I wish indeed that I had had a less valid excuse. But when M. Beza shall have confirmed it, I hope you will accept it. For the rest, Madame, I have much reason to glorify God for the great courage with which he has inspired you for advancing the reign of our Lord Jesus Christ, and for causing you to make a frank and pure declaration of following the truth of the gospel in life and in death, since all our happiness stands in being disciples of this great Master, and subjects of this sovereign King, who has been sent to us from heaven to withdraw us from perdition to the hope of eternal salvation, which he has purchased for us.

[1] Madeleine de Mailly, Comtesse de Roye, sister of the Admiral de Coligny, and mother-in-law of the Prince de Condé. Endowed, says the historian De Thou, with a superior genius and an intrepid mind, this lady embraced the Reform at the same time as her brothers, the Seigneurs of Châtillon, shared the perils of the Prince of Condé her son-in-law, recovered her liberty like him at the death of Francis II., and showed herself constantly faithful to the cause of the Reformed, in good as well as in bad fortune. Living at Strasbourg during the first war of religion, she returned to France after the conclusion of the peace of Amboise, and died in 1567.

Wherefore without this heritage, woe to all the riches, delights and honours of the world. And yet as we see how this inestimable treasure is despised by most men, and held in no esteem, so much the more reason have you for rejoicing that God has made you a partaker of the privilege of renouncing all the vanities of this world, which dazzle our eyes and cause us to float in continual anxiety, to find a true rest and abide therein. You have also another blessing in addition to those which have been already bestowed on you, in seeing your daughters, the princess as well as her sister,[1] keeping you company in tending towards the chief end of our existence, giving themselves up with one accord and dedicating their lives to the obedience of the pure truth. Now, Madame, though I have heard with what zeal you desire to serve God, nevertheless I pray you to take more and more courage, striving to overcome all the obstacles that might retard you, as you may be sure you shall always have many. And indeed these are the exercises of our faith, to fight against all the temptations which Satan devises and employs to turn us aside from the straight path. Aim then, Madame, at this perseverance, not doubting but the heavenly Father will conduct you even to the end, as he has a more than singular care about your salvation, and that Jesus Christ, that good Shepherd, who has undertaken the charge of you, will keep and protect you.

Madame, having humbly commended myself to your indulgent favour, I will supplicate our heavenly Father to govern you by his Holy Spirit, and increase you in all good and prosperity.

[*Fr. Copy.—Library of Geneva.* Vol. 107.]

---

[1] Eleonore de Roye, Princess of Condé, and Charlotte de Roye her sister, wife of the Comte de la Rochefoucauld.

DCXII.—To THEODORE BEZA.[1]

He compliments him on his noble attitude at the Colloquy of Poissy, and rejoices at his success.

GENEVA, 24th September, 1561.

If you receive from me two letters at the same time, he who undertook the charge of them must bear the blame of it for his inactivity. Certainly, as messengers were at his disposal every third day, he cannot exculpate himself for having neglected his duty till the ninth. We had been amply informed from other quarters of the magnificent transaction of which you write to us; but it was far more agreeable to have the whole affair set as it were before our eyes, and glean our information from your own testimony, than to listen to the accounts of others, who for the most part vitiate the purity of history by their fondness for embellishment. That was an auspicious day in which liberty was secured for the churches, a liberty which they will be obliged to concede, and which it will be most difficult for them to take away.

Your speech is now before us, in which God in a marvellous manner directed your mind and your tongue. That it stirred up the bile of the holy fathers was an inevitable consequence, but you could not help that, unless you had been inclined to tergiversate and expose yourself to their taunts. I am surprised that they broke out into tumultuous murmurs for that single reason, when in other passages they had been no less hardly hit. But it is a foolish pretence that the conference has been broken

---

[1] The letter of Beza to Calvin, containing an account of the first sitting of the Colloquy, still preserved in the Library of Geneva, is unfortunately truncated, but all the details of that important day are well known, and we can read in divers collections, the fine harangue pronounced by Theodore de Beza in the name of the Reformed churches. The orator showed himself full of moderation and dignity, and was listened to with the greatest attention, till the moment when he declared "that the body of Christ, though spiritually communicated in the Lord's supper, is as far removed from the bread as heaven is distant from the earth." The murmurs of the prelates who interrupted him were less the expression of a private dissent, than the revelation of the absolute incompatibility existing between the Church of Rome and that of Christ.

up for this cause of offence, for they would have found a hundred others, they who now so eagerly snap at one, as if with some modifications they assented to the rest of our doctrine. This circumstance then also fell out very fortunately. I rejoice that De Spina has frankly and publicly declared his adherence to the cause of Christ. In a letter which I have written to him I exhort him to persevere.[1] I am anxious to learn with what adroitness the Cardinal will attempt to put a good face on these proceedings.[2] An end has been put as I conjecture to all lighter bickering, and yet I do not apprehend that there will be any serious contest. Now though I have advised you not to demand too promptly your dismissal, nevertheless the Legate will do me a welcome service if he send you off as speedily as possible. It is with truth that you speak of the remains of my friends, for among the few that have been spared to me, I seem to myself to stand almost alone. All our colleagues very warmly salute you.

Farewell, most excellent brother. May the Lord always govern you, strengthen you with invincible constancy and courage, stand by you in your holy labours, and preserve you safe and uninjured. I desire to salute all your associates. As often as you shall keep silence longer than ten days, which has now happened to you the second time, I shall proclaim you a sluggard.

[*Calvin's Lat. corresp.*, Opera, ix. p. 157.]

[1] Jean de Spina, an old monk and celebrated Catholic divine, converted to the Reformed faith. Beza announced in the following terms this event to Calvin, "De Spina has fairly joined us and submitted himself to the judgment of the church. We on our part, with every demonstration of joy, have held out to him the right hand of fellowship and have clearly concluded that that day has shone out a most auspicious one for us."

[2] The reply of the Cardinal de Lorraine, though very skilfully conceived, but halfsatisfied the assembly. He himself recognized the superiority of Beza by this avowal, "I wish he had been dumb, or that we had been deaf."

DCXIII.—To the Comte of Erbach.[1]

He urges him to employ his influence to prevent every attempt to introduce the Confession of Augsburg into France.

Geneva, *30th September,* 1561.

It is against my inclinations that I am now troublesome in writing to you, most noble and illustrious seigneur, for considering the distance that separates us, my letter cannot convey to you any information which has not become obsolete, and which consequently cannot much interest you. But in the present moment a just motive, or rather necessity, urges me to address you, for I have been given to understand that the most illustrious Prince Palatine, and other confederated princes, having decided upon sending an embassy to France, are still deliberating among themselves respecting the instructions to be given to its members, and that thus the expedition has been hitherto suspended. If, then, I appear to mix myself up with this business more intimately than my condition warrants, I entreat you to pardon, with your usual indulgence, my solicitude should I labour to meet a danger which already presents itself so palpably to my observation. For I not only suspect but I distinctly perceive that a great many persons are obstinately bent upon obtruding the Confession of Augsburg on the French. The Duke of Wurtemberg had already made the same attempt four months ago, and Brentz, by the suggestion of the devil, certainly has actively and zealously, though fraudulently, busied himself, that by presenting to them the absurdity of his doctrine of ubiquity he might fascinate our French brethren. How pernicious that would prove, I shall briefly explain. First, a Confession has been published long ago by all the French churches, to which every one who is admitted into the rank of a pastor gives his assent by a solemn subscription. The same Confession has been repeatedly presented to the royal council. In an assem-

---

[1] See the Letter, page 56. This new letter to the Comte Eberard bore the following superscription :—" To the high-born and most noble Comte of Erbach, high chamberlain of the Palatine court, my very honoured and esteemed seigneur."

bly of all the princes and bishops, the king lately received the
same from the hands of our brother Beza, and delivered it to
the cardinals and bishops that the discussions of the colloquy
might turn upon it. What then could be more absurd than to
break off a course of proceedings so auspiciously commenced?
Should no other damage accrue from such a proceeding except
the delay, yet even that should be carefully guarded against.
But if the princes now interfere with a new Confession, not
only they will bring to nought all the noble transactions in
which the favour of God has been so marvellously conspicuous,
but by an obstacle worse than detrimental they will overturn
all our hopes for the future. For the Papists will eagerly lay
hold of this subject of quarrelling; and those among them who
excel in craftiness, after pretending in the first synod that they
are satisfied, as soon as matters shall have taken a new turn,
and they perceive the French Confession annihilated, will begin
to direct their attacks elsewhere. And what is to be thought
of the Germans prescribing laws to us, and dictating to us, as
if we were children? It cannot escape your singular perspicacity how plausible an argument this will furnish. In addition
to that, it will be difficult to violate the agreement which all
the pious have come to, and which they have publicly attested.
Unless, then, the princes avowedly wish not only to throw into
confusion their happy commencements, but to destroy entirely
the fruits which the incredible labour of numbers and the blood
of so many martyrs have produced, let them desist from this
inauspicious conflict. I say conflict, because, if they oppose
their Confession to the one which has been received, dreadful
disturbances will spring from it. And that no one may doubt
whence this project has proceeded, that has been already for
some time the object of the machinations of all those who in
France are the bitterest enemies of Christ, and who are hurried
on by the most deadly animosity to effect the ruin of his kingdom,
I forbear to mention that the Saxon furies, Brentz and his ac-
complices, have always made a bad use of the Augsburg Confession as a kind of torch to kindle a conflagration by which
the whole of Germany has been set on fire. For that reason,
we ought to be the more carefully on our guard lest the conta-

gion of the evil penetrate into France. But since, most excellent seigneur, not only in consequence of your affinity, but also of your virtues, you possess very great authority and influence with your most illustrious prince, I have not hesitated familiarly to confide to your friendly bosom this subject of anxiety, in order that you may provide a remedy in time. I would exhort you more earnestly, were I not perfectly assured that from your own remarkable magnanimity, and the warmth of your zeal, you are sufficiently and more than sufficiently, of your own free-will, disposed to this cause. In what regards my own duty, I have sincerely and boldly reminded you. You, on yours, will decide according to your just discernment what shall be most expedient, and your own fidelity and religious sentiments will sufficiently stimulate you to strenuous efforts.

Farewell, most accomplished and truly honoured seigneur. May the Lord continue to direct you by his Spirit, and adorn and enrich more and more your most distinguished family with every blessing.

[*Lat. Copy.—Library of Geneva.* Vol. 107 a.]

DCXIV.—To Theodore Beza.[1]

Ecclesiastical news—Apostleship of Viret in France—Reply to Baudouin.

GENEVA, 1st October, 1561.

Yesterday I received a couple of letters from you. If the bishops have been pleased or have even been permitted to enter into discussion with you, you have already fairly entered upon

[1] Though the Colloquy was still officially assembled, its task was ended. Theodore Beza having asked permission in the sitting of the 16th September to reply on the instant to the speech of the Cardinal of Lorraine, the prelates violently opposed his demand, and the Cardinal of Tournon declared that "in the *very Christian kingdom of France* there should be but one faith, one law, one king." Discussion was then no longer unfettered, and the conferences which continued for some days with shut doors had no longer any object. They only proved one thing, the impossibility of bringing the two churches to unity by mutual concessions, the duty for the government of pacifying people's minds by the application of a principle of sage toleration, a grand idea conceived by the Chancellor L'Hôpital, and realized for a moment by the edict of January.

the conference. But unless all my conjectures very much deceive me, every hope of that kind has now vanished. I wish that at an early day we had an opportunity of embracing you here safe and in good health. But should you see any danger arising from your too hurried departure, let us both bridle our impatience. Meanwhile, do not expose yourself too much to the savage humour of those who neither value your life, nor the common safety of the church. I hear that you are quite emaciated, nor is that wonderful, considering how absorbed you have been by a multiplicity of affairs. But though you must often give way to necessity, yet, unless you be careful of your health, you do not consult well for your desires, nor for the benefit of the church. If you listen to my advice, you will follow up what you have begun in such a manner as speedily to take leave of these deceitful maskers, whose honied flatteries savour of the most deadly poison. I should be unwilling that the others were left destitute by you, but unless my desire of seeing you blinds me, your absence for a short time will be advantageous. Only you must wait for an opportunity, which you should willingly seize when it offers itself. Respecting the Confession of Augsburg, I have written most carefully to the Comte of Erbach, in order that he may check any evil designs. I have pointed out the fountain-head of the treachery, and what an inundation might be expected to flow from it. I admit what you have written to me respecting our brethren that, in fact, they are not at liberty, since their names have been consigned to the public registers. But as my brother by his arrival has put an end to all our strifes, there is nothing to prevent Merlin's return. I dare not press the matter with regard to De Coulonges, for it is impossible to obtain the Duchess's permission. And even if we had him here, the inhabitants of Bordeaux have begged so eagerly to have him, that we have no hopes of being able to retain him, and the day before yesterday Chevalier was installed in his house. You know what attacks I had to endure from the latter. At last, I did not openly yield to him, but I put a constraint on myself, and kept silence. Before your departure, you know that we had a discussion respecting his successor. Why the affair was not yet settled, you

shall know at length. The senate conceives that it is freed from
all obligation, since by the common decision of our society a
simple discharge was asked for. But the death of our oldest
pastor has made it necessary for us to recall Merlin. I lately
made no mention of this motive; yet it would have been most
unfair for Vincent to have been abandoned by us after having
incurred so much expense. But why should I insist on the
private rights of one individul, and not rather plead that it is
most infamous that the church should be defrauded of its rights?
Moreover, I add, that it is your duty to bring along with you, or
to send a man well versed in our language. If Merlin will bring
any one along with him, his arrival will be doubly welcome to
us. I entreat you, however, occupy yourselves seriously respecting this matter. Among your cares, let it not be the last.
Only take care that whoever shall come he may be a pious man,
no pompous boaster, but one quietly disposed to endure labour.
Respecting his knowledge of the language, Merlin will judge.
It is not my fault if those who so eagerly desire Viret have not
yet obtained their wish.[1] For the present, he has gone to Montpellier, because he thought himself unequal to support the colds
of this country in winter. At the end of the winter, he will go
into Gascony, and having traversed the whole region of the
Garonne he will pass on to the Loire, whence he will advance
as far as Normandy. I feel dissatisfied that without a cause,
or the least colour of reason, I should be suspected by certain
persons of entertaining jealousy, and being hurt because I had
not been summoned to France.[2] The Admiral wrote to me
lately, just as if an apology had been necessary to appease my
irritation. You, however, are the best witness how carefully I

---

[1] Since his secession from Lausanne, Viret had exercised the ministry at Geneva,
though already, he said, his body was reduced to such a state of debility that he could
expect nothing except to be interred. He asked then for a leave of absence, which,
with much regret, was granted him to go and re-establish his health in the south of
France. From all parts calls were sent to the eloquent minister who had been one
of the first apostles of the Reformation in Swisserland. On the 30th of December,
the seigneurs of Geneva consented to grant him to the Church of Paris, " in hopes
that he would produce much fruit, and that he would convert the Parliament." But
Viret's health did not permit him to undertake this journey, and the last years of his
apostleship were devoted to the churches of the south.

[2] See page 219; note 1.

shunned that office. I was much dissatisfied that when I had besought you at your departure not to say one word about me, you had not been sufficiently mindful of that duty which I thought was due to me. But I am afraid that something or other has been suggested from some other quarter, for there are many who judge of me from their own character. For the rest, as glad and sorrowful tidings are conveyed to you from all the provinces, I make no doubt but that you are very solicitous, as it is your duty, to procure relief for the brethren. The inhabitants of Auvergne are very worthy of compassion, and their cause ought, from its justice, to conciliate favour for them. It is the interest of the whole church that the Lyonese should be promptly relieved. At present, all over that neighbouring region, the consciences of men are roused, as if from their lethargy. One would say, that they had been stung by gadflies. For my part, I answer that I have a fear of sudden changes. For why do they now, at last, begin to feel the evils to which they had been so long callous? Till your return, they will apply what remedies they can, or as you were wont jocularly to express it, will follow the smell of their own trail, but if this matter is to depend on us, they will quickly lose the scent.

Farewell, most excellent brother, along with M. Martyr and your other colleagues, to whom my brother and I beg to send our best respects. May the Lord stand by you, govern you by his Spirit, and keep you in safety under his protection.

Yours,   CHARLES PASSELIUS.

A short reply to Baudouin is now in the press, which you will receive next week. This was no very agreeable solace of my grief, nevertheless it was necessary that the criminal audacity of the scoundrel should be repelled. I wished, also, to have an indirect cut at the sloth of the tortoise. Let him enjoy his pleasures, provided we are at liberty to expose to his disgrace the deadly evils which he fosters. For this reason, it will perhaps be translated into French, though as yet I have not decided.

[*Lat. Orig.—Library of Geneva.* Vol. 107 *a.*]

DCXV.—To Theodore Beza.[1]

Blames the excesses committed by the Reformed—Favourable dispositions of Catherine
de Medicis—Escape of the Duke of Nemours.

GENEVA, 19th November, 1561.

Yesterday having gone out to supper after my ride I found
the stove much heated. Your former letter was put into my
hands at my first entrance, and as I was wholly absorbed in the
perusal of it, I did not remark that the vapour had affected my
brain. For though the food kept down the sneezing, yet after
my return home I felt my complaint aggravated. A short time
after I received your second letter. You will see what I have
written to Salignac. When you have read over the contents of
the letter, you may suppress it or have it delivered to him just
as you shall judge most proper. I have not thought fit to treat
too gently a man whose sluggishness by the long lapse of time
has degenerated into a lethargy. Would that now at least he
may wake up, and by his activity study to efface the disgrace
of his former indolence. I have touched upon the affair of the
Bishop of Troyes in this matter as you desired.[2] You will

---

[1] The Colloquy of Poissy, though without any results, everywhere increased the
audacity of the Reformed, and people saw the number of their churches multiplied.
In a great many localities the mass was abolished, and the temples till then consecrated to the Catholic worship were invaded by the new worship. These acts of violence which the ministers could not prevent, and which were blamed by Calvin, Viret,
and Theodore Beza, gave rise to severe ordinances on the part of the king. On the
3d of November the Reformed were enjoined to restore the edifices of which they had
taken forcible possession, and thanks to the energetic exhortations of their pastors,
this ordinance was almost everywhere scrupulously obeyed. The part which Calvin
played on this occasion was conformable to the spirit of prudence and moderation of
which he had given so many proofs in the direction of the French churches. He
might well render to himself this testimony in a letter to Farel: "In writing to Beza
I have discharged my duty. If the king's council held the seizure of the churches to
be an odious act, it was also one which I never could approve of till something should
be definitively decided, which I trust will be done in a short time." (28th December, 1561.)

[2] John Caraccioli, Bishop of Troyes, was in the number of the Prelates, who renouncing their benefices made public profession of the gospel. The Reformed Church
of Troyes owed to him its origin and its first progress.

pardon my brevity, however, which was forced upon me on the present occasion, though indeed I am moreover naturally disposed to it. Add to that, my desire on this subject to preserve a tone of the greatest moderation, lest I should seem to be imposing conditions on the vanquished. What you write to me respecting the preposterous zeal of our brethren is exceedingly true, and yet no method of moderating it occurs to me. Everywhere I proclaim to them, because they do not listen to salutary advice, that if I were a judge I should punish not less severely these furious attacks than the king does by his edicts. Nothing can be more equitable than the letter you have obtained. Others, by their intemperate conduct, will quite ruin the effects of so great a benefit. We must persist, however, since God has so willed that we should be debtors to fools. Since the time I have been informed by your letter that the assembling of a new conference has been decided upon, you have learned that we have changed our purpose respecting your return. There is an absolute necessity for your remaining, unless we wished to betray and ruin the cause, which has now reached its most critical point. I am especially delighted to hear that the queen wishes to go through with the measure, because I think I am entitled to conclude from that, that she is not acting craftily. If nevertheless we should receive some apology for your delay, it will come very seasonably to allay fears and doubts. For you cannot imagine with how much anxiety the council is perplexed, since they conceive that it is scarcely possible that you shall ever be restored to them. You will ascribe their silence for the time past to me, because I had taken that task on myself. The trafficker who wanted to impose his German wares on us, has had the reward of his perfidy.[1] But what surprises me is that he had so shaken off all modesty as not at least to dissemble a little. If Hotman is to be believed, Boquin entirely disagrees with Baudouin. I congratulate our friend Normandie on his having been so graciously received at court. God grant it be not a mere courtier-like reception. But I hope the best, because I fancy that those who have spontaneously promised to interpose their good offices are speaking seriously.

[1] Alluding to Vergerio, p. 214.

Farewell, most excellent and well beloved brother. May the Lord always stand by you, govern you, and preserve you in safety. All our brethren fondly salute you. Bourgoin has forced us by his imprudence to dismiss him. I suppose it is known in your parts that the Duke of Nemours[1] has fled to his own nest. The Prefect of Sex was on the point of laying hands on him as he passed incognito. Escaping from his clutches, he arrived by night at Chancy. There he with much trepidation made enquiries whether his attendants were in the Genevese or the Bernese territory. Having procured a guide, they set out for the village of L'Ecluse, where of twelve horses they left three half dead with fatigue. Best respects to Gallup and whatever others you may think proper. Consult your health, I entreat you, and do not suffer yourself to be overwhelmed by harassing labours, for it is not without sorrow that I learn that you are worn to a shadow. Again, farewell.—Yours,

CHARLES PASSELIUS.

[*Lat. Orig.—Library of Geneva.* Vol. 107 *a.*]

DCXVI.—To SALIGNAC.[2]

Congratulations and encouragements.

GENEVA, 19*th November*, 1561.

If I write to you by the hand of another, most accomplished sir and venerable brother in Christ, my letter will not be the less

---

[1] Jacques de Savoy, Duke of Nemours, who had been actively mixed up with all the intrigues of Emmanuel Philibert, and the Catholic party against Geneva.

[2] Among the doctors commissioned to maintain the cause of the Romish Church in the private conferences which followed the Colloquy of Poissy, may be noticed a reforming Prelate, Monluc, Bishop of Valence, and a theologian secretly converted to the Reformed creed. It was the Doctor Salignac. Informed of his sentiments by Beza, Calvin hastened to address to him a letter of fraternal encouragement. Salignac was touched by it, as we have a proof in his answer to Calvin: "I am a soldier of Christ, of whom I shall never feel ashamed, and for whose decrees I would not hesitate to lay down my life; and that I shall always reckon my highest glory and prefer it to every triumph." Notwithstanding the energy of this language, Salignac does not appear to have publicly detached himself from the church whose errors he recognized, and is to be classed among that numerous category of pious but timid men, who

valued by you, I imagine on that account, when you shall see
that it was dictated by the most intimate sentiments of my heart.
And certainly so it is: nor should I ever have ventured to deal
so familiarly with you, unless the love I entertain for you, and
the care for your salvation arising from that feeling which
renders me not only solicitous but anxious also, as often as I
meditate on your state had given me confidence. I remember
tbat you are one of those whom thirty years ago God deemed
worthy of the light of his gospel. No vulgar honour this, to be
reckoned among the first fruits of those who have received a
pure doctrine and a remarkable knowledge of the Holy Scriptures. But how unworthily that incomparable treasure has been
buried which God had confided to you, I prefer that you should
yourself judge, rather than wait till you must give an account
before your heavenly Judge of your indolence. But why do I
say indolence? For so many illustrious gifts have not only lain
hid without producing any fruit, but smothered by corruptions,
have been idled away, to the disgrace and dishonour of the pure
faith.

Now though the integrity and purity of your private life has
been praiseworthy, you are nevertheless aware, and pious and
courageous men have seen, not without the deepest sorrow, that
the ungodly and the wicked have triumphed over you, as often
as, restrained by fear, you have held your peace. Too long a
time has elapsed, in which that bondage, not less miserable than
shameful, has stifled the vigour of your mind. Grant that some
indulgence is due to a common evil, because, everywhere surrounded by terrors, there were few who dared to profess themselves undisguisedly the disciples of Christ. Now, however, that
a better condition has suddenly burst upon the sons of God, so
that their freedom is exempt from perils, I am forced to give
utterance to my thoughts. How long, I pray you, will you be
pleased voluntarily to defraud Christ of his rights by your ter-
giversation? Hitherto God has indulgently spared you; while
by your hesitation you choked the light of a right understanding
within you, he has not permitted it to be altogether extinguished.

thought it possible to conciliate the adoption of purer opinions with the outward profession of the Romish worship.

But I beseech you by this indulgence by which he has borne with you until this day, in which he has assembled so many thousands under his banner, that these may stir you up to a like alacrity of zeal, and that you may diligently weigh in your own mind, how precious a sacrifice to God is the pure confession of God, and that in fine the residue of your life, consecrated with single-mindedness to Christ, may compensate for the dilatoriness of times past. Nothing indeed could give me greater pleasure than to hear that having thrown aside all faint-heartedness and vanquished all timidity, you had publicly and professedly given in your name as a follower of Christ. I do not ask, however, that you should give me this assurance privately, but that you should comfort all the churches which God has so marvellously raised up in France, which certainly will congratulate both themselves and you, if, abandoning the camp of the enemy, you betake yourself to the fold of Christ. Nor is the number small of those who are still vacillating, who will forthwith prepare to imitate your example. And if you prudently ponder how many will be swayed by you, how many have their eyes fixed upon you, you will easily recognize that, if the lukewarmness of others is excusable, it is utterly impossible to pardon your sluggishness. Perhaps my letter may find you already sufficiently animated, so that my exhortation will be superfluous. I was unwilling however to fail in my duty.

Farewell, most excellent and highly respected sir. May the Lord govern you by his Spirit, furnish you with fortitude, and preserve you in safety.—Yours,

JOHN CALVIN.

[*Calvin's Lat. corresp.*, Opera, ix. p. 163.]

DCXVII.—To Theodore Beza.[1]

Journey of Theodore Beza's wife to France—Difficult situation of the Academy of Geneva—Sending off of new ministers.—The Duke of Longueville, and the Duke of Nemours—Divers salutations.

GENEVA, 31st *November*, 1561.

As I am uncertain whether my letters may find you at court before your departure for your father's, I shall write to you more briefly. Your wife commenced her journey on Sunday. It is by no means desirable that she should be left at your father's, or make too long a stay at Paris. She herself, too, wishes to leave your city speedily. She would willingly remain at Paris, perhaps. But it will be better, believe me, that she should be sent back on the first occasion, and the time will be very convenient in the month of March. It is your interest, also, when you return, to be free from all impediments, because the passage through Burgundy will not be so safe that you shall not be obliged to guard against ambush. Your last letter but one, as it gave us great hopes, was very agreeable to me. From your last, also, I derived no small satisfaction, except that it renewed my sorrow for the complaints I had made, which were a cause of grief or anxiety to you. I repented of it almost immediately afterwards, but the letter was gone. I could not recall it. Now I am still more displeased with myself for having offended you. There is no occasion, however, that you should make excuses for not having the interests of our Academy at heart, since you cannot be more convinced of that fact than we are ourselves. I, too, am sorry that we have been deceived once, but I am particularly angry with myself for having knowingly and willingly fallen into the trap. For the present moment, he seems to have made up his mind to stay with us, but

---

[1] In addition to the cares for the important interests of which he was the representative, Theodore Beza was occupied with domestic anxieties. He was about to visit his aged father, whom he had left at Vezelay in Burgundy, in order to present to him his young wife, Claudine Denosse, who had been the companion of his voluntary exile at Geneva. This introduction, delayed till then by religious differences, was not to take place without some painful circumstances, as Beza himself testifies in his unedited correspondence with Calvin (1561, 1562) *passim*.

we are resolved not to trust him, for he has neither laid aside
his project about going away, nor does he make any promise
about his return.   But of the character and acts of the man
we shall talk more fully when you come.   It will not be amiss,
however, if by the aid of Mercer, we could procure a successor
for him.   For even should he whom we had counted on put off
his departure, it will be convenient for us to have another person
on account of Sanraver's complaint, which, though the physicians pronounced it not to be mortal, will, nevertheless, be lingering, as I think.   It will give us pleasure if the person who
is to succeed to Baduel could be here as soon as possible.   I
have handed to Barnouin a copy of the letter, of which he is the
bearer, that he may deliver this copy to you.   I have also caused
to be copied out the reply I have made to Baudouin, that you
may con it over at leisure, and that you may not quite lose
your time, since you will be a little more disengaged while you
remain at your father's.   The Parisians, who had been sent to
fetch M. de Passy, came here.   At their request, I shall exhort
the inhabitants of Issoudun to let him go.   He himself, as I
hear, will comply with my advice.   For they have a letter by
which Viret is sent for, and the senate has granted him permission to pass through Paris, on condition, however, that he be
back by summer.[1]   The inhabitants of Tours stand up stoutly
for detaining M. de Spina,[2] who they pretend was definitely
assigned to them, when I was asked to allow him to go to them.
Certainly, the Parisians seem too greedy.   As I am about to
close my letter, I return to yourself.   You act wisely, indeed,
in voluntarily dismissing all foreign deliberations, in order to
embrace with both arms the duties which more properly belong
to our ministry.   I would not have you abstain altogether, however, from other cares.   You should still watch, not only what
is publicly going on, but even the more secret counsels should
not escape your observation.   For it is your province not only
to correct abuses where any thing has been done amiss, but

---

[1] See page 235, note.

[2] Jean de l'Epine, a distinguished divine, who had quitted the cloister to join the
ranks of the Reformed, whose doctrines he maintained at the Colloquy of Poissy.
He was also called Acanthius, Crottet.   *Chronique Protestante*, p. 252.

also to guard against the occurrence of evils. When you assert that you will always belong to our society, this is exactly the opinion which the senate entertains of your dispositions, nor did your brethren suspect any thing unfriendly on your part, but they were afraid you might not be at liberty to dispose of yourself. When your letter, then, was communicated to them, they were exceedingly delighted, just as if they had received some new piece of intelligence. Indeed, till I see you here, I shall seem, I know not how, in a certain fashion abandoned.

Farewell, most worthy and excellent brother. Our colleagues and friends most affectionately salute you; among others, the Marquis de Vico, who is still suffering from the third attack of a quartan ague. He is now, however, out of danger, we trust. The Duke of Longueville, who did not dare to visit us, till he had been to Berne to renew the league, writes to us that we may expect him here very soon. He and his mother wish to take me to Neuchâtel in the beginning of February, that I may be present at the synod. I shall hardly escape, because the senate makes no opposition. The Duke of Nemours feigns to be afraid. The gates of the city are carefully guarded. The Duke of Savoy lately ordered all his carriages and wagons to be conveyed to Chambery. Why all this stir we know not. Again and again, farewell, most worthy brother. May the Lord always stand by you, govern and protect you, and bless your labours. Our senate salutes you. I do not write to our friend Normandie, because I have nothing new to communicate to him. I wish he could be sent back to us earlier than what I conclude from your letter. If, in the mean time, he can settle the business which concerns his paternal inheritance, he will consult properly and advantageously for himself.[1] I had almost forgotten one thing. Canaye, having laid aside all thoughts of his mission, has resolved to stay among us till he again occupy himself with polite literature, between which and him there had been a long divorce. He will send to Viret another in his stead.

---

[1] See vol. ii., p. 219, note 2. Availing himself of the tolerating edicts which signalized the first years of the reign of Charles IX., Laurence de Normandie took a journey into France, found a favourable welcome at court, and obtained restitution of a part of his property.—*Normandius Calvino*, Sept., 1561. (MSS. of Gotha.)

This is the brevity of which I had spoken to you in the beginning of my letter.

Yours,   CHARLES PASSELIUS.

[*Lat. Orig. Autog.—Library of Gotha.* Vol. 405, p. 206.]

DCXVIII.—TO THE QUEEN OF NAVARRE.[1]

Regret for the prolonged absence of Beza—Writing against Baudouin—Letter to the Queen of Navarre, mother of Jane d'Albret.

GENEVA, 24th December, 1561.

MADAME :—It is not without great regret that we are still to be deprived for some time of the presence of our brother, M. Beza ;[2] for the church incurs a loss by it, and the students, who are here for the purpose of following a course of theology, have their studies retarded, inasmuch as I cannot satisfy all the demands that are made on my time. But since there is no help for that, I will pray God that the fruits which will accrue from his labours for the advancement of the reign of Jesus Christ, may be to us as a reward to gladden us, or, at least, in part to mitigate our distress.[3] In the mean time, we have wherewithall to bless God for having wrought so efficaciously in you, Madame, and caused you to surmount every thing that might have turned you aside from the right path. It were·much to be wished that the king, your husband, would, once for all, form a firm resolution not to swim any longer between two cur-

---

[1] Confirmed in the creed of the Reformed, by Theodore Beza, the Queen of Navarre employed her influence at court to prepare the way for the tolerating administration ushered in by the edict of January.

[2] Detained at St. Germain by the instant entreaties of the Queen of Navarre, Beza wrote to Calvin the 25th November :—" By the grace of God, we have begun to found a church here, and God aiding we shall celebrate, next Sabbath, the sacrament of the Lord's supper. I saluted, in your name, as you ordered me, the Queen of Navarre, the Prince of Conde, Possidonius, and their wives, which they took in very good part. She (I mean the Queen of Navarre) ceased not to ask me for a minister, and moreover declares that she will not suffer me to quit her."—Theodore Beza to Calvin, (Library of Geneva, vol. 117.)

[3] Theodore Beza quitted France definitively to return to Geneva, only in April, 1563, after the first civil war, and the conclusion of the peace of Amboise.

rents. I know, Madame, how much you are labouring to bring that about. But I entreat you, if you do not succeed so oon as we could wish, that the delay do not exhaust your patience, nor cool your zeal. For the rest, Madame, whatever happen, you know how carefully we should beware of withdrawing ourselves from God to gratify mortal creatures, which ought to give you courage zealously to persevere, aiming at the end which is proposed to you, whatever winds blow from opposite directions. I have also to apprize you, Madame, of one thing which I could gladly dispense with, were I at liberty to do so. But I fancy that having heard the motive which obliges me, you will easily excuse me for what I have done. There is a certain boor whom the king, your husband, has appointed to be the *tutor of his natural son,*[1] who, being an apostate and a traitor to religion,[2] has vomited out in a printed book all the abuse he could invent against me.[3] Now, besides pluming himself on the name of your husband, not doing him too much honour by that, he makes also a buckler against me of the late queen, your mother, because for some time she was displeased that I had so sharply confounded the sect of the Libertines. At that time, I answered her on the subject, and I send you, Madame, a copy of the letter written by the hand of our brother Des Gallars, fourteen years ago, in order that you may judge of the merits of the cause.[4] I have no intention to animate you against

---

[1] " *Magister de son bastard.*"

[2] Allusion to Francis Baudouin. As a reward for his efforts to bring about a reconciliation between the Catholics and Protestants, he had been appointed tutor of Charles de Bourbon, the natural son of the King of Navarre, with a salary of twelve hundred livres.

[3] The origin of this controversy, in which the precepts of charity were but little observed by either party, was the publication of Cassander's book, De officio pii viri in hoc religionis dissidio (of the duty of a pious man in these religious dissensions) of which Baudouin superintended the printing. It was the manifesto of the trimmers (moyenneurs) in religious matters. Calvin replied to it in one of the most virulent of his treatises:—*Reply to a certain double-dealing go-between, who, under pretext of pacification, has been intriguing to cut short the course of the gospel in France.* 1561, in 8vo., translated into French in the Recueil des Opuscules, p. 1885. The reply of Baudouin, full of abuse against the Reformer, provoked a second reply from Calvin:—*Answer to Baudouin's scurrilous railings;* and the contest continued by Theodore wandered still farther from the ways of moderation, from which it had deviated from the beginning.

[4] It is the letter to the Queen of Navarre, vol. i., p. 453. This letter, as Beza re-

him. You will act as God shall direct you. But I cannot forbear, Madame, from begging you to take steps to prevent him
from bringing into the question the name of the said lady, your
mother, lest I should be forced, in maintaining the cause of God,
to say more than I should wish. The malice and artifice of
these beggarly wretches is to allege, on false pretexts, the names
of princes, in order to shut the mouths of God's servants under
such a screen—the greater reason why princes should make a
point of stopping their mouths.

Whereupon, Madame, having very humbly commended myself to your indulgent favour, I will supplicate the heavenly
Father to keep you under his protection always, to govern you
by his Spirit, and increase your majesty in all good.

Your very humble servant,

CHARLES D'ESPEVILLE.

[*Fr. Minute Autog.—Library of Geneva.* Vol. 107.]

DCXIX.—To the King of Navarre.[1]

Severe judgment respecting the conduct of this prince, a renegado from the Reformed religion.

GENEVA, 24th December, 1561.

SIRE:—The fear we have of being importunate prevents us
from writing to you as often as we should do, and as possibly

lates, was approved of by Jane d'Albret :—"When I had shown her the copy of the
letter which I now send back to you, there was no need, she said, for any apology,
for I would by no means excuse my mother's fault, and I am perfectly well acquainted
with the whole affair. *She read the letter over, nevertheless, and approved of it.*"
Beza to Calvin, 6th January, 1562. (Library of Geneva, vol. 117.)

[1] Without the date of the month. Written in December, 1561, delivered to the king
in January, 1562, which is proved by the following passage of a letter of Calvin to
Beza : "If you think fit, you will see that this letter be delivered to the King of
Navarre. If it give offence, you will take the blame on yourself."

Circumstances imposed on the Reformer imperious duties with respect to the King
of Navarre. Betrayed by his servants, and deceived by the Guises, this prince float-
ing between the two parties had allowed himself to be seduced by the hope of espousing
the Queen of Scotland, and obtaining Sardinia in exchange for Spanish Navarre.
One of his confidential followers the Sire d'Escars had gone to convey on his part
terms of submission to the court of Rome—"Apprised of that, Theodore Beza, who

might be advantageous to you. But though we necessarily felt
some reluctance in addressing you, yet the letters of the queen
your consort have not only emboldened us, but also deprived us
of every excuse for delaying any longer to do so. For as God
has sensibly touched her heart, not content with holding on and
marching in the right path to which she has been called, she
has exhorted us, and that too most affectionately, to do all that
lay in our power to increase in you the courage and magnanimity
which you have so much need to display. As her desire is
laudable, so it ought to animate the zeal of us all; and as you
are her chief, Sire, you ought to set her an example, that she
may thereby be still more ardent for the glory of God, when in
so holy a matter she shall have it in her power to act conformably to your views. And in fact you have great reason to rejoice and bless God for having so disposed her mind, and that
whereas formerly she did not co-operate with you, she now strives
directly to second you as her duty demands. Still, Sire, inasmuch as she is firmly resolved to acquit herself of all that she
is in arrears to God and compensate for the defects of the
past, so it behoves you to make haste, in order that you may
always march before her in your order and degree. For it is
the first of all your titles of pre-eminence to bear yourself with
such courage, that she who desires to please you may have double
cause of rejoicing, when in submitting to you, she at the same
time glorifies God. And even should none of these motives
exist, Sire, still you would not be exempted from the duty you
owe to God. But such advantages certainly deserve to be
turned to account in urging you to vigorous action, as they leave
you without excuse, if you proceed with coldness and indifference.
Now you will be pleased to pardon us, Sire, if we cannot dissemble that hitherto you have been far from acquitting yourself

had ready access to him, did not fail to make to him excellent and warm remonstrances on the subject, to which the king replied, that he did not advance farther
than it was easy for him to extricate himself. . ." *Hist. Eccl.* vol. i. p. 688. In a
letter written with great moderation and energy, he endeavoured to enlighten the
king. All was to no purpose: "He broke," says Varillas, "with all his friends. He
put himself at the head of the Catholic party, and all that the tears of his wife could
obtain from him, was a permission to retire to her principality of Bearn, and live in
her Calvinistic fashion.

of what God is so justly entitled to require of you. Not that we do not take into account, Sire, the obstacles by which you are beset on all hands, but when you reflect that we are God's attorneys, as it were, you will, in your piety, permit us not to flatter you while we are maintaining his rights. Especially we entreat you to note what is written in psalm cxix., in which the prophet prays God not to take the word of truth utterly out of his mouth. There in the first place he is not ashamed to confess that he has neither shown himself so sincere, nor so entirely given up as he should have been, to maintaining the glory of God, and yet he protests in the same psalm that he has been as it were the preacher of the law before kings and princes. But well knowing that in a cause so worthy and precious, he who has done his best is still a debtor, he is displeased with his own weakness, in order that he may have satisfaction when he shall have profited more. Inasmuch as he had not been sufficiently zealous in maintaining God's quarrel for a time, he seeks the remedy where we may find it, that is, in being fortified by the power of the Holy Spirit. But at any rate, he falls not asleep in his coldness, but cuts short every cause of delay, as if he could never arrive soon enough at the end to which he is aspiring. That is the reason why he asks of God not to suffer him to remain in this state of weakness in which he feels himself to be.

Now as by the word *mouth* he shows that faith ought not to be buried, but that it ought to display itself before men, it cannot be doubted but that he means here to speak of the exterior service of God. Now, Sire, it is for you to consider whether you have been, we do not say as free as was requisite in bearing testimony to our faith, but whether you have even been half way in such a duty. It is then time to run lest the night surprise you. In general how far have you been, Sire, from maintaining the quarrel of Jesus Christ according to your rank and dignity, which required more of you than of private persons? If any man in a poor and humble condition appears to consent to having the name of God blasphemed, religion disgraced, and the poor church trodden under foot, he cannot avoid condemning himself of not having the word of truth in his mouth. What then shall we say of you, Sire, raised to such dignity, honour, and authority, if not to flatter you, you were called to give an account to Him from whom you hold all?

It would also be cowardice in us to pass over in silence the particular act which in the eyes of great and small has produced so much scandal. We speak of that unfortunate speech made at Rome on your part, Sire, which has caused to blush, weep, and groan, and almost burst with anger, all persons justly zealous either for the glory of God or the good reputation of your majesty. It is certain, Sire, that you cannot labour too hard, to follow manfully a directly opposite course, till once a fault of such a character be repaired both before God and men. We speak not of the man who was employed to pronounce the discourse, because no honest man could have been found who would have undertaken such an office. But it seems that he and your enemies wished to make a triumph of the reprobation you have incurred by printing an account of that disgraceful transaction, which was already but too well known. We see perfectly well, Sire, how you were induced to act so; but whether the perplexities by which you were then surrounded, caused you to yield in spite of your wishes, or you were swayed by considerations of personal safety to defeat the intrigues of your enemies, and break the nets which were spread for you, or whether you were lured by the hope of recovering for the future what belongs to you,—none of all these considerations will be admitted in the presence of God to absolve you. And in fact, what should we say if you were told that the whole world was to be bestowed on you, provided you fell down and worshipped him who is the principle of evil? You will pardon the necessity, Sire, which constrains us to speak thus, inasmuch as we are concerned for your salvation, and also for a thing still more worthy and precious, namely, the glory of God and the advancement of the reign of Jesus Christ, in which consists the salvation of you and of the whole world. Not, Sire, when we entreat you henceforth to bear yourself more manfully in making an upright and pure profession of true Christianity, that we do not take into account the opposition and alarms which you will have forthwith to struggle with. At the very least you will have to count on an interdict. But nothing can be more reasonable than that to serve Him to whom all is due, nothing should be spared. And though you should never be able to decide upon marching where God calls you, till you have learned to rely for everything on his promises, it is nevertheless true that to relieve you he holds out to you a helping hand in many ways. For if on the one hand there are threats and terrors, there are also good and suitable remedies, which will promptly present themselves when you shall be pleased to accept them. And even if every door should be shut against you, Sire, still it is your duty in this circumstance to apply to yourself what David says: God enables his children to leap over the highest walls. But when he so far supports you as to give you an opening, fail not, we pray you, Sire, to enter. Seize the favourable opportunity of which even the ungodly are wont to say that we should not allow it to escape. But though the affairs of this world are often conducted by long and tortuous ways, God will have us advance in a more straight-forward manner in maintaining his quarrel, so that the temporising method which you have hitherto followed, will never be found good at his tribunal.

We do not mean by this to urge you to precipitate action. Nay, there is an inconsiderate zeal in others which we do not approve of, and which we would fain moderate if it were in our power. But since we cannot, we entreat your majesty to be content to support it. What is more, we are of opinion that God, to correct the tardiness of the great, has caused the little ones of this world to put themselves so prominently forward that it would be difficult now to make them give ground. Now if it has pleased him so to *work* in them, the more the ungodly shall strive to resist, the more should you be whetted on, Sire, to put to use the weak instruments by which at last will be made apparent the power of the Holy Spirit. It is true that we had endeavoured to persuade them to be satisfied with preaching in secret in their own houses. Hearing that a contrary course has been pursued, we have been much surprised, but we cannot fail to conclude that God has wished to give free scope to his word without the aid of man, in order that the council may not think it so extraordinary to grant permission and toleration to what

is already established. Be that as it may, Sire, according as
you shall be faithful to the end, and as perfectly disposed as
were to be desired to procure the prosperity and repose of the
king and the good of the country of France, we entreat you also
with no less zeal and ardent affection to strive that God be
glorified, by resisting openly all superstition and idolatry, showing yourself at the same time the protector of the poor church,
until she shall no longer be so cruelly oppressed. For though
the Devil and the world vent all their rage, the liberty which
the faithful shall have of serving God, will procure from him
this blessing, that the king will peaceably rule all his subjects,
and you will be preserved in your rank, both to govern his
territory as chief of his council and also to reign in your own.

Sire, having humbly commended ourselves to the indulgent
favour of your majesty, we will supplicate our merciful Father
to have you in his keeping, to strengthen you with invincible
courage, to bestow on you prudence and address in the management of all affairs, and increase you more and more in his
grace.[1]

Your humble servants,

JOHN CALVIN, THEODORE BEZA.

[*Fr. Copy, in the hand of Th. Beza.—Library of Geneva.* Vol. 107.]

DCXX.—TO M. DE COLONGES.[2]

Answer to three questions.

GENEVA, *10th January,* 1562

MONSIEUR AND WELL-BELOVED BROTHER :—I should most
probably have been more expeditious in giving you an answer
respecting the three points about which you had asked my opi-

---

[1] The manuscript bears 1562, the date of the presentation of this letter to the King
of Navarre—early in January.

[2] *For title* : Answer to three questions. Francis de Morel, Sieur de Colonges,
minister of Geneva and of Paris. See p. 38. He presided in 1559 in the first synod
of the Reformed churches of France, and was present at the Colloquy of Poissy. He
was at this time minister of the Duchess of Ferrara.

nion, had I not felt some scruples in touching on so delicate a subject as that of ministers lending money upon interest. For to condemn absolutely such a manner of lending would be an instance of too great rigour, and might provoke many replies. In fact, I dare not assert that it is not lawful. But on the other hand, when I consider to how many calumnies and scandals such a practice may lead, and also that many persons are apt to pass the bounds of moderation in following it, and think themselves warranted to make such profits as may be deemed illicit, I willingly abstain from giving any answer to this question. The safest and most expedient conduct would be not to engage in such practices or contracts, and it is not without reason that Jeremiah protests that the contestations in which he was involved arose neither from borrowing nor lending. Thus, when a minister shall dispense with such gains, he will act most wisely. But as this practice is more supportable than pursuing mercantile speculations, or conducting any traffic by which he might be diverted from his functions, I see no reason why the thing should be condemned in general. Nevertheless, I could wish that so much moderation were observed that people should not desire to derive a certain profit from it, but should content themselves with lending their money to some merchant, a man of integrity, and trust to his good faith and loyalty for making an equitable gain out of it, when God should cause his industry to thrive.

With regard to taking an oath to the consistory, it is proper to proceed in that matter with prudence, in order to guard against detraction and murmurs. It is lawful to summon persons and adjure them, setting before their eyes the presence of God and his judgment, so much the rather that he presides over such a society. But we must carefully beware of every formality which might imply a kind of jurisdiction, or any thing that bore the semblance of it.

Respecting the last point, it appears to me that no objection can be made to admitting into the consistory officers of justice and chiefs of police, provided they sit in it in the capacity of magistrates. But always let there be a due distinction observed between the two functions and conditions. To exclude

persons that belong to the civil government from all superintendence in the spiritual administration, seems to me contrary
to reason.   What is essential is that when fitting persons shall
have been elected to such an office, there should be no blending
of their functions, nor the power of the sword confounded with
what ought to be carefully kept distinct from it.

You have here an abstract of what God has enabled me to
communicate to you respecting the three questions, and my
opinion is corroborated by that of all our brethren.   For I
thought right to adhere to their sentiments, in order that the
decision should not proceed from me alone.   Whereupon, . . .
etc.

[*Fr. Orig.—Library of Geneva.*   Vol. 145.]

DCXXI.—To M. de Passy.[1]

He urges him to accept the functions of an evangelical minister.

GENEVA, 24*th January*, 1562.

MONSIEUR AND HONOURED BROTHER:—When I wrote to you
not long ago on the part of the society, and at the request of
the Church of Paris, I begged you to consider, according to
your prudence, what should be most expedient, as you can best
judge by your experience of the past time, and also from your
greater proximity to the place.[2]   Before receiving an answer, I

[1] Jacques Paul Spifame, Seigneur de Passy, Bishop of Nevers, voluntarily resigned
his bishopric to withdraw, in 1559, to Geneva.   He was there made a burgess and a
minister of the city; became, in 1561, pastor of the Church of Issoudun, and was
employed by the Prince of Condé on several important missions in Germany.   Called
to the court of the Queen of Navarre, he incurred the blame of that princess by inconsiderate acts which caused the sincerity of his convictions to be suspected at Geneva.
His past life was subjected to a severe scrutiny.   This brought to light disorders
which Spifame had endeavoured to conceal by the fabrication of a false contract of
marriage.   Imprisoned as an adulterer, he confessed his guilt, and in vain solicited
the indulgence of his judges, who, from an excess of rigour, condemned him to death.
He died on the scaffold, the 23d March, 1566, "with a deep repentance for his faults,
which he testified by a good exhortation which he delivered to the people." . . .
Spon. *Hist. de Geneva*, vol. ii., p. 112; note 2, de Gautier; et Senebier, *Hist. Litt.*,
vol. i., p. 384.

[2] Spifame was then minister at Issoudun.

am solicited by Monseigneur, the Comte d'Eu, and the Church of Nevers, to pray, exhort, summon, and, if need be, adjure you to go and acquit yourself of your duty towards that poor people to whom you are indebted, and, above all, to compensate for the defects of the time past, by showing that if you were then a bishop so far as the title is concerned, you will now be so in reality.[1] The whole of our society have found this claim so just that I must entreat and beseech you, in the name of God, if you do not find a journey to Paris useful for the edification of the whole church, that you will accept this charge. We are well aware that in that case it will be necessary to provide the Church of Issoudun with some one to succeed you ; but we have on our part made provision for that necessity, for even before we had learned your intentions, we heard of a man whom they have presented to us, in order that if you go to them, they may have wherewithal to recompense the Church of Issoudun.

Whereupon, Monsieur and honoured brother, after having presented to you my affectionate commendations, and those of all our society, I will supplicate our heavenly Father to have you in his holy keeping, to sustain you by his power, and increase you in all good, making your labours profitable for the advancement of his kingdom.

Your servant and humble brother,

JOHN CALVIN.

Know that you are still continued a councillor. Now we are unwilling either to lose or to give you up.

[*Fr. Orig.—Library of Geneva.* Vol. 107.]

---

[1] The Reformed of Nevers assembled for the first time the 23d of March, 1561. Their church was established by the minister La Planche, under the auspices of the Comte d'Eu and of the Marquis d'Isles, son of the Duke of Nevers, governor of the province.

DCXXII.—To THEODORE BEZA.[1]

Catholic League—Recommendations of the family of Guillaume de Frie—Last words
of that Seigneur.

GENEVA, 11*th February,* 1562.

Since your two melancholy letters, we are yet ignorant whether any change for the better has taken place, and rumour has brought us no accounts that can diminish my anxiety. Unless God speedily interfere, a new opportunity will be sought for oppressing our cause. Of your first meeting[2] something has got wind, from which I conjecture that you argued but too truly when you wrote that all would vanish in smoke. Our neighbours are in great trepidation; we as yet are quietly waiting to see in what quarter the attack of Philip will break out, who is said to be gradually leading troops in no small numbers out of Spain, and enlisting other soldiers in Italy. I cannot yet persuade myself that he is preparing to wage a common war at once with the Pope and the Venetians. If you can fish out any news respecting these matters, it will be very advantageous for our interests to be made acquainted with them as early as possible. Certainly, a matter of such moment cannot be a secret at court. See then that you cram your earliest letters with details of these preparations. We are perfectly on our guard, and God, I trust, will keep watch over us, so that the enemy may not catch us unprepared. If it is an open war that is to be made

[1] At the moment in which L'Hôpital endeavoured to seal by reciprocal concessions the reconciliation of the religious parties, the Catholic monarchs of Spain and Italy, confirming their alliances, were preparing to destroy his work by attacking, with arms in their hands, Geneva and the French churches. The massacre of Vassy, which was about to usher in so sadly the period of the civil wars, was but the partial realization of the plan traced out in the counsels of Philip II. "The audacity and effrontery of the enemy," wrote Beza to Calvin, "is incredible. If the edict against our opinion were known, I am fully persuaded that they would attempt all extremities. I know, however, that they will not effect all they desire, nor is it a new thing for us to suffer injustice."

[2] An unseasonable controversy respecting the church and the sacraments, provoked by the adversaries of the Reformed, then divided the Doctors of the two religions still assembled at Poissy. On the one hand, Beza, Marlorat, Perucel; on the other, Salignac, D'Espense, Bouthelier.

on us, there will be time enough to summon auxiliaries to our
aid.   As to the new buildings adjoining to the gate, I had
already written that their outcries were ridiculous, for no one
there is as yet suspected by us.[1]   You will communicate the
contents of my letter to the Admiral, and see that you be a
faithful advocate of the cause which I entrust to you.[2]   I beg
of him to aid us with his influence and authority in obtaining
letters patent of which I send you a model, and also a copy
of a petition.   As the brother of De Frie is not only proud and
foolish, but also treacherous and cruel, and, in one word, perfectly unprincipled, nothing will be wrung from him except by
main force.   But we are asking for nothing illicit or difficult,
but what has been already every where granted to a great many,
viz., that minors be admitted to reclaim their rights.   Until this
preliminary step for the proceeding be gone through, we dare
not bring an action, because we have to do with a man more
than usually desperate.   Bernant, I trust, will undertake the
whole charge, but as much as it will be in your power, even if
it should put you to some inconvenience, I entreat you with all
the earnestness I can muster, to employ also your influence in the
matter ; though, in truth, I forbear to express all my zeal, since
I am sufficiently, and more than sufficiently aware of what you
will do for my sake, even without being solicited.   But be thoroughly persuaded, nevertheless, that of all private acts of friendship you can do none that will be more grateful to me.   I owe
it to the memory of a singularly excellent friend to cherish his
children just as if they were my own.   He has deserved that
from his incredible affection towards me, from the filial piety
with which he cherished me, and the deference which he paid me
up to the moment of his death ; and it would be a stain of infamy on my character, if the confidence which he reposed in me
should be disappointed.   His last dying words will ever remain
engraven on my memory, when he addressed me in presence of

---

[1] Beza had warned Calvin to be on his guard against a soldier, named Ferrand, "and
especially to keep a strict watch over the gates during the sermons."—Letter of the
6th January, 1561.

[2] Guillaume de Trie, at his death, had left several children stripped of their father's
fortune, by the application of the penalty that had been pronounced against the refugees.

his wife and children. "Here are your children, and as God is now taking me away, I entreat you, according as I have been to you a dutiful son, not to disown those that remain to you. I disavow them if they do not bear towards you more honour and obedience than towards myself. I resign to you all they owe me, and also all I owe to you it is their duty to acquit." I have thought proper to quote these expressions to you, that if you should encounter any obstacle from the indolence of others, you cease not to stimulate them, until what we have in view be accomplished.

Farewell again and again, most excellent brother. We shall shortly know, I suppose, whether our friend M. Normandie is still irresolute. I thought that for the settlement of his business the form of separation of which I had written to you was sufficient, but we shall see what his next letters will announce. If the ties by which he is bound are inextricable, let him rather, in fine, burst them asunder, than that we should always be deprived of him.

Farewell, both of you, again and again. May the Lord protect and govern you, enrich you with every blessing, and support you even to the end with his invincible courage. Our colleagues very zealously salute you.

Yours,   CHARLES PASSELIUS.

[*Lat. Orig.—Library of Geneva.*   Vol. 107 *a.*]

DCXXIII.—To THEODORE BEZA.

Imprudent concessions made to the Catholic prelates—Regrets and warnings of Calvin.

GENEVA, 18th February, 1562.

I have had no news from you since you briefly related to me a pleasant account of the result of the second conference.[1] It is true, that the court being full of intrigues that are ever transpiring, many rumours penetrate as far as us, and we are com-

---

[1] See page 256, note 2. This second colloquy had no greater results than the former, as we see by the letters of Theodore Beza to Calvin, 1562, *passim.*

pelled to hear more things than you are aware of. This is one of the effects of distance that many folks among us fancy they know more than ocular witnesses who are on the spot. I am surprised that in the first colloquy you did not perceive into what snares you threw yourselves. The method you adopted always displeased me, viz., your making one-half of your cause repose on the testimony of antiquity. On this matter, the agreement between us is like that which subsists between fire and water. But because you committed this slip, not from error or want of reflection, I leave that decision free to you. The wound, however, which was beginning to be cicatrized is again evidently bleeding afresh, and compels me to profess how greatly I differ from you. There was a certain plausibility in opposing the authority of antiquity against images. But with such an argument, how are you to deal with the chrism in baptism, auricular confession; and the wax-tapers of Easter? But I will not give free scope to my reflections, lest I should appear to see farther than Marlorat and such persons. Meanwhile, I am sorry for you whom their folly has plunged deep in the mire. I have briefly touched upon what I conceive to be expedient in what concerns a council.[1] After reading it you will perhaps not pay much attention to it, because it contains little but what is commonplace; but I preferred to comply with your wishes, though producing nothing, to refusing what you demanded. I now pass on to other subjects. Our neighbours recently made a serious application to the senate for the purpose of warning your graceless Absalom to be on his guard against the immense forces that are now being levied against him.[2] They relate a great many things which, I fancy, are brought to your ears from other quarters. On the other hand, you will learn from his letter what occupation Bullinger is creating for us. I did not venture to suppress this letter, lest the affair should be betrayed by our silence. I charge this task upon you, lest either party should complain that an excellent opportunity had

[1] Calvin had already developed his opinion on this subject in a special memorial to the Reformed churches, page 158.

[2] Allusion to the menaces uttered by Philip II. against the young King Charles IX., and his mother, on the occasion of the promulgation of the Edict of January, which had appeared to the sovereign of Spain a dereliction of the Catholic faith.

been neglected through our fastidiousness.   One thing I earnestly entreat of you, (mark the emphasis of my expression,) it is that you give me as early an answer as possible.   I have not many Dallers to furnish with information people who are half famished for want of news.   Then you are well aware that they who are slower than snails strangely abuse our French hastiness.   As soon as possible free me from my inquietude. But what, after all, if this is nothing but a little smoke got up to strike terror?   That does not concern me, provided only you make haste to give me news.   In such a press of business I wished to spare you.   I could not, however, do otherwise than send you Sulcer's letter, a proof of his fatuity and impudence, which I would have you despise as it deserves.

Farewell, most excellent and friendly brother.   May the Lord always stand by you, sustain you by his invincible courage, and preserve you in safety.

Yours,   CHARLES PASSELIUS.

All your colleagues salute you very earnestly, as also the new syndics, and the senate.

[*Lat. Copy.—Library of Geneva.*   Vol. 107 *a.*]

DCXXIV.—To the Duchess of Ferrara.[1]

League against the Reformation—Complaints respecting the conduct of the Duchess of Guise.

GENEVA, *February*, 1562.

MADAME:—I am delighted to have the means of writing to you in surety by the bearer, not that I have anything of importance to communicate to you at this moment, but that I may acquit myself of my duty, and also because I fancy my letters, in consequence of your favourable indulgence, are not unwelcome to you.   If they could be in any way profitable to you I should make an effort to let you have them more frequently.   But you have, thank God, in your household a man every way qualified

---

[1] Without date.   Written a short time before the massacre of Vassy, that is, in February, 1562.

to exhort you and confirm you in all you stand in need of.[1] I
have no news to send you that you may not learn from other
sources, especially none that can afford you pleasure, and I dislike to put you to pain, though I am compelled to disburden my
mind, not without great regret, of a sorrow common to all the
children of God. You know, Madame, what the enemies of the
truth are hatching; witness the league of the Pope with the
King of Spain, the Venetians, and the potentates of Italy, in
which our neighbour is included. They verily think that it is
their duty to banish all Christianity out of the world. Now in
the mean time, Madame de Guise is pursuing a course which can
only lead to her own confusion if she continue in it; for though
she does not think so, yet it is most certain that she is seeking
the ruin of the poor churches in France, of which God will be the
protector in order to maintain them.[2]

Again I protest, Madame, that I would fain abstain from
giving you uneasiness, but on the other hand I should wish that
she were induced by your authority to moderate her passions,
which she cannot obey as she does without making war on God.
I tell you frankly, Madame, what everybody knows, that you
may devise what good means can be applied to divert her from
conspiring with those who seek for nothing but to abolish pure
religion, and prevent her from being mixed up with intrigues of
which the issue cannot but be unfortunate, inasmuch as they are
directed against God.

Madame, having very humbly commended myself to your indulgent favour, I will supplicate our heavenly Father to keep
you always under his protection, to fortify you by his power,
and increase you in all good and prosperity.

[*Fr. Copy.—Library of Paris, Dupuy.* Vol. 102.]

---

[1] 3d July 1561 : " A minister is accorded to the Duchess of Ferrara on condition
that it be neither M. Calvin nor M. Beza." *Registres du Conseil.* This minister was
Francis de Morel.

[2] Anne d'Este, daughter of Renée of France and Duchess of Guise. Brought up at
the court of Ferrara, in the Reformed faith, she was obliged to abandon it in contracting an alliance with the house of Lorraine, but she always gave proofs of a generous
mind equally removed from the excesses of both parties. The massacre of Vassy,
which she vainly endeavoured to prevent, caused to fall upon her the hatred and unpopularity attached to the name of Francis de Guise among the Protestants.

DCXXV.—To Bullinger.[1]

News of France—Disorders at Aix—Progress of the gospel—Negotiations with the
court—Synod of Neuchatel.

GENEVA, 12th March, 1562.

When I wrote lately to our friend Blaurer I was prevented
from doing so to you, because, before I was quite recovered from
an attack of fever, a domestic sorrow, occasioned by the dishonour of my step-daughter, compelled me to seek the privacy
of solitude for a few days. When I was in my rustic cottage
your letter was presented to me, with the contents of which many
rumours from other quarters perfectly agree. We have, then,
good reason to be afraid. But how to take measures of pre-
caution is difficult. How great the confusion is in France, you
will learn partly from a letter of our brother Beza, of which I
send you a copy, and I will myself partly briefly allude to it.
At Aix, which is the seat of the Parliament, a sedition has been
stirred up by the Papists, that they might exclude from his
government, the Comte of Crussol, who had been appointed to
command there with supreme authority. But he having assembled a few companies of soldiers forced them to open their gates,
and gave orders to have some of them hanged. A part of the
faction which had found means to escape still keeps possession
of a neighbouring city, which is tolerably well fortified. But
want of provisions will ere long force them to a surrender, for
hitherto they have spread themselves up and down the country
like men on a chess-board. The Parliament itself is pronouncing
severe sentences on the rebels, although many of the judges
themselves are implicated in the same crime. They are spared

[1] In a letter written to Dr. George Tanner, the 10th March, 1562, Calvin thus de-
picted the state of France at this period. " I dare scarcely allude to the affairs of
France, they are in such disorder and confusion. The number of the godly indeed
daily increases. The alacrity and zeal are astonishing. But the fickleness of one
man (*the King of Navarre*) is the cause why the Parliament of Paris assails Christ
with obstinate fury." Disorders break out everywhere in consequence of the refusal
of the Parliament to register the *Edict of January.*

in the mean time till the violence of the tumult be a little spent. Marseilles and some other cities, which were meditating a revolt, have been reduced to subjection by having garrisons placed in them. The Parliament of Toulouse would willingly have thrown everything into disorder, but the magistrates of the city who are called *capitouls*, because to them belongs the ordinary jurisdiction, having assembled a powerful and energetic body of men so completely subdued the arrogance and cruelty of the Parliament, that now in the suburbs of the city there are free meetings of the godly to the number of ten thousand men. Indeed fifteen thousand have proclaimed their adherence to the gospel. In Auvergne the nobility still rages most obstinately. Among the Armoricans, that is, in Britanny, the nobility have almost to a man embraced the gospel. Also in Picardy, but the populace cannot be brought over. In Champaigne and the district of Sens they are rather lukewarm. The Burgundians begin to show a bolder spirit. They obey the edict of the king, but to see such numerous bodies proceeding in an orderly manner, instead of God's being worshipped in an obscure corner of the city, is what still more galls their adversaries.

Certainly nothing retards so much the progress of Christ's kingdom as the paucity of ministers. Beza indeed informs us that Julian[1] is attempting to ruin everything at court, but whatever evil he is creating will fall on his own head. He had not, however, yet received my last letter. The queen too, now that she will see that they are coming to her aid, will probably be more violently exasperated against us. I will only urge, as I have hitherto done, that our brethren who but too late have made head against these extreme measures, should not allow so fine an opportunity to escape them. The advice which Beza asked of me I had already sent to him.[2] I send you a copy of

---

[1] The King of Navarre: "You can scarcely believe what deplorable scenes he creates, whom it least of all becomes to do so. If I have any occasion in future to write of him, I shall denominate him Julian. In one word I will say that we have need that the Lord should execute his judgments; hardly any such instance of fickleness, perfidy, and profligacy exists." *Beza Calvino*, 26th February, 1562.

[2] "They inquire earnestly upon what conditions we should establish a free and Christian council. I ask you to aid us on the earliest occasion with your advice." *Ibidem.*

it in Latin, though I have preferred to render literally in barbarous style my French reply, rather than aim at expressing
myself with the elegance of a pure Latinity. I have also endeavoured to be concise, but without, however, omitting anything
that is essential. If I shall seem to have made more concession
to the adverse party than I ought, you will remember that I
was not at liberty to consult my own wishes. I was under the
necessity of accommodating what I said to the capacity of the
queen. I had two objects in view: first, that the Papists
should repudiate our conditions, should they chance to be
favourably received by the council, which it is certain they
will be next, if they shall be forced to submit to the yoke, that
no council of any sort shall have in their power to do us any
injury. I judged it more advantageous for us to sit in it as
tribunes of the people, than being confounded with the senators
to be overwhelmed by the majority of votes. You will look to
what our brother Beza asks of you, and determine with your
colleagues what shall be most expedient, and with all convenient
speed. If anything of greater importance take place, endeavour
to be early made acquainted with it. When Cognet arrives, he
will aid us in carrying letters backward and forward. The approbation of France will expose the hypocrisy of those who place
all their reliance on men, will increase the courage of the godly,
and teach them to rely more upon God alone, and the agitation will at the same time stir them up to have recourse to
prayer.

In reading over what I have written, I perceive that I have
omitted to allude to a subject which I had determined to do.
Already about the middle of February a report was circulated
in this neighbourhood, that the senate of Berne had been induced
by your advice to change its resolution respecting the convocation of a Synod, and that those who were preparing to set out
for it had been suddenly countermanded by an edict. I am
quite aware that you have acted with proper intentions, but a
slight experience will show you that your advice was far from
being salutary. You have no occasion to solicit my co-operation, for I declare that all our prospects are ruined. I dispense
with saying anything more. Being lately summoned to a synod

at Neuchatel, I begged to be excused, lest those who feign to
have need of my assistance, should exclaim that I go beyond
my bounds. I am summoned to it a second time. I am uncertain what I shall do. This I know that you are greatly and
too greatly mistaken in thinking that they desire to consult for
the good of the church. I could wish I were in the remotest
corners of the earth,[1] when I see them so insultingly making
game of me.

[*Lat. Orig. Minute.—Library of Geneva.* Vol. 107 *a.*]

DCXXVI.—To PETER MARTYR.[2]

Disorders the precursors of the civil wars in France—Opposition of the Reformer to
the Council of Trent.

GENEVA, 16*th March*, 1562.

Now, at last, I have received your letter, most accomplished
and venerable brother, to which if I give a short reply without
adding any apology you will know how to account for it. The
Bernese have not changed their resolution about calling a synod.
A report had gone abroad that by the advice of Bullinger they
had done so. From whatever quarter that rumour arose, still
from the contempt of a remedy in mortal diseases, I augur nothing but what is disastrous. But not to entangle myself in
such a labyrinth of matters, I pass on to others. Our brother
Beza is exercised with hard trials. By the treachery and
wickedness of Julian, he narrowly escaped, a short time ago,
from being dragged to execution, along with many others, but
God miraculously brought to naught such infamous attempts.[3]

[1] Ultra Sauromatas.

[2] This letter is the last of Calvin's correspondence with Martyr, who died at Zurich
on the 12th November, 1562.

[3] Is this an allusion to the journey of Theodore Beza to the court which was then
assembled at the Chateau of Monceaux, and to his eloquent protestation against the
massacre of Vassy? It was at that time he addressed to the King of Navarre, in
the face of the Guises, this proud saying:—"It is, in truth, the part of the church ·
of God to endure blows and not to inflict any; remember, however, that it is an an-
vil on which many hammers have been broken."

Now though that *apostate* has summoned the Guises to court, in order to have recourse to the worst extremities, Beza, nevertheless, trusts not only that these efforts will be unavailing, but that the church will receive so great an increase that they will not dare to attempt any thing afterwards. The first collision is to be dreaded, unless God speedily come to our aid, which we should ask by continual prayers. But though serious threats and terrors are impending everywhere over us, I nevertheless augur that something prosperous will come out of it. Since the Pope will not satisfy King Philip, and the Duke of Florence is under apprehensions from both of them, I doubt not but our brethren will present to the king and his council a form of protestation against the Council of Trent. The queen, also, would wish us to interfere, as I reminded M. Bullinger. You will see what advantages may arise from it. It would be absurd for us to attempt any thing apart, but we will willingly subscribe to the words of the resolution.

Farewell, most illustrious sir and honoured brother. May the Lord always stand by you, long preserve you from danger, and bless your labours. The Marquis and the others salute you. I beg also to present my best respects to your wife and family.

Yours,   JOHN CALVIN.

[Lat. Copy.—Library of Paris, Dupuy. Vol. 102, p. 59.]

DCXXVII.—TO THE QUEEN OF NAVARRE.[1]

Expression of warm sympathy for the trials of this princess.

GENEVA, 22d March, 1562.

MADAME:—My compassion for your sorrows makes me feel, in part, how severe they must be to you, and how bitter to sup-

---

[1] Offended in her dignity as a wife and a mother, by the disorderly conduct of her husband, deeply afflicted by his union with the enemies of the Reformation, this princess was a prey to the most poignant distress. "The Queen of Navarre, however, like a prudent and virtuous princess as she is, endeavoured to bring back her husband, supporting every thing which she could, and pointing out to him what he owed to God and his followers. But in vain, to such a degree is he infatuated. Seeing that she

port. But be they what they will, assuredly it is infinitely better to be sorrowful for such a cause than to live in contented
indifference to the perdition of your soul. It is a desirable
thing to live at ease when God affords such a blessing to his
children, as to put it into their power fully to rejoice, and since
that is a privilege which does not always last, if it please him
to try us sharply, it is also desirable to follow him through
rugged and difficult ways. You have been taught, Madame,
that we cannot serve him without fighting. The kinds of combats are diverse, but in whatever way it shall please God to
exercise us, we ought to be prepared for it. If the assaults
you have to sustain are rude and terrible, God has long ago
furnished you with an opportunity of meditating on them beforehand. The king, your husband, has already been long
assaulted by two of the devil's horns—I mean D'Escars[1] and
the Bishop of Auxerre.[2] Not only has he allowed himself to
be cast down by them, but, of his own accord, he arms himself
against God and God's children. I speak as of a thing that is
notorious. I know, Madame, that the first batteries are directed
against you. But though the difficulties should be a hundred
times greater, the courage which comes from on high, when we
have recourse to it, will be victorious. Remember only never
to weary of holding out, having God for your guaranty, for we
do not obey him at random, inasmuch as his promise cannot fail
that he will give a favourable issue to our constancy when it is
founded on his word. Therefore, should the whole world be
turned upside down, if our anchor is cast in heaven, however
tossed we may be, most assuredly we shall arrive in safety at
the harbour. St. Paul says that He is faithful to keep that which

had recourse but to tears and prayers, filling every one with compassion, except the
said sieur, the king, the queen-mother, in the mean time, tried to persuade her to
humour the king, her husband. At last, she made this reply, that rather than go to
mass, if she held her kingdom and her son in her hand, she would throw them both
into the bottom of the sea, if they should be an obstacle to her in the performance
of her duty. On receiving this answer, they ceased to trouble her on that point."—
Beza, *Hist. Eccl.,* vol. i., p. 689.

[1] Francis d'Escars, servant of the King of Navarre, "a man," says Mezeray, "who
sold himself for money to every body except his master."

[2] Philip de Lenoncourt, Bishop of Auxerre, suborned by the Guises to bring back
the King of Navarre to the bosom of the Catholic Church.

we have committed to him. Thus knowing in whom we have believed, let us persevere, pitying those who amuse themselves with such paltry attractions as even little children would laugh at. In the mean time, Madame, you shall not be forgotten in our prayers, as we learn both from our brother M. Beza and others that you desire them. I feel very confident, Madame, that God will hear your groanings, as well as ours, provided we offer to him the sacrifice of humility which he desires. For, though we may and should be bold in maintaining his quarrel, still we ought to attribute it to our sins that the course of his gospel is retarded. Whatever happen, in the midst of all your distresses remember the saying of St. Paul: "Let us rejoice in the Lord continually, and I say unto you again rejoice;" words uttered, no doubt, that we may have an invincible courage amid all our afflictions.

Madame, as the bearer will return to you to know whither it will please you to direct him, I cannot help declaring that he has conducted himself here so well that we could have wished to retain him altogether, which we should have done had he not been dedicated to your churches. I know he has not lost his time in coming here, as the fact will show.

[*Fr. Copy.—Library of Geneva.* Vol. 107.]

DCXXVIII.—To Sturm.[1]

Mission of Budé into Germany—Duplicity of the Guises.

Geneva, 25th March, 1562.

For what reason our friend Budé has undertaken this mission, he himself will better explain to you orally than it would be safe for me to do by letter. I doubt not but the cause when it shall be laid before you will meet with your warmest support.

---

[1] At the moment when the massacre of Vassy rendered the civil war inevitable, Calvin, devoted to his peaceful mission, tried the effect of a last measure upon the Protestant princes of Germany, in order to obtain from them an embassy to the king with instructions to exhort him to maintain the Edict of January, and not suffer himself to be led on by the fatal influence of the Guises. Sturm was the confident and natural intermediary of these steps, which produced no result.

Nay, as it is a cause common to you and us, I deem it superfluous to exhort you in many words to embrace it. If the liberty which has been promised us by an edict be not destroyed, the Papacy will fall to pieces of itself. The Guises will therefore have recourse to all extremities, in order forcibly to deprive us of it. But to repress their assaults it is of the highest importance that the princes of Germany should interfere to exhort the king to constancy, and declare that their good offices will be employed in his favour as far as opportunities will permit. If those furies lately made any dissembling promises at Saverne,[1] the atrocious act which immediately followed has revealed how vain and deceitful all their flatteries were. For scarcely had they quitted the colloquy, when they hurried to the perpetration of the most barbarous massacre.[2] But these things, and whatever relates to the cause, you will learn from Budé.

Farewell, most accomplished and honoured sir. May the Lord always stand by you and preserve you in safety.

[*Lat. Orig.—Library of Geneva.* Vol. 107 *a.*]

DCXXIX.—To the Church of Lyons.[3]

Severe admonitions because of the conduct of one of its ministers.

Geneva, 13*th May*, 1562.

Dearly beloved Brethren :—We have already long waited for letters from you, in order to have an opportunity in answer-

---

[1] Adding craft to hatred, the Cardinal of Lorraine and his brother Francis de Guise had attracted the Duke of Wurtemberg to Saverne, and affected in their interview with this prince the warmest desire to labour for the Reformation of the Church, at the moment they were hatching the most odious plot against the Reformed. Schmidt, *Vie de Sturm*, pp. 110, 111.

[2] The conferences took place in February, and the massacre on the 1st of March, 1562.

[3] Exasperated by the news of the massacre of Vassy, and supported by several captains of the Prince of Conde's army, the Protestants of Lyons took possession of the town on the 30th April, 1562. This audacious act, accomplished in a few hours, and almost without bloodshed, was followed by excesses greatly to be regretted. The Church of St. John was sacked, and given up to be pillaged by the Huguenots, and these violent deeds remained unpunished. Informed of what had taken place at

ing them, of disburdening our hearts of what lies so heavily on them. But since the change which has taken place at Lyons, we have not received a single word either from you or the society of the elders, which leads us to suppose that there is much disorder, seeing that we are solicited by certain persons to succour your church, and you drop not one word about it. Nay, when the Sire Jerome des Gouttes, passing by here a short time ago, asked us to send ministers to aid you, he declared that he was the bearer of no letters from you. In the mean time, we have news which causes us great distress. We are perfectly aware that in such disturbances it is difficult to preserve so much moderation as that no excesses shall be committed, and we could easily excuse you for not having held the bridle so tight as might have been desirable. But there are things quite insupportable concerning which we are forced to write to you with greater asperity than we could have wished. We should be traitors to God, to you, and to Christianity itself, if we dissembled what to our great regret is spoken of you here. It is an unbecoming act in a minister to play the trooper, or captain, but it is much worse when one quits the pulpit to carry arms.[1] But the worst of all is to go to the governor of a town, pistol in hand, and glorying in force and violence, to threaten him; here are the words that have been repeated to us, and which we hold from trustworthy witnesses: " Sir, you must do it, for we have force in our hands." We tell you frankly that we feel as much disgust at expressions of that sort as at the sight of a monster. We were also exceedingly displeased at the seal appended by the governor and the ministers. We pronounce the same judgment about the passports, and such like things, the enormity of which has disgusted many people; that is to say, alienated them from the gospel, and troubled and grieved all persons who have any piety and modesty. Nor was this enough for them, but they must scour the whole country, carrying off booty and

Lyons by the minister Viret, whose eloquence had greatly contributed to calm the passions that had been let loose, Calvin addressed severe reproaches to the ministers of this church.—See De Thou, Lib. xxxi.; Beza, vol. iii., p. 221.

[1] The Minister Jacques Rufi, a man of energy and action, had put himself at the head of armed bands, and had powerfully contributed to the taking of the town.— See Beza and De Thou, ut supra.

pillaging the cows and other cattle, and that too even since the Baron des Adrets arrived invested with authority,[1] who did not approve of such misdeeds with which those who boast of being the ministers of God's word were not ashamed to mix themselves up.　Now these old wounds have been again ripped up, for we have been told that the booty which had been taken from St. John's church has been exposed to sale to the highest bidder, and knocked down for a hundred and twelve crowns; nay, they promised the soldiers that they would distribute to each of them his portion.　It is true, that M. Rufi is expressly charged with the direction of all these affairs.　But it seems to us that you are partly to be blamed for not having checked him when you had liberty and power to do so; for if he does not submit to your correction, let him seek where he may erect a church apart.　We cannot remonstrate gently with you on these matters, which we cannot hear mentioned without shame and bitterness of heart.　Now, though it is late to remedy them, still we cannot refrain from entreating you, in the name of God, and exhorting you as much as it depends on us, to strive to compensate for past faults, and, above all, to put an end to all these acts of plunder and robbery.　For you should much rather quit these people, and separate yourselves from them, than bring disgrace on the gospel by associating with them.　Already there was an inconsiderate zeal in devastating as they have done the temples, but as it was done in the heat of passion, and from some feelings of devotion; people that fear God will not pass a very rigorous judgment on that act.　But of the plunder, what can they say?　By what title shall it be lawful to take away by force things that belong not to any private person?　If petty thefts are punishable, it is a double crime to plunder public property.　Wherefore, if you wish not to be hated and detested by all men, take measures to repair such offences.　For if you delay any longer, we are greatly afraid that you will set about it too late.　Wherefore, we will pray God to guide you by a spirit of prudence, direct you in all equity and uprightness, fortify you with constancy and virtue, that the pains which

---

[1] See the following letter.

you take may not be useless, but that your doctrine may fructify and his name be glorified.

[*Fr. Copy.—Library of Paris, Dupuy.* Vol. 102.]

DCXXX.—To the Baron des Adrets.[1]

He exhorts him to repress severely the disorders of those of his party at Lyons.

GENEVA, 13*th May*, 1562.

MONSIEUR:—We know very well that God, to curb our self-sufficiency, always tempers the joys which he allots us with some admixture of disappointments, and yet we were not greatly astonished to learn that people had overstepped the bounds of moderation in the change which took place at Lyons. And though it grieved us that they had allowed themselves too much license in some respects, still we supported that without breaking silence. But since your arrival there to take the direction of affairs, it is high time for them to moderate their impetuosity, and what is more that some order should be established instead of this confusion. We doubt not but you have laboured as much as possible to that end. As the charge, however, is heavy and difficult, we easily imagine that you cannot remedy all the evils which displease you, as it were to be wished. Most assuredly, however, you should make every possible exertion for that purpose, and above all correct one abuse which is altogether insupportable. I allude to the pretensions of the soldiery to have a right to plunder the chalices, reliquaries, and other furniture of the temples. What is worse, it has been reported that one

---

[1] Francis de Beaumont, Baron des Adrets, one of the principal chiefs of the Protestant party, which he dishonoured by his cruelties: "He was," says Beza, "one of the most vigilant of men, bold and successful in his enterprises, and truly gifted with many of the qualities requisite in a great captain; but in other respects extremely ambitious and cruel, which vices tarnished the lustre of his other virtues, and at last deprived him of all conscience and reputation." *Hist. Eccl.*, vol. iii., p. 224. After the taking of Lyons by the Huguenots, the Baron des Adrets took possession of the government of this city, which he was obliged soon after to put into the hands of M. de Loubise. Dissatisfied with the Prince of Condé, he entered into negotiations with the court, became again a Catholic, and turned his arms against his own party. He died in 1586, equally the object of the reprobation of both churches.

of the ministers had so identified himself with these plunderers as to cause to be exposed for sale a quantity of such booty. First of all, if that is true, it will cause dreadful scandal and make the gospel evil spoken of, and even if the mouths of the wicked should not be opened to blaspheme the name of God, still it is quite unlawful without a public authorization to touch public property. And in fact we are very certain that the Prince of Condé and all the worthy Seigneurs that have embraced our party, will not only disavow but stamp with infamy such an act, inasmuch as it is calculated to bring disgrace upon a cause so good and holy in itself, and render it odious. We are thoroughly persuaded that you will not suffer such extortions and acts of violence, and that without being greatly solicited you will be ready and inclined to lay hands on the authors of them. But the only means to provide against this evil is, we think, to have proclaimed about the public squares and crossways, that all those who shall have taken such booty, or received and concealed it, shall have to bring back what part of it is in their possession within a delay of eight days, on pain of being reputed guilty of larceny, and proceeded against as thieves, and that all those who know any persons that keep back or possess any part of it, shall have to make a declaration to that effect, within the aforesaid term, on pain of being punished as receivers. If the evil is not corrected by these means, at least we may be sure that the remedy will not be without some good effects; for by it you will close, as far as it will be possible, the mouths of evil speakers.

We have made no difficulty, Monsieur, in sending to you privily our opinion, and in praying and exhorting you in the name of God to bestir yourself and act vigorously as the case deserves. Whereupon, Monsieur, having affectionately commended ourselves to your indulgent favour, we will supplicate our heavenly Father to keep you under his protection, fortify you by his power, and increase you in all good.

[*Fr. Copy.—Library of Paris, Dupuy.* Vol. 102.]

DCXXXI.—To Monsieur de Diesbach.[1]

He urges him to send succour to the Reformed who were besieged in Lyons.

Geneva, 13*th June,* 1562.

Most honoured Seigneur:—As I have this very day received a pressing charge from Lyons to solicit the speedy dispatch of the succours, I have prayed the present nobleman, bearer of this letter, to take horse immediately, that the troops, if it be possible, may straightway begin their march; for as the town of Lyons is quite unprovided with troops, the enemy will be emboldened to throw themselves into it. Thus we must anticipate them in time. Add to this, that there is danger, lest the passages of Savoy be intercepted, for we have discovered, notwithstanding his fine protestations, that his highness[2] intends to join our enemies. Wherefore I pray, that conformably to the affection you bear us, you would furnish the bearer with all necessary directions, and give him advice respecting what he shall have to do.

Whereupon, most honoured Seigneur, having humbly commended myself to your indulgent favour, I will pray our heavenly Father to have you in his keeping and increase you in all good and prosperity.

Your servant and humble brother,

John Calvin.

[*Fr. original.—Archives of Berne.*]

[1] *On the back :* To the most honoured Seigneur Monsieur de Diesbach, Bailiff of Lausanne.

Threatened by the united forces of the Catholic armies of Burgundy and Dauphiné, under the command of the Duke of Nevers, the Protestants of Lyons invoked the succour of the Reformed Cantons of Switzerland. The bookseller Jean Frellon, their deputy, obtained for them eight companies from Berne, four from the Valais, three from Neuchâtel, on condition that these troops should be inscribed for the service of the king and destined for the protection of Lyons. De Thou, lib. xxxi. Calvin actively urged the sending off of these auxiliaries.

[2] The Duke Emmanuel Philibert.

DCXXXII.—To Bullinger.[1]

An appeal addressed to the Seigneurs of Berne in favour of the French Protestants—Succours from England and Germany—Juridical massacres at Toulouse—Preliminaries of the civil war.

GENEVA, 15*th August*, 1562.

It is not from negligence, believe me, venerable brother, that I write to you so seldom, but because I see things ever and anon changing. Shame, to a certain extent, makes me lazy, for fear I should afterwards be obliged to retract what I have written. At last, the Bernese have been prevailed on to make preparations for recovering the cities of Burgundy. Their progress, however, is slow, and we are afraid that the whole expedition will shortly come to nought, because the senate has replied too timidly and too servilely to Mendoza. They always insist with puerile chicanery that they only came to garrison the city, as if, forsooth, there had not been quite men enough to eat up the provisions without them. If Chatillon be captured, and a strong garrison placed in it, the navigation of the Soane will be secured, which supplies a copious abundance of many kinds of provisions. This will be the true defence of the city. But something else is required which, if that district be pacified, can easily be accomplished; it is that they should march straight to join the prince. But they obstinately refuse to do that, nor can the senate be induced to permit it. For what purpose, then,

---

[1] Active negotiations were entered upon to determine the Protestant cantons of Swisserland to interfere in favour of their fellow Protestants of France in the struggle that had already commenced. Beza, associated in all the trials of the churches which he had supported by his eloquence at Poissy, had repaired to Bale, in order to act at the same time on the German courts and the Helvetic councils. In a letter of the 15th of September, he transmitted to Calvin useful information respecting the results of the negotiations, of which the object was to unite in one common cause all the Protestant forces. He announced the arrival of D'Andelot with eight thousand German Lansquenets, and expressed his wishes that Swisserland should contribute not less efficaciously for the defence of the Evangelical cause. " Oh if some universal league could be concluded among us ! Nor do I doubt but that will take place. But the consternation of men is incredible. Whatever may be the issue, however, of these times, our redemption is at hand, which thing alone consoles me."—(*Library of Geneva*, vol. 117.)

did they need to bring out troops? The prince himself lately
sent word that he was again assembling his dispersed forces,
and that in a short time he would have a powerful army. The
enemy has been greatly terrified by the arrival of the English,
who have pitched their camp in the heart of Normandy, and in
a short time the Scots will join them. For that reason, the
queen, again having recourse to her intrigues, is covertly sending
envoys to treat about a peace. For which cause, however, the
Admiral bids us not to be alarmed. The auxiliaries which we
expected from Germany, unless I am mistaken, will be no more
heard of, because they had never touched any money. Our
senate has enjoined Budé to procure a loan of twelve thousand
gold crowns, either at Bale or Strasbourg. If all had good-
will in proportion to their means, we should not be thus destitute. God is then to be entreated that he may provide for us
from some other quarter. The Queen of Navarre is furnished
with a small army which will be sufficient for keeping in check
a part of Guienne, but unless it be reinforced by new auxiliaries, it is not strong enough to fall upon the enemy, a thing
much to be desired, however, in order that it might render useful service to the public cause. It is also much to be lamented
that it has not yet been possible to repress the cruelty of the
senate of Toulouse, which has put to death, by the hand of the
executioner, upwards of thirty individuals, wealthy and honourable, noble, also, and who had discharged public functions. If
you perceive that your authority can have any influence in deciding the senate of Berne to permit their troops to join the
prince, I entreat you to strain every nerve for that purpose,
because if the war is protracted any longer, we are completely
ruined, as well as the kingdom. Would they had never left
home! but in your wisdom you must conclude how much it
concerns the fame of the war that they should not depart; nay,
if the affair is to be decided by a battle, that they should be stationed at no great distance from the German fusileers, whom the
enemy has engaged as mercenaries. One company has deserted
to our side; others have promised that they will not engage
with us. The favourable disposition of the French cavalry, towards us, also, makes the party of the Guises very uneasy. The

King of Navarre has been sent to draw the king into the camp, in order that the Swiss and the other foreign troops, as well as the French who profess to be devoted to the king alone, may no longer decline the service. This compact, however, will turn out, I hope, to be a fable. A whole month has now elapsed since Beza ought to have been among us. But from the time when he arrived in safety in Champaigne, along with his companion, Porcien, we have not heard the slightest rumour respecting what quarter of the world he may be in; because I am unwilling to augur any misfortune, I conjecture that he has been detained in that province where at present grave commotions are reigning. As soon as any thing certain and worthy of being known shall have transpired, I will compensate, by my diligence in writing to you, for my fifteen days' silence.

Farewell, most illustrious sir and honoured brother, along with M. Peter Martyr, Gualter, and all your colleagues. May the Lord preserve you all in safety, and crown your labours with a happy success.

Yours,   JOHN CALVIN.

[*Lat. Orig., in Calvin's handwriting.—Library of Zurich, Hottinger, F. 80, p. 343.*]

DCXXXIII.—To BULLINGER.

A petition in favour of a prisoner of the inquisition at Milan.

GENEVA, *9th September,* 1562.

I am obliged, at the request of those who do not comply with my advice, to be troublesome to you, venerable brother. A worthy man has been thrown into prison at Milan, because he had expressed himself rather too freely against the Papistical impiety. He is, indeed, a native of Burgundy, but has long been settled in our city, and has been to Italy on business. Our senate would have been ready to intercede for him, but forbore because their letter would only have been turned into ridicule. I gave an advice which his friends rejected, for they imagined if four Swiss cantons that profess the pure doctrine of the gospel should intercede for him, the Milanese would scarcely venture to attempt any thing against him. And yet I am afraid lest your authority also may be slight, and of small weight in this affair; nevertheless because the cause itself deserves no common recommendation I entreat you again and again to aid our initiative, by procuring letters with what fidelity and diligence you can.

Farewell, most illustrious sir and honoured brother. May the Lord govern you by his Spirit, sustain you by his power, and preserve you in safety.

Yours, JOHN CALVIN.

[Lat. Orig.—Arch. of Zurich, Gest. II. 166, p. 52.]

DCXXXIV.—To the Churches of Languedoc.[1]

A collection for the benefit of the German soldiers enrolled under the banner of the Reformed churches.

GENEVA, September, 1562.

MESSIEURS:—Very dear and honoured brethren, I should wish indeed to transport myself among you to make you understand with what disposition of mind I write the present. But since it is not in my power to do this, I trust that the thing itself being properly understood by you will suffice to touch your

---

[1] Without a date. The end is wanting. September, 1562.

The massacre of Vassy gave the signal for the civil war. While the Prince of Condé, fortified in Orleans, addressed an appeal for men and money to the Reformed churches of the kingdom, d'Andelot went to solicit the support of the Protestant princes of Germany, and brought back a body of 6,000 reitres or lansquenets, with which he marched towards the frontier of Lorraine. He wrote on the 26th August, 1562, to Calvin: "It is a thing of which we must not become tired, but for which we should always be importunate, I mean the research of every means of procuring money, for it is of that we stand excessively in need, having, thank God, found so much favour on the other side of the Rhine, among the princes, that I hope to lead with me 3000 horse, and as many lansquenets. And if I now see them all disposed to do their utmost for us, I was a long time before I brought them to favour my views at all, and had almost begun to despair. I trust that our gracious God still wills to make use of human means to favour his church." Coll. de M. Tronchin à Geneve. Calvin addressing himself to the churches exhorted them to provide liberally for the expenses of the war provoked by the violation of the Edict of January.

hearts to devote yourselves to the good cause without reserve, each one according to his means. The point in question is to find money to support the troops which M. d'Andelot has levied. This is not the moment to enter into inquiries or disputes, in order to find fault with mistakes that have been committed in times past. For whatever may have been the cause of these, God has reduced us to such an extremity that if you are not succoured from that quarter, we can expect nothing, according to human probability, but a pitiful and horrible desolation. I know very well that though all should be ruined and lost, God has incomprehensible means of re-establishing his church as if he raised it from the dead, and it is that trust in which we must repose and patiently wait—that should we be abolished, even at the worst he knows how to create out of our ashes a new people. Nevertheless we have good reason to think, if we would not designedly shut the door against his grace—not to be negligent in discharging the duties which fall to our own share. It is certain that dilatoriness and indifference, or rather the niggardliness of the churches has occasioned us greater detriment than it is possible to express. Several who have spared a part of their goods have been doomed to lose them all. What is worse, there is an infinite number of poor people who have answered for them with their lives, though it was not their fault. If this evil continue, it is much to be feared that God will bring a greater number of rods to scourge us, and in fact it is a great shame that the enemies of God consume body and substance for a miserable quarrel to the perdition of their souls, and that those who should maintain the truth should be so stingy and close fisted. But it is a double shame that the necessity. . . .

[*Fr. Orig.—Library of Geneva.* Vol. 107.]

DCXXXV.—To Sulcer.[1]

Political and military news of France—Catherine de Medicis—The Emperor Ferdinand —The Turks—The Queen of England—Complaints against Peter Toussain.

GENEVA, *6th December,* 1562.

If I write to you less frequently than you might desire, you will be indulgent to my indolence, most excellent sir and venerable brother, for I am so weighed down by grief as to be sluggish in the performance of every duty, except when urged and dragged to it, as it were, contrary to my inclinations ; and also in so troubled a state of affairs I feel a reluctance to write about matters which are doubtful, lest to my shame I should have to retract what I believed to be true. For you cannot believe what licence people take in publishing lies. Wherefore from suffering from ennui, I have contracted such a habit of callousness that no reports affect me. Besides the roads have been so blocked up for six months that nothing certain reaches us. To-day we are ignorant of what our princes are doing, unless that about the end of the first month they were still at Corbeil. This is a small and poorly fortified town, about four hours' march distant from Paris. The advantages of the position of this place had induced the enemy to strive by every means to keep possession of it, because in consequence of its bridge the passage of provisions conveyed from Burgundy can easily be intercepted. St. André had therefore occupied that post with a strong garrison, but he deserted it before the storming of it. The queen had again recurred to her wonted arts of pacification, but the enemies will be too stupid if, after having been so often deceived by her treacherous caresses, they should again expose themselves to her snares. Their deputies were courteously received by the emperor, by his son, and by the Electors, but have not had an answer given them. What has been circulated among you respecting the Turk is, I suspect, a vain rumour, for certainly a word would have been dropped about it in his letter, by the one of the deputies to whom your princes disclose familiarly whatever it is our interest to be made acquainted

with. The Queen of England has boasted too greatly of the
aid afforded by her. It is by her vanity that we have lost
Rouen. The Duke of Nemours had concluded an armistice
with the Baron des Adrets, which has now expired. Because
the Prefect of Lyons was ill, he asked for an interview with him
which was refused. There is tranquillity at Lyons, but a penury
of money. The Danes had already learned from others they
would not find a convenient retreat among us. When they said
then that they would return on the following day, there was no
need of making a lengthened apology, and certainly our city
was never at any previous period so crowded with wretched
exiles. They flock hither in bands stripped of all their fortune,
many of them orphans, many widows. In these straitened circumstances in which we are placed, it is not an easy thing for
men unacquainted with our language to find a position. But
before they had spoken a word, they had resolved to remain at
Bale till Easter. I pass now to another subject.

Though often reminded of the atrocious perfidy and cruelty
of Peter Toussain,[1] you preferred to suspend your judgment
rather than give up an opinion you had once conceived of him.
And that crocodile maintains his influence by his fawning manners, so well calculated to deceive. Now having attacked his
colleague by fresh acts of treachery, he has succeeded in having
him ordered to be suspended from his functions for a season. I
am unwilling to enter on a long discussion on a subject that is
quite manifest. The point in question is the doctrine of predestination, respecting which he wished the worthy man to
abjure his sentiments. Need I recommend to you the cause of
Christ? Lest, however, you should suspect that something had
escaped him which might cause offence, you will see from the
whole course of the proceedings that he was only too modest
when attacked by that enemy of all godly men. It is very far
from being becoming that a learned and pious man should be
unworthily molested, while we stand by and wink at it. But as
I have no means of aiding him, I implore your faithful assistance;
you enjoy a very rare degree of influence with Balius and the
Prefect. Now though Toussain has fascinated them by his

[1] See vol. iii. p. 477.

cunning pretences, it will not be a matter of great difficulty for you after all to bring them back to the right path. I do not wish you to be mixed up with an obscure quarrel. I have exhorted the brother that he should lay his whole case before you. Having duly examined the whole matter, you will decide according to your equity and prudence what is fitting to be done. This at least I desire to obtain from you that you will endeavour to mollify the Prefect, though I am confident that you will have still greater success, and that a man otherwise of intrepid character will voluntarily undertake the defence of a just and pious cause. If then you set to work seriously, we have no doubts about the successful issue.

Farewell, most excellent and respected brother. We have a new subject for sorrow in the death of Peter Martyr. Our brother Beza is still in the camp. Ribitté went to Orleans about six months ago, being called thither to discharge the functions of a teacher. May the Lord preserve you in safety, and enrich you more and more with his gifts. My colleagues very respectfully salute you.—Yours,

JOHN CALVIN.

[*Lat. Orig.—Library of Geneva.* Vol. 107 *a.*]

DCXXXVI.—To BULLINGER.[1]

First religious war—Respective force of the two parties—Siege of Lyons—The Duke of Nemours—Des Adrets—News of Germany, and the Council of Trent.

GENEVA, *27th December*, 1562.

Although I dislike to write to you respecting things that are but uncertain, venerable brother, yet as this excellent young

---

[1] This letter is but the abstract of several letters addressed by Beza to Calvin. In it we see negotiations continually mixed up with hostilities during this first period of the civil war. Before coming to action, and inflicting on each other decisive blows, the parties seem to shrink from the terrible extremity to which they are henceforth reduced. A witness of these vicissitudes, Beza deplores them, as he sees the Protestant army allowing to escape more than one occasion of gaining a signal advantage over the Catholic enemy, and he bewails the painful necessities which detain him in France without his being able to exercise a decisive influence over events. "Would

man offered me his services to convey a letter to you, I was unwilling not to profit by the opportunity. What the Prince of Condé is meditating it is impossible for us to conjecture. About the beginning of this month, he had advanced his troops to the walls of Paris, and had almost reduced the city by famine after a blockade of fifteen days. The soldiers of Guise had made a sally, but being vigorously repulsed they then remained quiet behind their ramparts. Afterwards the queen had recourse to her usual intrigues, and the prince, with his indolent good nature, lost much time in deceitful conferences which he had better have employed in vigorous action. The common opinion was, that the preliminaries of a peace had been settled, when, contrary to expectation, Spanish and Breton troops came to the help of the enemy by which his activity was immediately increased. The prince withdrew his army to a greater distance. The soldiers of Guise went after him. On the fifteenth of this month, both parties had their camps in the Beauce, between the territory of the Chartrain and Maine. Letters were brought from Paris, and their contents were confirmed by certain proofs that the two armies had engaged in a trifling skirmish, and that seven hundred of the Spaniards had fallen. The news is not improbable, since a great many wounded had been conveyed to the city on carts and wagons. The enemy is stronger in infantry, the prince much superior in cavalry. The report that had reached us of the recovery of Rouen is now found to be false, and yet I fancy there must have been some foundation for it. Something which ought to have been kept a secret was blabbed out before the time by some babblers, and got too wide a circulation. If, however, it is true, and I have good reasons for believing it, that six thousand English have joined the prince, this will be no contemptible reinforcement. Assuredly, if he did not advance to meet these troops that he might animate still more their resolution, we should have to pronounce his retrograde movement an act of base cowardice. The Parisians themselves are rushing on more furiously than ever. Private

that God would avert the things I fear. Nothing is more wretched than I who can neither stay here with any great advantage, nor yet absent myself. But God is with me."—Letter of the 14th December, 1562. (Vol. de Geneve, 117.)

individuals are in the habit of obtaining as a boon from their sovereigns a dispensation of the legal age, and thus advancing the period when they have a right to administer their own affairs. The Parliament has granted the king this dispensation, and declared his majority as it is called. In the mean time, as if he were still in his nonage, they have appointed him guardians. The *conseillers* who refused to condemn the Admiral and his brother D'Andelot have been thrown into prison. These are tokens of a most desperate state. Against Lyons, the Duke of Nemours as yet attempts nothing by force of arms, because he hopes that he will be able to reduce it gradually by famine. The Baron des Adrets, who had hitherto acted with energy, allured by his wheedling promises, had allowed him to be made governor. But yielding to the unanimous wishes of the nobility and the states, he desisted from his purpose. If Vienne, as we trust, will soon be recovered, the province of Languedoc, which at present abounds in wheat and wine, will supply a plentiful stock of provisions. A troop of horsemen, dispatched by the prince, which was advancing to Lyons, has been intercepted. We now entertain great hopes of the Baron des Adrets, and he has pledged himself to listen to good and salutary counsels. Assuredly, it was not from treachery, but error and foolish credulity that he compromised himself. If Crussol, whom the cities of Languedoc have created their governor, take up the matter seriously, the Lyonese will be out of danger. I am afraid that the Comte of Beauvais, formerly Cardinal de Chatillon, is too dilatory, and will with his hesitations be a drag upon his movements. Sulcer had written the same thing that you did respecting the Turkish embassy, but it was a false report. Our Frankfort friend, M. de Passy, formerly Bishop of Nevers, was the deputy of the Prince de Condé to the emperor and the princes. As he had not mentioned the circumstance to me, I fancied it was an idle report. But now that he has arrived, he assures us that it was true. He declared that he was very graciously received by the emperor, who expressed to him his sorrow at the dissensions in France, especially because the enemies were plotting the destruction of pure religion. I suppose the news has reached you of the change in the form of taking an oath, for he promised that he would be the defender not of the Roman but of the Christian church, and he omitted the mention of the saints, contenting himself with employing the name of God alone. You will perceive from his speech what kind of part the Cardinal of Lorraine has played in the Council of Trent. With him chimed in that famous apostate the legate of the king. Though the copies of their speeches are incorrect, you will nevertheless easily perceive how embarrassed they are, and that they cannot muster any other army, except there be the free exercise of religion in France. I remit copies of the letters which I had written to the Poles, because the second answer in which I had explained the question at considerable length miscarried, I dispense with handling that cause. I suspect it was lost by the negligence or forgetfulness of Beza. I am very desirous to hear more favourable accounts of your health. God has put fetters on my feet. The acute pains have ceased, however, but it is with great difficulty I can hobble in my room from my bed to the table. I preached to-day, but I was carried to the church.

Farewell, most illustrious sir and respected brother; I beg you will salute your fellow pastors and brethren. My colleagues and friends all salute you; among others, the amanuensis, whose hand you recognize. May the Lord keep you in safety, sustain you by his power, and bless your labours.

Yours,   JOHN CALVIN.

You wished me to engage with Brentz, but up to this moment it has been out of my power; to such a degree have I been pressed by other lucubrations. If I can procure a little more leisure, an excellent opportunity has now presented itself, because the ministers who are in the dominions of the courts of Mansfeld have exhorted in a stupid pamphlet to repentance the French whom they acknowledge and style their brethren.

[*Lat. Copy.—Library of Geneva.* Vol. 107 *a*.]

DCXXXVII.—To Bullinger.[1]

Battle of Dreux—Captivity of Condé—Imposing attitude of Coligny—Theodore Beza at Orleans—Mission of the Cardinal de Lorraine to Germany—False news from France.

Geneva, 16th January, 1563.

At last, we have received a letter from the Admiral, giving us details of the battle and its results.[2] The prince had led out his troops, that he might compel the enemy to quit the camp. If the infantry had done their duty, there is no doubt that immediately without much difficulty, and almost without any loss, they would have gained a victory. The cowardice of the infantry, which some suspect to have been treachery, retarded the success. When the prince saw them basely hanging back, he dashed through their ranks, that shame, at least, might compel them to fight. In that course, his horse was wounded in the shoulder, hence it was that the enemy who was at no great distance got possession of his person, as it was impossible for him to procure a fresh horse in time. Already the constable had been made prisoner, the Marshal de St. André slain, one of the sons of the constable, the Duke of Nevers, had received a mortal wound. A brother of Guise, called the grand prior, was dangerously wounded. Of the principal officers, about twenty had fallen, of whom three knights of the *ordre Royal*. Not a few of the nobility of the highest class have been made prisoners, who are now kept in close custody. The German troopers conducted themselves courageously, as became brave

---

[1] On the 19th of December was fought the battle of Dreux. During more than two hours, the armies contemplated each other in sombre immobility. Each one said to himself, doubtless, that he had before him relations, friends, fellow-citizens. At last, the conflict began, and eight thousand dead bodies soon covered the field of battle. The Calvinists, at first, had the advantage, and the fugitives having conveyed the news of it to Paris, "Well, then," said Catharine of Medicis," we shall have to pray to God in French." A skilful manœuvre of the Duke of Guise brought back the advantage to the Catholics, and Coligny retreated proudly and in good order.

[2] What interest a letter of the Admiral's and containing a narrative of the battle would afford us ! This letter unfortunately has been lost.

soldiers. A like gallantry was displayed by the French cavalry. A terrible carnage took place in all the ranks of the enemies' army, but not above a fifth of our troops fell. Among those who have been taken, there is none except the Prince about whom we feel very anxious, and another named De Mouy, a cornet of cavalry. As night fell, both armies betook themselves to their camps. Among the enemies there was the greatest trepidation. Our troops were so animated with confidence that on the following day they did not hesitate to attack the enemy. The Duke of Guise kept his men within their entrenchments. The Admiral contented himself with letting them see that specimen of the spirit of his troops. The Prince of Condé is detained a close prisoner in a fortress situated between the Chartain and Dreux. The queen has set out for Chartres. The king followed a short time afterwards. No doubt the prince had been already conveyed thither. What the result of the conference was is unknown, except that fears are to be entertained of his too great propensity to the vain hope of a pacification, the disposition of mind which has hitherto been the cause of all our misfortunes; for unworthily betrayed three or four times he could never be induced to take precautions against treachery. Nevertheless, he courageously made head against his keepers, so that one would say he had assumed a manly character since the day of the battle. He alleges to them the edict which, in the king's name, the enemies had promulgated in the month of July, and in which it is declared that the war had been undertaken, in order to set him at liberty. He denies, then, that consistently with justice he should now be held to be a captive. He adds, too, that as he had been created the king's guardian by the suffrages of the orders, in order to represent the person of the king, it was unlawful for any one to lay hands upon him who was the second person of the kingdom. The day before the engagement, the prince had named the Admiral his successor. All the troops again took the oath of obedience to him. Of the infantry, he reassembled no contemptible number. A thousand Lansquenets, or thereabouts, returned to their own country. The Reitres remained quite cheerful in the cause, as before. There was no insubordination, no sign of desertion.

The general himself harangued them and exhorted them to perseverance, and entertains the highest hopes. He also entreats
them not to lend any credit to letters from the prince until he
be restored to liberty. You can scarcely believe what I tell
you, and yet it is perfectly true, that the constable was conducted to Orleans by only twelve men, and with so much speed
that they entered the city in a little more than twenty-four
hours after the battle, having accomplished a march of thirty
French leagues. The Admiral had resolved on joining the
English to the troops under his command, and if circumstances
required it, he did not shrink from another engagement. If he
chance to advance towards Lyons, do not imagine that this
movement is a flight. A report is spread, indeed, that he is
seeking a quiet district to recruit his troops. But there is some
deeper design concealed under this measure, and assuredly it
is of great importance that Lyons should receive supplies as
speedily as possible before it suffer still more from a want of
provisions. Add to this the defeat of the Baron des Adrets.
Now if the Duke de Nemours were put to flight, the whole territory of Gaul as far as Guienne would be cleared of these robbers. The province of Languedoc is so productive of corn and
wine, that the roads once opened up there is no danger of the
Lyonese suffering from famine. Thus a blockade need no
longer be feared in that quarter. Two thousand horsemen
have come to their relief, and these having brought along with
them not a few companions, this will be a strong reinforcement.
The messenger who was bringing to me the letter of our friend
Beza, has either been intercepted or wandered out of his way.
Beza had written to me four days before the battle, but by the
stupidity of the bearer the letter has made a long circuit before
it reached me. I send you a copy. He himself is now safe
and sound at Orleans. In the battle he stoutly harangued the
soldiers, and took his place in the front ranks, as if he had
been one of the standard bearers. This is the state of our
affairs. No doubt, the enemies imagine that they have done
something very advantageous for themselves by disseminating
false and boastful reports of the affair, in order to throw dust
in the eyes of silly people. But the matter is exactly as I

have described it. There is one thing which I most earnestly
entreat of you and all worthy men; it is, that should there be
any rumour about the arrival of the Cardinal of Lorraine, you
would speedily drop a word about it to me. He pretends that
he is undertaking this journey, in order to see the new king of
the Romans, and negotiate a marriage between his daughter
and the king of France. But he has something else in view.
Do you most carefully sift the whole matter, and if you gain
any information respecting it, fail not to let me know on the
instant, even if you should send a courier expressly for that
purpose, that we may have it in our power to provide against
his criminal projects. I wish there had been some one to undertake the defence of my cause when Baudouin passed through
your town. Certainly, either justice would have been denied
me, or he would never have escaped hanging. When I had
resolved at this time not to intermeddle with the Polish blasphemies, your entreaties prevailed on me to expose an impious
error which had fascinated some of our countrymen. His foolish pride, then, in threatening us with so much assurance surprised me, though I suspect that the author of the epistle is a
certain snappish Frenchman, whose temper I think I can recognize in it as in a mirror. At your request, then, I have exposed my judgment, and since the answer respecting an arbiter
has miscarried, lest any thing similar should take place, I have
taken care that this should be published, for it will be useful
that it should be known everywhere.

While my letter is waiting for the departure of the messenger, a report is spread about of a new engagement in which
two thousand of the enemy have been slain. There is, also, a
talk of the death of the Duke of Guise, at Cambray, but it
does not seem to me very probable.[1] Three thousand men have
been sent from Lyons to pillage the neighbouring district.
Corn has already been conveyed there by a great many ves-
sels. If they get possession of Macon, as they hope, there will
be a sufficient supply of provisions, on account of the naviga-

---

[1] The Duke of Guise fell by the hand of an assassin on the 18th of February following, at the siege of Orleans.

tion from Burgundy being open. For the Soane will furnish them abundantly with wheat, wine, wood, and hay.

Farewell, most distinguished sir and respected brother, along with your fellow pastors. May the Lord preserve you all in safety, govern you by his Spirit, and bless your labours.

Yours,   JOHN CALVIN.

I would have sent off this letter earlier, if De Frie had not earnestly begged me to put it off till the moment of his departure; for he fancied he would receive a warmer welcome among you if he should be the bearer of it. I had no other messenger at hand, but it was my intention to hire one, who should go as far as Berne. I suppose the report has also reached you, which has been afloat here, about the assassination of the German deputies in Champaigne. I do not believe it. Because the Comte Palatine had given that very inauspicious advice to M. Spifame, the prince's legate, not to be in a hurry about sending off an embassy, the affair had been broken off. What is said, that the one was of the family of Luneburg and the other the Comte of Mansfeld, is by no means probable.

[*Lat. Orig.—Library of Geneva.* Vol. 107 *a.*]

DCXXXVIII.—To THE QUEEN OF NAVARRE.[1]

Counsels for the abolition of the Catholic worship and the establishment of the pure gospel in Navarre.

GENEVA, 20th January, 1563.

MADAME:—Since it has pleased God, in removing from this world the late king, your husband, to put into your hands the

---

[1] Letter written to the Queen of Navarre after the death of her husband.

Severely wounded at the siege of Rouen where he commanded the Catholic army, this prince whom fortune seemed for a moment to call to great things, but whose incurable weakness rendered him the sport of all parties, died at Andelis the 17th November, 1562, in the forty-fourth year of his age. He appeared, if we may believe the account of one of his servants, to repent, during his last moments of having betrayed the Reformed faith: "Towards the evening the queen mother who had been informed . . . came to see him, and, having begun to converse with him, said:

entire charge of your country and subjects, you do well to think of acquitting yourself of your duty, as having to render an account to a Master and Sovereign Prince, who desires that his right should be maintained. For in commanding that he himself should be feared and kings honoured, thus doing you the honour of associating you with himself, it is every way reasonable that you should strive to do him homage and show him gratitude for the state and dignity which you hold from him; and just as you would not suffer the superiority which belongs to you to be taken from you by your officers, so you are bound, if you desire to be maintained under the protection of God, to take measures as far as it shall be in your power to have him served and honoured, showing to others the example. And in fact, Madame, it is only in subjecting your majesty to him that your reign will be established before him. You know that every knee should bend under the empire of our Lord Jesus Christ, but kings are specially commanded to pay him this mark of homage, for the purpose of showing better how much more they are held to cast down the loftiness which has been bestowed on them, and exalt him who is the chief of the angels of paradise and consequeutly of the great ones of this world. Wherefore, Madame, since the government is now come into your hands, know that God wishes to prove more and more the zeal and solicitude you have to acquit yourself faithfully in giving the pre-eminence to the true service which he demands. There are several reasons which prevent me from pushing this argument any farther. For all who have any dominion are also enjoined

---

Brother, how do you spend your time? You should make some one read to you. He replied : All my servants or the greater part of those who are around me are Huguenots, to which the lady replied : They are no less your servants." The queen having retired, he called for his physician, and had the history of Job read to him, to which he listened attentively. He then said : "Ah! Raphael, I see very well that I am dying, you have served me seven and twenty years, and now you see the deplorable days of my life. . ." And hereupon, he began with tears in his eyes, to beg pardon of God, and make a confession of his faith, according to the manner of the Reformed Church, protesting that if God should give him the grace to recover, he would cause the gospel to be preached in purity all over the kingdom, but that he would keep by the Confession of Augsburg." Account of the King of Navarre's death. *Archives curieuses de l'Histoire de France*, vol. v. p. 70, and the following. See also Beza, vol. ii. pp. 665-667.

to purge their territories of every kind of idolatry and corruption, by which the purity of true religion is defiled.   And
when St. Paul commands to pray for kings and all who are in
authority, it is not without cause that he adds this reason, "In
order that we may live under them in all godliness and honesty."
Before speaking of civil virtues, he enjoins the fear of God, by
which he signifies that the office of princes is to see that God be
adored with purity.   I take into consideration the difficulties
which may retard you, the fears and doubts which may debilitate
your courage, and I am persuaded that the numerous councillors
you shall have around you, if they think only of the world, will
endeavour to stay your hand in this good work.   But it is
certain that all fear of men which will divert us from paying to
God the homage he deserves, and induce us to deprive him of
his due, proves that we do not fear him in good earnest, and
make but small account of his invincible power, by which he has
promised to protect us.   Wherefore, Madame, in order to surmount all difficulties, lean upon the assurance which is given
you from on high, after complying with all that God requires.

These are the two points on which it behoves you to have
your eyes constantly fixed, which should serve you even as
wings to raise you above all the obstacles of the world: namely,
to know what God commands you to do, and that he will never
fail so to strengthen your hands that you will succeed in all you
shall attempt in obedience to him.   I know indeed the arguments that several bring forward to prove that princes ought
not to compel their subjects to live in a Christian manner.   But
it is a dispensation far too profane—that which permits the man
who will give up nothing that belongs to himself, to defraud his
superior of his rights.   If God's command does not move us,
this threat should cause us to tremble; every kingdom that will
not be subservient to that of Jesus Christ shall come to nought.
For that refers properly to the state of the Christian Church.
Thus whatever fine excuses the persons produce who wish to
colour over their own cowardice, I entreat you, Madame, to
reflect seriously with yourself, and judge whether the empire
of God should not be preferred to the honour which he has

bestowed on you, and you will be able speedily to resolve this point.

In the second place it remains for you to arm yourself with his promises that your faith may be victorious over the world, as says St. John, and here let me remind you of what is said by the prophet Isaiah and quoted by St. Peter, not to be alarmed by the terrors of the multitude, but to sanctify the Lord of Hosts that he may be our sanctuary. I know, Madame, how you are watched by your neighbour, who will not fail, if he can, to take an opportunity of raising disturbances,[1] but while you fear God you need not fear him. It will not be zeal which will actuate him, though he makes of that a false pretext. Seeing then that he is lying in wait for you, fortify yourself with the best defence you can have, and if God permits that the wicked make efforts to do you some despite, call to mind the memorable history of Hezekiah, for though God gave loose reins to his enemy to assail him soon after he had done away with superstitious rites, and even though Rabshakeh had cast in his teeth that God would not aid him, seeing that he had overthrown the altars, yet for all that the admirable succour which suddenly came to him from heaven is a sufficient example for you to set at defiance all those who fancy they shall have any advantage over you under colour of the changes you may introduce.

I do not say however, Madame, that all can be done in one day. God has given you prudence to judge of what proceedings you shall have to adopt, circumstances also will teach you what shall be the most suitable means; and as I cannot enter into every detail on paper, I have left to the bearer to explain more fully to you my opinion on the greater number. I have chosen him as the person most fitted for such a mission that I could find, and I trust that from experience you will find that he deserves this character.[2] I have obtained from our society

---

[1] The ferocious Monluc, Governor of Guienne and Gascony. He had ravaged these two provinces with fire and sword in order to pacify them. "I resolved," says he in his memoirs, "to cast from me all fear and apprehension, and make use of every act of cruelty in my power." It is well known that he kept his resolution. The states of the Queen of Navarre were threatened on the one hand by Monluc, and by Philip II. on the other.

[2] The minister Raymond Merlin, who had been restored the year before to the Church of Geneva, by the Admiral de Coligny. See p. 224, note 2.

as well as from our seigneury, that you should have the advantage of his services for the time that you have asked him, and all of them have willingly acceded to the request. I have only one remark to make, however, Madame, which is that you will find it far more easy to begin with those places which seem to you the most difficult; that is, where the evil is most apparent. For the others will submit with less reluctance when you have secured one, and it will draw after it a long train. I need not apprise you that your presence on the spot will be especially necessary, as also that it will be proper to make such preparations of every kind as that the enemy may be defeated or greatly weakened before matters come to an open struggle.

If you are pleased, Madame, also to put in execution what you have deliberated about, viz: to send to the princes of Germany to beg and exhort them to continue their countenance to the cause of our Lord, that will be an act worthy of your majesty, and one of the highest advantage to Christendom. It will be necessary to address yourself to Augustus Duke of Saxony, to the Duke of Wurtemberg, and to the Landgrave of Hesse; and the sooner you set about it the better. I beg you then, Madame, to expedite this mission. The bearer will explain by word of mouth all the rest.

Madame, having very humbly commended myself to you, I will supplicate our heavenly Father to have you in his holy keeping, to govern you by his Spirit in all wisdom, to fortify you in virtue and constancy, and increase your majesty in all good.

[*Fr. Copy.—Library of Paris, Dupuy.* Vol. 102.]

DCXXXIX.—To M. DE SOUBISE.[1]

He exhorts him to lay down arms after the conclusion of a treaty disadvantageous to his party.

GENEVA, *5th April,* 1563.

MONSIEUR :—The time is come when God wishes to afflict you. Thus our duty is to fortify ourselves against temptation, however hard it may be. I shall not insist on this subject any farther, inasmuch as it would only be ripping up old sores. And, in fact, I know why you have directed the present bearer to me. It is to have my opinion how you ought to decide, when they shall come to put in execution what has been concluded without you. Now observe, that the question is not about delivering your sentiments in a council in which you should have a vote, for the matter is concluded and done. If you had been on the spot, it would have been your duty not to spare your life, in order to resist with all due liberty the evil they wished to accomplish. At present, the question is how you are to act in the execution of a decree which takes the subject out of your power. Here you must consider what you ought to do, and what you can do. I understand by *what you can do*, what God permits you to do, and nothing more. Now thus stands the case : you have been sent to your present government on the part of that unhappy man who, having by his vanity betrayed God, has thrown every thing into confusion.[2] You have then to

---

[1] To M. de Soubise, Governor of Lyons. Jean de Partenay, Seigneur de Soubise, son of Michelle de Saubonne, a lady of honour to Anne of Brittany, and governess of Renée of France. Instructed by Calvin himself, at Ferrara, in the Reformed faith, he fought in the ranks of the Protestant party which he honoured by his moderation and served with ability till his death (in 1567.) Appointed by the Prince of Condé governor of Lyons (May, 1562,) he kept possession of this town in spite of the reiterated attacks of the Duke of Nemours, commander of the Catholic army, and gave it up with regret only after the conclusion of the peace of Amboise. In this latter conjuncture he repeatedly demanded the counsels of Calvin. His letters to the Reformer, full of deference and respect, are signed : *Your obedient son and faithful friend, Soubise.*

[2] Impatient to recover his liberty, the Prince of Condé had hastened to sign the peace of Amboise, which introduced grave restrictions into the Edict of January. In his precipitation he had not even waited for the arrival of De Coligny, who loudly accused him " of having sacrificed the cause of God, and ruined more churches by

practise the doctrine of the holy Scriptures, which is, that if God takes away the sword from those he had girt with it, this change should make us give way and regulate our conduct accordingly. Wherefore, I do not see that you have any reason or power, approved of by God, to resist a council of which it is impossible to say now that it is not legitimate. If it decide badly, since God is pleased to afflict us, let us stoop quietly to his will. For the rest, Monseigneur, here is the conduct, I fancy, you shall have to hold. I take it for granted, that before the bearer of this letter reach you, M. de B——[1] will have communicated to you the object of his commission. The first thing you must do, then, will be to surrender your office of governor, both in respect to him and to the community.

I leave to your own judgment, which on this point stands in no great need of instructions, what you shall have to do with regard to details. For it is impossible to specify in a letter, what, if I were present on the spot, I could do by word of mouth. I doubt not, however, but you will watch carefully over the interests of the city, and not allow it to fall into bad hands.[2] Only in suffering what you cannot prevent, you will take care to demand a delay for many particulars which are not sufficiently well and duly ascertained. This delay cannot be interpreted as an act of insubordination, nor is it possible that they can reproach you with wishing to impose conditions on your sovereign, when you grant the principal thing demanded, and ask only to have a sufficient and explicit declaration before any thing be put in execution.[3] I know that this submission will be a thing which your people will be hardly brought to

one stroke of his pen than all the united forces (of the enemy) could have overthrown in ten years."—*Hist. Eccl.*, vol. ii., p. 335.

[1] Le Sieur de Boucart, commissary of the king in Dauphiné and Languedoc, passing by Lyons "with ample instructions for the execution of the edict of peace."—*Ibid.*, vol. ii., p. 242.

[2] After having successively refused to give up the town to the Duke of Nemours, and to M. de Gordes, a nobleman of Dauphiné, Soubise consented to surrender it to the Marshal de Vicilleville, who, by the moderation of his character, had known how to merit the esteem of both parties.—*Ibid.*, vol. ii., p. 243, and De Thou. Lib. xxxiv.

[3] Religious liberty was solemnly guaranteed to the Protestants of Lyons, and diverse places were assigned them for the construction of their temples, "which they afterwards built at great expense, and of which one was called *Paradise* and the other *Fleur-de-lys*."—*Ibid.*

digest. But I believe they will, at last, consider what God permits them to do. On your side, I know that you will not fail in any one thing which you shall perceive to be lawful. But I have already declared to you that God having taken from us a worthless man has inflicted on us such a stunning blow that we must remain cast down till it please him to raise us up.

Monsieur, having humbly commended myself to your indulgent favour. . . .

[*Fr. Copy.—Library of Geneva.* Vol. 107.]

DCXL.—To BULLINGER.[1]

Treaty of Amboise—Strictures on this treaty concluded by the Prince of Condé without the approbation of Coligny and the principal Protestant chiefs.

GENEVA, *8th April,* 1563.

We have then been basely betrayed by the other brother also. He had promised by an oath, which he desired to be printed, that he would conclude nothing without the consent of his associates. Whilst he was clandestinely negotiating with the queen mother, he wrote to the governor of Lyons that he would leave the affair undecided till the return of the Admiral. Meanwhile, he advises his mother-in-law to send away all the troops, and affirms that every thing has been settled. The woman, who has not much cunning, confessed this in a letter to me at the same time she endeavours to appease me by her flattering compliments. What fortunate results he has completely destroyed in one moment, you will learn, moreover, from the letter of Beza, who, nevertheless, did not venture to write all the circumstances, nor what it was which disarmed us, even before this execrable treaty was generally known. The lust of power has entirely blinded the man. Meanwhile, he thinks he has

---

[1] The death of Francis of Guise deprived the Catholic party of its chief, and delivered the court of a redoubtable protector. The queen regent profited by that circumstance to propose negotiations, accepted with too much facility by the Prince of Condé, who was impatient to recover his liberty. These led to the treaty of Amboise.

achieved something important, because he is enrolled among
the knights of the royal order, and exults in puerilities of that
sort.   But as God is wont to work in a marvellous manner
through this infirmity, he will exalt his own power.

The articles of this peace are the following :—

1st. All nobles who are Barons, and all possessing a jurisdiction of life and death in their domains, or those who possess
fiefs by a noble tenure, shall remain in their castles without being molested in their conscience, and in the free exercise of the
religion which they style Reformed, along with their families,
and it is permitted to such of their vassals as of their own accord, without being forced, may desire it, to join them in their
worship.   But the nobles not possessing jurisdiction shall enjoy
that same liberty for themselves and their families, only provided
they do not live in cities, towns, and villages, under the jurisdiction of others; in which case they shall not be permitted to
exercise their religion, unless they obtain the consent of their
seigneurs.   The king, however, in his immediate domain concedes liberty to all.

2d. In all the *bailliages* from which there lies an appeal to the
courts of the Parliaments, one city shall be designated in the
suburbs of which religious worship may be celebrated by all
the persons of the same 'bailliage, who may wish to be present,
but not otherwise.   Every one, however, may remain perfectly
at liberty in his own dwelling, nor shall he be molested, nor
shall any inquisition be made after him, nor any violence offered
to his conscience.

3d. In all the cities in which religious worship has been celebrated, up to the seventh day of the present month, except the
other cities already designated, the same religious worship shall
be exercised within the walls in one or two places, provided the
persons exercising that religion be not allowed to apply the
temples to their use.   For all their property shall be restored
to the clergy, that they may celebrate divine worship as they
were accustomed to do, before the breaking out of the disturbances.   If any thing, however, shall have been ruined, the
clergy themselves shall not be permitted to institute a process.

4th. In the city of Paris, however, and within the precincts of its jurisdiction, the exercise of the Reformed religion is not permitted. But those who shall remain there shall enjoy the peaceable possession of their property, nor shall it be permitted to molest or force them, nor harass them by any inquisition respecting matters of conscience, either for what respects times past or future.

5th. All cities shall return to their ancient condition, commerce shall be free, all foreign troops shall be dismissed as soon as it may be conveniently done, and all subjects shall co-operate with all their influence to effectuate this object.

6th. Every one shall be restored to his rights, privileges, immunities, state, honours, and functions of whatsoever kind they may be, and shall be preserved and protected in them, notwithstanding all processes, decisions, sentences, and decrees that have followed the death of King Henry, either for the cause of religion or on account of the taking up of arms in the cause of religion. For decisions of that sort shall be null and void, of no effect or value, so that under pretext of such decisions heirs shall not be barred from the tranquil possession of their rights.

7th. And that the Seigneur Prince of Condé, Lieutenant General of the kingdom and Governor of Picardy, be freed from all anxiety, and that no reproach or odium be attached to him in time to come, and that he be declared a good relation and cousin and faithful subject of the king as he deserves to be by his proximity to the blood royal; and further that all knights, nobles, gentlemen, burgesses, whether of cities or country towns, and in fine whatever may have adhered to his party in this war, whithersoever they may have carried their arms during these troubles, shall be declared and reputed to be faithful subjects of the king ; because it is fully recognized that whatever they have done up to the present moment, they have done with a good intention and in obedience to the king. Wherefore they are exonerated from all blame.

8th. The said seigneur prince shall be relieved from all pecuniary obligations, and whatever by his orders may have been disbursed of the royal revenues, whatever may be its amount, the king shall place to his own account. He shall remain, moreover, free and exempt from all law suits, prosecutions, or molestation, in all that concerns contributions levied upon cities or towns, silver vases taken from temples, ecclesiastical revenues and incomes, and whatever may have been expended in the present war—so that neither he, nor his friends, nor his agents may be called to give an account for the past, nor in time to come. Also that for coining of money, casting of cannons, manufacturing of gunpowder, building of fortresses, or devastating and demolition of buildings, no action shall be brought against them, demanding damages either from the prince himself, or from communities, or from individuals.

9th. That all captives, whether by right of war or on account of religion, shall be dismissed by both parties with full liberty and without any ransom; though in this category the king will not have robbers and assassins included, to whom the benefit of this treaty shall not be extended.

10th. All injuries and damages committed during the present war, are held for the future to be effaced, extinguished, and buried in oblivion, and every one of whatever condition he may be, and to whichsoever of the two parties he may belong, is hereby interdicted on pain of capital punishment from injuring, provoking to quarrels, litigating, or insulting another, under pretext of religion.

11th. Those who profess the Reformed religion will break up all leagues they have contracted either within the kingdom or beyond its bounds; nor shall they in future, impose taxes, or levy troops, or raise contributions in money; moreover they shall hold no assemblies, or consistories, or public meetings, except for the exercise of religious worship. Amboise, 19th March, 1562.

Thus signed with our own hand,

CHARLES.

And underneath:

For the king in his council,

ROBERTET.

You see, my worthy brother, to what we have been reduced by the inconsistency of one man; for he might have obtained without any difficulty from the queen whatever conditions he pleased, but he has voluntarily prostituted himself to the most abject obsequiousness. We are now anxiously looking out for the issue of all this. We have much reason to fear disturbances, in appeasing which I shall not cease to put forth every effort in my power. As soon as Beza shall be back, you will learn the more secret details of the proceeding. The Duke of Nemours is so seriously ill of an intermittent fever that the doctors despair of his life. The secretary of the royal deputy was at Deux Ponts.

When the cardinal came there, he says that at a public banquet a very ancient and broad cup was produced, on which were carved verses, which confirm our doctrine respecting the Lord's supper, and that the cardinal gazed at the sight for a long time like one almost thunderstruck.

Farewell, most excellent sir, and honoured brother. In my hurry I had almost forgotten that within the last two days I have received from you a couple of letters, one of which was accompanied with books for which I return you my thanks. I beg you to present my best respects to all your fellow pastors, to your sons and your sons-in-law. May the Lord preserve you all in safety. My colleagues and friends all salute you, especially Jonvillers.—Yours,

JOHN CALVIN.

[*Lat. Orig.—Library of Geneva.* Vol. 107 *a.*]

DCXLI.—To the Comtesse de Roye.[1]

He blames the conduct of the Prince of Condé, and deplores the condition of the French churches badly protected by the last treaty.

GENEVA, *April*, 1563.

MADAME :—The conditions of the peace are so much to our disadvantage that we have great reason to invoke God more

---

[1] Without a date. Written after the conclusion of the peace of Amboise; that is, early in April, 1563. At a distance from France during the negotiations which were to end in the treaty of Amboise, the Comtesse de Roye could not exercise, in favour

than ever that he would have compassion upon us, and remedy such extremities. One thing is certain, we must hold down our heads and humble ourselves before God who has admirable issues in his hand, though the beginnings are such as to astonish us. I cannot dissemble that every body is displeased with the prince for showing himself so accommodating, and still more so for being in such a hurry to conclude. It seems pretty evident, also, that he has provided better for his own personal safety than for the common repose of the poor brethren. But be that as it will, this single consideration ought to shut our mouths, that we know that it is the will of God again to exercise us. I shall always give my advice to abstain from arms, and that all of us should perish rather than have recourse, a second time, to the disorders which we have witnessed. I hope, Madame, that you will do all in your power to advance that which for the moment seems put back. I pray you, in the name of God, to make every effort. Nay, I imagine that the habitual rage of our enemies will so nettle the queen and those who heretofore were far from being favourable to us, that every thing will finally turn out well. It is thus that God knows how to make light arise out of darkness. This expectation alleviates, in some degree, my sorrow. But I do not cease for all that to pine away with anguish which consumes me since the news.

Madame, having very humbly commended myself to your indulgent favour, I will supplicate our heavenly Father to have you in his holy keeping, and restore you sound and safe with your grand-children, whom God has honoured by making them pilgrims in a foreign land.[1] This they will have occasion to

of the Reformed party, the influence which her credit at court and the ascendency she possessed over the Prince of Condé assured her. She wrote from Strasbourg to Theodore Beza:—"I have had no other news from France, except the confirmation of that which was brought me by Millet, viz., that the queen and the prince give excellent orders throughout all the provinces that peace be maintained. I have hopes that you shall see with God's help that all those who show themselves still refractory will be punished as they deserve. There arrived here yesterday a man from the court who assures me that the prince is welcome there, and that he daily has one to preach in the king's household, where he has a numerous audience. . . . I am on my way to France, where I shall spare no pains that contribute to the advancement of the glory of God."—Letters of the 7th May, 1563, (*Library of Geneva*, vol. 196.)

[1] The Comtesse de Roye had taken with her to Strasbourg the young children of the Prince of Condé, with the exception of the Marquis of Conti, then nine years of

remember when they come to a riper age, . . . with like . . .
affection all their life.[1]

[*Fr. Orig. Minute.—Library of Geneva.*   Vol. 113.]

DCXLII.—To the Marquise de Rothelin.[2]

He congratnlates her on her firmness in the midst of troubles, and exhorts her to
perseverance.

Geneva, *April*, 1563.

Madame :—Though since a year I have often had news of
you, and such too as afforded me ample matter for rejoicing
and praising God, nevertheless I am very glad to hear from
your own letters what I could not so well comprehend from the
accounts of others.   True it is, you do not say any thing about
those matters of which we have heard from other sources : namely,
that in the midst of the greatest troubles you have never been
either ashamed or afraid to confess that you belong to the flock
of Jesus Christ ; nay, that your house has been an hospital to
receive the poor scattered sheep in which God has been glorified by the mouth of all his faithful ones.   The humanity you
have shown towards those who were afflicted for his name, has
also been to him a pleasing sacrifice.   If the wicked have been
exasperated by it, it is enough for you to have the promise of
our Lord Jesus Christ, that he who shall give a cup of cold water
in his name to one of the least of his disciples shall not lose his
reward.   What has most delighted me, Madame, in your letters

age, who remained at Orleans with the Princess of Condé, his mother.—Beza, vol. ii.,
page 11.
   [1] The concluding words of the letter are illegible.
   [2] Without a date ; written after the conclusion of the peace of Amboise ; that is,
in April, 1563.   Living in retirement during the first civil war, at the Château of
Blandy, near Melan, the Marquise de Rothelin had not ceased to testify her attachment to the gospel which she publicly professed, along with the Duke of Longueville,
her son, since the year 1561 :—" The Duke of Longueville, a young man of the principal nobility and of great hopes, at the last festival of Easter, sat down along with
his mother at the Lord's table, and fully abjured idolatry." (*Beza to Calvin*, 24th
May, 1561.)   The marriage of the Duke of Longueville, with Marie de Bourbon,
widow of Francis of Cleves, Duke of Nevers, brought back this young man to the
ranks of the Catholic party, whilst his mother remained invariably faithful to the Reformed faith.

is the hope that you give us of having the pleasure of seeing you here ere long, and if you find here wherewithal to alleviate your sorrows our satisfaction will be doubled. I doubt not but you have endured many vexations and torments, but we must always put in practice the doctrine which teaches us to lay all our cares upon God, and I know very well you do so. I shall add nothing more, reserving what I have principally to say for your arrival, which I pray God to accelerate. Since you have thought proper that our brother Pierre should go to your town of Noyers, we have decided upon that measure, and given our consent to his departure.

Madame, having very humbly commended myself to your indulgent favour, I will supplicate our heavenly Father to keep you under his protection, to fortify you more and more, and increase you in all good and prosperity.

[*Fr. Orig. Minute.—Library of Geneva.* Vol. 107 a.]

DCXLIII.—To M. DE CRUSSOL.[1]

Sad condition of France, presage of new troubles—Double message to the Prince of Condé and De Coligny.

GENEVA, 7th May, 1563.

MONSEIGNEUR:—If I had the means of writing to you more frequently, it would not depend on my inclinations if I did not acquit myself of the duty. And, in fact, though the roads were blocked up, I did not fail to do so when it seemed to me there was a necessity for it, for without necessity I was unwilling to

[1] Antony de Crussol, governor of Abbeville, and Montreuil, councillor of state, knight of honour of the queen mother, Duke of Uses in 1565, and peer in 1572, occupies with D'Acier, his brother, an important place among the chiefs of French Protestantism. Appointed in 1561 Lieutenant General in Dauphiné, Provence, and Languedoc, with instructions to pacify the religious disturbances in these provinces, he acquitted himself successfully of this mission, and showed himself equally the faithful servant of the king, and sincere partisan of liberty of conscience. The violation of the Edict of January made him join the ranks of the Protestants. He fought valiantly for their cause without entirely partaking their religious opinions, and did not lay down arms till the conclusion of the peace of Amboise. As well as the Chatillons, Soubise, and the chiefs of the party, Antony de Crussol deplored the precipitation with which the Prince of Condé had signed a peace disadvantageous to the Reformed churches.

hazard a letter. As to the state of France, I see so much confusion on all sides that I am much afraid we shall be obliged
more than ever to begin again. Not that the remedy was not
easy, and in our own hands, had we but wished to make use of
it, but you see the position in which we are at present. We
have nothing else to do, then, but patiently to humble ourselves,
waiting till God open up some way. Indeed, I doubt not but
we shall ere long see some signs of his doing so. In the mean
time, we must busy ourselves more courageously than ever, for
God wishes to prove his followers by this blow, setting before
them on the one hand great difficulties, and a second time furnishing them with an opportunity of employing themselves in
good earnest in his service. Thus, Monsieur, I beg you to take
courage. And since you see that God has done you the honour
of setting you as an example and a mirror, you should spare
nothing in his service. But I am so confident of your zeal in
this respect, that I will spare you further exhortations. Nay,
as I see that you have at heart that others should be exhorted
to do their duty, I have written to the prince,[1] for he also had
furnished me an occasion by his letters brought to me by Theodore Beza. But excuse me if I have not adopted the style you
could have wished ; for to make him believe that black is white,
is a thing too much opposed to my natural disposition, and which
it would be impossible for me to do. I have, likewise, answered
the Admiral, begging him more privately to keep a firm hand
on many things, not so much for the need he has of being stimulated, as because he begged of me to do this. When he
shall think proper to show the letters, there is no tartness in
them that can give offence, and there are some goads to prick
on him who shall see them.

Monsieur, having humbly commended myself to your indulgent favour, I will supplicate our heavenly Father to have you
in his keeping, to govern you in your undertakings by his Spirit, to fortify you in upright constancy, and increase you in all
prosperity.

[*Fr. Copy.—Library of Geneva.* Vol. 107.]

[1] See the letter to the Prince of Condé, of the 10th May, a date later than that on
which it was written.

DCXLIV.—To Madame de Crussol.[1]

Wishes for the happy success of the journey to court, which she is about to undertake —Pious exhortations.

Geneva, *8th May,* 1563.

Madame:—I write to you at random, not knowing whether my letters will find you in Languedoc, since the queen has written to Madame de Roye, that she would meet you at court. But as it is just possible that you may not have been ready so soon, I think it right not to omit an opportunity of acquitting myself of my duty, in declaring that I shall not forget to pray God to prosper your journey, and wherever you may be to guide you by his Holy Spirit, in such wisdom that you shall never make more account of the world than of him. I know that he has hitherto derived good services from you, but you can never during the whole course of your life perform the hundredth part of what you owe to him every single day. Wherefore, Madame, bethink yourself how you can pay your arrears, that you may show by deeds it is no vain pretence when we protest that we wish to separate ourselves from all filthiness and pollution, in order to dedicate ourselves purely to our Lord Jesus Christ, who died and rose again that we might live and die in obedience to him.

[1] Louise de Clermont, Comtesse de Tonnerre, wife of Antony de Crussol, and lady of honour to Catherine de Medicis. She added to much intelligence, a lively wit and promptness in repartee, as the following anecdote will show. A few days before the colloquy of Poissy she was present along with the Queen of Navarre and the princes, at a private interview between Theodore Beza and the Cardinal of Lorraine : " The said Cardinal caressing Beza, pronounced these words : I am delighted to have seen and heard you. I adjure you in the name of God to confer with us that I may hear your reasons, and you mine, and you will find that I am not so black as people have represented me . . . This remark being made, the lady of M. de Crussol, who does not scruple to say what she thinks, observed that they ought to have paper and ink to make the Cardinal sign what he had said and avowed, for, added she, to-morrow he will say quite the contrary. In this observation she was found to have guessed rightly." *Hist. Eccl.,* vol. i. p. 497. This same trait is related somewhat differently in a letter of Beza's to Calvin : " Madame de Crussol has proved a prophet, for holding the Cardinal by the hand, she said to him aloud; Good natured man this evening, but to-morrow what?" 25th August, 1561. (Geneva, vol. 117.)

Above all, Madame, because I fear lest you be solicited to swim between two currents, I entreat you to be on your guard, for when the matter in question is how to glorify God he cannot endure any neutrality. Nay more, what might have been tolerated formerly is now no longer permitted you, for you have advanced so far that you cannot go back without running the risk of a mortal fall. Now though this exhortation is superfluous in respect of you, still I have wished to confirm you, almost unnecessarily, in your good zeal, that you may know the desire I have to see you holding on constantly in the right way, and that I may have wherewithal to praise God and rejoice in the cares I bestow on your salvation.

Madame, having humbly commended myself to your indulgent favour, I will supplicate our heavenly Father to maintain you always under his protection, and enrich you more and more with the gifts of his Spirit.

[*Fr. Copy.—Library of Geneva.* Vol. 107.]

DCXLV.—TO THE PRINCE PORCIEN.[1]

He exhorts him to glorify God in life as in death.

GENEVA, *May*, 1563.

MONSEIGNEUR:—Though hitherto I have not written to you, I have not ceased to entertain towards you the respect which you merit, and a wish to employ myself in rendering you a service, desiring that God would furnish me the means of doing so; for I cannot be his servant without loving and honouring

---

[1] Antony de Croï, Prince de Porcien, one of the most brilliant seigneurs of the court of France, attached himself at a very early period of life, to the cause of the Reformation and the party of the Admiral de Coligny. Mixed up in an active manner with the first civil war, he signalized himself by his valour at the battle of Dreux, kept up after the conclusion of the peace, a correspondence with Calvin and Theodore Beza, and died of poison, it is said, at the age of twenty-six. There exists in the archives of Colonel Tronchin at Lavigny, a fine epistle of consolation addressed by Theodore Beza to his widow Catherine of Cleves, Comtesse d'Eu. She contracted a second marriage with Henry de Guise, called the Balafré, and abjured the Protestant faith upon forming this new alliance.

the choice virtues which he has implanted in you. But as I could do nothing better, I have contented myself till now with holding you in my remembrance, praying our heavenly Father to preserve and increase in you the gifts of his Spirit. I am then so much the more delighted, having heard from the bearer who is in your service, that of your kindness you have given me an opening to do what I did not dare though I had a very great desire. I thank you humbly then, Monseigneur, for having deigned to let me know the favourable dispositions you cherish in' respect of me; not only because I put a high value upon standing well in your opinion, but also because you have furnished me with an opportunity of declaring how much I am your affectionate servant. However, inasmuch as I have no other means of demonstrating my disposition of mind towards you, except in procuring your salvation, and in applying to that end whatever faculties God may have bestowed on me, it is to that object I shall have recourse, praying and exhorting you, Monseigneur, in the name of God, to take courage and pursue what you have so well and so happily begun. For some time you have been for a man of your rank and quality put to the severest tests, and God has given you that invincible courage which has enabled you to stand them all. This has been an excellent proof of your faith. But you cannot be too much reminded that this is not the end, and that there still remain many temptations against which you will have to do battle. For our Christian life is not only shown in bearing arms and exposing our bodies and wealth in order to maintain the quarrel of the gospel, but also in subjecting ourselves entirely to the obedience of Him who has bought us at so dear a price, that he may be glorified in our life as well as in our death. Here it is then, Monseigneur, where we are called to persevere, in not becoming weary, not only of fighting with the sword against invisible enemies, but against everything that might turn us aside from walking in the right path. What is more, besides that we are so frail in ourselves, and have inward combats infinite in number to maintain, the devil fails not to raise up against us many crosses, either to make us turn bridle or become lukewarm.

Thus when we think of repose let us only look up to heaven,

even though God give us here below a long period of respite.   I
say not this from any feeling of distrust, because I am convinced
that God, who has given you such excellent tokens of his goodness, will never abandon you. But you feel by experience,
Monseigneur, that we can never be too well fortified in order to
resist so many temptations, by which we are incessantly assailed.
Nevertheless doubting not but you diligently exercise yourself
in reading and hearing the holy exhortations which should serve
you for sword and armour, I shall pursue this topic no further.
I know not if God will ever grant us the blessing (of which you
give us some hope) of one day seeing you in this world; but the
main point is that we should all be assembled in his eternal
kingdom.   I long notwithstanding to enjoy this accessary
pleasure.

Monseigneur, having very humbly commended myself to your
indulgent favour, I will supplicate our heavenly Father to have
you in his holy keeping, to fortify you more and more by his
power, and increase you in all good and prosperity.

[*Fr. Copy.—Library of Geneva.*   Vol. 107.]

DCXLVI.—To the Prince of Condé.[1]

Instructions respecting the greatest advantages to be derived from the treaty of Amboise—The sending off of a confession of faith to Germany—Alliance with Swisserland—Recommendation of Geneva.

GENEVA, 10th May, 1563.

MONSEIGNEUR :—I have no need on the present occasion to
present you with any lengthened excuses for having delayed so

[1] Louis de Bourbon, Prince of Condé, chief of the illustrious house, forming a col-
lateral branch of the monarchy, and which was destined to give to France the great
Condé, and become extinct in the person of the Duke d'Enghien.   The rival of the
Guises and early gained to the cause of the Reformation, by the influence of his mother-in-law, the Comtesse de Roye, the Prince of Condé was imprisoned after the
conspiracy of Amboise, condemned to death, and restored to liberty by the death of
Francis II.   Having become from that period the avowed chief of the Protestant
party in France, he supported the Reformation with his credit in the councils of the
king, and with his sword at Dreux, St. Denis, and Jarnac, where he was assassinated
in 1569.   Arbiter of peace, after the death of the Duke of Guise, and having it in
his power easily to conclude one that would have been advantageous to the Reformed

long to write to you, since I was precluded, for want of means, from acquitting myself of that duty. And even at present I am afraid that the routes are far from being safe. But since you have graciously anticipated me, by your letters brought to me by my brother M. Beza, I am ashamed to delay any longer, especially having an opportunity in the bearer who is obliged to undertake a journey to court.

Respecting the conditions of the peace, I know very well, Monseigneur, that it was not easy for you to obtain them such as you could have wished. Wherefore, if many people desire they had been better, I pray you not to think it extraordinary, for in that respect they are exactly of your own opinion. Meanwhile, if God has thrust us back more than we imagined, it is our duty to humble ourselves under his hand. Be that as it will, as I doubt not but you have striven as much as it lay in your power to advance the kingdom of God, and procure the repose and liberty of the churches, I also hope, and am persuaded, that for the future you will continue to bring every thing to a better state. Nevertheless, Monseigneur, I pray you not to take it amiss if on my part I solicit you to that effect, considering the difficulties by which you are environed. In the first place, if you do not make good by your authority what has been concluded to the advantage of our brethren, the peace will be like a body without a soul; and experience has already proved to you how audaciously the enemies of God undertake to do evil, unless they be vigorously resisted. Next, without any one saying a word to you, you see sufficiently, in your wisdom, Monseigneur, how many people are watching for an opportunity of getting the upper hand. You know their manœuvres; if you give them leisure to surprise you, they will not fail to profit by it, and when once they have their foot in the stirrup, it will be no longer time to wish to restrain them. That should induce you to take steps for being so well supported in the direction of affairs, that the door may be shut against all opponents who

churches, the Prince of Condé did not know how to resist the perfidious seductions of the queen mother, and signed on the 12th March, 1563, in opposition to the opinion of seventy-two ministers assembled at Orleans the convention of Amboise which contained grave infractions of the Edict of January. This fault, bitterly blamed by Coligny, was judged with no less severity by the Reformer.

want to breed mischief.   In the mean time, there will be several means of enlarging the course of the gospel.   I am perfectly aware, Monseigneur, that all cannot be done in a day, but I think, in order to let slip no opportunity, you will do well to remember the proverb—"*what is soonest is best,*" for fear they hatch new plots to dissipate all we have gained, when we fancied that every thing was going on favourably.   And it is at this moment that you should labour more than ever, since God seems to be holding out his hand to you, and as he has done you the inestimable honour of charging you to maintain his quarrel with your sword, it seems also that he has reserved other means for bringing to perfection what he has been pleased to commence.   Since, then, it is his will to try and exercise us in diverse manners, you have the greater occasion to quit yourself manfully, without sparing any thing, that you may prove yourself more worthy in his sight.

I have also another point to touch upon, Monseigneur.   Before the Imperial diet was held at Frankfort, to which you sent M. de Passy,[1] I was required and exhorted by M. d'Andelot to draw up a short confession in your name, that it might be presented to the diet.[2]   I drew it up as God gave me means.[3]   The Count of Beauvais[4] having seen it, could have wished very much it had been signed.   But neither Madame de Roye, nor M. de Soubise, could find means of putting it into your hands.   At

---

[1] In November, 1562.   The former Bishop of Nevers, now become a minister of the gospel, was charged with the mission of justifying before the Emperor, the recourse which Condé had to arms, and of refuting the calumnies spread in Germany about the Reformed churches of France.—*Hist. Eccl.,* vol. ii., p. 152, and the following.

[2] The following is the passage of D'Andelot's letter to Calvin:—"For the rest, in handling the affairs of this country, I have discovered that it is very expedient that the Prince of Condé, and the other principal seigneurs, . . . should cause to be drawn up a confession of faith, signed with their names, to be presented by some notable person to the emperor, the electors, and other princes and seigneurs of Germany.   And, as you know well, that it is impossible but that in so large an assembly there must be great diversity of opinions, I pray you most affectionately to take your pen and draw up the said confession of faith, so that the honour of God and the purity of the gospel being maintained, the ears of so many great princes may not be scandalized by it.

[3] This was the confession of faith, in the name of the Reformed churches of France, drawn up during the war to be presented to the Emperor in the diet at Frankfort, 1562.—*Opuscules,* p. 1991, and *Hist. Eccl.,* vol. i., p. 156.

[4] Odet, Cardinal de Chatillon.

last, I sent it to you by a poor lad, but he arrived too late.
Thus this opportunity is gone by, though it appears to me that
the said confession would not be unseasonable even now ; but,
on the contrary, it would be productive of great advantages,
both within the kingdom and without. For the rest, it would
be necessary to consult about changing the preface, and instead
of being addressed to the emperor that it should be more general, and also without any particular mention of what relates to
the incident of the war. If such a change should meet with
your approbation, I have undertaken to apprise you where
it would be proper to begin, as you will see by the copy which
I send you. If you prefer to leave it such as it is, it would be
necessary to prefix a brief advertisement by way of apology
for its not having been produced at the proper time and place.
As to the advantages which would result from it, I shall only
say a word or two. You know, Monseigneur, that it would
attract many poor ignorant people to have the patience to read
about what otherwise they would reject. Thus it would be a blessed
means of gaining an infinite number of persons, but we might
hope for still greater fruits from it out of the kingdom, inasmuch as many Germans who have been alienated from the
French on account of the question of the Lord's supper would
not abstain from casting a look at it, appearing under the sanc-
tion of your name. In the mean time, that can only tend to
procure you more favour. Besides, you ought to anticipate a
danger which you have perhaps already felt in part, which is, that
they will not cease to stretch nets to entangle you in the Confession of Augsburg, a confession which is neither flesh nor fish, and
is the cause of great schisms and debates among the Germans.
Now, Monseigneur, having made such a declaration, you would
have shut the door on all the importunities with which they
could assail you, having always this word to reply, that you
cannot retract the confession which you have made, unless they
show you some reason why. I shall not give myself the trouble
to protest that in this matter I am seeking but the glory of
God, the common welfare of his church, and even your own
honour, because I do not think that you deem me a man to
consult only my own personal interests. Thus I shall wait for

your answer to learn your good pleasure in order that I may
obey what you shall command me.

But one thing more:—As I have learned that they are treating of an alliance in which the Swiss are included, I pray you
for the good of the king to take care that this measure be vigorously pursued. I urge this because there were some difficulties
that you might find tiresome. But when every thing is maturely
weighed, such a cause is not to be given up slightly. I dare
not recommend to you that this city of ours should be included
in the treaty, though the seigneurs of Berne, our fellow-bur-
ghers, have promised to aid us in that matter, the rather too
that everybody clearly sees that it is the king's interest, and
that he will incur an actual detriment if we were left out.[1] I
dare not offer my services, but it is enough that you shall always
find me disposed, if you see that my co-operation can be of any
use.

Monseigneur, having very humbly commended myself to your
indulgent favour, I will supplicate our heavenly Father to have
you in his holy keeping, to conduct you by his Holy Spirit,
fortify you with invincible courage, and increase you in all
good and prosperity.

[*Fr. Copy.—Library of Geneva.* Vol. 107.]

DCXLVII.—To the Duchess of Ferrara.[2]

He congratulates her on her noble conduct amidst the civil wars—Exhorts her to
keep her house free from all scandal, and recommends to her an ancient servant.

GENEVA, 10*th May,* 1563.

MADAME:—I have experienced during these troubles arising
from the war, in what confusion everything was plunged in

---

[1] See page 166, note 1.

[2] Living retired at Montargis during the first troubles, the Duchess of Ferrara there
displayed the noblest character and knew how to conciliate the respect of all parties.
In spite of the threats of the court and of her son-in-law the Duke of Guise, she
offered an asylum to the unhappy victims of the civil wars. "That was the cause,"
says an historian, "that towns and villages of the flat country all fled to Montargis,
where several had been preserved from the commencement of the wars under the pro-

France, the more that I have had no means of writing to you
at a time when you stood more in need of it than ever.   Now I
hope that the communications are more open, and though for
some time yet there will be robbers and bandits, yet at last God
will provide a remedy for all disorders.   And indeed if he did
not interfere we should be in a worse state than before, for
if those who are in authority do not put in execution all the
provisions of the peace, advancing the honour of God still more
than others oppose it, religion will be like a body without a
soul.

I know, Madame, how God has strengthened you during the
rudest assaults, and how by his grace you have courageously
resisted all temptations, not being ashamed to bear the opprobrium of Jesus Christ, while the pride of his enemies rose above
the clouds.   I know, moreover, that you have been as it were a
nursing mother to those poor persecuted brethren who knew not
where to betake themselves.   I know that a princess, considering things only with the eyes of the world, would have
been ashamed and taken it almost for an insult that her castle
should have been called God's hostelry.   But I cannot do you
a higher honour than in expressing myself thus, to commend
and recognize the humanity which you have exercised towards
the children of God who found a refuge with you.   Oftentimes
have I thought, Madame, that God had reserved such trials for
your old age, that you might have an opportunity of paying him
the arrears due to him for the timidity of times past.   I speak
after the manner of men; for though you had done a hundred,
nay a thousand times more, it would not pay a tithe of each
day's debt you are contiuually contracting for the infinite blessings he continues to bestow on you.   But what I mean is, that
he has done you a singular honour in employing you in such a

tection of the duchess, who being of the blood royal, and connected by affinity with
the Guises, had had a special privilege. She and her ministers blamed those who took
up arms in terms which rendered her and the Prince de Condé enemies, and this
quarrel afforded a pretext for not paying her proper respect." D'Aubigné, *Hist.
Univ.*, vol. i. p. 415. The peace having been signed at Amboise, Calvin wrote to the
Duchess of Ferrara, and as he had formerly reproved her acts of weakness, he praised
the constancy and magnanimity which she had displayed amid the most difficult circumstances.

duty, and making you carry his banner in order to be glorified in you, while you hospitably entertained his word which is the inestimable treasure of salvation, and afforded an asylum to the members of his son. So much the more then it is your duty, Madame, to preserve for the future your house pure and uncontaminated that it may be wholly dedicated to him. And on this subject I cannot refrain from mentioning to you a cause of scandal of which I have heard rumours heretofore.

There is a young man whom you have brought up and settled in marriage, who has dismissed his wife to keep up intercourse with a strumpet. I inquired of M. Biry, the circumstances of the affair, knowing that he was such an affectionate servant to you that you would not feel offended if I disclosed to him what people reported on this subject. He at first replied that you had taken pains to correct such a disorder. However, he at last avowed to me, that though there had been apparently some amendment, people did not know if it would last.

I pray you, Madame, in the name of God to be vigilant in this and similar cases, to keep your household unsullied from all disgraceful stains, in order to shut the mouths of the ungodly who ·ask for nothing better than to blaspheme the name of God. And nevertheless, rejoice, as you have good grounds for joy amid so much sorrow, for it is no slight blessing that God has so approved of you as to choose you out in order to be glorified by your means.

You will be pleased also, Madame, to excuse me for not having immediately satisfied your desire in sending you a preacher. But I shall not fail to occupy myself with this commission till you be provided with one. One cannot find at every instant such ministers as one could wish, and we are importuned from so many quarters that we scarcely know on what side to turn ourselves. At any rate you may count upon being served in preference to all others, and were you present here you would see that it is not without cause that I beg of you to have patience.

There is a private matter about which your old servant Messire Francisco[1] has begged me to write to you. The subject

---

[1] Francis Porto of the island of Candia, formerly professor of Greek in the Uni-

of his communication is this: Since you were pleased graciously to promise him that you would interest yourself in favour of his daughter, and do something towards procuring her a husband, as she is now of a marriageable age, he would fain know your good pleasure and what he is to expect from it. You know that I am not in the habit of soliciting you for any one, and were it for myself or any of mine I should not venture to do it. But since the person in question is your old servant, whom you were pleased to recommend to me, I did not dare to refuse his request, more especially as he faithfully discharges his duty, and conducts himself to the satisfaction of all good men. On the other hand, his salary, like that of all of us, is so small, that it would be impossible for him to live upon it, did he not derive support elsewhere to enable him to cover his expenses.

Madame, having very humbly commended myself to your indulgent favour, I will supplicate our heavenly Father to keep you always under his protection, to strengthen you with invincible courage, and increase you in all good and prosperity.

[*Fr. Copy.—Library of Geneva.* Vol. 107.]

DCXLVIII.—To MONSIEUR DE SOUBISE.[1]

Counsels respecting the conduct he ought to hold in very difficult conjunctures.

GENEVA, *25th May*, 1563.

MONSIEUR :—Both your letters found me in so bad a state of health that it was impossible for me to answer them sooner,

versity of Ferrara. Banished from this town as a Lutheran he retired first to Venice and afterwards to Geneva, where he obtained the rights of citizenship as well as the chair of Greek literature in the Academy. He received during his old age numerous tokens of the affection of the Duchess of Ferrara, and died in 1581, leaving many writings which procured him the esteem of Joseph Scaliger. Senebier, *Hist. Litt.*, vol. ii. p. 24.

[1] See letter, page   Dissatisfied, as well as all his party, at the treaty signed by the Prince of Condé, Soubise still hesitated to surrender Lyons into the hands of the king. The presence in Dauphiné of Protestant troops, commanded by the Comtes de Beauvais and of Crussol, encouraged him to tempt again the fortune of arms. Calvin, in dissuading him from this latter measure, exhorted him to temporize. The arrival of the Marshal de Vicilleville, " a man of a peaceable disposition who had

and even at present I know not if I shall be able to do it, inasmuch as the pains, or rather the tortures, of a desperate colic do not give me a moment's respite. Wherefore, I pray you to excuse my brevity, for my bodily sufferings have in a manner stultified my mind. Having observed the current of your affairs, I always return to my old conclusion to see and judge what is lawful and what is possible. If the question were to fight in good earnest, I do not see by what title you could do so, since God has disarmed you. To put off and shuffle, I do not think right, and especially that you may have leisure to put to the proof what are the intentions and abilities of the two comtes to succour you, for without them I do not see how you can maintain your position.

Besides, even if they should join you, you would still require to have some show of right on your side; for to attempt any thing, unless we be called and warranted to do so, can never come to any good. I do not say that some just occasion may not be found, but hitherto I do not know of any, and that is the reason why I should not dare to advise you to decide upon making war at least till I be better informed. These means seem to me altogether inadequate, unless the Comte de Beauvais engage his associate to do more than I expect when I consider the character of both parties. I do not say, however, that you should quit the place at the very first summons, in order to throw yourself into the jaws of the wolf; but to act in direct opposition to the command of the king, I do not see that God permits you. What remains, then, is to reflect to what point excuses are admissible, both for your delay in laying down arms, and for your refusal to admit M. de Nemours as governor. I feel the importance of the inconveniences you allege, but for sole answer I stick to the saying of Abraham, God will provide for the matter, as indeed the apostle reminds us that he is faithful, and thus will not suffer us to be tempted above what we can bear. Into particulars I will not enter, except that it would be useful, in my opinion, to write to the comtes openly, offering to join them in all that will be found

never shown himself partial during these troubles," put an end to the hesitations of Soubise, and caused Lyons to come again into the power of the king.

proper to keep up their courage. I doubt not but you have written to the Admiral, on account of your position which will serve as a summons to make him undertake the charge and so relieve you.

Monsieur, having commended myself to your indulgent favour, etc.

[*Fr. Copy.—Library of Geneva.* Vol. 107.]

DCXLIX.—To the Queen of Navarre.[1]

Sending off ministers—Claiming of a debt contracted by the King of Navarre.

GENEVA, 1st *June*, 1563.

MADAME:—It has grieved me that the bearer did not find me in a condition to busy myself as I could have wished, in order to satisfy your holy desire; but I have been tormented during fifteen days by colic of so extraordinary a kind, that all my senses and my intellect have been rendered almost useless by the violence of the pain. At present, though the complaint has not left me, it begins to assume a milder form which gives

---

[1] Docile to the councils of Calvin, and without allowing herself to be terrified by the anathemas of Rome, and the threats of Spain, Jane d'Albret had courageously undertaken the work of reformation in her states. She abolished the worship of images, forbade public processions, suppressed the monasteries, and transformed the churches into Protestant temples. The ecclesiastical lands were united to the domain of the crown, their revenues consecrated to the relief of the poor, and the education of youth. Missionaries of Bearn and the Basques country preached the gospel in their own language. But their number was insufficient. By the cares of Calvin and Beza the society of Geneva, who had already granted Merlin to the Queen of Navarre, associated themselves more actively in this work by sending off twelve ministers. So complete a revolution could not be accomplished without great difficulties. The genius of the queen happily triumphed over them. " I receive here," Merlin wrote to Calvin, " so many molestations that my health suffers. These molestations are not caused by the queen, for I can affirm that I have her constancy in admiration, and I entreat you to confirm it more and more by your letters. . . . They set before our eyes marvellous dangers at one time from a sedition of the natives of the country, at another, from the Spaniards, then from Monluc, and even from France. They spread about reports that the preparations for war are all made, in order to fall upon us if we make any innovations in religion. The constancy of the queen surmounts all that."—Letter of the 23d July, 1563. This religious revolution was completed in 1574, and was crowned by the celebrated ordinances, a monument of the faith and the genius of the Queen of Navarre.

me hopes of further relief. In short, however, my brother M.
Beza, along with the society, has supplied my absence. The gentlemen of this city, also, having learned from me the recommendations which you addressed to them have prayed and exhorted
us to acquit ourselves to the best of our abilities. At last, we
have procured for you a dozen of men. If they are not in all
respects as accomplished as we could have wished, I beg you,
Madame, to have patience, for ministers are a merchandize one
cannot lay one's hands on as easily as it were to be desired.
At any rate, my colleagues trust that they will be tolerably
proper and fitting to instruct the people to your satisfaction.
Nothing remains, Madame, but to set them to work and to
strengthen their hands, as your authority will be very requisite
to arm and protect them against the keen opposition they shall
have to encounter. For this purpose, Madame, you are duly
warned that you yourself must be armed and fortified from on
high, in order not to flinch, but to hold on to the end in your
holy enterprise. When you shall have established some order,
which will be ere long I hope, I very humbly entreat you to
dispense with the services of our brother Merlin,[1] whose absence is felt by us, considering the smallness of our numbers.

For the rest, Madame, with respect to the sum of which I
have given you information: Here is how the matter stands.
The late king, your husband, being at that time well disposed
to the cause, and seeing himself involved in considerable em-
barrassments, asked us if we could afford him some pecuniary
relief. I bestirred myself so effectually that he was promised,
on the part of this city, forty thousand franks. Before they
could collect them, he sent to Lyons M. de Malligny, now Vi-
dame of Chartres, whom he ordered to send him twenty-five
thousand franks for certain expenses which he was about to
incur, of which I despatched ten thousand to him at his own
request. But when the time came round for the payment, I
did not know in what direction to turn myself, for I have never
been a man of finances, and I can assure you, Madame, that of
the little I possess, which is almost nothing, I would willingly
have stripped myself, even to the money which I required for

---

[1] He returned the following year (1564) to Geneva.

the purchase of my daily provisions. But thank God, at last, the contribution was completed, which the late king, your husband, who had not yet been turned aside from us, promised M. Beza to liquidate, as the latter can certify. Wherefore, what I say about it is not in order to be reimbursed of even one penny which I contributed of my own money, but to acquit myself of what I owe my friends who aided me in this strait, and also to clear up my honour. Madame, I would by no means importune you in any manner whatever, but I thought that at least you would not take it amiss to be informed of the truth of the fact, in order to take such steps as your humanity shall dictate, and as you shall see to be reasonable.

Madame, having presented my very humble respects to your majesty, I will supplicate our heavenly Father to keep you always under his protection, to enrich you with the gifts of his Spirit, and increase you in all good and prosperity.

[*Fr. Copy.—Library of Geneva.* Vol. 107.]

DCL.—To Bullinger.[1]

Sufferings of Calvin—News of the court and kingdom of France—Precautions against the Confession of Augsburg.

GENEVA, 2d *July*, 1563.

The inconsiderateness of a worthy but thoughtless man obliges me to dictate these words in a hurry. Being about to send his

---

[1] Rendered incapable of writing by multiplied sufferings, Calvin was obliged to resign himself not without regrets to the necessity of dictating his letters. His secretary, Charles de Jonvillers, assisted from that time in the occupations of his vast correspondence, as he himself informs us in an affecting letter to Bullinger: " When some years previously I saw M. Calvin almost succumbing under the burden of his correspondence, yet unwilling to employ an amanuensis, I entreated him to spare himself, and added that his letters would not be less cherished, though written by the hand of another, provided they were signed by his own hand. He replied that he was afraid that people might put a wrong interpretation upon it, or think themselves slighted, if he did not write letters with his own hand. I, in my turn, rejoined, remarking something which I thought to the purpose. At length, he allowed himself to be persuaded, so that now he makes use of the assistance of another."—(MSS. of Zurich, 10 Aug., 1565.) The last letters of Calvin to Bullinger are all in the handwriting of Charles de Jonvillers.

sons to your city he did not apprise me of his intention till the
moment of their departure. At present, I am relieved from
very acute suffering, having been delivered of a calculus about
the size of the kernel of a filbert. As the retention of urine
was very painful to me, by the advice of my physician, I got
upon horseback that the jolting might assist me in discharging
the calculus. On my return home I was surprised to find that
I emitted discoloured blood instead of urine. The following
day the calculus had forced its way from the bladder into the
urethra. Hence still more excruciating tortures. For more
than half an hour I endeavoured to disengage myself from it by
a violent agitation of my whole body. I gained nothing by
that, but obtained a slight relief by fomentations with warm
water. Meanwhile, the urinary canal was so much lacerated
that copious discharges of blood flowed from it. It seems to
me now that I begin to live anew for the last two days since I
am delivered from these pains.

Of the state of France, I should have written to you with
more details if I had been at leisure. At Lyons the churches
have been restored to the priests. Four only have been left to
us, of which one was obtained by craft, and under a false pretext. The former governor of the city has been recalled, a
man of a peaceable and mild character, detested by the Papists,
because he is favourable to us. The godly are everywhere recovering their courage. The enemies are still raising disturbances in many places, and their fury breaks out in fires and
massacres. It will proceed, at last, to such lengths that even
their protectors will feel that they are implacable. The Constable grows milder every day. Though the queen caresses the
Prince of Condé, yet the versatile and crafty woman inspires
us with but very little or no confidence. But though she is entirely destitute of sincerity, she would nevertheless comply with
the prince, if she saw in him a prudent and magnanimous man.
Though the Parliament of Paris has, at length, readmitted those
counsellors who had taken to flight, many have nevertheless
abdicated their functions. The chancellor is much offended at
that, because he would wish to see in it as many persons as possible favourable to our party. He therefore severely represses

these resignations as much as it depends on him. The Admiral hitherto remains quiet. His brother is at court. It is with great difficulty that the Constable has been at length induced to lead an army against the English. Either the faint-heartedness and cowardice of Condé outstrips all belief, or we shall have some favourable change ere long.

Farewell, most accomplished sir and honoured brother. May the Lord prosper you and yours. Carefully salute all your fellow pastors. My colleagues, who are now present with me, also salute you. I have retired for a moment from their society to dictate this letter to you.

Yours, JOHN CALVIN.

I am carefully on the watch that Lutheranism gain no ground, nor be introduced into France. The best means, believe me, for checking the evil would be that the confession written by me in the name of the Prince of Condé and the other nobles should be published,[1] by which Condé would pledge his good faith and reputation, and endeavour to draw over the German princes to our party. I am waiting for his answer. The Admiral is urging him. If we could bring people to subscribe it, this proceeding would procure us some pleasant sport. Meanwhile, the condition of the churches is better than you imagine. They are permitted to make use of the confession presented to the king, as well as the catechism. In one word, things are strangely mixed up. There is no reason to fear, however, that the Papists will admit the Confession of Augsburg, should it be offered to them a hundred times. As my commentaries on Jeremiah will be published about the time of the next fair, I have resolved to dedicate them to the Prince Palatine. In my preface I have introduced an abstract of our whole controversy. So there is no doubt Brentz will have at me.

The father of the boys who will deliver to you this letter begs me to recommend them to you. But he does not wish you to be put to any inconvenience on their account, only when an opportunity may present itself he would be delighted if you

---

[1] See page 311.

inquired whether they behaved modestly, and that you should make it your business that they be kept to their studies.

[*Lat. Orig. —Library of Geneva.* Vol. 107 *a.*]

DCLI.—To Bullinger.

News of France—Reply of Coligny and Theodore Beza to a calumnious accusation—
Siege of Havre.

GENEVA, 19*th July*, 1563.

Since I wrote to you we have heard nothing new from France, except that God seems to turn children's sport into serious earnest. The Duke of Orleans,[1] provoked by the petulance of a child of the Duke of Guise's, struck him with an arrow which he held in his hand. The boy ran immediately to his mother, and his mother to the queen, who advised her son after slightly reprimanding him to pardon young Guise. The Duke boldly replied, that he could never bring himself to endure the sight of him, and that not only he detested the boy, but the whole family which had been so fatal to the kingdom. The queen mother was thus obliged to send him out of her presence. But at Paris she encourages and inflames the furious passions of the people. Every day new disturbances are breaking out. The Parliament is entirely without authority. An armed rabble sets aside with impunity all its decisions. This is a very just judgment, that where robbers govern, licentiousness should prevail. Condé keeps silence. The Admiral makes apologies, saying he prefers remaining at home and waiting for a favourable opportunity to throw himself into manifest danger. Since he, the Comte de Rochefoucaud and Beza have had their attention called to the assassin of Guise, they have published a common defence which was immediately presented to the king's council.[2]

---

[1] Henry, the third son of Henry II. and Catherine de Medici, afterwards Duke of Anjou, and king under the name of Henry III.

[2] In a letter of Beza's to Calvin of the 8th October, 1563, are the following words : That tyrannicide (τυραννοκτονος) Poltrot, in his trial, and even amid his tortures a hundred times declared me innocent of all participation in the murder of Guise. Dis-

But because all men had not sufficiently got over their scruples, the Admiral published a declaration. If there is any good translator among you, it would be very desirable that it were published in German for the time of the next fair. The book would be salable, so there would be no fear of the printer sustaining any loss. But you would need to make haste. We entrust the affair to your wisdom, and that of your brethren. If you judge it expedient that it should be brought out, perhaps some means of doing it might be found among you. All things are still in a very peaceable state at Lyons. The priests conduct themselves with moderation; nay, fawn upon our brethren. They have only got up the representation of one mass as yet, and that too on a profane altar, for there was no consecrated one. At Montpelier, Nimes, and other cities, our brethren are still in possession of the churches, because no one of the opposite party ventures to claim them. In Normandy, Havre de Grace, which the English have occupied, is besieged.[1] That is all I have to add for the present to my former news. I beg that you and Gualter would superintend the publishing of the defence, if your time permit, and a good printer undertake it.

Farewell, most illustrious sir and respected brother. You will salute all your colleagues in my name and that of my brethren, and your own family at the same time. May the Lord stand by you, govern you by his Spirit, and bless your labours.

Yours,   JOHN CALVIN.

[*Lat. Copy.—Library of Geneva.* Vol. 107 *a*.]

charged, in his turn, from all imputation, Coligny nevertheless thought it necessary to reply by a public declaration.—*Memoires de Condé*, vol. iv., p. 312.

[1] This place had been given up to Elizabeth by the Protestants. They repaired their fault in assisting the Royal army to recover it. Every body knows the bon mot which Brantome lends them : "We are foolish enough to take Havre from the English."

DCLII.—To Bullinger.

Disturbances at Rouen—Uncertainty respecting the projects of Coligny—Calm at Lyons.

GENEVA, *29th July,* 1563.

I know nothing worth writing about except that the inhabitants of Rouen vie with the Parisians in audacity and perversity. One of the marshals was therefore sent to curb their fury, and procure our brethren some security. It would not be difficult to remedy all these disorders, nay they would disappear of themselves, did not the queen by her clandestine arts foment them. She pretends indeed the contrary; it is certain, however, that by her emissaries she is acting in such a manner as will enable worthless men to render by their profligacy everything unavailing that has been publicly decreed in the council of the king. Certes the impunity allowed to crimes sufficiently demonstrates that she approves of everything that has a tendency to crush us. What the Admiral intends I know not. Yesterday I had a letter from him in which he only lets Beza and myself know that very soon he will send an express messenger to inform us of his designs. From a letter of Soubise, who I conjecture was along with him, I learn that he still keeps away from court, partly because he is unwilling uselessly to expose himself to danger, and partly for fear he should be forced to take in hand the expedition against the English.[1] The Comte of Lancy, Governor of Lyons, with whom I had previously no intercourse, congratulates me on the tranquil state of the city. But in the provinces they obstinately refuse to admit our brethren. In the long run they will have to be compelled by force of arms, and despair is driving them on to reckless courses.

Farewell, most illustrious sir and respected brother. Best respects to all your colleagues, your wife, and your whole family. May the Lord preserve you all in safety.—Yours,

JOHN CALVIN.

[1] See p. 323.

Your friend Jonvillers respectfully and affectionately salutes you.

[*Lat. Copy.—Library of Geneva.* Vol. 107 *a.*]

DCLIII.—To MONSIEUR DE CRUSSOL.[1]

Answer to some scruples expressed by this seigneur.

GENEVA, 31*st July,* 1563.

MONSEIGNEUR :—The person whom you charged to propose to me the scruples which you desired to have resolved has acquitted himself of his commission. Before I proceed to answer you, I thank God for having so touched your heart by his Spirit that you do not stretch your conscience to give yourself liberties as so many others do, who nevertheless after having excused themselves before men are constrained to condemn themselves before God. Now to come to the point, I know that you do not mean to disguise your sentiments, like one that wishes to swim between two currents.

You only ask if having made a free and open profession of your Christian faith, it will be lawful for you to accompany the queen in certain processions as well as in other acts of idolatry. Whereupon, Monseigneur, you have to consider two things : first, not to grieve the children of God, or be a subject of scandal to them, or disgust the infirm or ignorant ; secondly, not to give an occasion to the enemies of the truth to raise their crests and triumph, nay, not even to furnish them a pretext for opening their mouths to blaspheme the name of God and turn into ridicule the true religion. We ought to be carefully attentive to these two considerations, as they are also strongly recom-

---

[1] See the letter p. 304. Recalled to court after the conclusion of the peace this seigneur seemed to incline towards a public profession of the Protestant faith, as is proved by the scruples which he submitted to Calvin, and the directions he received from him. But he did not persevere in these sentiments and died a Catholic. D'Acier his brother, who succeeded him in 1573 in the title of Duke of Usès, long persisted in the Reformed confession, which he nevertheless abandoned in the latter years of his life.

mended to us. Since then the Holy Spirit expressly forbids
you to grieve your brethren in this respect, reflect how many
poor people there will be cut to the heart, when they shall see
you parading with a band marching to do despite unto God.
As to the scandal you see how great it will be, and how far it
will extend. For many will shelter themselves under your example, even the hypocrites who till now have been ashamed of
their cowardice will screen themselves under your shadow. On
the other hand, there can be no doubt but you will make proud
the ungodly, not only to despise the gospel, but also to harden
themselves in their cruelty towards those who shall be unwilling
to square their sails to the wind. In one word, the more you
shall consider all the circumstances, the more you will conclude
that God would be offended in divers ways by such conduct.
There remains but the example of Naaman. But the difference
is so great here between the persons, that you cannot apply
what was done by him to your case.

There was nobody but himself in the land of Syria, who feared
God or had any devotion to his service, wherefore there was no
danger of scandal. No true believer could be grieved that he
had exposed to disgrace the true religion. He could not
turn aside those who were already in the good way, nor disgust others from entering upon it. On the contrary he irritated
his whole nation by having an altar apart to worship the God
of Israel. The main point here is not to adhere to the literal
fact, but to consider what edification is to be derived from it.
The rest is to see if for that you should rather abandon the
state than not show complaisance to the queen. In this matter
we should hold by the rule of St. Paul, not to do evil that good
may come of it. I see very well what advantages may accrue
to the church from your occupying your present post, and what
detriment we should have to fear if you gave it up. But in
such perplexities we should do God the honour of putting full
confidence in him, trusting that he will know how to provide for
everything.

Nevertheless it seems to me that you might have a sufficiently
feasible excuse, since the queen is not ignorant, that according to
the religion you hold, you cannot mingle in their ceremonies with-

out offending God, because your conscience condemns them. What is more, I trust she will find your courageous independence preferable to a mean act of condescension. For she has suffered you to be long absent, she will then permit you to be ill during three days in the year. I do not say that, however, by way of cunning artifice, for to feign illness would be a disgrace to the gospel. When you shall have weighed all these circumstances, I doubt not but you will conceive with St. Paul, that we cannot be partakers of the Lord's supper, and show ourselves among idolatries, especially when we should thus set a bad example. But I entreat you, Monseigneur, to quit yourself like a man, and pray God to strengthen your hands, and clothe you with the armour which he has given you, to do battle constantly, that is, to exercise yourself diligently in his word.

Monseigneur, having presented my humble commendations to your indulgent favour and that of your wife, I will pray the Father of mercies to have you in his keeping, to guide you prosperously and grant you a happy arrival.

Your humble servant,

JOHN CALVIN.

[*Fr. Copy.—Library of Geneva.* Vol. 107 *a.*]

DCLIV.—To the Admiral Coligny.[1]

Communications respecting the printing of a memorial—Wishes for the prompt return of the Admiral to the court

Geneva, *5th July*, 1563.

Monseigneur :—Having received your letters from the Seigneur de Verac, we readily perceived that there had been a mis-

---

[1] On the back : *à Monsieur l'Amiral.* Without the date of the year : 1563. The attention of the whole of Europe was occupied during several months by the process between the Guises and Coligny, in consequence of the assassination of the Duke of Guise at Orleans. This crime, the work of a fanatical sectary who had taken counsel only from himself, was imputed to a whole party. Poltrot himself in his interrogatory had designated the Admiral as the instigator of this assassination, but he continually varied in his depositions, and made a solemn retractation before his death. The noble character of the Admiral should have set him above all such suspicions. He thought

take respecting the printing of your reply. But the excuse is
not difficult, so far as we are concerned. For having heard
that the copy which you sent might be already published, and
that thus any diversity might have been found bad, though the
advertisement came very late, nevertheless we put off till we
had letters from you in which you made no objection, and thus
we thought that your intention was that we should not mind it.
So we proceeded. Now, since the arrival of the Seigneur de
Verac, we could do nothing better than to prepare actively for
having the said answer translated into Latin and German. We
thought it preferable to defer printing in French the copy which
he has brought us till the return of our messenger. At present,
we shall use dispatch that you may be satisfied as soon as possible. There is one evil more, which is, that a part of the first
impression was sold. The rest shall be kept locked up.

We are very sorry the journey of the Comte[1] has been retarded, because it was very desirable that he should arrive at
court. But we see very well that he had good reasons for his
conduct, in order not to expose himself to danger, and also to
sound people's dispositions of mind which were uncertain. If
the answer is such as we desire, it will contribute greatly both
to his safety and your own, and will prepare the way for your
adopting some more certain decision.

Touching the Cardinal's hat,[2] we know very well that it is not
a thing of such importance as many people would make it. But
you are aware we cannot altogether exculpate him, nor under-

it his duty, nevertheless, to reply by a public declaration to these calumnious imputations spread about by his enemies. It is the answer of which the Reformer makes
mention and which one may read : *Hist. Eccl.*, vol. ii., p. 291, and the following.
Printed at Paris and Geneva, translated into Latin and German, this piece was disseminated all over Europe.

[1] Francis, Comte de Rochefoucaud, and de Roucy, Prince of Marsillac, one of the
principal chiefs of the Protestant party. Incriminated like the Admiral, then excul-
pated in the depositions of Poltrot, he perished like him in the massacre of St. Bartholomew.

[2] Allusion to Odet de Coligny, Cardinal of Chatillon. After his conversion to the
Reformed faith this prelate had laid aside the name and dress of his ecclesiastical
dignity, and assumed the title of Comte de Beauvais. Excommunicated by the Pope,
he put on the costume of a Cardinal in great ceremonies, to show his contempt for
the Pontifical censures. He went farther still. He married, and wore his Cardinal's
dress on his marriage day.

take the defence of his cause, as really in conscience we cannot help saying that there was a certain degree of levity in his conduct in that matter.   It will be sufficient, we think, if some persons should be too violently offended at it, to moderate their zeal and humble a little those who should make war on him for that reason, so that without approving the deed we may show them that it is pardonable, and that we should not cease to esteem him, as he deserves, the less on that account.   As for yourself, we thank God that you have resolved to go to court as soon as the Comte shall have arrived there and informed you that you run no risk, for we have learned by your absence from it how profitable it would have been had you always remained there. It seems even that every thing must go from bad to worse if God do not speedily prevent it, which we trust he will do by means of you.   Thus persuaded that he has reserved you for this purpose, we entreat you most earnestly not to let slip any opportunity.   For your presence, at any rate, will impose upon your enemies.

Touching the alliance, we defer to another time to speak of it, for at the present moment you could not undertake any thing on that subject.

Monseigneur, having humbly commended myself to your indulgent favour, we supplicate our heavenly Father to keep you under his protection, to fortify you by his power, and increase you in all prosperity.

Your humble servants,

JOHN CALVIN—THEODORE BEZA.[1]

[Fr. Orig. Autog.—Library of Paris, Bethune, 8702, p. 76.]

[1] The name of Beza is in Calvin's handwriting.

DCLV.—To Madame de Coligny.[1]

The Christian uses of sickness.

GENEVA, *5th August*, 1563.

MADAME :—That my letters were sent off without having my signature affixed to them did not occur so much from any stupidity or negligence of mine as from the too great haste of M. Beza, who took them from me while I was ill, and without looking whether they were signed and dated, folded them up and put them in the parcel. But it is enough that you know whence they came, for my handwriting would scarcely have added any thing to their gracious reception. However, another time I will pay more attention. For the rest, Madame, I thank God who has put you in the way of recovery from an illness which we had great reason to fear might have been mortal, although I confess I had no inquietudes on that score. Nevertheless, I did not fail to have you in remembrance, for it is but just that both the Admiral and yourself should be objects of the deepest interest to all true servants of God, in the number of whom I hope to be reckoned, though I am more than unworthy of that honour. You know, Madame, how we should turn to our profit both the chastisements we receive from the hand of our merciful Father and the succour which he sends in time of need. It is certain that all diseases ought not only to humble us in setting before our eyes our frailty, but also cause us to look into ourselves, that having recognized our own poverty we may place all our trust in his mercy. They should, moreover, serve us for medicines to purge us from worldly affections, and retrench what is superfluous in us, and since they are to us the messengers of death, we ought to learn to have one foot raised to take our departure when it shall please God. Nevertheless, he lets us taste of his bounty as often as he delivers us from them, just as it has been a most salutary thing for you, Madame, to have

---

[1] Written at the same time as the preceding, after a serious illness of Madame l'Amirale.

known the danger in which you were and from which he has delivered you. It remains for you to conclude with St. Paul that
when we have been delivered from many deaths by his hand, he
will also withdraw us from them in time to come. And thus
take courage, so much the more to give yourself up to his service, as you do well to consider that it is to that end he has reserved you. I am very glad that the Admiral thinks of going
to court, on the first occasion that will present itself. I hope
that this journey will be productive of much good, and in divers
ways, and we pray God also to make it prosper.

Madame, having humbly commended myself to your indulgent favour, I will supplicate our heavenly Father to keep you
always under his protection, to enrich you with his spiritual
gifts, and to conduct you always, in order that his name may
be glorified in you.

[*Fr. Orig.—Library of Geneva.* Vol. 107.]

DCLVI.—To the Comtesse de Seninghen.[1]

He exhorts her to show herself firm in the profession of the faith and patient in
affliction.

Geneva, 28th *August*, 1563.

Madame:—Though I have never written to you hitherto, it
was not for want of devotedness to occupy myself in doing you
a service. I have you also in remembrance before God, as my
duty requires. But because my letters cannot much benefit
you, and my brother M. Beza, moreover, can amply discharge
his own duty and mine too towards you, I have put off writing
to you. But, at last, fearing that I might be too neglectful, I
have resolved to defer doing so no longer.

Now, Madame, I thank God, in the first place, for the con-

---

[1] Françoise d'Amboise, wife of Charles de Croi, Comte de Seninghen, and mother
of Prince Porcien and of the Marquis de Reuel deserves a place beside the Comtesse
de Roye, the Marchioness of Rothelin, and Madame l'Amirale de Coligny, among the
illustrious ladies of the Reformation in France. She died in 1565. The Marquis de
Reuel, the eldest of her sons, was in the number of the victims of the St. Bartholomew.

stancy he has bestowed on you which has kept you from being shaken by the troubles which have taken place in France. By your perseverance you have shown that your faith was well grounded, and had taken such deep root as not to be impaired. You have still to take courage for the future, for though the assaults are not so rude as those we have witnessed, the devil has many ways of turning aside the children of God from the right path, were it but the bad examples with which we are surrounded on all sides. Several are fickle, some altogether profane; some become lukewarm, others are fond of luxury, and others again give themselves up to a dissolute manner of life. In a word, everywhere we meet with stumbling-blocks. For that reason, you have the more need to be ever on the watch, and to fortify yourself, so that you may be, as it were, a mirror to bring back to the good way those who are in train to stray from it.

In the mean time, I hear that God exercises you in order that you may put your patience in practice, and place your life entirely in his hands, for as much as you are weak in body and afflicted with many diseases, of which I too have my share to exercise me in the same manner. But however that may be, we have great cause to be satisfied that in our languishing we are supported by the strength of God's Spirit, and moreover, that if this corruptible tabernacle is falling to decay, we know that we shall be very soon restored, once and for ever. But however that may be, we have occasion to know better the value of the gospel, and that there is no repose nor satisfaction for us in this world.

Madame, having humbly commended myself to your indulgent favour, I will supplicate our heavenly Father to fortify you by his power, to keep you under his protection, and increase you in all good and prosperity.

[*Fr. Copy.*—*Library of Geneva.*   Vol. 107.]

DCLVII.—To Bullinger.

GENEVA, *9th September,* 1563.

If your neighbours[1] make so much ado and utter such vaunts, I am surprised that you make yourselves weary at such trifles which are rather matter of contempt, not deserving that we should attach any real importance to them. For in what place they displayed those warlike arts of theirs is a thing quite unknown in France. Two companies had been placed in garrison at Orleans. Our men wakened up some drowsy fellows among them, but without effusion of blood. Up to this moment they have remained there very peaceably. At present, their most active exploits consist in preying on the provisions of the villages, on which they pounce like so many starving thrushes. Those who were at the siege of Havre de Grace, rendered more prudent by their former check, have not ventured within the reach of missiles. The French, who had shown more courage, were vigorously repulsed, and when they had opened their trenches a great quantity of water was let out by the English which cut them off from the main body. There was then a great slaughter of them, and from that time they confined themselves to the bombardment, till their powder failed. The English not being aware of that fact were forced to surrender. At present, there is no doubt but that the war is about to break out afresh, for by both parties envoys have been detained prisoners, contrary to the law of nations. That is the reason why your neighbours are blowing their trumpet so lustily about their own feats. Our men are not in the least alarmed about the troops which you remind us are being levied at Luzerne. After all, they may be arming against the enemy. For the king's council do not approve of soldiers being enlisted in Germany at their expense, and they are strictly forbidden to pro-

---

[1] The Catholic cantons which furnished the King of France with his best troops.

ceed any further in such measures. A conspiracy, also, has
been detected which infringes upon their authority. Meanwhile, the queen is straining every nerve to have the majority
of her son pronounced, though he has scarcely completed his
thirteenth year. He has himself, however, proclaimed his
majority in the Parliament of Rouen, and that by the advice of
his mother and the nobles, among whom his brother the Duke
of Orleans, a boy eleven years old, is reckoned the first. You
see into what a ridiculous mockery the lustre of that ancient
kingdom has degenerated. For though there are seven supreme
courts of Parliament in France, six of them have been erected
merely for the purpose of taking cognizance of causes connected
with the administration of justice. That of Paris alone has been
in the habit of deciding questions that embrace the general interests of the kingdom. But if anything is to be settled in a
reasonable manner, it will be necessary to convoke an assembly
of the states general of the three orders. But whatever be done
the king even in despite of nature will be declared major, nor
will he obtain the dispensation of age from any other than from
himself—a dispensation which the laws teach is only to be conceded to others at the good pleasure of the prince.

As soon as he shall have made his entry into the city, it has
been resolved to put some restraint on the madness of the
tumultuous populace. The Constable unflinchingly defends the
edict which confers liberty on our churches, guaranties security
to them, and gives it as his opinion that the edict ought to be
maintained intact. Respecting the Confession of Augsburg, I
see no reason for our feeling any great uneasiness. It will be
obtruded on us in vain, for no one of the Papists will admit its
claims, and our brethren firmly reject it. We are nevertheless
making the most strenuous efforts, and we shall continue to
make them lest any detriment should arise from our negligence.
But what are you about in the meantime? Your senate consults
privately its own interests according to its wonted manner, and
imagines that its authority will remain unimpaired, though all
others should go to ruin. Excuse me if I express myself rather
harshly, because hitherto they have not shown any tokens of
that solicitude which the necessity of the times so imperiously

demanded. The Bernese in their deliberations are certainly complaining that they have never manifested any zeal for the public safety.

If the three balliages are now restored to the Duke of Savoy,[1] hemmed in on every side and far from all auxiliaries, we shall easily fall a prey to our enemies. For the Duke will not remain satisfied with this acquisition, and will not hesitate to recover that part which will afford him the most favourable opportunity for making war. But though we are brought into the greatest danger, I do not demand of you to take our case into consideration, but only to take into account the common danger. Again, excuse me if, till your fellow citizens conduct themselves otherwise, I shall consider them to have no more fellow feeling with our misfortunes than so many blocks. But God suffers us to be abandoned of men, that we may learn to divert our thoughts to himself and keep them fixed upon him alone.

Farewell, most accomplished sir and respected brother. May the Lord long preserve you in safety, continue to direct you by his Spirit, and bless your labours. Salute very kindly all your colleagues.—Yours,

JOHN CALVIN.

Your devoted friend Jonvillers respectfully and affectionately salutes you.

[*Lat. Orig.—Arch. of Zurich, Gallicana Scripta, p. 55.*]

---

[1] Viz., the territory conquered by the Seigneurs of Berne from Savoy, in 1536, and the territory contiguous to the southern banks of the Lake of Geneva.

DCLVIII.—To the Prince of Condé.[1]

Request concerning the publication of a confession of faith—Blame of the gallantries
of the prince.

GENEVA, 17th *September*, 1563.

MONSEIGNEUR:—Already we entreated you long ago to deign
to inform us of your good pleasure touching the confession which
had been drawn up during the war, in order to shut the mouths
of your enemies, who by their calumnies made people believe
whatever they chose. The person who drew it up had not put
himself forward from any caprice of his own, but had been duly
required and solicited by M. d'Andelot, who being at that time
in Germany knew how necessary and useful such a remedy
would be.

Now at that time this confession was addressed to you, but
the communications being interrupted we could not have an
answer whether you would approve of its being printed, which
we should never have thought of attempting without your permission. Since then, we have been persuaded and convinced by
valid reasons that the present time is quite as opportune as ever
for such a measure. We know not from what cause it happens
that we have never been made acquainted with your good pleasure, but we suppose indeed that amid the pressure of so many
affairs this matter may have dropped from your recollection.
At present we are obliged, Monseigneur, to refresh your memory,
and if need be to importune you respecting it. For we have
been informed that the Duke of Wirtemberg has had a catechism
translated into French, expressly for the purpose of confuting
the doctrine which we hold respecting the Lord's supper. We
foresee many objections which it will be necessary to obviate.
We have no doubt but he will make you a present of it, if he has
not already done so, in order to induce you to renounce that

---

[1] See the letters pp. 212, 309, as well as the notes concerning the intrigues of the
Ultra-Lutheran party in Germany to impose on the Reformed churches of France the
Confession of Augsburg.

pure simplicity in which you have been instructed. If he cannot succeed, as we are indeed convinced that he will be disappointed in that respect, his design is to set at defiance this man and that man, everybody in short, in order to render the faith which you possess odious. He will pretend also to gain over some, to stir up animosities, and array one party against the other. Now it seems to us that you can find no remedy more effectual against such evils than to publish a confession, both to cut short his intrigues and humble by your constancy the impertinence of those who might think of intimidating you under such pretexts. It will also have the effect of instructing the ignorant, and putting a stop to the blasphemies with which you should be chargeable were your cause not known. You cannot imagine, Monseigneur, what advantages would accrue from it to Germany. It is even possible that he who thinks of making a proselyte of you will be caught tripping and converted in his turn. The opportunity is the finest in the world for paying him off in his own coin, since it was he who gave the first invitation. Wherefore we entreat you to send us word what we shall have to do, for the moment we have the watchword, we shall not fail to make all diligence. We give you a sure address, Mr. Aubrée Lyons. He is one of your faithful servants. Besides that the copy has been twice sent to you, and, we doubt not, read and approved by you, you may consult the opinion of the Cardinal de Chatillon to confirm more thoroughly your own judgment.

For the rest, Monseigneur, we cannot let pass this opportunity of beseeching you in general not only to take under your protection the cause of our Lord Jesus Christ, so that the course of the gospel may be advanced and the poor followers of God left in peace and security, but also that you would testify by your whole life that you have profited by the doctrine of salvation, and that your example may tend to edify the good as well as shut the mouths of all gainsayers. For being raised to such pre-eminent rank, just as you are an object of contemplation from afar, so ought you to beware that men find nothing to blame in your conduct. You cannot doubt, Monseigneur, but that we cherish your honour, almost as much as we desire your salvation. Now we should be traitors to you if we left you in ignorance of the rumours that fly about. We do not believe that at bottom there is any evil in your conduct or that God is directly offended by it; but when we are told that you are making love to ladies, we think that this greatly derogates from your authority and reputation. Good men will be grieved, and the malicious and ill-intentioned will laugh at it. There is also in that dissipation something which prevents you from attending to your duty, or at least retards you in the accomplishment of it. Nay, it is possible that in all this there may be a portion of worldly vanity, and you should especially take care that the light which God has set within you be not dimmed or extinguished.

We trust, Monseigneur, that this admonition you will take in good part, when you reflect how very useful it may be to you.

Your very humble brethren,
JOHN CALVIN, THEODORE BEZA.

[*Fr. Copy.—Library of Paris, Dupuy.* Vol. 102.]

DCLIX.—TO BULLINGER.

News of France—Humiliation of the Parliament of Paris and of the Guises—False news of the death of the Duke of Savoy.

GENEVA, 20th October, 1563.

There is nothing changed in the state of France since I wrote to you,[1] except that the Parisians are every day more and more abating their arrogant presumption. First the Parliament is crushed, or at least tamed by a decree of the king. Next measures have been taken with the population of the city. As a very bad precedent indeed, all the acts of the Parliament have

---

[1] In the letter which is here alluded to, we remark the following passage: "The affairs of France are still perplexed. The Parisians have abated in some degree their obstinacy, but the king who had almost approached their walls has directed his course elsewhere. The queen mother pretends to mediate between the parties, but many tokens of her perfidy are remarked. The Chancellor is liberal as usual in his edicts, but few obey them. Unless the queen speedily come to a rupture with the Guises, formidable convulsions will again break out." Letter of the 30th September, 1563.

been rescinded, and whatever dignity resided in that body has been abrogated. I am very sorry for my part that by an arbitrary order and almost in a despotic manner, that authority has been overthrown which has flourished for upwards of two centuries, for it was expedient that there should be an intermediate power to impose some restraint on royal decrees. But on the present occasion all the counsellors were compelled to be present, and with open doors the sentence was pronounced which brands them with infamy. For nothing could be more disgraceful than that all the acts in which they had exceeded the bounds of moderation should be torn up in their presence, and themselves strictly enjoined not to dare to attempt anything similar in future. The king himself contumeliously received the messengers whom they repeatedly sent to him. By terror then they were all reduced to obedience. The ferocity of that turbulent populace being now subdued, others will cease to breed disturbances.

The inhabitants of the provinces have received severe injunctions not to retard any longer or throw obstacles in the way of the execution of the edicts. The Guises also have been bridled, nor indeed did they dare to interpose while the king menaced, for the Admiral was present with superior forces. Hope has again shone out on us, as far at least as evil broils are concerned; but that plague spreads itself to an incredible degree in Gascony and over the whole tract of the Loire. It has not yet gained Lyons. Twenty-five battalions had been dispatched, who were to halt on their march till news was brought of the death of our neighbour, who now, however, is reported to have recovered. He has not yet proclaimed war on the Bernese. I will not wrangle with you for excusing the conduct of your fellow citizens—God who is a just judge will lend an ear to our complaints. If, however, you inquire more carefully, you will learn that your deputies, after they had fulfilled the object of their instructions, gave their aid more strenuously to the cause than the citizens of Lucerne. We shall hold our peace till an opportunity invite us to speak. For having obtained from your senate for worthy men the thing which they demanded, I return you thanks both in my own name and in theirs.

Farewell, most illustrious sir and venerable brother. May the Lord preserve you in safety, sustain you by his power, and bless your labours. Best respects to your fellow pastors, your wife, and your whole family.—Yours,

JOHN CALVIN.

Your devoted friend Jonvillers respectfully and affectionately salutes you.

[*Lat. Copy.—Library of Geneva.* Vol. 107 *a.*]

DCLX.—TO MERCER.[1]

New proposals of a chair in the Academy of Geneva.

GENEVA, 23*d October,* 1563.

I could have wished, when I called you hither two years ago, that your engagements had permitted you not to hesitate in conferring your services upon our church and school. But it was not so disagreeable for me at that time to be disappointed in my expectations, as it has been matter of sorrow and regret since, that in the miserable dispersion which has taken place at Paris, you have been excluded from your functions of teaching. It was certainly a laborious and modest situation to which I called you. In one respect, however, you formed a false estimate of it, when you felt convinced that your labours would be more useful and productive of greater results on a celebrated theatre than in this obscure corner. For though the number of students is small, yet you would have found among them pupils to whose advancement it would have given you much satisfaction to contribute, and if you repair here, as I hope, you will see that the field was by no means to be despised. But since those calamitous events which have so suddenly fallen out

---

[1] See vol. iii. p. 412. Always attentive to the development of the Academy, Calvin never allowed an opportunity to escape of attracting to Geneva the most distinguished professors. Mercer did not respond to this second appeal, but he called Calvin's attention to the learned Matthew Beroald, the nephew of Vatable and professor at Orleans.

and ruined everything at Paris, I Nave been much astonished that you have sought for a retreat elsewhere than among us, for never would you have found a more tranquil nor a more suitable position. And in truth I should never have delayed so long to write to you, if I could have guessed in what quarter of the world my letter would reach you. Now that a friend has pledged himself that he will find a means of having it delivered to you, it would have been an act of unpardonable negligence on my part to delay any longer. For here a task awaits you which I think you ought to prefer to any other, even if you were at liberty to choose. But now that God has detached you from the spot with which you fancied yourself indissolubly connected, why you should delay one moment, or why you should not immediately on the receipt of this decide upon what public utility demands of you, I can see no reason whatever. It would be difficult for me to explain to you minutely all the details of this affair, but if my entreaties have any influence with you, I beg and beseech you that you let us obtain this favour at least of you. For at the present moment I plead for nothing else but that you will become one of us until the necessities of your duty may call you somewhere else. And if you are not to be moved by my prayers, I interpose my advice, with which if you comply, I promise you, you shall reap greater satisfaction in the discharge of your office than you could have believed before making the experiment. Make haste then with all the speed you may, and settle among us.

Farewell, most accomplished sir and very honoured brother. May the Lord always direct you by his Spirit, and prosper your journey that we may see you in safety ere long.—Yours,

CHARLES PASSELIUS.

[*Lat. Copy.—Library of Zurich, Simler.* Vol. 108.]

DCLXI.—To M. DE LOINES.

Councillor in the court of Parliament of Paris—Exhortation not to abandon his office
of councillor and still less the truth.

GENEVA, *5th November,* 1563.

MONSIEUR:—Though till the present moment I had never
received any letters from you, yet it was with pleasure that I
often had good news of you, which were communicated to me
several times, and for which I thanked God. But letters from
your own hand have given me much greater satisfaction, because I see by them the good and friendly disposition you entertain towards me. I was already aware of that, but I am
delighted to have a new pledge of it in order to be still more
certain of it. For the rest, as I see, God has sorely tried you
since you were appointed to your present charge. I had no
doubts indeed but that while your colleagues were demeaning
themselves like madmen you must have been in great perplexity.[1]
But now that in consequence of the very excesses of their
mutinous disposition they have been subdued and tamed, you
may continue to exercise your profession or rather pursue the
object you had in view in adopting it, and in doing so it appears
to me you will have no reason to regret it, and I am so far from
turning you aside from that purpose that I would take pains to
stimulate you were it necessary.

Since you are pleased to ask my advice, besides the general
principle that it is not lawful to quit a public vocation and disengage ourselves from its duties at our good pleasure, without
being constrained to such a measure by necessity or violence,
the present state of things imposes on you a double obligation
to persist in your task, were it but to ascertain how God will be
pleased to employ you. I will not enter into any discussion to

---

[1] The Parliament of Paris had signalized itself among all the courts of the kingdom
for its animosity against the Reformed. It long refused to register the edict of
January, and saw but with regret the conclusion of the treaty of Amboise which
granted to the Protestants a limited liberty.

persuade you how you ought to surmount all difficulties, since it is certain that the greatest virtue you can possess is to shut your eyes on everything that may happen, marching simply whither God has called you. It would be desirable that you had many associates in your task, but let this consideration satisfy you, that God has called you to a combat, which you have already no doubt duly meditated, in order to carry you through the struggle manfully.

It is a marvellous thing that the devil has agents who are inflamed with zeal, and spare no pains to lay hold of all the seats of justice, thinking that it is a means of oppressing God's church, and that in the mean time those who ought to resist the evil quit the place. This is very far from putting in practice St. Paul's rule, to take away the occasion from those who seek it. On the contrary, we should rather strive to make some vacate their places, to put in their stead men who hold out for the good party. I should only ask for a dozen of honest men to put some heart into the bosoms of those who are neither flesh nor fish, that is to say, of more than sixty individuals. But since God has already shown you what you ought to do, I have only to pray him to fortify you with invincible courage, as I am sure he will. Only make haste without boggling, for we are certain of gaining every point, being stayed by His power to strengthen us to do whatever he commands.

Whereupon, Monsieur, having humbly commended myself to your indulgent favour, I will supplicate our heavenly Father to keep you under his protection, to conduct you by his Spirit, and make you prosper in all good.

[*Fr. Orig. Minute.—Library of Geneva.* Vol. 107.]

DCLXII.—To Bullinger.

Versatile policy of Catherine de Medicis—Departure of Condé—Favour of Coligny—Intolerance of the Guises—Oppression of the Protestants in the provinces—Necessity for assuring to them some guaranties.

GENEVA, 2nd *December*, 1563.

Since I wrote to you, venerable brother, these are the latest news from France. As nearly all the members of the king's council are hostile to us, in a sudden impulse of fury it was decreed that the walls of Orleans should be demolished. The military governor began to pull down some towers and to fill up the fosses with rubbish. If, however, we may believe the rumour, its authors are ashamed and repent of so pernicious a decree. They had come to a similar decision respecting many other cities, under the pretext that it was by no means expedient that there should be any fortified places except near the frontiers for the purpose of repelling the enemy. The Prince of Condé left the court about a month ago, because the queen mother had craftily kept in suspense the marriage of her son with the daughter of Saint André. Thus in truth betraying the cause of Christ, he has consulted only his own interest and personal advantages. Although nobody feels any great solicitude to have him appeased, his indignation will evaporate of its own accord. Now I shall tell you what intelligence we received the day before yesterday.

When the Admiral had come to salute the king, he was very graciously received by him. After that he went to Paris with a very numerous escort. The Constable, that he might stir up the bile of the envious, went to his lodgings and after breakfast took him to the king's palace. There he was present at a deliberation, in which it is supposed that a great many matters were canvassed. The partisans of Guise decamped with bag and baggage to another quarter of the city. Through the Duke of Nemours they let the queen mother know that they were astonished why she suffered the Admiral to come into such close contact with her son. She replied that he was an old servant

of the king, and that there was no reason why he should be excluded from visiting him; then that such was the king's pleasure, but that at the same time there was room for everybody;
that she advised them consequently to come; which advice they
did not take. But the parliament sent intercessors to the Constable that he might appease the resentment of his grandson.
The Maire and the magistrates did the same thing. The king
was on the point of going to the Parliament and taking the
Admiral along with him. In a short time we shall hear how
that proceeding terminated, which, however, has inspired our
party with the greatest hopes of a favourable issue. The Prince
Porcien was expected at court as well as the Duke of Bouillon,
son of the Marquis and great grandson of the famous Robert.
They are both the most decided enemies of the party of the
Guises. The Chancellor who was our friend begins to recover
from his timidity and take heart. The king, under pretext of
visiting the lady who has just been confined, was about to be
dragged to Lorraine, and Athaliah[1] was so bent on going there
that it was to no purpose that everybody opposed her resolution.
Now it is reported that she has changed her mind respecting
that journey. The minds of all are occupied with concluding a
peace with the English. In this manner all the intrigues of the
Cardinal of Lorraine to his great disgrace will come to nothing.
The king is nominally major, but is in reality governed by the
will of another, and that too almost like a slave. He would not
be unfavourable to us, if he durst express an opinion. In the
mean time you could hardly believe how great is the audacity
of nearly all the judges in their efforts to oppress us. The innocent are thus miserably tormented, and license is increased
by impunity. The inhabitants of Orleans have obtained one
object of their wishes in having the garrison removed from there,
as the garrisons have been from other cities.

Wherefore I remind you that you must take care that travelling expenses be provided for our neighbours, who will speedily
return. Now I come to a point of the greatest importance of
all, and to which I particularly desire you to apply all your attention and zeal. You are aware that the time is fast approach-

1 That is to say: Catherine de Medicis.

ing in which the league is to be renewed with the Helvetians. If your senate can be brought to contract an alliance with the king, this will be the only and the shortest method of establishing the gospel in France. I do not know if you have heard of the conspiracy of the enemies. They fancy that when a national assembly shall be appointed, it will be an easy and prompt method of overturning at one moment almost all the churches, both because they will decide in it everything at their own pleasure, and because they will have the means of putting their resolutions in execution. The pope in the mean time, with the king of Spain, the Venetians, the Italian princes, and the Duke of Savoy is preparing to destroy this city entirely and cut us all off. Good men are afraid that the queen mother, unless she be bridled, is but too much inclined to lend her aid to that faction. It will then be the safest, and indeed the only remedy, if the Helvetian states that have embraced the gospel should form a league on this condition, that provision should be made for the French churches and their liberties. That might be obtained without great difficulty. Three other cantons would follow the example set them by your senate. Nor would it be advantageous to the French and us alone, that the king should be bound to protect the churches in the modest privileges which they now possess, but it would also be extremely desirable for yourselves in order to put a check upon your neighbours, whose arrogance would thus be humbled, and their intemperate fury calmed down. I entreat you then, venerable brother, in the name of God, and I implore you by the common safety of all our brethren, that forgetting the numerous obstacles that may stand in your way, you would strive to bring about this alliance which will preserve the interests of religion safe and intact in France, and close the door on the wicked plots of the ungodly. You see how frankly I deal with you. I am very anxious to know what you think on the subject. This one thing I will venture to testify freely; if your fellow citizens refuse, they will be liable to be charged both in the presence of God and men with more than one species of crime. But perhaps there will be no necessity for making a great effort to decide them, when they perceive not only how sacred a duty it is to rescue from all inquietude the churches now in danger, but also how much it will promote their own interests to have the king bound down not to abjure the cause of protecting religion.

Farewell, most illustrious sir and respected brother. Be careful to salute all your colleagues in my name, as all mine salute you. May the Lord stand by you, sustain you by his Spirit, and long preserve you in safety.—Yours,

JOHN CALVIN.

Your devoted friend Jonvillers respectfully and affectionately salutes you.

[*Lat. Copy.—Library of Geneva.* Vol. 107 *a.*]

DCLXIII.—To the Duchess of Ferrara.[1]

Counsels for the direction of her household—Present of a medal.

GENEVA, 8*th January*, 1564.

MADAME:—I believe you have received my last letters, to which I expect an answer in order to acquit myself of my duty respecting the subject on which you had been pleased to write to me. In the mean time I was unwilling to neglect the opportunity of recommending the present bearer to you, that you might learn from him the state of things here, for it is better to assign to him the task of informing you orally than charge the paper with such details, seeing that he is one of the most intimate friends I have, and a man in whom one may repose the

---

[1] The minister Francis de Morel, almoner of the Duchess of Ferrara, had complained to Calvin of the difficulties he encountered in the exercise of his ministry and in the application of ecclesiastical discipline at the small court of Montargis : " Great danger arises from a woman being the sovereign. The church is in a miserable condition, I was obliged to forego dispensing the sacrament of the Lord's supper on the bypast month of September, because from other quarters came so many *dogs* and *swine* that I should have been obliged to admit along with the sheep. The festival of Christ's birth is at hand. At that time it is customary to administer the Lord's supper. I do not know how to act. Do you then, my most worthy father, advise me." Letter of the 6th December, 1563. The Reformer exhorted the duchess to maintain the authority of the Consistory and preserve a severe discipline in her household.

most absolute trust.[1]   He is a son of the late M. Budé the king's
master of the rolls, who was much renowned for his erudition.
For the rest, Madame, you have shown by your decision that a
residence at Paris was very little to your taste.[2]   It is true that
it would have been desirable that you had remained constantly
at court for the relief of the poor churches, but I am not surprised that you seek for a quieter manner of life.

Now, since God has brought you back to your own town, it
behoves you to redouble your care for administering rightly
both your subjects and your household.   I know, Madame, how
obstinate the people are, and how you have laboured heretofore
without much profit, to bring them into subjection.   Be that as
it will, I pray you to follow out completely the doctrine of St.
Paul on this head, never to be weary of well doing, whatever
malice you may encounter to damp your ardor.   Above all let
your household be a mirror to set the example to those who
show themselves rather indocile, and to confound those who are
incorrigible and entirely hardened.   To accomplish this, I beg
you to keep a firm hand, to the utmost of your power, to
establish a good discipline for repressing vices and occasions of
scandal.

I do not mean a police with regard to political matters, but
also in respect of the Consistory of the church, and let those who
are established to have an eye over the conduct of others, be
men fearing God, of holy life, and such sincerity and straightforwardness that nothing shall prevent them from doing their
duty, having such a zeal as becomes them in maintaining the
honour of God in its integrity.   Now let no one, whatever be
his rank or condition, or in whatever esteem you may hold him,
be ashamed to submit to the order which the Son of God himself has established, and bend his neck to receive the yoke.   For
I assure you, Madame, that without this remedy there will be
an unbridled licentiousness which will engender only confusion.
Those who make some profession of Christianity will be for the
most part dissolute.   In one word, there will be a pliant, and as

[1] John de Budé.
[2] Contrary to the desires of Calvin, the Duchess of Ferrara had quitted the court,
where her counsels were not listened to, to return to her château of Montargis.

it were many-coloured (*sic*) gospel, for we see how every one flatters himself and is disposed to follow his own appetites. It is wonderful to see how those that have voluntarily subjected themselves to the tyranny of the pope, cannot endure that Jesus Christ should bear gentle rule over them for their own salvation. But it is true that the devil makes use of this device to bring the truth of God into opprobrium, to cause pure religion to be contemned, and the sacred name of our Redeemer blasphemed. Thus, Madame, to have a church duly Reformed, it is more than ever requisite to have people charged with a superintendence to watch over the morals of each; and that no one may feel himself aggrieved in giving an account of his life to the elders, let the elders themselves be selected by the church, as nothing can be more reasonable than to preserve to it this liberty, and this privilege will tend also to produce greater discretion in the choice of fitting men, and approved of as such by the Consistory.

I am persuaded, Madame, that you have aided our brother de Colonges with your authority in establishing some such order. But knowing to how much corruption the courts of princes are subject, I have thought that it would not be superfluous to exhort you to maintain it. Nay, it is right that you should be reminded of one thing: namely, that at all times the devil has striven by sinister reports and defamation, to render the ministers of the gospel contemptible, in order that they may become the object either of aversion or of disgust. For that reason all the faithful should be carefully on their guard against such wiles. For, in fact, to quarrel with their spiritual pasture is something worse than finding fault with their bodily food, since the matter at stake here is the life of their souls. Be that as it will, if there are any who aim, were it but indirectly, to discourage you from pursuing what you have so well begun, you ought to shun them as deadly plagues. And in sooth the devil stirs them up to alienate people by indirect means from God, whose will it is that He should be recognized in the person of his servants.

Above all, Madame, never allow yourself to be persuaded to change anything in the state of the church, such as God has consecrated it by his blood. For it is he before whom every knee should bend. If to wheedle you they allege that your house ought to be privileged, reflect that they cannot do you more dishonour than in cutting it off from the body of the church; as on the contrary you cannot be more highly honoured than in having your house purged of all pollutions. Where, I ask you, Madame, ought we to apply the remedies sooner than in the cases where the diseases have most chance to spread? Now only judge if courts are not more apt to break out into all kinds of licentiousness than private families, unless precautions be taken against the evil. I do not say, if there is any subject of scandal among the members of your household, that you, who are the principal member of the church, should be the first to be reminded of it, in order to deliberate in perfect concord how it may be corrected; but what I recommend is that your authority should not interfere to interrupt the course of discipline, since if your domestics were spared, all respect for the Consistory would disappear like water from a leaky vessel.

Madame, I pass to another subject. I have long had a great wish to make you a present of a gold piece. Think how bold I am; but because I supposed you had a similar one, I have not ventured hitherto, for it is only its rarity that can give it any value in your esteem. Finally I have delivered it to the bearer to show it to you, and if it is a novelty to you, will you be pleased to keep it? It is the finest present that I have it in my power to make you.[1]

Madame, having very humbly commended myself to your indulgent favour, I will supplicate our heavenly Father to have you in his holy keeping, and increase you in all good and prosperity.

[*Fr. Copy.—Library of Geneva.* Vol. 107.]

[1] It was a gold medal which King Louis XII., the father of René, had caused to be struck at the time of his disputes with the Pope Julius II. with this exergue: Perdam Babylonis nomen: *I will destroy the name of Babylon.* This gift was very agreeable to the Duchess : " As to the present you have sent me, I assure you, I have seen and accepted it with very great pleasure, and I never had any like it. I have praised God that the late king my father had adopted such a device. If God did not grant him the grace to put it in execution, perhaps he reserves for one of his descendants to take his place to accomplish it." (Library of Paris, Dupuy, vol. 86, p. 120.)

DCLXIV.—To the Duchess of Ferrara.[1]

Answer to a letter of this princess concerning the condemnation of the Duke of Guise and the beatification of the King of Navarre—Is it lawful to hate our enemies— Eulogy of Coligny.

Geneva, 24th January, 1564.

Madame:—When by your last letter you had intimated to Messire Francisco, that it would be expedient that I should exhort to charity those who make a profession of being Christians, I understood that to refer to some ministers that you have found not to be very charitable according to your judgment. In the mean time, I can gather that you alluded to the too great asperity with which they have condemned the late Duke of Guise. Now, Madame, before I proceed to examine more closely that question, I pray you in God's name to reflect seriously, that on your part also it is requisite to observe

[1] Sincerely devoted to the cause of the Reformation which counted only adversaries and persecutors in her family, mother-in-law of the Duke of Guise, aunt of Catherine of Medicis and Charles IX., the Duchess of Ferrara had a painful struggle to maintain between her affections and her faith. The memory of the Duke of Guise, her son-in-law, was particularly odious to the Reformed, who accused him of being the author of the massacre of Vassy. Assassinated at Orleans by the fanatic Poltrot, the hatred of the Protestants pursued him even after his death, and the ministers devoted his soul to eternal damnation. These violent sentiments grieved the Duchess of Ferrara, who eloquently complained of them in several of her letters to Calvin : "I have no wish to excuse the faults of my son-in-law for not possessing the knowledge of God, but against the accusation that he was the only one that kindled these fires of discord. It is well known that he had retired to his house, and was unwilling to stir from it, and also that he was urged by letters and messages to make him leave it; and now that he is dead and gone, there is so envenomed and deadly a hatred, which never ceases to blacken his memory by all the falsehoods that can be raked up or imagined, that I am compelled to declare that I cannot hold or esteem such lying words to proceed from God. I know that he was a persecutor, but I do not know, nor do I believe, to speak out to you undisguisedly, that he is reprobated by God, for he gave signs of a Christian man on the contrary before his death. But they will not allow that he said anything, and they wish to close and lock up the mouths of those that know the fact . . . And do you not see how they can never sufficiently satiate their rancour even after his death ? And had he been ten times more unhappy and reprobate than he ever was, it is strange that they will never speak of anything else . . . etc." Letter of the Duchess of Ferrara to Calvin. (Coll. Dupuy, vol. 86,) published for the first time in the Archives Curieuses de l'Histoire de France. Vol. v. p. 399.

moderation. For it is only one void of reflection who will fancy that we can ever have too much of it. And without taking into account the report of others I have perceived in your letter, that affection makes you forget what otherwise you should have sufficiently known. Respecting what I had alleged to you that David teaches us by his example to hate the enemies of God, you reply that it was only during those times when people lived under the rigour of the law, that it was permitted to hate enemies. Now, Madame, this gloss would lead to the over-throwing of the whole Scriptures, and for that reason we should shun it as we would a deadly plague. For we see that David surpassed in kindness of character the best of those that would be found in our days. Thus when he protests that he has wept and in secret shed tears for those who were plotting his death, we see that his hatred consisted in mourning for their death, that he was as meek spirited as could possibly be desired. But when he says he holds the reprobate in mortal aversion, it cannot be doubted that he glories in an upright, pure, and well regulated zeal, for which three things are requisite: first, that we should have no regard for ourselves nor our private interests; next, that we should possess prudence and discretion not to judge at random; and finally, that we observe moderation not to exceed the bounds of our calling. All this you will see, Madame, more in detail in several passages of my commentaries on the Psalms, when you shall be pleased to take the trouble to look into them. So that indeed the Holy Spirit has given us David as a model, that in this respect we might follow his ex-ample. And in fact we are told that in this ardor he was the type of our Lord Jesus Christ, and if we pretend to surpass in meekness and humanity him who is the fountain of pity and compassion, woe to us.

But to cut short all disputes, let it satisfy us that St. Paul applies to all believers this passage: " *The zeal of thy house hath eaten me up.*" Wherefore our Lord Jesus, reproving his dis-ciples because they desired that he should cause fire to come down from heaven as Elias had done, and consume those who rejected him, does not allege that we are no longer under a law of rigour, but simply shows them that they are not led by the same spirit as the prophet. Nay, St. John, of whom you have retained nothing but the word love, clearly shows that we ought not, under show of an affection for men, to become indifferent to the duty we owe to the honour of God and the preservation of his church. It is when he forbids us even to salute those, who, as much as in them lies, turn us aside from the pure doctrine. On that subject, I pray you, to pardon me if I tell you frankly, that in my opinion you have taken in a wrong sense the comparison of the bow, which we bend in an opposite direction when it has been too much bent on one side. For he who employed it doubtless only meant to say that in seeing you carried to excess he had been constrained to be more vehement, not that he might falsify the Scriptures or disguise the truth.

I come now to the fact which, not to annoy you by my prolixity, I shall only briefly touch upon. You have not been the only one to suffer much anguish and bitterness during these horrible troubles that have fallen out. True it is, the evil might sting you more keenly on seeing the throne with which you are connected by your royal descent, subject to such disorder. But certainly the sorrow was common to all the children of God, and though we might all have said: Woe to him by whom this scandal is come; nevertheless there was special reason for groaning and lamenting, seeing that a good cause had been very ill-conducted. Now if the evil distressed all good men, the Duke of Guise who had kindled the conflagration could not be spared. For my own part, though I have often prayed God to show him mercy, yet it is certain I have often desired that God should lay his hand on him in order to deliver out of his hands the poor church, unless it pleased God to convert him. So that I may protest that before the war, I had but to give my consent to have had him exterminated by those men of prompt and ready execution, who were bent on that object, and who were restrained only by my exhortation. To pronounce that he is damned, however, is to go too far, unless one had some certain and infallible mark of his reprobation. In which we must guard against presumption and temerity, for there is none can know that but the Judge before whose tribunal we have all to render an account.

The second point seems to me still more exorbitant, that of pronouncing the King of Navarre in paradise and the Duke of Guise in hell. For if we institute a comparison between them, we find that the former was an apostate, the latter always an avowed enemy of the truth of the gospel. What I should wish then in this matter would be more moderation and sobriety. In the mean time I have also to pray you, Madame, not to show so much displeasure at the expression, *not to pray for any one,* without having made a due distinction between the form and the reality of the subject in question. For though I pray for the salvation of any one, that does not imply that in all respects, and everywhere, I recommend him as if he were a member of the church. We demand of God that he would bring back into the right path those who are on the way to perdition. But it will not be in placing them in the rank of our brethren in order to desire for them all kinds of prosperity.

On this subject, I will relate to you an anecdote of the Queen of Navarre, very applicable to the matter in question. When the king her husband had fallen off from us, the minister at her court ceased to make mention of him in the public prayers. Irritated, she remonstrated with him that he ought not to make this omission, if for no other reason at least from consideration for his subjects. He excusing himself declared that if he had altogether abstained from doing so, it was to conceal the dishonour of the king her husband, inasmuch as he could not pray to God for him in reality, unless he made supplication for his conversion, which was only discovering his fall. If he asked God to maintain him in prosperity, it would be a mockery and a profanation of prayer. Having heard this answer she said not a word till she had demanded advice of others, and finding that they all agreed she mildly acquiesced. As I know, Madame, that this virtuous princess would be disposed to take a lesson from you as a thing due to your age and your virtues, in like manner I entreat you not to be ashamed to conform your conduct to hers in this matter. Her husband was a closer connection to her than your son-in-law to you; nevertheless she mastered her affections in order not to be the cause of having God's name profaned, which it would be assuredly if our prayers were feigned or militated against the repose of the church. And to have done with this pretext of charity, judge, I beseech you, Madame, if it is reasonable that at the capricious desire of a single man, we are to make no account of a hundred thousand—that charity should be so confined to one who had endeavoured to throw everything into confusion, that the children of God should be kept completely in the background. Now the remedy for all that is to hate evil, without taking persons into the account, but leaving every one to his Judge. If God granted me the favour of speaking with you, I trust I should speedily satisfy you. In the mean time I entreat you to weigh well what I have slightly handled, that you may not disquiet and irritate your mind for a little idle talk, which you could afford to treat with the most thorough contempt.

You are solicited to permit the shops of the Papists to be robbed and pillaged. I take good care not to approve of such a step, whoever may have taken it. I commend on the contrary your virtue and greatness of mind, in having been unwilling to acquiesce in so unjust a demand. I say the same thing of the other excesses which you mention. Touching the quarrel which has arisen in your household between the two persons whom you name, I know not what reason there is for speaking against the woman. I have no doubt of what you tell me, Madame; but I know not whether there have been any bad symptoms that have forced M. de Colonges to give such an admonition as a kind of preventive remedy, or whether he has gone too for, and there has been want of due reflection on his part. One thing is certain; that the husband gave loose to too much violence when they offered to satisfy him, and the answer and refusal of M. de Colonges also savours more of his ambition and of worldly vanity than of the modesty of a man of his calling, at which I am very sorry, for he must have forgotten himself too far. If the parties agree to lay before us an account of their affair, I will do all in my power to remedy the evil on whichsoever side it may be found.

On this point, Madame, I confess that it is much to be feared

that God will not leave us long to enjoy the blessings he has
granted us; since every one is so taken up with his self-interest,
that we do not know how to support our neighbour in a spirit
of meekness and humility. And so far are we from loving our
enemies, striving to overcome evil with good, that there is no
gentleness among us to keep up brotherly love between those
who boast that they are Christians. Nevertheless, I pray you
again, Madame, not to dwell any longer on that distinction
which deceives you, while you imagine that it was permitted
under the law to avenge one's self, because it is there said, "an
eye for an eye." For vengeance was as much forbidden then as
it is under the gospel, seeing that we are commanded to do good
even to the beast of our enemy. But what was addressed to
the judges each individual applied to himself. There remains
the abuse of the precept which our Lord Jesus Christ corrects.
Be that as it will, we are all agreed, that in order to be recognized as children of God, it behoves us to conform ourselves
to his example, striving to do good to those who are unworthy
of it, just as he causes his sun to shine on the evil and the good.
Thus hatred and Christianity are things incompatible. I mean
hatred towards persons—in opposition to the love we owe them.
On the contrary we are to wish and even procure their good;
and to labour, as much as in us lies, to maintain peace and concord with all men.

Now if those who are commissioned to dissipate all enmity
and rancour, to reconcile enemies, to exhort to patience, and
repress all lust of vengeance, be themselves brands of discord—
so much the worse, and so much the less are they to be excused.
At any rate, Madame, the faults which displease you ought not
to cool your zeal or prevent you from continuing as you have so
well begun. And I know that God has fortified you with such
courage that it is unnecessary to solicit you yet more. Wherefore I am confident that you will set an example of charity to
those who know not what it is, and by your integrity and plain
dealing cover with confusion those who practise towards you
hypocrisy and dissimulation. On the other hand I bless God
for having made known to you the real character of the Admiral,

to inspire you with a taste for his probity. When it will please
him he will do the rest . . .[1]

[*Fr. Copy.—Library of Geneva.* Vol. 107.]

DCLXV.—To the Physicians of Montpellier.

Medical consultation.

GENEVA, 8*th February*, 1564.

When the physician Sarrazin, on whose directions I principally rely for the re-establishment of my health, presented me
not long ago some remedies which you prescribed for the relief
of my complaints, I asked him, who had without my knowledge
taken that task upon him. He replied that at the request of
one of my colleagues, who is at present resident among you, he
had drawn up a short abstract of matters connected with my
case, in order that you might give me the benefit of your advice.
On my part, I cannot but recognize from the very minute answers you have transmitted, how much interest you take in my
life, about the prolongation of which you have spontaneously
shown yourselves so solicitous. If to have given yourselves that
trouble at my demand would have been no small token of kindness on your part, how much more must I feel indebted to you
for thus anticipating my desires by your unsolicited benevolence!
Moreover, I have no other means of testifying my gratitude to
you, besides that of recommending you to draw in your turn
from my writings what may afford you a spiritual medicine.
Twenty years ago I experienced the same courteous services
from the distinguished Parisian physicians, Acatus, Tagant, and
Gallois.   But at that time I was not attacked by arthritic pains,
knew nothing of the stone or the gravel—I was not tormented
with the gripings of the cholic, nor afflicted with hemorrhoids,
nor threatened with expectoration of blood. At present all

---

[1] The end is wanting. We are furnished with the date by the answer of the duchess
to Calvin : " Monsieur Calvin,I have received your letter of the 8th January from M.
Budé, and that of the 24th in answer to my last . . .

these ailments as it were in troops assail me. As soon as I recovered from a quartan ague, I was seized with severe and acute pains in the calves of my legs, which after being partially relieved returned a second and a third time. At last they degenerated into a disease in my articulations, which spread from my feet to my knees. An ulcer in the hæmorrhoid veins long caused me excruciating sufferings, and intestinal ascarides subjected me to painful titillations, though I am now relieved from this vermicular disease, but immediately after in the course of last summer I had an attack of nephritis. As I could not endure the jolting motion of horseback, I was conveyed into the country in a litter. On my return I wished to accomplish a part of the journey on foot. I had scarcely proceeded a mile when I was obliged to repose myself, in consequence of lassitude in the reins. And then to my surprise I discovered that I discharged blood instead of urine. As soon as I got home I took to bed. . The nephritis gave me exquisite pain, from which I only obtained a partial relief by the application of remedies. At length not without the most painful strainings I ejected a calculus which in some degree mitigated my sufferings, but such was its size, that it lacerated the urinary canal and a copious discharge of blood followed. This hemorrhage could only be arrested by an injection of milk [1] through a syringe. After that I ejected several others, and the oppressive numbness of the reins is a sufficient symptom that there still exist there some remains of uric calculus. It is a fortunate thing, however, that minute or at least moderately sized particles still continue to be emitted. My sedentary way of life to which I am condemned by the gout in my feet precludes all hopes of a cure. I am also prevented from taking exercise on horseback by my hemorrhoids. Add to my other complaints that whatever nourishment I take imperfectly digested turns into phlegm, which by its density sticks like paste to my stomach. But I am thoughtlessly tasking your patience, giving you double labour as the reward of your previous kindness, not indeed in consulting you, but in giving you the trouble to read over my vain complaints.

[1] *Muliebri lacte.*

Farewell, most accomplished sirs whom I sincerely honour. May the Lord always direct you by his Spirit, sustain you by his power, and enrich you more and more with his gifts.

[*Calvin's Lat. corresp.*, Opera, ix. p. 172.]

DCLXVI.—To the Duchess of Ferrara.[1]

Homage rendered to the piety of this princess—Eulogy of her niece the Duchess of Savoy.

GENEVA, *4th April*, 1564.

MADAME:—I pray you to pardon me if I employ the hand of my brother in writing to you, in consequence of my weakness and the pains I suffer from divers diseases—difficulty of breathing, the stone, the gout, and an ulcer in the hæmorrhoid veins which prevents me from taking any exercise, which is the only thing from which I might hope to derive some relief. I will also pray you to excuse me if this letter is short in comparison of yours, inasmuch as I am still waiting for the return of M. de Budé, through whom you have promised to let me hear news of you. Add to that, I have received no letter from M. de Colonges to inform me what measures should be adopted to appease the differences of your household, and remedy for the future all that might breed troubles and tumults, or keep up animosities and rancour.

Touching other matters, if my advice has any weight with you, do not, I pray you, torment your mind any more about them, for whatever occur, too violent passions engender much uneasiness, and shut the door on reason and truth. Nay, I have been astonished, Madame, though in speaking of the reprobate I had distinctly separated the person of the Duke of Guise from the question, and protested that those who according to their fancy damn people are too presumptuous, that you have nevertheless taken my remark in quite a contrary sense. That is the reason why I refrain from saying anything more, either good or bad

---

[1] Dictated from his death-bed. This letter is the last of the French correspondence of the Reformer.

on that matter. I shall allude to one thing, however, that so far are virtuous people from entertaining sentiments either of hatred or horror for you, because you are the mother-in-law of M. de Guise, that they only love and respect you the more, seeing that connection did not turn you aside from making an upright and pure profession of Christianity, and that not only in words but by deeds so remarkable that nothing could exceed them. As for myself I protest to you, that that has excited me to hold your virtues in so much the greater admiration.

I pass to another subject. I have heard that your niece the Duchess of Savoy is in a fair train, and is even deliberating about making an open declaration,[1] but you know how many meddlesome intriguers there are to retard her or cool her zeal, and on the other hand she has always been timid, so that it is to be feared that this good disposition of mind will proceed no further unless it be stimulated. Now, Madame, I am of opinion that there is nobody in this world who has more authority over her than you; for that reason I would entreat you in God's name not to spare a good and earnest exhortation, in order to give her courage to take a decided resolution: in which I hold it for certain that you will do your whole duty according to your zeal for having God more and more served and honoured.

Madame, having very humbly commended myself to your indulgent favour, I will supplicate our heavenly Father to keep you under his protection, to govern you continually by his Spirit, and to maintain you in all prosperity.

[*Fr. Copy.—Library of Geneva.* Vol. 107.]

---

[1] Margaret of France, sister of Henry II., wife of Emmanuel Philibert, Duke of Savoy. Endowed with the most amiable and generous character, this princess had a secret inclination towards the Reformed faith. She died in 1574, leaving a memory that was venerated in the churches of the valleys of Piedmont, whose cause she pleaded several times with Emmanuel Philibert. See on this subject two letters of this princess to the Seigneury of Geneva, written in the month of June, 1566. *Archives de Genève.* No. 1680.

DCLXVII.—To Bullinger.

Sufferings of Calvin and the inefficacy of the healing art to relieve them—News of France and Germany.

GENEVA, *6th April,* 1564.

I do not claim your indulgence for my long silence, respected brother, because you must have learned from others how just an excuse I have had for my delay, and which excuse I may in a great measure still allege.[1] For though the pain in my side is abated, my lungs are nevertheless so charged with phlegmatic humours that my respiration is difficult and interrupted. A calculus in my bladder also gives me very exquisite pain for the last twelve days. Add to that the anxious doubts we entertain about the possibility of curing it, for all remedies have hitherto proved ineffectual; exercise on horseback would have been the best and most expeditious method of getting rid of it, but an ulcer in my abdomen gives me excruciating pain even when seated or lying in bed, so that the agitation of riding is out of the question. Within the last three days the gout has also been troublesome. You will not be surprised then if so many united sufferings make me lazy. It is with much ado I can be brought to take any food. The taste of wine is bitter. But while I wish to discharge my duty in writing to you, I am only tiring out your patience with my insipid details.

Respecting the affairs of France, Beza has promised to write[2]

[1] Already the preceding year Calvin had been repeatedly forced to interrupt his correspondence in consequence of the multiplied sufferings of his illness. His pious secretary Charles de Jonvillers wrote on this occasion to Bullinger: "These few words I have thought proper to add hurriedly, that you may know that M. Calvin is such a martyr to sufferings, that far from being able to write, he cannot even dictate anything to be sent to you, in consequence of the pressure of his disease. I know the high esteem in which he holds you, as you deserve, and I can scarcely write without tears. I entreat you then that in your prayers and those of your whole church, you in the mean time commend to God both him and all of us." Letter of the 11th June, 1563. (*Arch. of Zurich.*) The days of the Reformer were already numbered, and before a year had elapsed, that great light was withdrawn from the church and the world.

[2] In a letter of Beza's to Bullinger of the 4th May, 1564, may be remarked some affecting details respecting the malady of Calvin already so weak as to be incapable

to you. I dispense then with saying anything, not to repeat a twice told tale. I shall only allude to one subject however. You have heard long ago that the king has gone to Lorraine. The cause of his journey was a secret to the courtiers themselves, but it was revealed to me lately by the person who was charged to convey instructions backwards and forwards. The envoy of the king to the emperor, and who formerly was among you at the time he was Abbot of St. Laurence, is holding out to the queen mother great and dazzling prospects from King Maximilian. But in the mean time he stipulates that the queen should not openly declare that she entertains any hopes. I make no doubt, therefore, but he will sell himself to the cardinal of Lorraine. For after having failed in all his projects, he conceives that his only remaining resource is to gain time by giving out these ambiguous intimations. I see no other fraud or treachery concealed in this mission, except to amuse the queen with false expectations, and bring himself forward by his insinuations, to undertake affairs which he will never bring to any conclusion. For it is evident that Roschetelle has made a false use of King Maximilian's name, since he childishly advises the queen to dissemble and keep everything a profound secret. But my cough and a difficulty of breathing leave me no voice to dictate any more. Farewell, then, venerable brother, along with Mr. Gualter, your other colleagues, and your whole family. May the Lord protect you all, enrich you more and more with his benefits, and sustain you by his power. I am unwilling to lose my pains in writing to you about the state of our city.— Yours,

JOHN CALVIN.

[*Lat. Copy.—Library of Geneva.* Vol. 107 *a.*]

of acquitting himself of his epistolary duties. " But what gives us the most poignant distress is the uninterrupted sufferings of that most excellent man, our father and the faithful servant of God. Of his life, humanly speaking, we now utterly despair. He is alive, however, and thus indeed, as he had afforded us a rare example of an upright life, so now he furnishes us with one of a courageous and truly Christian death. But ah wretched, me! what shall I do upon whom so overwhelming a charge devolves?" (Library of Geneva, vol. 118.)

DCLXVIII.—To Farel.

Last adieus.

GENEVA, *2nd May,* 1564.

Farewell, my most excellent and upright brother; and since it is the will of God that you should survive me in the world, live mindful of our intimacy, which, as it was useful to the church of God, so the fruits of it await us in heaven.[1] I am unwilling that you should fatigue yourself for my sake.[2] I draw my breath with difficulty, and every moment I am in expectation of breathing my last. It is enough that I live and die for Christ, who is to all his followers a gain both in life and death. Again I bid you and your brethren Farewell.

[*Lat. Copy.—Arch. of Neuchâtel.*]

[1] It cannot fail to be interesting to produce along with this affecting adieu the noble testimony rendered by Farel to Calvin in a letter to Fabri of the 6th June, 1564 : " Oh why was I not taken away in his stead, and he preserved to the church which he has so well served, and in combats harder than death? He has done more and with greater promptitude than any one, surpassing not only the others but himself. Oh, how happily he has run a noble race ! May the Lord grant that we run like him, and according to the measure of grace that has been dealt out to us."

[2] In spite of his great age Farel took a journey to see again once more his friend, his fellow labourer now on his death-bed. " And nevertheless, that excellent old man came to Geneva, and after they had an interview together, the following day he returned to Neuchâtel." Beza, *Vita Calvini.*

LAST DISCOURSES OF CALVIN.

CALVIN'S TESTAMENT.

LAST ʼWILL AND TESTAMENT OF MASTER JOHN CALVIN.

In the name of God, be it known to all men by these presents
that in the year 1564, and the 25th day of the month of April,
I Peter Chenelat, citizen and sworn Notary of Geneva, have
been sent for by *Spectable*[1] John Calvin, minister of the word
of God in the Church of Geneva, and burgess of the said Geneva,
who, being sick and indisposed in body alone, has declared to me
his intention to make his testament and declaration of his last
will, begging me to write it according as it should be by him
dictated and pronounced, which, at his said request, I have done,
and have written it under him, and according as he hath dictated
and pronounced it, word for word, without omitting or adding
anything—in form as follows:

In the name of God, I John Calvin, minister of the word of
God in the Church of Geneva, feeling myself reduced so low by
diverse maladies, that I cannot but think that it is the will of
God to withdraw me shortly from this world, have advised to
make and set down in writing my testament and declaration of
my last will in form, as follows:

---

[1] Epithet marking respect, used in title deeds, etc.

In the first place, I render thanks to God, not only because he has had compassion on me, his poor creature, to draw me out of the abyss of idolatry in which I was plunged, in order to bring me to the light of his gospel and make me a partaker of the doctrine of salvation, of which I was altogether unworthy, and continuing his mercy he has supported me amid so many sins and short-comings, which were such that I well deserved to be rejected by him a hundred thousand times—but what is more, he has so far extended his mercy towards me as to make use of me and of my labour, to convey and announce the truth of his gospel; protesting that it is my wish to live and die in this faith which he has bestowed on me, having no other hope nor refuge except in his gratuitous adoption, upon which all my salvation is founded; embracing the grace which he has given me in our Lord Jesus Christ, and accepting the merits of his death and passion, in order that by this means all my sins may be buried; and praying him so to wash and cleanse me by the blood of this great Redeemer, which has been shed for us poor sinners, that I may appear before his face, bearing as it were his image.

I protest also that I have endeavoured, according to the measure of grace he has given me, to teach his word in purity, both in my sermons and writings, and to expound faithfully the Holy Scriptures; and moreover, that in all the disputes I have had with the enemies of the truth, I have never made use of subtle craft nor sophistry, but have gone to work straight-for-wardly in maintaining his quarrel. But alas! the desire which I have had, and the zeal, if so it must be called, has been so cold and so sluggish that I feel myself a debtor in everything and everywhere, and that, were it not for his infinite goodness, all the affection I have had would be but as smoke, nay, that even the favours which he has accorded me would but render me so much the more guilty; so that my only recourse is this, that being the Father of mercies he will show himself the Father of so miserable a sinner.

Moreover, I desire that my body after my decease be interred in the usual manner, to wait for the day of the blessed resurrection.

Touching the little earthly goods which God has given me here to dispose of, I name and appoint for my sole heir, my well beloved brother Antony Calvin, but only as honorary heir however, leaving to him the right of possessing nothing save the cup which I have had from Monsieur de Varennes,[1] and begging him to be satisfied with that, as I am well assured he will be, because he knows that I do this for no other reason but that the little which I leave may remain to his children. I next bequeath to the college ten crowns, and to the treasure of poor foreigners the same sum. Item, to Jane, daughter of Charles Costan and my half-sister,[2] that is to say, by the father's side, the sum of ten crowns; and afterwards to each of my nephews, Samuel and John, sons of my aforesaid brother,[3] forty crowns; and to each of my nieces, Anne, Susannah, and Dorothy, thirty crowns. As for my nephew David their brother, because he has been thoughtless and unsettled, I leave to him but twenty-five crowns as a chastisement.[4] This is the total of all the property which God has given me, according as I have been able to value and estimate it, whether in books,[5] furniture,[6] plate, or anything

[1] Guillaume de Trie, Seigneur de Varennes. He died in 1562, leaving the guardianship of his children to Calvin.

[2] Mary, daughter by a second marriage of Gerard Calvin. She had quitted Noyou in 1536, to follow her brothers John and Antony to Switzerland.

[3] Antony Calvin had espoused in first marriage Anne de Fer, whom he divorced for adultery in 1557. He married again the 14th of January, 1560, with Antoinette Commelin, the widow of the minister of St. André. He had by his first wife two sons, Samuel and David, and two daughters, Anne and Susannah; by the second, a son, John, who died without posterity in 1601, and three daughters, Dorothy, Judith, and Mary, who died of the plague in 1574. Galiffe, *Not. Geneal.* vol. iii. p. 113.

[4] This David, as well as Samuel his brother, were disinherited by Antony Calvin, because of their "disobedience."

[5] Calvin's books were purchased after his death by the Seigneury, as we see by the registers of the council, 8th July, 1564: "Resolved to buy for the republic such of the books of Mr. Calvin as Mr. Beza shall judge proper.

[6] A part of Calvin's furniture belonged to the republic of Geneva, as is proved by the inventory preserved in the archives. (No. 1426.) We extract from it the list of articles lent to the Reformer, 27th December, 1548, and restored to the seigneury after his death :

1st. A bedstead of walnut-tree wood, rough and unplaned; Item. A walnut-tree table of a square form jointed with iron; A bench turned on the lathe to correspond to this table; A buffet of walnut-tree jointed with iron; A walnut-tree wash hand stand; Another bedstead, planed by the joiner; A walnut wood chest, consolidated with iron; A high-backed chair of polished walnut tree; A square wooden table; A polished walnut-tree buffet (has not been found); A coffer buffet; A long bench turned on the lathe; Another square walnut wood table; A walnut wood bedstead;

else. However, should the result of the sale amount to anything more, I mean that it should be distributed among my said nephews and nieces, not excluding David, if God shall have given him grace to be more moderate and staid. But I believe that on this subject there will be no difficulty, especially when my debts shall be paid, as I have given charge to my brother on whom I rely, naming him executor of this testament along with the *spectable* Laurence de Normandie, giving them all power and authority to make an inventory without any judicial forms, and sell my furniture to raise money from it in order to accomplish the directions of this testament as it is here set down in writing, this 25th April, 1564.

Witness my hand,

JOHN CALVIN.

After being written as above, at the same instant the said *spectable* Calvin undersigned with his usual signature the minute of the said testament. And the following day, which was the 26th of the month of April, the said *spectable* Calvin sent for me a second time together with *spectable* Theodore Beza, Raymond Chauvet, Michael Cop, Louis Enoch, Nicholas Coladon, Jacques Desbordes, ministers of the word of God in this church, and *spectable* Henry Seringer, professor of letters, all burgesses of Geneva, in presence of whom he declared that he had caused me to write under him, and at his dictation, the said testament in the form, and with the same words as here above, praying me to read it aloud in the presence of the said witnesses sent for and required for that purpose, which I did with an audible voice, and word for word. After which reading he declared that such was his will and last disposition, desiring that it might be observed. And for still greater confirmation of the same, begged and requested the above mentioned persons to subscribe it along with me, which was also done on the year and day above written, at Geneva in the street called *Des chanoines*, and the dwelling

---

Four long tables with their trestles of fir, and another long table of walnut wood; A dozen forms good and bad (new ones given back in their stead); A desk for books. The present furniture given back this 25th September, 1564.

RUFI.

house of the said testator. In faith of which, and to serve for sufficient proof, I have drawn up in the form as here above presented, the present testament, in order to expedite it to whom it may concern, under the common seal of our most honourable seigneurs and superiors and my own usual sign-manual.

Witness my hand,

P. CHENALAT.

CALVIN'S FAREWELL TO THE SEIGNEURS OF GENEVA.

Taken down by the Secretary of the Republic.

[Follow the words and exhortations of *spectable* John Calvin, minister of the word of God in this church spoken this day, 27th April, 1564, to our most honourable seigneurs the Syndics and Council].

First, after having thanked Messeigneurs for the trouble they had taken in coming to his house, though his wish was to have had himself carried to the town house, he declared that he has always had the desire to address them once more; and though heretofore he has been very low, nevertheless he was unwilling to hurry, inasmuch as God had not given him so precise an advertisement as he does at present.

Then after he had thanked them, because they had been pleased to do him more honour than was due to him, and to bear with him in many circumstances in which he stood in great need of their indulgence, he still considers himself so much the more obliged to the said seigneurs that they have always shown him such marks of affection, that it was impossible for them to show more. True it is that while he has resided here, he has had many combats and subjects of vexation, as no doubt all good men must be tried, yet none of these were owing to Messeigneurs. He prays them then, if he has not done what he ought to have done, that Messeigneurs will be pleased to take the will for the deed, for he has desired the good of this city, and has contributed to it, but he is far from having accomplished all his duty

in respect to it.   It is true he does not deny that God has made
use of him as an instrument for the little he has done, and if he
said otherwise he should be a hypocrite; he begs then again to
be excused for having done so little in proportion to what he
was bound to do, both in public and private, and he feels persuaded that Messeigneurs have borne with his natural disposition
by far too vehement, and with which he is offended, and with his
other vices as God also has been.

Moreover, he protests before God and before Messeigneurs,
that he has made it his endeavour to speak in purity the word
which God has confided to him, making sure not to walk at
random nor in error.   Otherwise he should expect a condemnation on his head, not doubting, as we see, but that the devil,
whose only aim is to pervert, stirs up wicked people, having the
spirit of madness to aim at the same end.

For the rest, it is necessary that Messeigneurs should have a
short word of exhortation.   For they see in what position they
are placed, and whether they fancy they shall stand in surety
or shall be threatened, it behoves them always to keep in mind
that God wishes to be honoured, and that he reserves to himself
the right of maintaining both public states and private conditions, and wills that we do him homage, by recognizing that we
are wholly dependent on him.   We have an example in David,
who confesses that when he was quietly settled in his kingdom,
he forgot himself so far as to have stumbled mortally, if God had
not had compassion upon him.

And if a man who was so excellent a . . .[1] both trembles and
stumbles, what should we who are nothing feel?   We shall have
much occasion to humble ourselves, keeping ourselves concealed
under the wings of God on whom should repose all our confidence.   And though we are, as it were, suspended by a thread,
we should trust that he will continue to protect us as in times
past, since we have experienced already that he has saved us in
divers ways.

If our Lord gives us prosperity, we rejoice.   But when we are
assailed on all sides, and it seems that there is a host of evils
encompassing us, we ought not for all that to cease to have con-

---

[1] A word is here left in blank in the registers.

fidence in him, and how often soever, and in what manner soever we may be taken by surprise, let us know that it is God who wills to awaken us, to the end, that we may humble ourselves and take shelter under his wings.

And if we desire to be maintained in our present condition, we must beware that the seat in which we have been placed be not dishonoured; for he says he will honour those who shall honour him, and on the contrary will bring to disgrace those who shall despise him.

There is no superiority but from God, who is King of kings, and Lord of lords.

This is said in order that we may serve him in purity according to his word, and think of him more than ever. For we are very far indeed from acquitting ourselves fully of that duty, and with such integrity as we ought to do.

For the rest, he has said that all our conduct and whatever we do is open to his eyes; we stand then in great need of being exhorted.

Every one has his imperfections. It is our duty to examine them. Wherefore let each one look to himself and combat them.

Some are indifferent, absorbed by their own affairs, and but little concerned about the public good; others are given up to their passions.

Others, when God has bestowed on them a spirit of prudence, do not make use of it.

Others are wedded to their opinions, wishing to be held for oracles, to seem something, to be in credit and reputation.

Let the old not bear envy towards the young, for the grace they may have received, but let them rejoice and bless God for having bestowed it on them.

Let the young continue to be modest, without wishing to put themselves forward too much; for there is always a boastful character in young folks, who cannot bridle themselves, and who push on in despising others.

Do not discourage one another, be not an obstacle to one another, do not make yourselves odious to one another. For when animosities are kindled, people fall off from their duty.

And to avoid inconveniences, let every one walk according to his rank, and busy himself according as God has given him means to support this republic.

As to civil or criminal processes—cast from you all favour, hatred, crooked means, recommendations, and renounce all self-interest, holding by integrity and equity ; and if ever you are tempted to swerve from them, resist and be firm, looking unto Him who hath established us, and praying him to conduct us by his Holy Spirit, and he will not fail us.

Finally, after having again begged to be excused and supported in his infirmities, which he will not deny (for since God and the angels know them, he will not deny them before men), and to accept with good will his small labours, he prayed God to conduct and govern us, continually increasing his grace in us, and causing it to turn to our own salvation and that of all this poor people.[1]

[*Orig. Minute.—Arch. of Geneva*, 1564.]

CALVIN'S FAREWELL TO THE MINISTERS OF GENEVA.

Taken down by the minister Pinant.[2]

[On Friday, 28th April, 1564, taken down by (Pinant) and written as pronounced as nearly as the memory could preserve it word for word, though in a slightly different order with respect to some words and phrases.]

Brethren, inasmuch as I have had something to say to you,

---

[1] Whereupon, says Beza, having prayed [Messeigneurs] to forgive him all his faults which no one thought greater than himself, he held out his hand to them. I do not know if there could have happened to these seigneurs a more sad spectacle, who all with great justice considered him, in respect of his office, as the mouth of the Lord, and in respect of his affection as their father. Indeed he had known and instructed a part of them from their youth.

[2] There exists in the fine archives of Colonel Henry Tronchin, a second account of Calvins' Farewell by an unknown person, B. B., called Corneille. With less precision and naïveté, in the details, it fully confirms the exactness of the former in all essential points. Perhaps we shall give the reader pleasure in quoting as variations, some traits borrowed from this second account, likewise unedited.

which concerns not only this church, but also several others, which in a eertain manner depend on it, it will be good to begin with prayer, in order that God may give me grace to say every thing without ambition, always having a respect to his glory, and also that every one may retain and profit by what shall be said.

It may be thought that I am too precipitate in concluding my end to be drawing near, and that I am not so ill as I persuade myself; but I assure you, that though I have often felt myself very ill, yet I have never found myself in such a state, nor so weak as I am. When they take me to put me in bed, my head fails me and I swoon away forthwith. There is also this shortness of breathing, which oppresses me more and more. I am altogether different from other sick persons, for when their end is approaching their senses fail them and they become delirious. With respect to myself, true it is that I feel stupefied, but it seems to me that God wills to concentrate all my senses within me,[1] and I believe indeed that I shall have much difficulty and that it will cost me a great effort to die. I may perhaps lose the faculty of speech, and yet preserve my sound sense;[2] but I have also advertised my friends of that and told them what I wished them to do for me, and it is for this very reason I have desired to speak with you before God call me away; not that God may not indeed do otherwise than I think; it would be temerity on my part to wish to enter into his counsel.

When I first came to this church, I found almost nothing in it.[3] There was preaching and that was all. They would look out for idols it is true, and they burned them. But there was no reformation. Everything was in disorder. There was no doubt the good man Master William,[4] and then blind Courant (not

---

[1] "As to his senses he is in full possession of them, and they are more subtle than ever, but nature is fast sinking." . . *Relat. de B. B. dit Corneille.*

[2] "That he has often predicted that he should be deprived of speech some days before his death, and he still believes it." *Ibidem.*

[3] "When he came to this town . . . he found it without morals, discipline, or life." *Ibid.*

[4] Farel.

born blind, but he became so at Bâle).[1] There was besides
Master Antony Saulnier,[2] and that fine preacher Froment, who
having laid aside his apron got up into the pulpit, then went
back to his shop where he prated, and thus gave a double
sermon.[3]

I have lived here amid continual bickerings. I have been
from derision saluted of an evening before my door with forty
or fifty shots of an arquebuse. How think you must that have
astonished a poor scholar timid as I am, and as I have always
been, I confess?[4]

Then afterwards I was expelled from this town and went
away to Strasbourg, and when I had lived there some time I was
called back hither, but I had no less trouble when I wished to
discharge my duty than heretofore. They set the dogs at my
heels, crying, Hère! hère![5] and these snapped at my gown and
my legs. I went my way to the council of the two hundred
when they were fighting, and I kept back the others who wanted
to go, and who had nothing to do there; and though they boast
that it was they who did everything, like M. de Saulx,[6] yet I
was there, and as I entered, people said to me, "Withdraw, sir,
we have nothing to say to you." I replied, "I will do no such
thing—come, come, wicked men that you are; kill me, and my
blood will rise up against you, and these very benches will require it." Thus I have been amid combats, and you will experience that there will be others not less but greater. For you

---

[1] Enlightening souls—though he had become blind as to his body." *Hist. Eccl.*,
vol. i. p. 15.

[2] Banished from Geneva in 1538, Saulnier became the minister of the Church of
Morges. The date of his death is not known.

[3] It is known that Froment first presented himself at Geneva as a schoolmaster.
Of a vain and inconstant spirit, he was incapable of maintaining his dignity in the
glorious part of a missionary of the Reformation. In 1553 he abandoned the office of
the ministry, bought the charge of a notary, and merited on more than one occasion
for his inconsiderate conduct the censures of the seigneury.

[4] . . . "and repeated twice or thrice these words : I assure you I am naturally
timid and fearful." Beza, *Vie de Calvin.* The same confession is several times expressed in the preface of the Commentary on the Psalms, a real autobiography of the
Reformer.

[5] Term of the chase—a young fawn of a year old.

[6] Is it the minister Nicholas des Gallars, otherwise called M. de Saules? He was
pastor in 1564 of the church of Orleans.

are a perverse and unhappy nation, and though there are good men in it the nation is perverse and wicked, and you will have troubles when God shall have called me away; for though I am nothing, yet know I well that I have prevented three thousand tumults that would have broken out in Geneva.[1] But take courage and fortify yourselves, for God will make use of this church and will maintain it, and assures you that he will protect it.

I have had many infirmities which you have been obliged to bear with, and what is more, all I have done has been worth nothing. The ungodly will greedily seize upon this word, but I say it again that all I have done has been worth nothing, and that I am a miserable creature. But certainly I can say this that I have willed what is good, that my vices have always displeased me, and that the root of the fear of God has been in my heart; and you may say that the disposition was good; and I pray you, that the evil be forgiven me, and if there was any good, that you conform yourselves to it and make it an example.[2]

As to my doctrine, I have taught faithfully, and God has given me grace to write what I have written as faithfully as it was in my power. I have not falsified a single passage of the Scriptures, nor given it a wrong interpretation to the best of my knowledge; and though I might have introduced subtle senses, had I studied subtilty, I cast that temptation under my feet and always aimed at simplicity.[3]

I have written nothing out of hatred to any one, but I have always faithfully propounded what I esteemed to be for the glory of God.

As to our internal state, you have elected M. Beza to hold my place. Advise how to relieve him, for the charge is great, and so weighty that he might well sink under the load. But

---

[1] "That this town would be assaulted from without, but that God wished to make use of it, who ought to be for us an inexpugnable rock to induce us not to quit it." *Relat. de B. B. dit Corneille.*

[2] "He prays his brethren to forgive him for having been so violent, choleric, and hasty." *Ibid.*

[3] "Made no use of sophistry, and wishes to live and die in the doctrine which he had, and prays his brethren to persevere in it." *Ibid.*

advise how to support him. Of him I know that he has a good
will and will do what he can.

Let every one consider the obligation which he has not only
to this church but also to the city, which you have promised
to serve in adversity as well as in prosperity; thus let each
keep by his vocation and not endeavour to retire from it
nor enter into cabals. For when people go under ground
to seek for shifts, they may say indeed that they did not
reflect, and that they did aim at this or that. But let them
consider the obligation that they have here contracted before
God.

And study too that that there be no bickerings or sharp
words among you, as sometimes biting gibes will be bandied
about.[1] This will take place, it is true, in laughing, but there
will be bitterness in the heart. All that is good for nothing,
and is even contrary to a Christian disposition. You should
then guard against it, and live in good accord and all friendship
and sincerity.[2]

I had forgotten this point: I pray you make no change, no
innovation. People often ask for novelties. Not that I desire
for my own sake out of ambition that what I have established
should remain, and that people should retain it without wishing
for something better, but because all changes are dangerous and
sometimes hurtful.

On my return from Strasbourg, I composed the catechism
and in haste, for I would never accept the ministry till they
had taken an oath respecting these two points: namely, to
preserve the catechism and discipline; and while I was writing
it, they came to fetch bits of paper as big as my hand and carry
them to the printing office. Though Master Peter Viret was
then in this town, do you think I ever showed him a word of it?
I never had leisure; I have sometimes indeed thought of putting
a finishing hand to it if I had had leisure.

As to the prayers for the Sabbath I adopted the form of

---

[1] " He has not known such love and kindly feeling to exist among you as he could
have wished, but rather covert piques and banterings. That all should be on a more
friendly footing than formerly." *Ibid.*

[2] " Love one another, support one another. Let there be no envy." *Ibid.*

Strasbourg, and borrowed the greater part of it. Of the other prayers, I could not take any part from that formulary, for it contained nothing of the kind; but I took the whole from the Holy Scriptures.

I was also obliged to compose a formulary of baptism when I was at Strasbourg, where people brought me the children of Anabaptists from five or six leagues off to have them baptized. I then composed this unpolished formulary, which I would not advise you, notwithstanding, to change.

The Church of (Berne)[1] has betrayed this one, and they have always feared me more than they loved me. I am desirous they should know that I died in the opinion that they feared rather than loved me, and even now they fear me more than they love me, and have always been afraid lest I should disturb them about their eucharisty.[2]

This remark ought to have been introduced before in some place of which I have not a distinct recollection.

He made use of the aforesaid words. I have not set them down in doubt or uncertainty. I doubt not but he himself would have set them down better, and would have said more. But what I did not recollect with the most perfect distinctness I have left out. He took a courteous leave of all the brethren who shook him by the hand, one after the other, all melting into tears.

Written the 1st day of May, 1564, on the 27th day of which month he died.[3]

Ultima Calvinus nobis quae verba locutus,
Quae meminisse mihi licuit, certoque referre,
Hic mihi descripsi monumentum, sed mihi soli.

J. P. M.[4]

---

[1] There is a blank space left for a word in the two narratives.

[2] "That those of . . . betrayed this church at the time of his banishment for the sake of the eucharisty and even now fear him more than they love him. He desires that they should know that he departed this life with such an opinion of them." *Relat. de B. B. dit Corneille.*

[3] "In the Minutes of the Consistory of Geneva, we read these words with a simple cross † opposite to the name of Calvin: "Gone to God, May 27th of the present year, between 8 and 9 o'clock, P. M."

[4] Jean Pinant, minister.

["The last words which Calvin addressed to us, as far as I could remember, and with certainty relate them, I have here written down as a memorial for myself, but for myself alone."]

[*Orig. Minute.—Arch. of M. Tronchin at Geneva.*]

APPENDIX.

APPENDIX.

I.—To Francis Daniel.[1]

Preparations for his departure for Switzerland—Recommendation of a physician.

PARIS, 1534.

I had resolved not to write to you at so unpropitious a moment, but a subject for doing so has presented itself to me, which I could not anticipate. While I was occupied with the preparations for my departure I had a severe attack of diarrhæa, to check which I called in the bearer of this letter, a man well skilled in the healing art, and perfectly free from quackery. While treating me he mentioned his intention of going to settle at Orleans, where he expects to find a good opening for the exercise of his profession. I have thought it my duty to furnish him with a letter of recommendation, that he might not arrive in your city a stranger to everybody. I ask of you then, as a pledge of our friendship, to welcome him and give him what assistance may be in your power. I am not ignorant how grave a responsibility he assumes, who recommends a physician, for should you commend an unworthy one, you hold out a sword to an assassin for the destruction of the public, as you prepare the way for one to inflict death on great numbers; since the

---

[1] Without a date. Written according to all probability from Paris, in June or July, 1534, at the moment when Calvin was preparing to quit France in order to retire to Switzerland.

(381)

physician, as it has been remarked, may commit murder with
impunity. Of this man, however, I am not afraid to affirm that
he is thoroughly instructed in the theory of his art, and so well
versed in its practice as not readily to make any slips from ignorance. With that, his probity is equal to his talent. For these
things I pledge my honour both to you and others, and I beg
you to do all in your power to induce those to have recourse
with all confidence to his talents, who otherwise might not
venture, where their lives are at stake, to make trial of a man
quite unknown. What my projects are, you already know from
our friend Francis, and you may learn from the bearer. Salute
for me, your mother, wife, sister, etc.

                                        JOHN CALVIN.

    [*Lat. Orig.—Library of Berne.* Vol. 141.]

II.—To BUCER.[1]

Unsuccessful results of the Colloquy of Berne—Sacramentarian discord—Remarkable
judgment concerning Luther—Violence of the Bernese Minister Conzen—Appeal
to Bucer.

                                        GENEVA, 12th January, 1538.

    I have a good many things to write to you about, things too
by no means agreeable, had I a little more leisure; write how-

---

[1] One of the first acts of Farel and Calvin during their common ministry at Geneva,
was the drawing up of a confession of faith which the citizens solemnly took oath to
observe. But this confession resolutely opposed by an ardent minority, which was
at a later period stigmatized under the name of the *Libertines*, encountered every day
grave difficulties in practice, particularly in what concerned ecclesiastical excommunication. The Seigneurs of Berne, chosen for arbiters, showed themselves but little
disposed to resolve the difficulties in a sense conformable to the wishes of the ministers. Pre-occupied above all by the rights of the civil authority and the demands of
external unity, they urged the ministers of Geneva to conform to the usages of the
Church of Berne, "in order to deprive their enemies of every subject of calumny."
Whilst at Berne they communicated with unleavened bread, administered baptism on
fonts of stone, and celebrated the great religious festivals, not one of these usages was
followed at Geneva, and this difference in practice occasioned much coldness between
the two churches. Several Bernese ministers had even been censured and revoked
for having shown themselves too favourable to the doctrine of Calvin. Among them
was Gaspar Megander. (Vol. i. p. 47, 141). Calvin deplored these differences between the Swiss Churches, just as he bewailed the discords which the Sacramentarian

ever I must, as much as my very limited time will permit, since
to me it will be no slight consolation, to confide to your friendly
bosom, the evils which oppress us.   In the letter which I wrote
to Capito from Berne, I exulted as if matters had been terminated to our satisfaction; and who would have entertained any
doubts about the success of so good a cause?   For our confession, which was then the point in question, was judged by the
ministers to be a devout production, and an oath in confirmation
of it was with the highest propriety exacted by the people; what
remained but that a deputation should be named to cure the
wound which had been inflicted by the former deputies of Berne?
That was not obtained without the greatest difficulty, but when
even those who were actuated by the most iniquitous sentiments
could not oppose our demand, deputies were appointed to settle
this question, who it was very sure would never undertake the
task for which they had been selected.   As soon as they refused, the duty was entrusted to those among whom the evil had
arisen; but that you may understand how little seriousness there
was in this measure, the moment that the feeblest rumor of
public report indicated to what issue things so well prepared
were tending, these new deputies were immediately recalled.

I dare not give way to too malignant suspicions, but all declare that those who take such delight in disturbances and seditions are watching for an opportunity of making innovations.
A short time after that, it was announced that Megander had
left the country by a sentence of banishment.   This news was
as great a blow to us as if we had heard that the Church of
Berne had for the most part fallen off.   I begin to fear, my dear
Bucer, that we are aiming at an agreement[1] which will have to

question had given birth to in Germany, and without perhaps making all the concessions necessary to appease them, he pronounced the most remarkable judgment respecting Luther, while at the same time he addressed to Bucer pressing exhortations
to determine him to accomplish unequivocally and without weakness his duties as a
conciliator between the parties.

[1] Calvin had drawn up in concert with Bucer, Capito, Farel, and Viret, a declaration on the subject of the sacrament of the Lord's supper, which, keeping at an equal
distance from the interpretation of Luther and that of Zwingli, seemed calculated to
conciliate people's minds, (Opera, vol. ix. p.   ,) but it only envenomed the discords
which were destined at a later period, in Germany especially, to end in a veritable
persecution against the Calvinists.

be sanctioned by the sacrifice and blood of many pious men, nor
is this the phrase of a man who wishes to draw back, but of one
who desires such an agreement as all good men could join us in.
And if we have this at heart, all those perplexing difficulties
which it seems might restrain the more timid, will be swept
away. But these, which we ourselves thought were to be opposed, are that Luther should not give scope to his wild fancy,
about our flesh being as it were a graff into that of Christ's, or
that of Christ's into ours, nor feign that Christ's body is of infinite extension, nor impose upon us a local presence: for there
is hardly any one of those who have hitherto protested who does
not suspect something of this kind. If Luther can cordially
accept of us along with our confession, there is nothing which I
could more willingly desire; but in the mean time he is not the
only one in the church of God to be looked up to. For we
should be cruel and barbarous if we made no account of the
many thousands who are cruelly domineered over under pretext
of that agreement.

What to think of Luther I know not, though I am thoroughly
convinced of his piety; but I wish it were false, what is commonly said by most people, who in other respects would be very
unwilling to be unjust to him, that with his firmness there is
mixed up a good deal of obstinacy. His conduct affords us no
slight grounds for entertaining this suspicion. If that is true
which I understood to be rumored about lately in the churches
of Wurtemberg, that they had compelled nearly all the churches
to recognize error, how much vainglory, pray, is there in such
conduct? If we were not afflicted with the malady of ambition,
would it not have been enough for us that Christ should be
deemed veracious, and that his truth should shine forth in the
hearts of men? I see indeed what will come of all this. Nothing
can be safe as long as that rage for contention shall agitate us.
All recollections of past times must then be buried in oblivion,
if we look for a solid peace. For the contest was so keen and
so much embittered, that it is not possible to bring it to mind
without kindling at least some sparks of strife; and if Luther
has so great a lust of victory, he will never be able to join along
with us in a sincere agreement respecting the pure truth of God.

For he has sinned against it not only from vainglory and abusive language, but also from ignorance and the grossest extravagance. For what absurdities he pawned upon us in the beginning, when he said the bread is the very body! And if now he imagines that the body of Christ is enveloped by the bread, I judge that he is chargeable with a very foul error. What can I say of the partisans of that cause? Do they not romance more wildly than Marcion respecting the body of Christ? If the Swiss should take upon them to inveigh against such mistakes, how would this pave the way for an agreement?

Wherefore if you have any influence or authority over Martin, use it to dispose him to prefer subduing to Christ, rather than to himself, those with whom he has hitherto wrangled in the most inauspicious of strifes; nay, that he himself submit to the truth which he is now manifestly attacking. Here what should have been done was that every one should ingenuously confess of his own accord his own error, and I could not help protesting to you as I think you yourself recollect, that those wily insinuations by which you attempted to excuse yourself and Zwingli displeased me. It is not in the mean time by any means becoming to insult one another. Would that all these reproaches might fall upon my head, and yet I am fully convinced in my own mind that I have never been so abandoned by God since I began to taste of his word, as not to preserve a pious sense of the use of the sacraments and of our participation of the body of Christ. There is nothing certainly in my introduction to contradict this; and even should we grant that there was an absurd shame in one party of confessing their fault, who would not after all excuse this feeling compared with what is said of the insolent fury of Martin?

Wherefore, my dear Bucer, you must strive that all things be properly adjusted on both sides. A difficult task, you will say; I admit it, certainly; but since you have taken it upon you, you must labour seriously, I do not say to fulfil it, but to endeavour to do so. How intolerable do you think it appears that so many, and by no means contemptible churches of the whole of Saxony, when they have shown their readiness to come to an equitable agreement, should be kept so long in

suspense! If then you ask of the Swiss to lay aside their obstinacy, contrive that Luther in his turn cease to bear himself
so imperiously. But I return to Megander (Grossman). He
was forced to go into exile, because he could not bear to subscribe to your corrections.[1] Will you not say it was sufficient
cause for bearing hard upon him, that without reason he opposed
the truth? What would you say if on the contrary he was prepared without any constraint to bear witness to the truth?
What then was the cause why he did not accept the things
which had been well said by another? Grant that here he
showed some of that infirmity which is incident to our nature:
was it not better that such a man should have been retained,
by looking over that trifling weakness, than that he should be
driven from his ministry with so much scandal, to the great
contempt of God everywhere, with so great a loss to the church,
and greater danger for the time to come? How saucily the
enemies of the gospel now triumph on all sides, because pastors
begin to be driven into exile! How licentiously they make
a mock of the gospel of God! In what derision they hold us,
who, having the most powerful and well appointed adversaries
drawn up in battle array against us, are nevertheless dispatching
one another with mutual wounds! What moreover will the weak
do when they see their pastors punished with exile on whose
mouths they formerly hung?

Finally you are not aware how immense the loss which the
Church of Berne has sustained in being despoiled of such a
pastor. I confidently declare, you do not know what we all
know, viz: that in this matter you are blinded, or certainly
grievously mistaken. Sebastian (the elder) and Conzen no
doubt are left to them. But what can the former of these do,
but subvert by his wild errors the purity of the gospel? For I
lately detected what superstitious principles he cherishes, with
what difficulty he admitted that the dogma of the schoolmen
about the seven sacraments is but empty trifling, and how
wickedly he fumed up because marriage and absolution were
not received by us into the number of the sacraments. And
should we wink at these absurdities, he is not the less, as all

[1] On Megander's catechism.

men see, totally unequal to the task of governing the church,
especially in times so difficult. He has so bad a memory withal
that he stutters and hesitates at every third word. If you irritate him, he is carried away by the violence of his temper to
such a degree as no longer to seem in his right senses; and if
you assent to him, you may lead him like a child wherever you
please. You will say that I am accustomed to fulminate in my
letters, but to soften down when I come to grapple with actual
business. Certainly it is not one of my habits to wrangle. But
I cannot refrain from expressing what I feel in plain words, both
before people's faces and in my letters. You will estimate that
disposition as you please, but when I have carefully weighed how
much sincerity is preferable to cunning, I fancy you will not
think I should do such violence to my natural character as not
frankly to open my mind to you about what I see to be true, for
I know the man·to whom I reveal my thoughts. I dare hardly
express what sort of person Conzen is. By your moderation
and forbearance indeed he seemed to us a little tamed, and a
short while ago, he made a wonderful show of activity in our
business; the moment is gone by, and he is become worse than
his very self. Farel declares he never saw a wild beast more
rabid, than he found him lately. His countenance, gestures,
words, his very colour breathed, as he says, fury. Whatever excuses therefore may be made for him hereafter, until I
perceive that he is changed, I shall deem him charged with
venom, for what is his reason, pray, for hating us so mortally,
as to be incessantly plotting against us every extremity of evil?
If you are not convinced of this, the Lord sees it, who in time
will show himself an avenger, and satisfied with his judgment,
we are not very anxiously concerned about the opinions of the
mass of men, though we make it our study so to conduct ourselves that no one may be able with justice to condemn us. For
which reason we act towards him so that he may understand
that we are not unfriendly to him, however hostile he may be to
us; we soothe him with so much moderation that he cannot give
loose to his fury against us unless by an act of open insanity.
In our judgments I confess we differ as widely as possible from
him, for those whom he raises to the ministry of the word, we

deem very fit subjects for the gallows. And that you may know
how preposterously he acts, I will tell you that the good men
who have been approved by us, he dare not choose, unless they
have been examined by the whole class of that district for which
they are intended; but those who have by the whole class
been judged unworthy, he not only invests with ecclesiastical
functions, but cherishes as his bosom companions. Those who
have been stigmatized as Anabaptists, or detected in thefts, he
obtrudes on the unwilling brethren. In the mean time the most
pious, learned, and prudent man in this neighbourhood is called
in question by two magistrates, apprehended, vexed with more
than usual inhumanity, and treated with an extreme violence by
those two creatures of Konzen's, plying all their arts to ruin
him. What can we augur from such beginnings? While he
thinks he is getting up scourges to lash us, I suspect he is plotting his own destruction. And in sooth, if such be the will of
the Lord, may he be caught in the snare which he has set, and
fall headlong into the pit he has dug, rather than he should
create so many vexations to the church of Christ any longer.
What renders your cause so very odious to many judicious men
at Berne, is that, their pastor being sent into banishment, they
see this truculent wild beast left among them. To what purpose these complaints? you will say. To this end then, that, if it
is in your power, you diligently cast about for some remedy.
If none is within your reach, that along with us you pray the
Lord, that he would not suffer us to be driven from the right
path by these menaced terrors, but would deliver his flock from
the gluttony of beasts of prey.

And now, we think it expedient (I speak in my own name
and in that of my colleagues) to put in a word of admonition for
yourself, and we venture to take that liberty with you, trusting
to the singular moderation of your character. What we would
suggest to your consideration is this: In expounding the word
of God, and especially in those points that are so much the subject of controversy in our day, you study to soften down your
expressions, so as to give offence to as few persons as possible.
You do so, we are persuaded, with the best intentions. But this
manner of proceeding meets with our greatest disapprobation.

You know that we formerly expressed our sentiments on that subject, and now we are compelled to reiterate anew the old complaint, because we perceive that those precautions of yours to treat all things smoothly is becoming every day more hurtful. I know what you used to allege as an excuse—that the minds of the more simple are not to be alienated from religion by contentious disputes, whom it were better to attract by every means, provided they be conciliated by nothing which may not be conceded without impiety. I answer you, as I always have done, if you wish to make Christ acceptable to all, you are not, however, to construct a new gospel; and certainly it is manifest to what these things will tend. When you have heard that the invocation of the saints was devised by the superstition of men rather than founded on the word of God, you immediately add, however, we owe that deference to the authority of the holy fathers that an invocation of the kind that is recommended in their writings is not to be entirely condemned. Thus you are continually in the habit of obtruding their authority under colour of which any falsity may pass for truth.

Is it truly sanctifying God, to pay such deference to men, as that his truth should not alone bear sway over us? Does that man not sufficiently honour the fathers who conceives that they are not to be contemned, even though they are found to have erred in many things? If human wantonness cannot be restrained, but must needs go farther and farther astray when once you have given it loose reins, what moderation, pray, shall we keep, when it shall be granted that we may with impunity overstep the limits of God's word? Nor is it in one point you do that, but everywhere you seem to wish to share a kind of divided empire between Christ and the Pope. We do not say that you actually do this; we do not even suspect it. But quick-sighted people who are of a wily turn of mind fancy they can detect such a tendency, while the more simple interpreting your conduct as a retraction of the truth are thrown into terrible perplexity. You began this practice in your commentaries on the psalms, a work but for that of superlative merit, but that pious shuffling of yours, under another title, was to a certain extent overlooked, though to confess to you frankly, it always appeared to me a thing utterly intolerable that in the work in question you overturned from its foundations the doctrine of justification by faith, yet people thought they might in some measure tolerate a treasure so precious in certain respects to be disseminated over all Europe. But when your celebrated pamphlet against Cerealis began to be read, there was no pious man who did not exclaim, that it was a most unworthy thing that the gospel should be shrouded under so many enigmatical explications by such a preacher of the gospel. It is a book which no one will deny to be full of the most profound erudition, written, with exquisite art and no ordinary degree of research, but so thickly bestowed with blemishes that many people would wish them corrected by a single sweeping erasure. I doubt not but you yourself will have the same opinion when you know what fruits this book will produce in France and England. Whatever you published since has likewise an admixture of baser matter. And do not fancy that, carried away by any desire of differing with you, I am judging rather unfairly and maliciously of your writings.

The Lord is my witness that it is not with the mind alone, but with my very bowels, that I dissent as often as I see that I do not agree with pious men, and especially with you whose most excellent gifts besides your piety I cannot but cherish and look up to. But when I have brought myself to the greatest kindliness of feeling, still there are certain things which I cannot assent to without doing violence to the testimony of my conscience. And indeed, I am wont to wonder what can be your drift in this manner of acting. For while you exhort us to seek for an agreement with Luther, you attach just so much value to your advice as to affirm that nothing should appear in our eyes of greater importance, than with united minds and arms to join in battle against the falsehoods of Satan. In that moderation you are so unlike Luther, that I imagine he himself would be more gravely offended by your manner of acting, should he chance to light upon your works, than he formerly was with the opinion of Zwingli and Œcolampadius. For the most odious imputation with which he loaded the Sacramentarians was that by them justification by faith was overthrown, or certainly shaken and compromised.

These things, well beloved and most honoured brother, we jointly complain of to yourself, not without the most poignant distress, because we perceive the commencements of a mighty ruin to many, if you determine to go on as you have begun. For you know what powerful instruments for good and evil those are whom the Lord has furnished and equipped with superior learning, genius, and wisdom. Certainly you have been raised to such an eminence, and hold such a rank in the church of Christ, that most men have their eyes fixed on you. Wherefore be not surprised if we exact more rigidly a certain faultless perfection from you, than we generally do from others, since we know that you ought to march in the van, and point out the way to vast numbers. When we petty dwarfs fail in our duty, as the consequences are less disastrous, so greater indulgence is shown us. But you, from whose example much more serious evil arises, it is the duty of the church to confine by much stricter ties. May the Lord preserve you and increase in you his gifts, most worthy and dearest brother. May I beg of you to salute Capito very respectfully in my name. Farel and two of my other colleagues salute you both.—Yours,

JOHN CALVIN.

I had omitted what should not have occupied the last place in my letter. All the ministers that officiate in the churches of our neighbours, have been interdicted from having any intercourse or holding any communication whatever with us. See to what these subjects of strife lead—to nothing truly but the total ruin of the churches. But we have to thank Conzen for this good turn.

[*Lat. Copy.—Arch. Eccl. of Berne.*]

III.—To Bullinger.

An account of the conferences at Berne—Vain attempt at reconciliation between
Geneva and the exiled ministers—Sad state of this church after the banishment
of Farel and Calvin.

BASLE, *June*, 1538.

As it is not in our power to treat with you in your presence,[1]
which is what we should above all desire, we have recourse
to what next remains to us, viz: to lay before you, or at least
slightly indicate by letter, the main points of our business. You
already knew from another letter that at length on the 8th day
after our arrival at Berne, Konzen and Erasmus[2] had repaired
thither. They seemed to have been in no great hurry. We
thought they were purposely putting our patience to trial, that,
if impatient of so long a delay we had thrown up the cause, the
whole blame might with some plausibility be thrown upon us.
When their arrival was announced, we immediately as-

---

[1] This letter signed by Farel and Calvin contains a very circumstantial account of
the events which took place between their banishment from Geneva and their arrival
at Bâle. (April, May, 1538). After having appeared at the Synod of Zurich, they
repaired to Berne to confer with the ministers of that city on some points in dispute,
and lay the foundation of an ecclesiastical concord. But the conferences were without any result, notwithstanding the conciliatory spirit of which Farel and Calvin gave
proofs on this occasion, and the intervention of the Seigneurie of Berne to bring them
back to Geneva was equally unsuccessful. Calvin had already explained himself respecting the controverted points with the Bernese clergy, and had given a summary
of his opinion in a short memorial, of which the following are the principal points :
" Of the three articles of conformity which have been proposed to us, the first, which
concerns the establishment of baptismal fonts, we have already declared that we should
by no means object to, provided that in other things nothing which has been observed
hitherto respecting this rite be changed ; namely, that baptism be administered at the
hours in which the church is wont to assemble, and that the doctrine concerning it
be read from the pulpit, that it may be the more distinctly heard. 2. In the change
introduced respecting the bread we feel a little more difficulty . . . 3. Respecting
the festivals we are in very great perplexity. 4. But this appear to us the best and
most suitable manner of settling a uniformity, if the deputies of Berne openly attest
that they by no means censure the ceremonies that have hitherto been observed among
us, nor desire any innovation in them because they judge them contrary to the purity
of Scripture, but that they have in view nothing but unity and concord which are
most commonly settled on a more solid basis by a similarity of rites."

[2] Erasmus Ritter.

sembled in Konzen's house. Sebastian[1] and Erasmus were
present.   Here Konzen began with long expostulations, a
thing for which we were by no means prepared, from which
at last he made a transition to taunting insults. We on the
contrary endured that atrocity with as much good temper as
we were masters of, because we saw we should gain nothing
by greater vehemence, except to stimulate to the last degree of
phrensy a man who was already mad without any provocation.
His colleagues also assisted us in calming his transports. He
then began to ask us whether we wished him to interpose his
services in the settlement of our business. He added, as a
reason for declining this office, that he foresaw that if the affair
turned out badly he should be accused by us of bad faith ; and
when we had answered three several times that it was not our
wish to take from him the task which he had once undertaken,
in consequence of the decree of Zurich, he nevertheless kept on
repeating every now and then the same cuckoo's note. Fatigued
at last by his own violent humour, he pledged himself not to
abandon us. The following day was fixed upon for pleading
the cause. We then went up to the council house. After a
lapse of two hours, it is announced that the ministers were too
much occupied with consistorial business to have leisure to attend to us. After dinner the following day we again waited on
them, but found them then still less prepared than they had been
the day before, for, said they, they had to consider deliberately
the articles which had been submitted by us to the meeting,
but they had resolved that we should have a full and patient
hearing. Though we saw that they were acting unfairly by us,
and bore that indignity without expressing our feelings, there
was scarcely one syllable about which they did not quibble.
During the discussion of the second article, which treats of the
nature of the bread, Conzen could no longer contain himself,
but burst out into many scurrilities of which we shall mention
but one as a specimen. For he reproached all the churches of
Germany, which in other respects were tranquil, with having
been thrown into anarchy by us from an importunate affectation
of novelty. We replied that the use of leavened bread had not

[1] Sebastian the elder.

been first introduced by us, but had been adopted from the
ancient practice of the church and thus handed down by tradition. Nay even among the Papists there had existed traces of
a purer form in administering the Lord's supper, in which
leavened bread was distributed. He would listen to no reasons,
but always stormed more savagely until the others interrupted
him by the reading of the third article. Here not content with
simply bawling, he rushed down from his desk and threw his
body into so many contortions, that his colleagues had a good
deal of difficulty, and only by laying hands on him, to keep him
quiet. When he had come a little to himself, he said, that our
insupportable craftiness was apparent in this, that the whole
paper was crammed full of our objections. We replied that we
had rather studied simplicity, when before the assembly we had
simply and openly made exceptions to things which seemed ob-
jectionable.

Now only mark the impudence of the man. He did not recollect that articles had ever been drawn up by us. As we had
no witnesses to refute such evident falsehood, we said that we
appealed to the judgment of the church, that we were prepared
to submit to any degree of infamy, if all these articles were not
recognized by the totality of the assembly, according to which
Bucer had pleaded our cause, and according to which he pronounced the final sentence of the brethren, which was in perfect
harmony with the things demanded by us, and that you yourselves may be more certain about that point, we send you those
articles faithfully copied out. As he wished to convict us of
falsehood, how, said he, can you reconcile it with this sentence
of the brethren that you wish your rites to be confirmed by the
testimony of our deputation, rites which all the brethren at
Zurich disapproved of? You see, my very worthy brethren, we
had to do with one who deserves not the title of a man, much
less that of a servant of Christ, in such a manner did he exhibit
himself in so arduous a business. When we plied him with
arguments too cogent to be eluded, I know, said he, far too
well your fickleness and inconstancy, for you declared in the conference, that you had been prepared to yield to us at Lausanne
with regard to two articles, that you had resisted concerning the

third only, yet when there you were unwilling to make the slightest concession, more than beyond giving us a hearing. What then, we replied, do you not remember, that everything was transacted between us with the greatest harmony, and that the only difficulty that embarrassed us was a controversy about festival days? When he kept bawling that all that was false, we appealed to Erasmus who had been present at the conference. He indeed admitted that our statement was correct; but notwithstanding all this, Conzen could not yet be checked from proceeding with greater audacity. The deputy who had presided in the synod gave a most irrefragable testimony in our favour, and added, that he would not hesitate, if we wished it, to protest against the falsehoods of that man, even before the consistories. He nevertheless with unabashed front persisted in his denials to the last. We then left the council house without entertaining any further hopes. When we had got into the street, Sebastian asked if we thought that true which was related by certain persons; namely, that there was so much of rigid feeling in certain of the brethren that they called wolves and false prophets, the men who had crept into our places; we answered that we ourselves entertained precisely the same opinion of them. Then, said he, by a parity of reason, we shall be condemned who are settled here after the banishment of Megander. We denied that the cause was identical.[1]   And we gave reasons for not thinking more favourably of these wolves. Learn from this what a pretext he seized upon for disengaging himself from us, for the moment he heard that remark, he renounced the whole management of our cause, though previously he had solemnly promised that there was nothing he would not do for us. Erasmus alone now remained to us, who promised, however, that he would faithfully bestow all his labour on our business. But he can be of very little· service to us while he is opposed by the others. A

---

[1] Mr. Henry has appended the following note in German to the Latin text: Diese Stelle scheint Kirchhofer nicht richtig zu nehmen. Farel's Leben, i. 248: "Auch er halte sie dafur, wie diejenigen, die nach Vertreibung Meganders in Bern blieben." Sie antworten im gegentheil: "Negavimus." (Kirchhofer appears not to have rightly understood this passage, Farel's Life, i. 248: "He also held them for such, as he did those, who after the banishment of Megander remained in Berne." They answer on the contrary; "Negavimus," *we deny*.)

few days after we were admitted into the senate house and
called back three times in the course of one hour, in order that
we might recede from our articles—for we wished that by a
legitimate order, conformity should be adopted in the church.
The senate wished that we should abide by that which was
already in some sort adopted. But this conformity had been
adopted by a few seditious persons in consequence of the same
decree by which it behoved us to be flung into the Rhone. We
preferred, however, at last to stoop to any conditions rather than
occasion good men to believe that it was through our fault that
nothing had been effected. A decree of the senate was passed
that two deputies should accompany us to the fourth milestone
from Geneva, that then they should go before us into the city
to prepare the way for our return; that if they succeeded in their
mission they would conduct us into the town and procure our restitution to the ministry. Because this proposal did not give us
great satisfaction, we again asked an audience of the senate.
When this was granted, we showed them that out of their
measure would arise what we chiefly dreaded; namely, that we
should seem to be restored by having implored pardon for our
fault; we also complained that none of the ministers had been
adjoined to the embassy. A new decree of the senate was then
passed that we should be conducted straight back into the city
by the deputation, and first of all an opportunity of pleading our
cause should be obtained for us, that at length we might be duly
reinstated in our pastoral functions, if it should be made clear
that we could be charged with no delinquency. In addition to
the others, Erasmus and Viret were given to us. We were now
about a mile's distance from Geneva, when a messenger met us
who forbade our entrance. Though that was contrary to justice
and civil rights, we nevertheless complied with the advice of the
deputies, otherwise we should have gone boldly forward, if they
had not rather firmly opposed our design, and in that they had
wisely consulted for our lives. For it appeared afterwards that
at no great distance from the gates an ambush had been laid for
us, and at the gate itself twenty armed banditti were lying in
wait for us. Both the councils decided that the examination of
the affair should be left to the people. Among them Louis

Amman, one of the deputies, and Viret, who spoke in his own name and that of Erasmus, handled the cause with so much dignity, that the minds of the multitude seemed to be induced to act with fairness; until as the meeting was breaking up, one of the presidents of the council· began to read to them our articles, putting on them as invidious a construction as he could, a good many others at the same time chiming in with him. For it had been settled beforehand, that while he read they should keep raising an outcry to inflame the minds of the populace. They had only three topics to carp about to get up ill-will against us—that we called the church of Geneva ours—that we called the Bernese by their name, without prefixing to it any honorary appellation—and that we made mention of excommunication. See only, they exclaimed, how they dare to call the church theirs, as if they had already come into possession of it. See with what arrogance they despise the seigneurs themselves. See how they are aiming at a despotism. For what is their excommunication but despotic domination?

You perceive how frivolous and nugatory these calumnies are, for they had long ago admitted of excommunication, the very name of which they now shrank from with such horror. These firebrands were nevertheless able to inflame to madness the minds of all. They decreed that they would die sooner than that we should be allowed a hearing to explain the reasons of our conduct. Certain deputies had brought the articles, but with this injunction that they should not lay them before the people before we should be present, that we might have a prompt opportunity of removing any scruple, should any arise. But our friend Konzen had other designs to serve, and so he clandestinely sent those articles by a certain notorious traitor named Peter Vandel, and that you may not fancy we are grounding our assertion on obscure conjectures, we have in our hands clear proofs of his perfidy in this matter. For he and Sebastian were the only persons who had copies of them—and the fellow Vandel had vaingloriously prated to many while he was on the way, that he was the bearer of what would prove a deadly poison to us. In truth he could not dissemble the state of his feelings towards us, for in a meeting of the brethren held at Nyon, we have heard that he spoke thus: "The senate was deliberating whether I should not proceed to Geneva for the purpose of restoring those banished fellows," (so he contemptuously styled us,) "but I would rather have abdicated my ministry and retired from my country than aid those by whom I know that I was savagely defamed." This forsooth is the faith solemnly pledged to you and to the church of Christ, the power of violating which you supposed had been taken from Conzen. Now believe after the proof that it was no vain terror by which we were frightened to such a degree as scarcely to be induced even by the authority of the church to venture upon losing ourselves in this labyrinth. We have now gone through with our task.

We now think we have fully complied with your advice and that of all godly men, though we have effected nothing by it, except perhaps that the evil has broken out with twofold or threefold violence, and worse symptoms, than it did before, for though no sooner were we expelled than Satan triumphed wantonly, both there and all over France, yet the presumption both of him and his agents has been increased in no ordinary degree in consequence of that repulse. It is incredible how licentiously and insolently the ungodly there revel in every species of vice, how petulantly they insult the servants of Christ, how arrogantly they scoff at the gospel, how outrageously they exhale their fury in all ways. This calamity ought to be the more bitter to us, because, as the discipline, though very gentle of late, forced the keenest adversaries of our religion to give glory to God, so that mad license given to the perpetration of all sins, in consequence of the celebrity of the place, will be but too much remarked to the greater scorn of the gospel. Woe to him by whom such scandal has been raised—or rather woe to those who have conspired together for this accursed purpose. A good many, though they desired that we should retain our functions, yet as they could not obtain what they coveted, unless the light of truth were extinguished, did not hesitate to gratify their perverse lusts even at that price. Conzen, as he could not subvert us without the ruin of the church, did not hesitate to betray it along with us, and he fancies he has pulled down what we had built up; but we stand unshaken in the Lord, and we shall stand yet more firmly when he with the whole race of the ungodly shall perish; at present it would be better that the church should be entirely destitute of pastors than that it should be invaded by such traitors skulking under the mask of pastors. For there are two who have usurped our place, of whom one was a Franciscan monk about the beginning of the reform, and one of its bitterest enemies, until at last he contemplated Christ under the form of a woman, whom as soon as he had persuaded to live with him he corrupted by every means of seduction. Even while he continued a monk he led the most corrupted and debauched life, not only not observing the superstitious rules of his order, but not even making a show of observing them. Thus then, lest it should be thought that he is one to be justly driven from the order of bishops, he often cries out of the pulpit that a bishop is not required by St. Paul to be a man that has been blameless, but who begins to be so, as soon as he has been raised to that dignity. From the time in which he has professed to follow the gospel, he has so conducted himself as to make it evident to all that his heart is utterly void of the fear of God, and consequently of all religion. The other, though exceedingly cunning in concealing his vices, is nevertheless so remarkably and notoriously vicious that he imposes only on strangers. Both moreover are grossly ignorant and intolerably silly, not only unable to speak, but even to prate to any purpose, and yet they are puffed up with the most insolent pride. They have now connected themselves with a third, taxed not long ago with habitual fornication, and on the point of being convicted had he not escaped a condemnation by the favour of a few. Nor do they display more address in the discharge of their functions, than they did in usurping them; for they have interfered with the ministers of the whole district, partly against the wishes of some and partly against the protestations of others, though in that they make evident rather their quality of hirelings than of servants of Christ. But nothing grieves us more than that by their ignorance, their levity, and their stupidity, the ministry is prostituted and brought into contempt. Not a day passes in which some blunder of theirs is not plainly remarked either by men or women, sometimes even by children. But my letter is plucked from my hands by the hurry of the messenger.

Farewell then, well beloved and most honoured brethren, and with serious prayers call upon the Lord that he may speedily arise.—Your affectionate brethren,

FAREL AND CALVIN.

These words in the writing of Calvin.

We beseech you, brethren, beware lest the publicity given to this letter should bring us into trouble. For we confide matters more unreservedly to your bosom than we should relate them to men in general. Remember then that these things are entrusted confidentially to your good faith.

[*Lat. Copy.—Arch. Eccl. of Berne.*]

IV.—To ZEBEDEE.[1]

Pressing invitations to concord—Apology for Bucer—Judgment respecting Zwingli, Luther, Carlostadt—Necessity of union.

STRASBOURG, 19*th May*, 1539.

Your letter gave me uneasiness for other reasons, but greatly agitated my mind, because I see that you still entertain so great an aversion to the agreement which I imagined had been duly established in your parts. As you do not seem, however, to have taken up your views of the subject without some reasons, I shall first endeavour to satisfy you as well as I can respecting the things which you object to, then I shall slightly touch on the cause itself. You say that those men whose talents and) hearts I so highly commend, have diminished their own authority among most persons whom you know, both men of small and of great importance. I confess it indeed. But whose fault is it? "I wish it were not their own," you say.

[1] John Calvin to Zebedee, faithful minister of the Church of Orbe. André Zebedee, minister of the Church of Orbe, " a red-haired and very haughty man," says an ancient chronicle of this town, after having long kept up a friendly intercourse with Calvin became at a later period one of his most violent adversaries. See vol.

Take care, lest you do injustice to the servants of Christ, whom you suspect so maliciously when they themselves have given you no grounds for doing so. Bucer conducted himself in such a manner in the affair of the agreement, that while many exclaim that his actions displease them, no one can point out the slightest point in which he did wrong. I know what complaints are everywhere heard about him among those who cry out against the agreement. But if you examine a little more closely, it will be clear to you that they are mere invectives. If we condemn, with so much facility, a man endowed with so many excellent gifts, and whose services the Lord has made use of for such excellent things, what, pray, shall we say of those who have hitherto approved themselves by no notable action? But should you persist in flattering yourself by depreciating men who do not deserve it, you shall never, for all that, persuade me not to feel and declare those to be sincere men whose sincerity I see with my eyes. It is to no purpose you recur to that commonplace remark, we should not from admiration of men let ourselves be led away from the certain truth of religion. For I am not enslaved by so preposterous and blind an admiration of any man, as to be detached by it from a sound judgment, much less from the authority of the faith; and I know that Farel has too much firmness to leave me any room for fearing that he could in this manner be turned aside from the word of God. But as I know that all who stand up for the opinions of Luther are suspected of too much wiliness by the men of our party, I was unwilling to allow Farel to be tormented by a needless mistrust. But to what purpose dread the astuteness of that man of whose candour you can be assured? I shall not cease then loudly to proclaim that virtue which I think I perceive in Melanchthon. Meanwhile there are certain things in which I myself confess him to be deficient, so far am I from wishing to subject any one to his opinions. For this is my purpose, that banishing all suspicions which are an obstacle to us, we should confidingly on the one side and the other listen to each other's reasons, reserving for our own judgment the question itself intact till the truth be discovered. I know that there is an immense fear of the Gorgon as far as Bucer is concerned. But it vexes you, that he has overthrown a doctrine, which lately (1537, Sept.), was so well established there, and you think it to be the more dishonourable, that he himself should bring into doubt a doctrine, which formerly he defended with the greatest firmness against most obstinate opponents. What kind of a truth it is we are wavering in, I do not perceive; but I venture to say, that we perfectly and firmly agree with Bucer, so that no part of sound doctrine is abandoned by us. What is there repugnant to the plain meaning of the Scripture in the formula I drew up some time ago? What is there in my articles, which could in any way give you offence? Nevertheless nothing prevents an agreement, but that those men, who wish to appear very conservative, entirely reject this doctrine. If we think that Martin dissembles, why do we not thoroughly draw him out? Let us simply assent to the teaching of the Scripture, and we shall either win him over, with or against his will, to the light; or he certainly will not be able to use evasion, but will disclose whatever poison may be in his heart. But since we have not fully found out his opinion, we even shrink from confessing the truth, lest we may seem to assent to his views. What harm could result from drawing up a clear confession of the participation of the body and blood of the Lord, which is the privilege of the faithful in the holy supper? Surely Martin would be compelled to accept it, or we would justly bid him farewell. You have no cause to take so great offence at the retractations of Bucer. Since his teaching concerning the use of the sacraments was erroneous, he justly retracted it. I would that Zwingli had made up his mind to do the same. For his opinion on this subject was both wrong and pernicious. When I saw that our friends eagerly accepted it with great applause, I did not hesitate to oppose it, while I was still working in France. I confess, he (Bucer) commits a mistake by endeavouring to soften the sentiments of Œcolampadius and Zwingli, because he makes them almost agree with Luther. But those men, who most spitefully censure him in every other respect, do not blame him for this. For they have nothing more at heart, but that Zwingli should remain untouched. But I wish, that they would cease to defend him so urgently, and would with singleness of mind give glory to God by a bare confession of the truth. I am very far from conceding to you that there was no rigidity in the doctrine of Zwingli. Indeed one can see at a glance that, too much absorbed with overturning the superstition of a carnal presence, he at the same time set aside the true efficacy of our participation, or at least threw an obscurity over it. So that what we required was that greater light should have been thrown on that point. You have reason to be offended that Luther retracts nothing, palliates nothing, but stubbornly maintains all his opinions.

But what could Bucer do? He might have waited, you will say. But it was better by his example to incite Luther and others to their duty. To what end that holy obtestation? For after he had retracted his own errors, he also adjures them in God's name to correct in their turn whatever mistakes they have committed. What Luther's book against the Arians contains, I know not, except that from the title I guess the main points of the subject. If in handling it he has given Carlostadt a good drubbing, it is not without reason. Wherefore they cannot feel wroth with him, except that it is matter of sorrow that by the unnecessary ripping up of old quarrels, minds should be exasperated. It is more certain than certainty itself, that the Church of Wittemberg has been pestered with that foolish dogma by Carlostadt. We have not Bucer's Latin book. If such are their acts of conciliation it is with reason they displease you, and I should not consider them in a more favourable light if I saw them. But it does not follow that every difference of opinion should immediately break out into an open rupture. Wherefore, though your conscience compel you to oppose in some respects his opinion, it is your duty to do your endeavour that the fraternal union between you and him be maintained. For it behoves us not rashly to break up our connection with those whom the Lord has joined with us in the fellowship of his work. And this alone I ask of you, that you constantly retain that faith in which you have hitherto stood, but in such a manner as that you may not appear of your own free will to seek

for a rupture with those to whom you cannot refuse the right
of being esteemed both by you and all pious men as among the
leading servants of Christ. Good God, to what a point have we
come. We ought to consider a separation from the ministers of
Christ, with the same disposition as if our own bowels were torn
out. Now it is almost a sort of sport not only to cut off certain
members, but to retrench the most vital parts from their connection with us. These things, as I have thrown them together
at random and without any arrangement, you will reflect on,
and endure patiently the just liberty I have taken. Moreover
you have no occasion to be under any apprehensions from me.
The things you have written I will keep by me as religiously as
I should wish them to be kept, if it were my own life that was
at stake.

[*Lat. Copy.—Arch. Eccl. of Berne.*]

V.—To Viret.

Tragical death of one of the chiefs of the Libertine party at Geneva—Discourse pronounced by Calvin on this occasion.

GENEVA, 14th *November*, 1546.

I thought I had sent word to some one or other to give you
an oral account of the story which you now require me to write
to you about. Well then, as you wish to know the matter more
thoroughly, here it is in a few words. When our brother Raymond said he had heard something about the horrid end of an
impious man, the matter seemed to deserve to be investigated by
the magistrate. By the orders of my brethren then I presented
myself before the senate. I showed them that it was of much
importance that some inquiry should be set on foot, while it was
yet possible to have the matter thoroughly sifted, for it was impossible that the rumour should not be speedily and widely
spread; so that, if it were a fable, it should be confuted by public
authority, but if what was reported should be found true, that
such a judgment of God ought not to be buried in oblivion; that
I had already seen very many who passed it off as a joke. But
I reminded them that there never had existed any miracle, even
the most evident, over which Satan did not attempt to cast a
mist; that not even when Korah, Dathan, and Abiram had been
swallowed up, had the hand of God been recognized. I made a
tolerably long speech. It was decreed that for the present
matter [1] . . . The four Syndics were present and the greater
part of the council, the burgomaster also with his suite. My
colleagues too assisted. There was a small cottage in a field
where his wife and four children had died of the plague. He had
been, all his life, a criminal and profligate man, a haunter of
taverns, a drunkard, a brawler, much addicted to profane swear-
ing, in a word, one of the most notorious despisers of God.
When his neighbours reproved him because he went so seldom to
church, he was in the habit of saying, as we heard, " What ?

---

[1] Something is here a wanting in the manuscript.

Have I hired myself to Calvin that I should go to hear him
talk?" Admonished by Ferron respecting his disgraceful life,
he showed no signs of repentance.

A short time before he fell ill, Raymond sharply rebuked
him, as was his duty, for having shamefully abandoned his wife.
He wickedly took occasion, from the contagious nature of the
disease, to indulge in slanderous remarks. After having lost his
children, he was himself attacked by the malady, and was now so
completely debilitated that he could scarcely lift his hand, when
he was suddenly seized one night with an inflammation of the
brain. He sprang out of bed. His mother and his wife, who
were watching by his bed-side, retained him. He chattered of
nothing but devils, that he was a man past all hope, that he
was a prey due to the devil. When he was admonished to pray
to God, he replied that this would be of no service to him, because he was already awarded to the devils, that he cared no
more for God than for the sole of a torn shoe. These were his
very words, as his mother and the maid servant testified. After
sun rise about seven o'clock in the morning, while he was reposing in bed, his mother was seated near the door. He rushed out,
passing over her head like a whirlwind. Both the women strove
to retain him, but he flew off to a great distance with so violent
an impetus, that he appeared to be carried off, not to run of his
own accord. There is in that part of the field through which
he rushed a very thick quick-set hedge. The place was pointed
out to us. Even if the ground were level on each side of the
hedge, there is no one, however vigorous he might be, who could
have crossed it at a leap without leaving some traces of his passage, but on the other side there is the high parapet of a haha.
At the bottom of this parapet there is a stony and rugged path
like that down which rush summer torrents. Over against this
place, but at a considerable distance from it, there is a parapet
similar to the first mentioned, which has also a thick and prickly
hedge. When there was no possibility of springing through
this hedge without tearing all one's limbs, and on the opposite
side there appeared no path leading upwards, in the sight of the
women he was whisked away like a hurricane into a vineyard
beyond that. With their finger they pointed out the place from

a distance where he vanished from their sight. His hat was found in that place by the bank of the Rhone. Boatmen were sent to look for the corpse; they lost their pains, and from that place he could not have reached the Rhone without being carried headlong down.

In a matter so very evident, there were nevertheless some of the principal persons who impudently endeavoured to explain away what was miraculous in it. I then exclaimed in a loud voice, "If you believe that there are any devils at all, here you clearly perceive the agency of the devil. Those who have no faith in God deserve to stumble in darkness in open day." As the Sabbath came round two days afterwards, by the advice of my brethren I handled the subject in my sermon, and sharply inveighed against those who treated a thing so convincingly proved as a fable, or who at least feigned so to treat it. Nay, in my warmth I was carried so far as to assert that during those two days, I more than twenty times with ardent wishes invoked death because I saw men of such hardened effrontery in contemplating the judgments of God. For now the impiety of our citizens was made more evident than it ever had been before. Only a few agreed with us in words; I know not if even one believed me in his heart. I added two other incidents that had taken place; not so striking, but which were still worthy of being mentioned.

An individual during the time of sermon on the Lord's day went into a wine shop to drink; by chance he fell on his sword that had slipped out of its scabbard and was carried out in a dying state. Another in the month of September last, on a day in which the sacrament of the Lord's supper was administered, as he was secretly attempting while intoxicated to creep through a window to get to a strumpet, had his bones broken in several places by a terrible fall. At last I said in conclusion, "Till hell swallow you up with all your houses, you will not give faith to God when he stretches forth his hand." I perceived that my zeal gave no great pleasure to a good many, because they would not be willingly wakened from their lethargy. For you can scarcely believe how torpid the conscience of many is, who seem puffed up to the skies. The greater part of them fear disgrace

to the city; a few of them, to our doctrine; but all of them quite
foolishly.   For what more glorious for us than this notable
vengeance of God against the despisers of our doctrine ?   And
what have the Papists to insult the Genevese with, if God thus
guards against contempt the doctrine which they profess ?   But
as I was saying, this place deserves that God should signalize it
more than others by remarkable instances of his judgment.   I
have not said much, and yet I have gone farther than I wished.

There is at my house a pious and learned brother, who was
minded to go to Strasbourg, to spend there a couple of years in
study, and afterwards come back here that he might give himself up to the ministry.   He has a brother tolerably rich, who
had promised to defray his expenses during three years.   But
he disappointed him at last.   Thus the good man, left destitute,
was looking about for what he should do.   Because I had the
best testimony respecting him from all good men, and because
he was personally known to me, I have taken him to my house,
where his table and lodging cost him nothing, till some situation
cast up for him.   Not to be burdensome to me, he asked me for
a recommendation to you, but I put him in mind that we should
watch for a suitable opportunity.   I therefore beseech you again
and again, if you shall happen to get rid of some of your teachers,
that you will let me know of it.   For this man deserves that we
should interest ourselves in his behalf.   If I did not think that
he would be a worthy minister of Christ, I should not busy myself about him, though, as it is, I am consulting the advantage of
the church as well as that of the man.   You too will never repent of having seconded us.   The brothers of Farel are here.
In what concerns himself, may God perfect what has been so
happily begun.   With regard to the man I have spoken of, I am
afraid of but one thing, that is, that he may be a little too
despotic, having once been set over children, but it will be your
business to moderate him.   You must be very cautious in
choosing a successor at Neuchatel, lest the brethren should be
too morose.   As far as I could divine, Thomas is not exceedingly well pleased that people's minds were so much alienated
from him.   Do you prudently try to meet the dangers.

Farewell, with your brethren and friends, whom you will

salute in my name. My colleagues salute you and them. My wife also. May the Lord preserve you and govern you by his Spirit. Amen.—Yours,

JOHN CALVIN.

[*Lat. Copy.—Library of Geneva.* Vol. 111.]

VI.—TO VIRET.[1]

Mention of Servetus—Marriage of the minister Merlin—Epistolary vexations.

1st September, 1548.

I think you must have read by this time the answers I made to Servetus. At length I have resolved not to contend any longer with the incorrigible obstinacy of a heretical man. And in sooth we must comply with what Paul mentions, but at present he attacks you. You will consider how far you ought to insist upon refuting his ravings. He shall not henceforth wring one word from me. For our friend Merlin I should wish a wife of distinguished merit, but when I look all about me I can scarcely find one that I dare venture to betroth him to, according to my hopes and wishes. If it were convenient for him under any other pretext to undertake a journey hither, he might himself look out better; he would then consult with me and confide to me with security and familiarity his ideas on that subject. Perhaps we might thus hit on some expedient. This seems to me the best method of proceeding.

The day before your letter to Martyr was delivered me, Dumoulin had left this town. A messenger to convey it back did not immediately present himself. If the seal is broken up, it is from inattention, for when I was tumbling over a mass of letters confusedly heaped up on my table at the time I was about to write an answer to you, fancying this to be one of those that were written to me I opened it. I had not perused a line

<hr>

Independently of the painful interest which is attached to the name of Servetus, this letter shows what minute precautions Calvin and Viret were obliged to take in carrying on their familiar correspondence, of which the effusions were incessantly maliciously interpreted both at Berne and Geneva. See vol. ii. p. 176.

of it before I perceived my mistake. This at least I have gained by my heedlessness, I perceived that I have been more indulgent in bearing testimony.

The flying rumours that are spread about respecting our letters among the evil disposed savour of their old worn out malice, so that it seems that those who would like to do a great deal of mischief, either do not dare, or as yet, are but ill-prepared for the onset. Relying on a good conscience I fear no attack. For what worse than death can they threaten? And yet if the minds of the Bernese shall at length be somewhat mitigated towards you, as Christopher gave me some reason to hope, you will perhaps be able to draw something from them, as it were by chance. What if either of us should attempt it through Zerkint? Reflect if that will not be more expedient. Respecting Guillaume's business, Allen and St. Privat will bring back word what has been resolved. Both willingly offer their services, and yet should the affair get wind I shall scarcely be able to persuade them to do so at this time. You will assist Allen with your recommendation, if by chance he should judge it necessary to go to Berne. I have collected into a parcel all the letters I have had from you, that you yourself in reading them over may signalize by a certain mark whatever things in them may seem to you to expose you to danger. Those which shall be so marked, keep by you in a place of safety. I will do the same thing by my own the moment I receive them from you.

Farewell, most worthy brother and friend. May the Lord preserve you, and ever accompany you with his grace. Amen. Carefully salute your wife and your colleague in my name. My wife also salutes you all, and commends herself to your prayers.

[*Lat. Orig.—Library of Geneva.* Vol. 111 a.]

VII.—To Brentz.[1]

Message of consolation and fraternal sympathy.

GENEVA, 5th November, 1548.

If anything could afford me pleasure in these unhappy times, your very affectionate and interesting letter would certainly have done so. Most grateful indeed it was, and furnished me with much consolation under my various sorrows, since it let me know that you, about whose life all good men had been so long in anxious suspense, had been rescued, as it were, from the jaws of death. And though in the present posture of affairs, life cannot but seem bitter to you, when you reflect that you have been torn from the church which you had begotten in Christ, and trained up with such anxious care, and which now deprived of its pastor, you perceive to be in a manner exposed to the unbridled caprice of Satan; nevertheless, you should bear in mind at the same time, that it is not without some special design, that your life has been preserved by the Lord. Though you still enjoy a green old age, you would have gone down to the tomb full of years. And in truth what is there in this world at present which should render us very solicitous about living? I am convinced then that God, who has hitherto so happily made use of your ministry for the edification of his church, and crowned it with such abundant fruits, has yet in reserve for you some work to us unknown, in which he wills still further to exercise you. Not that we have any prospect, at least, any im-

---

[1] Compelled to exile himself from Wurtemburg, after the proclamation of the *Interim*, Brentz, who had taken so great a part in the reformation of this country, had withdrawn to Bâle, where he waited for better days. In a letter to Calvin, of the 6th October, 1548, he expressed his regrets and sorrow: "And though I have found here all sorts of advantages—hospitality, a charming city, the friendly feelings of the inhabitants, intercourse with learned men, and, what delights me most of all, the courteous kindness of the ministers of the Gospel; yet when I call to mind the desolate state of the church, the abandonment of my own family, and the dangers which seem impending over other churches and their ministers, you yourself can easily imagine that no charm in external things is so great as to afford me pleasure in such a conjuncture."

mediate one of a better state of things. On the contrary, wherever we turn our eyes, the symptoms of fresh evils manifest themselves so clearly, that the final ruin of the church seems inevitable. And then, as our own impiety and ingratitude have been the primary causes of these evils, so our contumacy carries us headlong to such a degree, that more numerous and more terrible misfortunes than any we have hitherto experienced, are justly to be apprehended. One thought there is, however, which enables me to bear up, and revives my courage; it is when I reflect in my own mind that God would never have permitted this marvellous restoration of the church to proceed so far, merely to have inspired a fallacious hope, destined to vanish immediately away; but that he has undertaken a work, which not only in spite of Satan, but also notwithstanding all the malicious opposition of men, he will defend and establish. Meanwhile let us patiently endure the purgation of which we stand in need. Should the fury of the lion once be fairly let loose on us, we shall be far more cruelly handled. Assuredly up to the present time he has rather terrified us with threats, than ferociously assailed us. But he will give way to the rage which he has as yet curbed as soon as he shall see all the obstacles to his designs removed. It is for that reason we should be as fully prepared as if the unsheathed sword were already over our necks, and the fires lighted to consume us. But, as I said, I feel convinced that some limits will be set to our chastisement, and God will speedily re-assemble his church, after this most wretched dispersion. One thing I fear is, that he will severely avenge the disgraceful supineness of Germany, as well as its impious perfidiousness. But as he must recognize that many poor harmless sheep had been betrayed by the sturdier goats, he will, I trust, in his mercy, take into consideration the condition of the former, so as to mitigate his just indignation. Here having no other means of testifying our sympathy, we are unceasingly mindful of you and such as you in our prayers; would that we could aid you by other services. Thus, then, first of all, with one accord, we suppliantly entreat God, if, offended by our transgressions, he has given loose reins for a season to the cruelty of the ungodly, that in turn provoked by the scoffings and frowardness of these wicked men, he would again look with compassion on his own cause and that of his children; next we implore Jesus Christ not only to be our intercessor with the Father, but also to show himself the just avenger of his church.

Farewell, most distinguished sir, and my very honoured brother in the Lord. May the Lord whom you serve continue to govern you by his Spirit, and bless all your holy labours.

[*Calvin's Lat. Corresp.* Opera, ix. p. 47.]

VIII.—TO AMBROSE BLAURER.[1]

Sends him divers works—News of Italy—Belgium and France—Disturbances in Germany—Chastisement of Constance.

GENEVA, 14*th February,* 1552. (5 o'clock P. M.)

If I have delayed rather too long in answering your letter, my most worthy and much respected brother, it is the fault of Michael Muller, who every day on the point of setting out has kept me in suspense for upwards of a month and a half.

Yesterday, as I was proceeding to church to deliver a lecture, a boy put your letter into my hands. Three hours afterwards about supper time, I called at the inn, but the courier was not there. About midnight I was seized with a violent megrim, a complaint to which I am but too subject. To-day after sermon till midday I kept my bed. After that I had to lecture, and now having come back, I shall write to you very briefly, for I

---

[1] "A most excellent servant of our Lord Jesus Christ, faithful pastor of the church of Bienne, my very dear friend, and honoured fellow minister."

Banished from Constance, his native town, where the Catholic worship had been re-established by the Imperialists, Blaurer had found an asylum at Bienne. His brother Thomas, driven into exile like himself, wrote to Calvin, "I recommend to you my brother Ambrose now at Bienne, serving the Lord, and at no great distance from your church." 22nd October, 1551. By a letter written some time afterwards, 3rd of December of the same year, Ambrose Blaurer asked Calvin for some of his writings. This was the origin of the most affectionate intercourse between the proscribed minister and the Reformer.

have but little time before me. I am exhausted by my illness
and still feel a little inclined to be lazy. The courier will also
leave this to-morrow, as I have been told, for he was never to
be found at his inn. So I could not saddle him with my commentary on John as you desired. By the inscription you will
perceive that I had already destined it as a present to you. I
have added four sermons along with an exposition of one Psalm.
For the four copies of the treatise on predestination with the
answer of Etienne, I have reminded the servant that he is to
receive only as much as he paid to the bookseller. Our fellow
citizens occasion us much concern, inasmuch as nothing can exceed the disorder of this republic, and the church of God here is
tossed about by conflicting waves, like Noah's ark by the waters
of the deluge. But notwithstanding all that, such is the nature
of the commotion that it not only does not weaken the faith of
pious men, but does not even agitate their minds more than if
they were riding quietly at anchor in a secure harbour. And
assuredly in whatever corner of the world the sons of God now
take up their habitation, it is necessary for them to be fortified
by a rare constancy against the storms that are everywhere
raging. The emperor is at present carrying on war against the
people of Sienna with immense preparations. He has also a
second army in Piedmont, and is himself in Belgium re-assem-
bling fresh forces, that he may make a new incursion into
Picardy. France is everywhere collecting what troops and
money she can. I cannot easily divine what will be the issue
of the convulsions in Germany, and yet the obstinacy of the
Count of Mansfeld in carrying on the war is astonishing, since
even during the severe cold of the inclement climate of Saxony,
he continued the campaign during the whole winter.

In the mean time your wretched fellow-townsmen, the inhabitants of Constance, not only freely indulge themselves, but revel
in their wantonness. A terrible vengeance of God no doubt!
For it is very evident that God thus punishes their impious contempt of his doctrine, by giving them up to that brutal intem-
perance as to a spirit of giddiness and folly. And though I
am aware it is a sad and bitter thing for you to hear what you
write to me about the blindness of your native place, yet this

one reflection ought to afford you no small consolation, that God in this manner sets his seal upon your ministry, which was by them at that time so unworthily despised.[1]

It was my wish to lengthen out my letter a little more, but you must pardon my brevity for I can stand this long fasting no longer. Farewell, most accomplished man and honoured brother. My colleagues and many godly men salute you; will you, in your turn, salute very cordially for me, our brother Justin? May the Lord preserve you and your Church, watch over you, govern you by his Spirit, and bless your holy labour. From the whole heart—Yours,

JOHN CALVIN.

[*Lat. Orig. Library of Munich, Coll. Cameriana*, viii. p. 164.]

IX.—TO FRANCIS DRYANDER.[2]

Consultation on the subject of a new edition of the Bible—Troubles in Geneva—
Apology of Calvin for himself.

GENEVA, November, 1552.

If my delay in replying to you hitherto has given you offence, I should not be surprised at it, for though you make me no reproach, yet I cannot conceal from myself that I ought to blush for my too prolonged silence. One thing only I beg of you, which is that you will not suppose me to be so indolent nor so unpolite as to have neglected a friendly office which is due

---

[1] It is to this apostasy of Constance, of which he had been the reformer, that Blaurer alludes in a letter to Calvin, in which we read these words : " Unhappy that I am, who survive my country, which, though still alive, is virtually dead." MSS. of Geneva.

[2] See the note Vol. I. p. 3. It appears that independently of his translation of the New Testament into Spanish, Francis Dryander had undertaken immense labours on the Scriptures. " If God permit, I should wish to publish before my death the books of the Bible, upon which I have bestowed all my pains during fifteen years." This wish expressed in one of his letters to Calvin (Oct. 1552) was not realized. But Dryander nevertheless deserves a place among the propagators of the Reformation in Spain.

both to yourself and your pious wish, had an opportunity and the means of performing it presented themselves. But seldom, as far as I know in these unpropitious times, do any persons go from this place to your country to whom I might venture to entrust a letter. Besides these causes of delay, the penury of such matters as I should have wished to write upon, checked my desire to send you a very speedy answer. I have had a conference with eight more of my friends respecting the business of which you sent me word. Stephen Tremuleius still abides by his resolution. The others I found not quite so well disposed: some, because there are few at the present moment who can readily lay their hands upon their funds, having invested their money in other transactions; others, because they fancy that it would be a tedious and difficult matter to dispose of all the copies of such an edition; and others again there are who apprehend that the sale of the volumes would not cover the expenses which the publication of so extensive a work necessarily requires, even if it went off more rapidly than they have any reason to expect. For they imagine, as you yourself informed us by letter, that it is now a long time since you first undertook your task. They foresee how much your journey here will cost, and how expensive the correction of the press will be, especially as you are resolved to send to Paris for an assistant to superintend the impression. They conjecture, too, that you will not have many purchasers, because most of them will be deterred by the enormity of the price. Besides they are afraid of envy and unfavourable reports. I see, moreover, that the subsidiary and casual expenses which I spoke of never enter into their calculations. In the mean time, if they are called upon for anything which they imagine to be beyond what is just and moderate, they in their ignorance complain of it and set it down to the account of extortion. I am myself, too, of such a character that I dare not press them more sharply. Now in matters of so doubtful a character, and which afford so small a prospect of success (at least much smaller than I could have wished), I am at a loss what advice to give you. I have no need, however, to employ many words to prove that I have the greatest inclination to be of use to you, should an opportunity

of showing it occur, and that too not only for the sake of the
public good, which should always be a primary consideration,
but also because I am extremely grieved to see you living in
perpetual fear and amid various perils. Though when I look
around me and see from what quarter storms arise and where
they alight, I come to the conclusion that no where in this
world is to be found a harbour of undisturbed and lasting tranquillity. Certainly as matters stand here we are not far from
the range of hostile missiles; at least we stand in almost equal
jeopardy. But know that I have been so long inured to the
intestine strife of which rumours, as you write to me, have reached
you, that they find me quite callous. Still I take it kindly of
you to exhort me to moderation, for I have learned by long experience how difficult it is to preserve a just measure when
people have once come to wrangling. They are on a dangerous
descent on which they are very liable to be carried away by
passion. I am perfectly aware also that my own temper is
naturally inclined to be rather violent. Here, however, we
have competent judges who according to circumstances are in a
better position to pronounce what measures are to be considered as
excessive, and what tempered by a proper degree of moderation.
But you would be surprised, I dare say, did you hear, that in
all these turmoils I have been as unruffled as those who pass
for men of a sluggish and phlegmatic temperament.

After the condemnation of that monk, who had been let loose
on us from among the creatures of M. de Tralais,[1] a brawling
fellow suddenly sprung up who having clandestinely fomented
intrigues, went about incessantly repeating not only in private
houses, but up and down in taverns, that we had made God the
author of sin.[2] In other respects, too, he most contumaciously
traduced our ministry. When I perceived that these foul calumnies were everywhere disseminated, by means of which ungodly
men were openly plotting to overthrow the whole kingdom of
Christ in this city, I mildly admonished the people to be on
their guard against these men. I also pointed out to the senate
the danger of temporising amid such dissensions. Those who
had instigated him for the purpose of molesting me, spun out

[1] See Vol. II., pp. 322, 381.   [2] *Ibidem*, p. 363.

the affair in such a manner by their intrigues that for three
months they kept me in uncertainty. For among the judges
there were several supporters of the adverse party. But of the
numerous injuries I had to endure none was so bitter and cruel
to me as to see myself dragged into an invidious disagreement
with Melancthon, from which, however, I so dexterously disengaged myself, that during the whole proceding I continued to
say nothing but what was to the honour of so great a man.
The whole faction seeing themselves completely baffled, kindled
a new conflagration for the purpose of extinguishing the former
one. Three abandoned scoundrels, of the principal families of
the city, however, having contumeliously attacked our brother
Raymond, at last proceeded to such extremities as to throw the
ecclesiastical meeting for that day into utter confusion. We
came to an unanimous decision that our complaint should be
laid before the senate. When they had been thus condemned
by a judgment of the elders, one of them for the sake of trying
my firmness or my influence, presented a child for baptism. I
refused to inscribe the name of his sponsor. All of them began
to vociferate that there was a manifest conspiracy. Meanwhile
amid a horrid din, outcries, abusive language, and threats, I
maintained such empire over my temper that not one word
dropped from me that betrayed the least agitation. Were you
well acquainted with the present state of affairs here, you would
say that it is only by the marvellous wisdom of the Lord, that
swords have not been drawn a hundred times, especially as those
who had the greatest influence were provoked so often and in
so infamous a manner. First of all the man who had atrociously attacked my doctrine, and profanely traduced my whole
ministry, has escaped with impunity, though it was in my power
to crush him completely. I deemed it sufficient that the senate
should pronounce an opinion on the matter in dispute, without
any regard to the persons that had agitated it, so that others
might willingly return to fellowship with us. But it is better
to suffer a hundred deaths, rather than swerve a hair's breadth
from the straight line.

Farel and Viret were here ten whole days; they will bear
ample testimony, I trust, to my forbearance; for they saw how

many tragical matters that referred to ourselves alone, we passed
over in silence, what affronts we quietly devoured, how many
offences we pardoned, but there are many things, at which if I
should connive, I should perfidiously betray both Christ and the
flock which he has committed to my charge. So then you have
no occasion to feel any uneasiness on my account, when you
shall hear in future that I am engaged in controversies. One
thing, however, I entreat of you is that you would not deem me
so fond of power, as willingly to bring enemies and contentions
upon my head. Certainly nothing could be dearer to me than
tranquillity and lettered ease, did He under whose banner I do
battle, grant me such an indulgence; but I candidly confess to
you that I felt considerable surprise when you proposed Hedio,[1]
of all persons, as one whose example I ought to imitate. This
want of due discrimination in the choice of your model, is the
reason why you do not convince me that I ought to act in the
manner you recommend.[2]   *   *   *   *

[*Lat. Orig. Library of Geneva.*   Vol. 107, *a.*]

X. To Farel.

Misunderstanding between Farel and his colleague Christopher Fabri—Attempt to reconcile them.

GENEVA, 19*th July*, 1553.

I wish, my dear Farel, I could find a better remedy for your
evils than that which I here think of offering you. But as you
yourself are well aware that there are many things which we
must endure, because it is not in our power to correct them, I
shall not spend many words in exhorting you to show yourself
gentle and moderate, in a contest which is evidently not embittered by personal hostility; if, indeed, that should be called a
contest in which your colleague differs from you, without any

---

[1] Hedio, a minister and theologian of Strasbourg, died in 1552. A lover of ease, he
always kept aloof from the strifes and disputes of his time.

[2] The end is wanting. See the Letter to Nicolas Zerkinden. Vol. III., p. 428.

malevolent feeling, or desire to breed disturbances. In what
points I think him defective, as you yourself are my best authority on that subject, I shall for the moment forbear to mention; but one thing we know that the man is pious and zealous
in the discharge of his duty. Add to that—he loves you—is
anxious to have your approbation, and both considers and respects you as a parent. Now if he sometimes carries himself
rather more frowardly than he ought, the chief cause of such
conduct appears to me to be this: he fancies that you are too
rigid and morose, and so he aims at a certain popularity which
may smooth down offences. Thus the good man, while he is
consulting your tranquillity, and guarding against ill will, which
he believes neither of you can stand against, forgets the firmness and dignity which should belong to a minister of Christ;
and while he imposes on you the necessity of resisting him, he
furnishes the gainsayers with arms to assail your common ministry. I see how vexatious and provoking a proceeding this is,
nor am I ignorant how much blame his fault deserves. But
your own prudence and love of fair dealing will suggest to you
that you ought on the other hand to number up the good qualities which counterbalance his defects. If he is carried away
by an overwhelming self-confidence, you know that there is in
it not one particle of rankling malice; if he is chargeable with
obstinacy, nothing was ever farther from his thoughts than to
breed disturbances in the Church, or gain a triumph for himself,
by bringing his brethren into contempt. Then why not show
indulgence to his imprudence? You bore with Chaponneau,
not only a man of no mark, but one who seemed born for
kindling strife; who with his foolish arrogance trampled upon
all order in the Church; who with his malignant cavils impudently sought to overturn whatever had been duly and orderly
arranged; who was urged on to do mischief by some fatal genius,
as well as by his own rabid instincts; and who with premeditated
purpose set all the factions on to plot the ruin of the Church.
With how much greater reason, then, should you strive to foster
peace with a man who both desires faithfully to serve the Lord
along with you, and abhors all rancorous dissensions! But you

are bound not only to maintain peace with him, but to cultivate friendship also.

For if you bear in mind how few tolerably good ministers we have in the present day, you will be on your guard how you slight a man who is both honest and diligent, endowed, moreover, with other most estimable gifts. And as it will be expedient to bury in silence any little angry feeling you may have hitherto conceived against him, so also it will be better in future to remonstrate frankly with him, should he give you any grounds for offence; provided always such remonstrances do not break out into an open rupture. Let him only feel that you love him, and I answer for it, you will find him tolerably docile.

Last Sabbath a merchant was burned at Lyons, who marched to execution with astonishing firmness and no less moderation. His relations and fellow-townsmen attempted by all the motives they could suggest to urge him to a recantation. His mother flung herself three times at his feet, and with tears most suppliantly entreated him to spare his own life, but to no purpose. The storm of persecution is everywhere raging in France. In the Beauce it is the nobility who are chiefly molested.

Farewell, most upright and esteemed brother. May the Lord continue to direct you by his Spirit, and long preserve you in safety. Salute your brother and friends.

[*Lat. Copy.—Library of Geneva.* Vol. 111.]

XI.—To Christopher Piperin.

Trials and tribulations of Calvin at Geneva.

Geneva, 18*th October,* 1555.

It is true, my dear Piperin, when I hear that I am everywhere so foully defamed, I have not such iron nerves as not to be stung with sorrow. But it is no slight consolation to me that yourself and many other servants of Christ and pious worshippers of God sympathize with me in my wrongs. And yet if it were possible, I had rather devour in silence whatever insults are heaped upon me, that no portion of my annoyances should extend to my brethren. This it is, among other reasons, which makes me pass by, without notice, calumnies, which it would be very easy for me to refute, and which I should wish to shake off. For why should I worry honest people with my zeal for vindicating my own reputation? Did there exist a greater necessity for it, having entreated their indulgence, I should lay my defence before them. But the scurrilous calumnies with which malignant men bespatter me, are too unfounded and too silly to require any laboured confutation on my part. The authors of them would tax me with self-importance, and laugh at me as being too anxious about clearing up my character. One example of these falsehoods is that immense sum of money which you mention. Everybody knows how frugally I live in my own house. Every one sees that I am at no expense for the splendor of my dress. It is perfectly well known everywhere that my only brother is far from being very rich, and that the little which he has, he acquired without any influence of mine. Where then was that hidden treasure dug up? But they openly give out that I have robbed the poor. Well, this charge also, these most slanderous of men will be compelled to confess was falsely got up without any grounds. I have never had the handling of one farthing of the money which charitable people have bestowed on the poor. About eight years ago, a man of rank died in my house who had deposited upwards of two thousand crowns with me, and without demanding one scrap of writing to prove the deposit. When I perceived that his life was in danger, though he wished to entrust that sum to my management, I refused to undertake so responsible a charge. I contrived, however, that eight hundred crowns should be sent to Strasbourg to relieve the wants of the exiles. By my advice he chose men above all suspicion to distribute the remainder of the sum. When he wished to appoint me one of their number, to which the others made no objections, I refused; but I see what nettles my enemies. As they form an estimate of my character from their own, they feel convinced that I must amass, wherever I find a good opportunity. But if during my lifetime I do not escape the reputation of being rich, death will at last vindicate my character from this imputation. And I should never have done writing were I to direct my thoughts to composing a defence. If many flying reports are bandied about in your quarter, know that they form not a hundredth part of the rumors with which my ears are here continually stunned. I have nothing for it then but to give some explanation, and yet for all that I must hold out my cheek to the smiters. But let us go on, my dear Christopher, through evil report and through good report, and let us not suffer ourselves to be cast down by slanderous rumors. Though if we trace all this calumny up to its source, we shall find that we can only overcome it by patient endurance. For no one would think of breathing a syllable against us, did not a set of worthless fellows perceive that in so doing they are executing a task well pleasing to the princes, and are sure beforehand of their reward; these falsehoods, moreover, would speedily disappear, were they not carefully kept up by the very persons for whose sake they have been invented. Here I stop: for I am obliged suddenly to break off my letter.

Farewell, my best, and dearest brother. May the Lord always stand by you, govern you by his Spirit, and bless your labours.

[*Calvin's Lat. Corresp.* Opera, ix. p. 103.]

XII.—To Count Tarnow.[1]

An exhortation strenuously to promote the propagation of the Gospel in Poland.

GENEVA, 29*th December*, 1555.

Behold how much confidence the fame of your virtue imparts to me, a fame which N., a trustworthy and competent eye-

[1] " Most illustrious Seigneur, and distinguished for his excellent virtues, Governor of Cracow, and Commander in Chief in the Kingdom of Poland."

Notwithstanding the reiterated exhortations of the Reformer, this nobleman seems to have taken but a slight part in the evangelization of his country. While he encouraged Calvin to continue to write to him, and recommended himself to his prayers,

witness has extolled before me with no ordinary encomiums. This is the cause why I, a person perhaps unknown to you, venture not only to address you by letter, but also familiarly discuss with you a matter of the highest importance to all, and exhort you to undertake the weighty task which I now offer to your consideration. Some time ago we were led to entertain tolerable hopes of recalling the kingdom of Poland to the pure and genuine faith of Christ; and though by the crooked devices of Satan, manifold obstacles have been interposed to the progress of this good work, yet at length God has opened a door for his Son, by which he invites all reverently to receive him.

Now, many indeed, as I hear, eagerly rush to meet him, and offer to the heavenly Sovereign those duties of piety, which of right belong to him, and with such zeal, too, that in the ranks of the nobility a holy unanimity of purpose to welcome purity of doctrine, is no less prevalent, than is an untamable spirit of rancour among the enemies of Christ banded to hinder the free course of the gospel. But you, most excellent sir, who are invested with the highest authority, and on whom the eyes of the king, as well as of others are fixed, it would but ill become to remain quiescent, or to advance with tardy steps, while others are pressing strenuously forward; nor has God indeed raised you to your present eminence upon any other terms, than that from your lofty post you should bear high his standard in the sight of all, and quicken the alacrity of their zeal. For it would be passing strange, indeed, if, while so many illustrious men are now advancing to battle, spontaneously and undauntedly in the front ranks, you who are not less distinguished for wisdom and counsel than for your station, should not be found in the mean time marching at their head. For though I am aware that the leading part in this cause belongs to his most Serene Highness the king, yet since he seems sufficiently well

---

he started objections founded on his fear of the troubles which follow great innovations and the multiplicity of sects; and he wished to reduce the Reformation to the correction of some abuses. In a letter of a posterior date, (15th November, 1559,) Calvin addressed to him severe remonstrances which were softened only by the respect due to his rank. "Your excellency will pardon me, if I feel indignant that the sacred name of God and zeal for religion should be treated as if they were a subject for jesting and pleasantry."

inclined of his own accord to act properly, he will put forth much more confidently, I trust, all his energies, when he shall find in you a steady supporter and adherent. There can be no doubt, I think, but Christ deserves this at your hands, that you should accept the command of all his generous soldiers. And already you have advanced so far, that all doubt respecting the sincerity of your affections is at an end. My only fear is that by procrastinating, you allow too much time to escape. Assuredly by far too much blame has hitherto been incurred by tardy measures. Now that same God who has opened a door for his gospel is calling with a loud voice upon the king himself, and upon all the nobles, to make an open and unambiguous profession of his doctrine. Wherefore, most excellent sir, call to mind that admonition of the prophet—"in an acceptable time I have heard thee, and in a day of salvation I have helped thee," which solicits all the sons of God sedulously to embrace the time of his visitation, lest the grace once offered, if slighted through slothfulness, should at last be withdrawn. Because it frequently comes to pass that joyful beginnings, which promise a prosperous issue, produce in many men a sluggish disposition, every one should prudently beware not to extinguish the light which has begun to break forth, nor permit torpor to creep upon him. I am aware that a certain measure is always to be observed, that by urging you too sharply I may not seem to distrust your piety; still the importance as well as the difficulty of the work, compels me to dissemble none of the incentives which should stir you to action, in order that the faithful servants of Christ may not find you deficient in any one thing, to be expected from a man of your high reputation. As the sole end for which we live is to worship God in purity, the whole scope of my argument then comes to this—that attaching an inferior importance to all other concerns, we are bound to make it our principal occupation, by the extirpation of every superstition, to clear the way for the progress of true religion. Now indeed by what foul corruptions it has been well nigh extinguished under the Papacy can scarcely be expressed in words, or contemplated without the deepest horror. Nay, since popery altogether is nothing but a sacrilegious profanation of God's name, blended

with innumerable mummeries, if we are lukewarm in purging
away these pollutions, our sluggishness will be held to be inex-
cusable in the sight of God and his angels. Moreover, as the
confession of his truth is a thing most agreeable to God, and a
sacrifice of most sweet smelling odour, and as an unshaken constancy in maintaining it, is justly reckoned among the highest
duties of piety, there is no kind of office in which you can put
forth all your courage or exercise yourself with greater renown.
Again when you yourself behold with what courage the enemies
of Christ contend for their own usurped power, and how furiously
they oppose the doctrine which the Son of God has asserted
with his blood, it would be strange if their wickedness did not
animate you to emulate them; in other words, that you should
strive with less activity in vindicating the glory of God than
they do in destroying it. If you have remarked by how noble
a title the Holy Spirit has honoured those whom he styled the
first fruits of Achaia, certainly you will make an effort not to
be classed among the last, nor among any but the first of those
who are at present the defenders of a resucitating gospel in
Poland. Add that in nothing can you give a better proof of
your fidelity to his most Serene Highness the king. For though
the state of his kingdom is tranquil at the present moment, yet
if he would enjoy the continuance of this good fortune, he will
find that the best means of securing so valuable a blessing will
be to establish the kingdom of Christ. For though God,
that he may show himself to be the Protector of the human race,
does not permit political order to be overturned even among
pagans, nevertheless it is evident from numberless examples
that this blessing no where remains so permanently, as where
true religion flourishes. And when the gospel opens up to
us the inestimable treasures of eternal life, we must consider
it as no contemptible accession to the advantages which it brings
in its train, that God takes under his protection the kingdoms
and principalities in which it is established. From whatsoever
places then the impiety of popery has been expelled to make
room for the restoration of true piety, there too we see the laws
and tribunals in vigour, a greater respect for magistrates prevail,
and the people everywhere restrained within the bounds of

moderation and contentment. For this reason so much the more intolerable is the wickedness of those who perversely discredit the doctrine which we teach, as if it sapped the edifice of social order, when on the contrary experience everywhere proclaims that it cannot repose on a more secure foundation. Our brother, in a personal interview, will treat of these matters much more conveniently with you, than it is possible for me to do by means of a letter.

Farewell, most accomplished and illustrious sir. May Christ who has endowed you with such excellent gifts, direct your mind and thoughts to make a legitimate use of them. May he sustain you by his power, and accompany you with all his blessings even unto the end.

[*Calvin's Lat. Corresp.* Opera, ix. p. 104.]

XIII. To GODFREY VARAGLIA.[1]

Exhortation to Martyrdom.

GENEVA, 17*th December,* 1557.

Though the tidings respecting your bonds, my dearest brother, were very sorrowful to us, yet they would have afflicted us still more deeply had not God, who is wont to make light arise out of darkness, tempered our grief with some portion of gladness. For we have occasion to congratulate ourselves that your labours in the very prison have begun to be so fruitful, that they have contributed more to the glory of the gospel of Christ, than if you had been in the undisturbed possession of your liberty.

[1] The Reformation in Italy had not a more ardent missionary nor a more intrepid martyr than Godfrey Varaglia. Born in Piedmont and early enrolled in the order of the Capuchins, he quitted them in order to preach the gospel with an eloquence which equalled that of the celebrated Ochino. With greater constancy than the latter, he was destined to seal his confession with his blood. Apprehended in the valley of Angrogne in 1557, he nobly confessed the gospel in his dungeon, and before his judges. Questioned by them respecting the number of his companions, he replied that he lived with twenty-four preachers, most of whom had come from Geneva, and that the number of those who were ready to follow them was so considerable, that the inquisitors would not have wood enough to burn them. He was condemned at Turin, and perished at the stake with extraordinary courage, the 29th March, 1558, a few months after having received the last exhortations of the Reformer.

Not without reason, then, should you feel your courage strengthened by that boast of St. Paul's, that though the enemy holds
you captive, yet the word of God is not fettered, and that not
only a door has been opened up for hearers who might dissem-
inate more widely that life-giving seed which they had caught
from your lips, but that you have yourself seen its fruits spring
up before your eyes. So that if it is your lot to be bound with
fetters, this reward of your labour will afford you no common
source of consolation. For if the confession of the faith before a crooked and perverse generation, be a sacrifice grateful
to God, how much more sweet-smelling will that savour be, which
is diffused abroad for the salvation of many ! You see, moreover, my brother, to what a warfare you have been called, and
this is what you must carefully turn over in your mind. For
when Christ exacts even from private individuals their testimony
to his gospel, by how much holier a tie does he hold you bound !
—you whom he has appointed to be a public preacher of his
doctrine, which is now persecuted in your person. Remember,
then, that you are produced as a witness by that same Master
who thought you worthy of so high an honour, that what you
formerly taught with your lips you may, if need be, seal with
your blood. Mean while, doubt not but he will be a faithful
guardian of your life, and since he has promised that the death
of his saints will be precious in his eyes, whatever be the issue,
let this compensation suffice you, that through you the Son of
God at present triumphs to the end that he may finally receive
you into the fellowship of his everlasting glory. I shall not
dwell at greater length on this subject because I am persuaded
that you repose on the faith and protection of Him—to whom as
long as we die and live—we are happier in our death than worldly
and profane men are in their life. Farewell, best and dearest
brother. My colleagues salute you. May the Lord always
stand by you, govern you by the prudence of his Spirit, sustain
you with his invincible courage, and shield you by his protection—Yours,

JOHN ———,

a friend whom you know.

[Lat. Copy. Library of Geneva, Vol. 107, a.]

XIV.—To Macar.[1]

Congratulations on the zeal which he displays at Paris—Difficulties that stand in the way of sending off new ministers—Letter of the king of Navarre—Divers particulars.

GENEVA, 16th March, 1558.

I dare scarcely commend your punctuality in writing, because it would then be difficult for me to excuse my own negligence. It is better, however, to admit frankly my faultiness in this respect, than deprive myself of a favour which is so delightful to myself as well as to all of us. I, therefore, entreat you most earnestly, that though I should not reply to you in my turn, that you will not for all that cease to lessen in part by frequent letters, the ennui occasioned by your absence. Now if I am disposed to furnish you with some plausible excuses for my laziness, I fear I shall occasion you some uneasiness and distress. Nearly six weeks have elapsed since I was seized with a pain in my side, which yielding to medical treatment had abated a little its severity, but which again attacked me with such aggravated symptoms, that I am obliged to renounce all active employment. But I am so tired of doing nothing, that, happen what will, I feel that I shall be forced before six days to resume my wonted occupations.

In the mean time I am delighted to hear of that physical strength with which God has endowed you, in order that your

---

[1] John Macar, (or *Racham*,) a native of Crans, near Laon, in Picardy, and a refugee at Geneva for the sake of religion, devoted himself to the ministry, and soon became distinguished by his masculine eloquence and undaunted character. Called to Paris as a pastor in 1557, at the moment in which the most rigorous persecution prevailed, he did not hesitate to accept of functions surrounded by so many perils, and displayed in the discharge of them a zeal and charity worthy of the Apostolic Church. His correspondence with Calvin, which is kept at Geneva, is one of the most precious monuments of the faith, in those trying times in which the missionary was so often called to close his career by martyrdom. "The king," says he, "multiplies his threats, and declares that he will not give himself any rest till he has extirpated from his kingdom the very last heretic. As for us, who have our anchor fixed in heaven, we sail amid storms, as if we were in a quiet haven." Library of Geneva. Vol. 112.

activity of mind should be supported by a corresponding vigour of body. Now that La Roche Chandieu by his arrival will take a part of the burden off your shoulders you will go on with greater courage for the future. We are extremely sorry that La Rivière should be pining away under the effects of a lingering fever, but the mild weather of spring will, I hope, set him to rights.

It is scarcely at all in our power, however expedient it might be, to send off another person from our society, and your brethren will, in their equity, forgive us, if we do not comply with their wishes, because we thus consult their interests no less than our own. You can yourself bear witness that all were unanimous in wishing to devote themselves to your service. But we must also consider how far our duties permit us to act. The excuse you make about the expenses, I readily admit. Had they refused point blank, the refusal would have piqued me more slightly, but what offended me more seriously was their writing, not without a certain bantering tone, that the expedition had not been undertaken without having been solicited; and next, that it was by no means fair that they should pay away money for the prisoners.

The king of Navarre has returned me a very polite answer, and though I am aware that his secretaries for the most part write of their own accord in a more courteous style, still from certain indications I am warranted to conclude that the whole proceeded from himself. I wish that what Bussy promised in his name were made good in reality. But the timidity which usually defeats all his manly resolutions, is an object of suspicion to me. I am unwilling, indeed, before the time to augur unfavourably, but I fear me you will discover ere long that those preachers dealt in hyperbole, who so emphatically lauded his virtues among you. The silliness of the Baron is well known to me, and therefore, whatever is represented to me by him goes for nothing. Bussy, though he be scheming nothing with a treacherous intention, may yet do mischief by uselessly busying himself. You can scarcely believe with how much ambition he is inflamed, how inconsiderately he bustles, and with what audacity he intermeddles with matters that do not concern him.

I lately hinted to you that you ought to interfere. Now I more distinctly advise you to take care that they do not abuse your too easy temper, because from their character I conjecture that they are not aiming at any sober or moderate measures. Remember, moreover, that his loud vaunts are mere baits to catch the unwary. In the mean time, you must take care not to alienate them; but their good will is only to be cultivated to prevent them from doing mischief, which you will contrive prudently to prevent.

I had written thus far, when towards the evening, your last letter was brought to me. If I only allude briefly to a few of the principal points contained in it, you will excuse me, because the pain in my side prevents me from entering more into detail. I have not, moreover, brought an amanuensis along with me here, because the physicians condemn me to total inaction. These wretched men, upon whose constancy you counted, have either by their fickleness fallen off to a foul apostasy, or have yielded to a weakness unworthy of Christian men. It is not your business to be answerable for their fault.[1] I wish some one had been sent by you to the meeting of the princes. But our two deputies will make up, by their address, for anything that is deficient.

Farewell, most worthy brother and faithful servant of Christ. May the Lord always stand by you, govern and protect you, and bless all your pious labours—Amen. Salute very carefully your colleagues. I add no salutation from my fellow-pastors, because I write to you in the name of them all. From the chalet of my brother,[2] where he himself as my host, M. M. Villemongis, Normandie, and Varennes, have just supped with me. All of them desire to be kindly remembered to you.—

Yours truly,

CHARLES PASSELIUS.

[*Lat. Copy.—Library of Geneva.* Vol. 107, *b.*]

[1] See Vol. III, p. 390, Note 1.　　　[2] At Tussy, near Geneva.

XV.—To Macar.[1]

Community of sufferings between the churches of Paris and Geneva—Hope of better
days.

GENEVA.

My brother, my dearest brother, if exempt from all fear and
anxiety, I should urge you and your colleagues to meet the
struggles which now threaten you, such enormous garrulity
would deservedly appear contemptible, nay, disgusting in your
eyes. But now, while I am myself anxious and trembling at
your dangers, if I exhort you to confidence and constancy, this
letter of mine which will be the lively portraiture of my heart,
and reflect all its most intimate feelings, will affect you, I trust,
as if I were present among you, and the sharer of all your inquietudes. And assuredly, should matters come to the last extremity, I had much rather be joined with you in death, than
survive to bewail so great a calamity to the church. But whatever fall out, you know full well from the precept of our
heavenly Master, though I should say nothing, that you ought
to suffer death a hundred times rather than timidly desert the
post in which you have been stationed. I too feel horrified at
the reproach of sedition, with which wicked men attempt not
only to blacken your character, but also to defame the sacred
gospel of Christ. But as you are perfectly conscious that you
are falsely charged with the odium of such a crime, strong in

---

[1] Without date : April, 1558.

The correspondence of Macar with Calvin gives us an insight into the daily trials
and perils of the Church of Paris at this period. In spite of the confession presented
to Henry II., as an answer to the calumnies of their adversaries, the Protestants of
Paris were persecuted with unrelenting severity. We remark the following words in
one of Macar's letters to Calvin : " Pharaoh breathes nothing but destruction, should
God once grant him repose. We are groaning, and yet we labour to the best of our
strength. We have already begun to preach among the willows, since the rage and
vigilance of the enemy no longer permit us to assemble in the city." Macar himself
too much exposed to the fury of his enemies, was obliged to return to Geneva before
the end of the year, leaving his place to François Morel. (Library of Geneva, Vol.
112, passim.)

the testimony of your innocence, you should feel it to be your duty to endure this calumny with a patient and undisturbed mind—a calumny from which not even the Son of God could escape. It is consoling that even if you should hold your tongues, the truth which will speedily burst forth from the obscurity in which it is now enveloped, will dissipate this calumny of your enemies. For when three days shall have elapsed, the rumour will fall to the ground of itself, and the authors of it will be reduced to silence from very shame. No doubt the devil, as he is the father and the artificer of all lies, will put forth all his strength to overwhelm you with odium and disgrace. He will not, for all that, gain anything by his devices, but on the contrary, God, by this distinguished and memorable conflict, will illustrate his own name, and out of darkness will cause to shine the full effulgence of his glory. No free and unsophisticated confession had ever reached the ears of the king.[1] If the last things correspond to the first (which we have reason to hope,) this blood-red lion will grow pale, believe me a hundred times. If among the flock there shall be much trepidation, let it not disturb you, but do you rather calmly not less than vigorously provide remedies against its dispersion. Perhaps, contrary to expectation, some mitigation of your trials will ere long present itself. But should it happen that your patience is to be put to a still more severe proof, since such is the decree of your heavenly Father, let this remain graven on your hearts, that he is faithful who will not suffer his children to be tempted beyond what they can endure.

Farewell, beloved brother. May the Lord stand by you, and support you with his invincible fortitude.—Yours,

CHARLES PASSELIUS.

[*Lat. Copy.—Library of Geneva.* Vol. 107, *b.*]

[1] See Vol. III. p. 372.

AN HISTORICAL CALUMNY REFUTED.

[We read in the *Nouveaux Mémoires* of the Abbé d'Artigny, vol. iii. pp. 313–316: "An able Jesuit very fond of literary anecdotes has communicated to me the two following letters, the originals of which the Marquis du Poet preserves with great care . . . These two letters in which the patriarch of the pretended Reformed, has painted himself to the life, do him so little honour that no efforts have been spared to get them out of M. du Poet's hands, with such pertinacity indeed that a minister of the Cevennes having asked to read them wished to take forcible possession of them, which gave rise to a rather animated scene, the consequences of which, as may well be imagined, were not to the advantage of the preacher."

Such is the first mention slightly embellished of the two famous letters which, published in 1750 by the Abbé d'Artigny, were about to furnish Voltaire with a sarcasm, and commence their career of scandal in a celebrated chapter of the Essai sur les Moeurs. "The last feature in the portrait of Calvin may be taken from a letter in his own handwriting, which is still preserved in the Chateau of La Bastie-Roland near Montelimart. It is addressed to the Marquis du Poet, Grand Chamberlain of the Queen of Navarre, and dated the 30th September, 1561: 'Honour, glory, and riches will be the reward of your pains. Above all do not fail to rid the country of all those zealous scoundrels that stir up the people to make head against us. Such monsters should be smothered, as I have done here by Michel Servetus the Spaniard.'"[1]

Too circumspect to reproduce the sorry trash of the letters signalized by the *able* Jesuit, and accepted without examination by the Abbé d'Artigny, but too partial to discuss their value, Voltaire confined himself to a quotation, and flung as a challenge to the Reform a phrase in the handwriting of Calvin, containing

---

[1] *Essai sur les Moeurs*, C. i. 34.

an atrocious exhortation to murder, enveloped in a cruel allusion
to the death of Servetus.[1]

This was but the prelude to the fortune reserved for the two
documents of which the singular destiny has been to serve the
rancour of the philosophical spirit of the eighteenth century,
against the religious spirit of the sixteenth, and the hatred of a
school which does not shrink, we know, from a defence of the Inquisition and the massacre of St. Bartholomew, but which piously
veils its face before the funeral-pile of Servetus, and the incon-
sistent rigour of the Reform at Geneva.   The letters to M. du
Poet were destined to furnish ample matter for the declamations
of a party, not very scrupulous in the choice of its arms against
heresy.   It has not failed to lay hold of them.   Let us content
ourselves with recalling to mind that we find them invariably
quoted in a great number of writings of Catholic controversy,
from d'Artigny and Bergier,[2] down to the Abbé Amodru;[3] that
they have obtained the honours of a double mention in Audin,[4]
and a little insertion in one of the most vaunted works of M.
Capefigue.[5]   Let us add in fine that a writer of Dauphiny, M.
Aubenas, has renewed the accusation[6] reproduced by a learned
historian, M. Lavallée,[7] who does not hesitate to condemn Calvin
on the faith of Voltaire.

[1] It is the same tactics which make Catholic writers invariably quote a pretended
phrase of Calvin's of which there exists not the slightest trace in his writings.   The
point in question is nothing less than the extermination of the Jesuits: "*Jesuitæ vero
qui se nobis opponunt aut necandi, aut si hoc commodè fieri non potest ejiciendi, aut
certe mendaciis et calumniis opprimendi sunt.*"   "But the Jesuits who oppose us are to
be massacred, or if this cannot be conveniently accomplished, to be banished, or at
any rate crushed by falsehoods and calumnies."   Now this passage quoted by Alzog,
Universal Geschichte der Christlichen Kirche, Edit. of 1840, p. 913, commented on by
Audin, *Hist. de Calvin*, vol. ii. p. 434, and reproduced in innumerable libels, is the
work of the R. P. Jesuit Martinus Becanus, who in his aphorisms (*Opera*, Mayence,
1649, p. 855) ironically gives to his adversaries the most convenient receipt for crushing the disciples of Loyola, and it is Becanus' phrase (could it be believed?) that is
charitably attributed to Calvin.   Thus it is that history is written !   See on this subject the caustic dissertation of M. A. Réville, *Bulletin de la societé d'Histoire du Pro-
testantisme Français*, vol. iii. pp. 150, 153.

[2] *Dictionnaire Théologique*, i. 241.

[3] *La verité proposée aux Catholiques et aux Protestants.*   Valence, 1847, in 18mo.

[4] *Vie de Calvin*, ii. 179, 434, 435.

[5] *Histoire de la Reforme*, ii. 34, 35.

[6] *Notice Historique sur la ville et le Canton de Valreas*, 156, 157.

[7] *Histoire des Français*, ii. 362.

Such is the history of these letters which, quoted with the most unshaken assurance for more than a century, have acquired in passing from mouth to mouth, a mysterious authority which seems placed beyond dispute and doubt. Thus spring up and are propagated at the pleasure of passions interested in spreading them, those falsehoods consecrated by time, which cannot brook, however, the slightest examination, and yet of which the most palpable refutations can scarcely shake the empire. It is one of those pious frauds which we now attempt to unmask for the first time.

Among the seigneurs who embraced with the greatest ardour the cause of the Reform in Dauphiny, in the second half of the sixteenth century, we must reckon Louis de Marcel, Seigneur of Barry, Mornans, Saou, Baron du Poet near Montelimart. He united his exertions to those of the principal noblemen of the country, Monbrun, Blacons, and Mirabel, to obtain liberty of conscience, and vied with them in bravery for the defence of Lyons against the Catholic army.[1] He took part in the battles of Jarnac and Montcontour, and followed the fortunes of the King of Navarre through all the vicissitudes of the civil wars. His services were not forgotten, and when the cause, for which he had valiantly combatted, became triumphant, he was named successively Chamberlain of the King of Navarre, councillor of state, Governor of Montelimart, and lieutenant general of the Marquisate of Saluces, 1593.[2] We see already by these details that the importance of the Baron du Poet as a chief of the Calvinist party is much posterior to the death of Calvin. But he had declared for the Reformation before this period, and must have kept up with the Reformer an intercourse, of which we think we find the traces in a letter addressed "to a Baron of Dauphiny." This intercourse is attested besides by a tradition generally disseminated in the southern part of Dauphiny, and of which it is impossible not to recognize the value. It is in consequence of this tradition that must have arisen and gained credit in the district, the false letters fraudulently inserted in the archives of the family of du

---

[1] D'Aubigné, *Hist. Univ.*, vol. i. p. 247.
[2] D'Aubigné, vol. ii. pp. 455 et 1140. Aubenas, Notice already quoted.

Poet—at what period and by what hands? Of that we are ignorant.

Need we say that a simple perusal of these letters in the memoirs of the Abbé d'Artigny had inspired us with invincible doubts of their authenticity? But these doubts equivalent to a moral certainty could only acquire a scientific certainty by an examination of the documents themselves. No pains were to be spared by us to obtain such a result. The archives of the family of du Poet, long preserved in the seignorial manor of du Poet-Ceylar near Dieulefit, transported at a later period to the château of la Bastie-Roland, had at length fallen by inheritance to the Marquis d'Alissac de Valreas, whose kindness has permitted us freely to consult the correspondences which illustrious successions have accumulated in his hands.[1] Among all the documents which compose this family inheritance, among which we remark the distinguished names of Montmorency, Condé, Châtillon, Lesdiguieres, Henry IV., etc., two, the reader will easily conceive, almost exclusively attracted our attention. The simple inspection of them was sufficient to confirm all our doubts, and demonstrate with an evidence not to be resisted the spuriousness of these letters.

The proofs in confirmation of this conclusion are so numerous, that our only embarrassment would be to examine them. We must content ourselves with a summary enumeration of them.

1st. These originals, written by Calvin's own hand (as Voltaire affirms), are anything but autographs. They are neither in the handwriting of Calvin, nor in that of Jonvillers his secretary, nor of Antony Calvin, who sometimes held the pen under the dictation of the Reformer during the latter years of his life.

2nd. If these pieces are not in the handwriting of Calvin, still less do we find in them his style, admired by Bossuet himself and one of the finest in our language. That style is concise, nervous, and dignified, bearing the impress of a strong individuality more easy to caricature than to imitate.

3d. From the form let us pass to the substance. The two

---

[1] M. d'Alissac, at the moment we write these lines, is no more; but our gratitude and respect remain due to his memory for the courtesy with which he facilitated our researches.

letters swarm with mistakes and historical blunders which betray the work of an unskilful forger.   The first, dated the 8th May, 1547, and addressed to M. du Poet, General of the Religion in Dauphiny, bestows this title on this seigneur, fifteen years before the period in which he declared for the Reformation, and when the new faith, having neither church nor soldier in Dauphiny, could scarcely enumerate some obscure martyrs in that province.   The second, dated the 13th September, 1561, has for superscription—to M. du Poet, grand chamberlain of Navarre and Governor of Montelimart, dignities with which he was invested only twenty years later, in 1584.   It is one of Calvin's accusers, M. Aubenas himself, who informs us of that, without remarking that the notice which he has devoted to M. du Poet is the best refutation of the authenticity of the letters attributed to the Reformer.

We should have but too easy a task in pursuing in detail the analysis of these letters.   But how is it possible to go through with it?   How take up one by one the errors, the improbabilities, the nonsense, the enormities of every sort accumulated as if on purpose in these pages, in which the absurd vies with the odious, in which men and things are so sillily travestied, in which the grand and holy revolution of the sixteenth century is represented by a shameless scribbler as a coarse farce played by impudent mountebanks!   Here the pen drops from our hands!   When anonymous calumny dares to attack by abject defamation the most venerated names, it deserves not the honour of a reply; to confound it, it is enough to show it up in open day.   To quote these pretended letters of Calvin's to M. du Poet is to refute them!]

XVI.—To Monseigneur, Monseigneur du Poet, General of Religion in Dauphiny.

Monseigneur:—Who can resist your attack?   The Eternal protects you, the people loves you, the great fear you, the most distant regions resound with your acts of prowess.   Heaven has raised you up to establish in your countries its church. There remains for you but to receive the crown of glory which you desire. For the rest, Monseigneur, you have apparently heard of the progress of religion in our countries. The gospel is preached in our cities as well as in our valleys. People flock from all quarters to receive the yoke. In the missions there has been great fruit, and folks have gained no small riches. The Apostles never laboured with so much fruit, and if the Papists dispute the truth of our religion and whether it will last, they cannot dispute its riches. You alone labour without ceasing and without interest. Do not by any means neglect the increase of your means. A time will come in which you alone shall have acquired nothing by these new changes. Every one should think of his own interest; I alone have neglected mine, of which I greatly repent me. Thus those to whom I have furnished the means of acquiring wealth will take care of my old age which is unprovided for. You on the contrary, Monseigneur, who leave behind you a valiant lineage to support the little flock, do not leave them without great and powerful means without which good will would be useless. The Queen of Navarre has well fortified our religion in Bearn. The Papists have been entirely expelled from it. In Languedoc many an assembly has been held respecting our faith. In time shall be heard everywhere the praises of the Eternal. I pray the Creator to preserve you for his service, and for me—to furnish me with an opportunity of testifying to you how much I desire the quality of,

MONSEIGNEUR,

Your very humble and affectionate servant,

J. CALVIN.

At Geneva, this 8th May, 1547.

XVII.—TO MONSEIGNEUR, MONSEIGNEUR DU POET, GRAND CHAMBERLAIN OF NAVARRE AND GOVERNOR OF THE TOWN OF MONTELIMART, AT CREST.

MONSEIGNEUR :—What have you judged of the Colloquy of Poissy? We have conducted our business safely. The Bishop of Valence as well as the others have signed our profession of faith. Let the king make processions as much as he pleases, he will not be able to hinder the preaching of our faith, harangues in public, nor gain anything except to stir up the people already too disposed for rebellion. The brave Seigneurs de Montbrun and de Beaumont abandon their opinions. You spare neither courses, nor cares; labour, you and yours will find their turn (*sic*). One day, honour, glory, and riches will be the reward of so much pains. Above all, do not fail to rid the country of all those zealous scoundrels that stir up the people by their discourses to make head against us, blacken our conduct, and wish to make our belief pass for a reverie. Such monsters should be smothered, as I have done here, by the execution of Michel Servetus the Spaniard. Do not imagine that in future any one will take it into his head to do the like.

For the rest, Monseigneur, I forgot the subject for which I did myself the honour to write to you, which is humbly to kiss your hands, supplicating you to take in good part the quality which I shall covet during my whole life of . . .

MONSEIGNEUR,

Your very humble and affectionate servant,

J. CALVIN.

At Geneva, this 8th September, 1561.

[*Fr. Copy.—Arch. of M. le Marquis d'Alissac à Valreas.*]

[Besides the authors which we have just quoted, these two pieces have been triumphantly reproduced by M. Crétineau Joly (*Histoire des Jesuites*, T. I. pp. 421, 422,) and in an ironical pamphlet : *Les Protestants deboutés de leurs pretentions.* Brussels, 1776. These pretended letters will always find, in spite of our refutations, authors complaisant enough to invoke their authority; "for there are too many people that have an interest in keeping up stories that please them." This remark of Bayle is, unfortunately, quite as apposite now as ever, and we do not flatter ourselves that we shall take any thing from its applicability. Let the reader, however, compare these two pieces, the work of an impudent forger, who has not even given himself the trouble to save appearances, with the following letter written by Calvin to a Baron of Dauphiny, perhaps to M. du Poet himself, and he will see the distance which separates the language of calumny from the austere effusions of our Reformer. He will recognize Calvin by that inimitable accent, which his whole correspondence breathes, and which not even the most adroit Jesuit can catch. *Ex ungue leonem!*]

XVIII. To a Baron of Dauphiny:

GENEVA, *8th July*, 1563.

MONSIEUR, Your letter and the account which the bearer of it gave me of your state, have afforded me ample matter of rejoicing, and of glorifying God for the change he has wrought in you, when of his infinite will he has brought you into his flock, from which you had hitherto kept yourself so far aloof. In that, we see how he formerly created the world out of nothing. For in like manner, when it is his good pleasure to bring us back to himself, it is as if he were to form new creatures. Nay, he even displays a double portion of his energy, quelling the rebellion by which we resist his grace, as much as in us lies, just as he has reduced you to obedience to his truth, of which you were an enemy, in order that, knowing yourself to be his by a two-fold title, you should be stirred up to consecrate yourself entirely to him, as you are in duty bound. And it is for that reason that by the mouth of his prophet Isaiah, he magnifies his compassion, saying that he has been found of those who sought him not; and that he has declared himself to those that did not seek after him; saying, also, Here I am, to those that had not known him. Since then he has withdrawn you from the fathomless pit in which you were plunged; what remains, Monsieur, is not only that you do him honour and homage for so great a benefit, but also that you strive to acquit yourself of your arrears, putting forth a zeal in pursuing your course, so much the more ardent as you have entered upon it too late. If from our childhood we had battled manfully and done marvels, St. Paul tells us, that still we ought not at all to look at the past, for fear of being cooled or retarded for the future. But when we have been long unserviceable, and even opposed to the holy will of God, the recollection of our past faults should stimulate us to put forth our strength more and more. And I perceive, Monsieur, that God has effectually wrought in you, not only to make you receive the doctrine of salvation, but also to give you courage to labour, that your subjects should follow your example and keep you company in serving Him, to whom belongs the sovereign empire of heaven and earth. In which office I will aid you as far as shall be in my power, as will also my brethren and companions, nor is there a single individual who does not desire to bestir himself to render you service. We will then look out for what means we may find for sending to you apt and sufficient men, in order that Jesus Christ may bear peaceful rule in the country where he has given you preëminence. Only take courage, Monsieur, to persevere, as you have so well begun; and as God has raised you to a post of honour, may you set an example to all.

Whereupon, Monsieur, having humbly commended myself to your indulgent favour, I will supplicate our Heavenly Father to have you in his holy keeping, to strengthen you by his power, and increase you in all good and prosperity.

[*Fr. Copy. Library of Geneva.* Vol. 107.]

INDEX.

A